Race and the Archaeology of Identity

Foundations of Archaeological Inquiry

James M. Skibo, series editor

VOLUMES IN THIS SERIES:

Expanding Archaeology
James M. Skibo, William H. Walker, and Axel E. Nielsen

Behavioral Archaeology: First Principles
Michael Brian Schiffer

Evolutionary Archaeology: Theory and Application
Edited by Michael J. O'Brien

Unit Issues in Archaeology: Measuring Time, Space, and Material
Edited by Ann F. Ramenofsky and Anastasia Steffen

Pottery Ethnoarchaeology in the Central Maya Highlands
Michael Deal

Pottery and People: A Dynamic Interaction
Edited by James M. Skibo and Gary M. Feinman

Material Meanings: Critical Approaches to the Interpretation of Material Culture
Edited by Elizabeth S. Chilton

Social Theory in Archaeology
Edited by Michael Brian Schiffer

Race and the Archaeology of Identity

Edited by Charles E. Orser Jr.

THE UNIVERSITY OF UTAH PRESS
SALT LAKE CITY

Foundations of Archaeological Inquiry
James M. Skibo, editor

∞ Printed on acid-free paper

Manufactured in the United States of America
06 05 04 03 02 01
5 4 3 2 1

Library of Congress Cataloging-in-Publication Data

Race and the archaeology of identity / edited by Charles E. Orser, Jr.
p. cm. — (Foundations of archaeological inquiry)
Papers from a Foundations of archaeological inquiry roundtable held in Salt Lake City in early November 1999.
Includes bibliographical references and index.
ISBN 0-87480-693-3 (acid-free paper) — ISBN 0-87480-694-1 (pbk. : acid-free paper)
1. United States—Race relations—Congresses. 2. United States—Antiquities—Congresses. 3. Ethnoarchaeology—United States—Congresses. 4. Race—Social aspects—United States—History—Congresses. 5. Ethnicity—United States—History—Congresses. 6. African Americans—Race identity—Congresses. 7. African Americans—History—Congresses. 8. African Americans—Social conditions—Congresses. I. Orser, Charles E. II. Series.
E184.A1 R228 2002
305.8'00973—dc21

2001004436

Contents

Figures

Tables

Race and the Archaeology of Identity

I

Race and the Archaeology of Identity in the Modern World

Charles E. Orser Jr.

Race is not a subject that most people, including many archaeologists, might normally associate with archaeological research. The problems associated with the definition of race, racial identification, and the many stereotypic images of "the races" that confront us every day seem more immediate and thus far removed from the many pasts studied by archaeologists. Many people believe, either through personal commitment or from having been influenced by cinematic portrayals of archaeology, that archaeologists confine themselves to mysterious, ancient civilizations in faraway places. Being immersed in the intricacies and puzzles of ancient history, archaeologists have no time—and supposedly no professional interest—in investigating the troubling issues that confound and confuse today's world. After all, unlike their colleagues in cultural anthropology and sociology, archaeologists study human settlements only after their occupants have long since disappeared or moved away. The subject of race figures prominently in the litany of difficult issues that confront modern nations across the world today, and our personal experiences with the complexities, contradictions, and vagaries of race convince us that archaeologists will face profound difficulties when attempting any analysis of race. Cynics of the archaeology of race could well ask: What can archaeologists tell us about racial profiling in today's major cities? Where precisely is the relevance and value of an archaeological interest in race? What is the usefulness of archaeology when it comes to race?

In truth, archaeology can shed little if any light on the contemporary racial issues that today's modern societies have created and on the social systems of racial hierarchy that still exist as we begin the twenty-first century. Racial profiling is only one example of a serious social issue for which archaeological research is perhaps irrelevant. But even though archaeology may not be used as a tool to solve today's problems, it does have an important role to play in the investigation of race. It is the discipline's concentration on the past—perhaps its lack of perfect contemporaneity—that makes archaeological research not only pertinent to modern society but extremely significant. Archaeologists are especially well suited to provide unique understandings of the historical and material dimensions of some of today's most confounding social issues simply because of their interest in long periods of time, and the social and cultural changes brought about within these broad sweeps of history.

Men and women living in today's United States, like members of cultures everywhere, tend to interpret their way of doing things as simply "natural"; we act in certain ways because it "seems right" or "it has always been done that way." Most people seldom stop to consider that their present way of life did not just happen. Culture and tradition, though incorporating the "habitual forms of action" mentioned by Durkheim, Weber, and finally Bourdieu (Swartz 1997:115), are nonetheless created by real men and women going about their daily lives. People are free to change their viewpoints and perspectives as often as they wish as they move through life, constructing and reconstructing their personal and cultural histories. When we consider a topic as complex, historically persistent, and mutable as race, we can begin to imagine the important contribution that archaeologists, particularly historical archaeologists, can make to our current understandings. We can also glimpse the reason why this inquiry is so formidable and why progress is necessarily slow and tenuous.

Archaeologists of the modern world can no longer reasonably ignore race as a subject for several important reasons. First, race and racial categorization have been prominent ideas in world history, particularly within the United States, where racial constructs are inseparable from history. Many of today's most cherished beliefs about race have considerable historical depth, and to understand the many dimensions of modern race, we should be familiar with its antecedents. Using a transtemporal perspective, we can fully grasp, and be able to communicate, the artificiality of racial designations through history. As race is "one of the central conceptual inventions of modernity" (Goldberg 1993:3), it especially behooves modern-world archaeologists to examine the phenomenon as closely as possible. Second, since the beginning of the twentieth century, American anthropologists have been engaged in unmasking the "naturalness" of racial categorizations and their concomitant racial hierarchies. This substantive research began with the determined efforts of Franz Boas and was taken up by many of his most talented students.

A protracted concern for race provided a strong antiracist agenda for American anthropology, even though exposing the social construction of race was often characterized by a series of fits and starts rather than a constant, sustained effort (Harrison 1998:611). In 1998, however, the American Anthropological Association issued an explicit "statement on race" both to clarify the position toward race held by most anthropologists and to foreground the scholarly examination of race within the discipline. The companionship of American historical archaeology in this noble endeavor can strengthen the links between historical archaeology and anthropology. Historical archaeologists can use both their overt interest in race and the power of their interpretive insights to demonstrate the relevance of their field to their often-skeptical colleagues in cultural anthropology. But even if historical archaeologists ultimately fail to make their case for relevance within anthropology, they should not be deterred from the historical investigation of race, because the examination has anthropological relevance in any case. Finally, an archaeological interest in race can only serve to increase the sophistication of intellectual discourse in historical archaeology. Race is without question a serious subject that defies easy analysis. Rigorous archaeological studies of race conducted within the milieu of historic America will do much to strengthen the theoretical foundations of research in historical archaeology. The chapters in this book continue this process of disciplinary growth.

The present volume developed from a Foundations of Archaeological Inquiry roundtable held in Salt Lake City in early November 1999, sponsored by the University of Utah Press. The editor organized the meeting with the overt plan of bringing together some of America's most perceptive and talented historical archaeologists, individuals who were actively engaged in examining the historical and material dimensions of race. The goal of the symposium was to discuss our common intellectual interests and social concerns about race, to present scholarly papers about our research into the archaeology of race and identity, and to explore new issues raised by each presenter. The chapters in this volume, since revised, were originally delivered at the symposium. Our hope is that our concerted interest in race, material culture, and identity will serve as a catalyst to compel historical archaeologists to push the study of race to the forefront of the discipline. This research focus, albeit with an archaeological twist, is in keeping with the calls made both in the past by individual anthropologists (e.g., Blakey 1988; Harrison 1995; Willis 1974) and more recently by the American Anthropological Association (Harrison 1998) for a more foregrounded consideration of race in mainstream anthropological scholarship. American anthropologists have decided that race continues to matter in the United States, and that as committed intellectuals they have a social responsibility to throw their analytical weight and significant insights behind its examination. Unfortunately, racial categorization and the prejudice that accompanies it are not disappearing from the United States, and recent events such as the controversy over flying the Confederate flag demonstrate a reality recognized years ago by W. E. B. Du Bois: that race was not only *the* issue of the twentieth century, but many people will also find it to be *the* issue of the twenty-first. One of our collective hopes in this volume is to increase the profile of race and racism as legitimate topics of study in historical archaeology, and in the process, to assist in the intellectual maturation of the field.

Before proceeding with the individual chapters, however, we must provide a context for the study of race within historical archaeology, and to explore further the issue of why the investigation of race is important. This book is focused on the United States, but racial issues are important around the globe. As a result, the topics examined in this volume can be expanded to engage race in the many other regions where historical archaeologists are now conducting research.

CREATING ANTHROPOLOGICAL AND ARCHAEOLOGICAL CONNECTIONS WITH RACE

The anthropology of race, both as a formal topic within the academy and as a widely held belief system among nonscholars, is inexorably connected to the history of intellectual thought in the United States. Western science has had a tradition of assigning racial categorizations to disparate peoples around the world stretching back to Linnaeus's *Systema naturae,* first published in 1735 (Voget 1975: 57). Linnaeus believed that humanity represented a single species, which he termed *Homo sapiens,* but he also recognized the existence of four "varieties" of humans: European, American, Asian, and African. Though some Renaissance scholars, such as Johann Boemus (Hodgen 1971:131–133), had been intrigued by human diversity since the earliest days of Europe's global expansion, it was really Linnaeus who began the process of human categorization.

The subject of race and racial identification became a major topic of serious scientific concern in eighteenth- and nineteenth-century America, undoubtedly because of the undeniable presence of large populations of Native Americans and African Americans in the expanding nation. American men and women of European heritage were convinced of their moral and cultural superiority over these two peoples—one indigenous and the other imported against its will—and so the goal of much early American social science was designed to find ways to differentiate between peoples in the most basic ways. The usual medium for segmentation was physical because the observable, though often imaginary, differences between peoples could be perceived as ordained from above. Within this intellectual mind set, the different "races" simply existed; it was up to the scientists to substantiate the differences that God had created.

Samuel G. Morton was one of the most renowned nineteenth-century American scientists investigating human diversity, and his *Crania Americana,* published in 1839, was a major achievement of the period (Bieder 1986:68). This work, which focused on the exacting—and thus "scientific"—measurement of Native American skulls from North and South America, was a refined version of Johann F. Blumenbach's less rigorous study of skulls in his *On the Natural History of Mankind,* published in 1775 (Voget 1975: 105). Morton's "science" included the ideas that racial types actually existed, that moral and mental characteristics were attached to these racial types, and that Linnaeus's four varieties of humanity represented separate creations (Bieder 1986:83). Science in Morton's hands thus confirmed the biologic differences between the human varieties.

America's pioneering archaeologists were not strangers to the contemporary controversies about race, and many of them were eager to enter the intellectual fray. Many found their cause when they took up the case of the so-called Moundbuilders.

The earliest European explorers and colonists encountered their first earthen mounds soon after they landed on the shores of eastern North America. Pioneering settlers came upon larger and more complex mounds as they moved farther west into the Ohio and Mississippi Valleys. Surrounded as they were by these silent, often majestic monuments from antiquity, it was not long before America's archaeologists were involved in a controversial scientific quest to explain who had built these impressive earthworks.

Theories about the Moundbuilders abounded in early America. Some antiquarians did not believe that the builders were ancestors of the Native Americans because the mounds were simply too sophisticated and required too much labor and America's indigenous cultures were considered to lack the ingenuity and perseverance needed to produce such wonders. As a result, many early archaeologists argued that the only reasonable conclusion was that the Moundbuilders had to have been non-natives. Among the possible candidates were courageous Welsh seafarers, wayward Irish monks, and even a mysterious, highly advanced culture, possibly from Atlantis. Other archaeologists, however, believed that ancient Native Americans had to have been responsible for the mounds, and they set about proving it with controlled excavation and careful analysis (Patterson 1995:27–28; Silverman 1986:9–49).

Speculation about the racial origins of the Moundbuilders continued to be expressed long after the publication of Samuel F. Haven's *Archaeology of the United States* in 1856 (Willey 1968:33–34; Willey and Sabloff 1993:45). Many proponents of the Moundbuilder myth incorporated into their arguments ideas that were intended to help build the ideology of the American nation as a place once inhabited by a great and mysterious people (Hinsley 1989:83). Others believed that if they could intellectually distance the mysterious and culturally sophisticated Moundbuilders from the "primitive" Native Americans of nineteenth-century America, they could provide a rationale for the displacement and even destruction of the "simple" Native Americans who stood in the way of America's heavenly ordained Manifest Destiny (Trigger 1989:126; Willey and Sabloff 1993:45). Attributing the mounds to Native Americans would only demonstrate that the indigenous peoples of America were capable of being creative, intelligent, and industrious.

The Moundbuilder controversy created charged emotions on both sides of the issue, and American archaeologists could only put the myth to rest once they had fully adopted stratigraphic excavation in the late nineteenth century, largely under the direction of the archaeologists of the Bureau of American Ethnology (Stiebing 1993:193). Careful excavation, coupled with a complete lack of pre-Columbian evidence of European presence in those regions of North America that contained mounds, finally destroyed the myth of the Moundbuilders in serious archaeology. The myth is promoted today only by the most outrageous of the pseudo-archaeologists.

The widespread adoption of scientific excavation techniques, when added to the growing anthropological understanding that only one true race could be said to exist, caused American archaeologists to lose interest in race as a topic of investigation. Rather than focus on identifying the spurious, independently created "races" acknowledged in the late eighteenth and early nineteenth centuries, America's archaeologists turned their attention to unraveling the many cultural divisions that existed among Native Americas in prehistory. The use of large-scale, culturally defined regional chronologies contributed to the anthropologization of American archaeology through the compilation of prehistoric culture histories (Lyman et al. 1997;

McKern 1939; Willey and Phillips 1958). But what about American historical archaeology?

DISCOVERING RACE IN HISTORICAL ARCHAEOLOGY

Historical archaeology, as a specialized subarea within American archaeology, developed in a haphazard fashion during prehistoric archaeology's cultural history phase. Historical archaeology could simply find no suitable role in the development of regional cultural chronologies because the broad post-Columbian history of North America could be established without recourse to archaeological research. During this period, then, historical archaeology was largely marginalized from mainstream American archaeology, and historical archaeologists responded by focusing their skills on physical reconstructions and other tasks that could be said to have only limited, if any, interest to anthropologists or prehistoric archaeologists. The rise of the New Archaeology in the late 1960s, however, provided the intellectual rationale for historical archaeology to establish more purely anthropological goals. The New Archaeology, for all its faults, was instrumental in providing historical archaeologists with legitimate reasons why they could contribute to the larger anthropological endeavor. The research program that would eventually develop would necessarily incorporate some of the most challenging questions facing social scientists in the late twentieth century. Race, a tenacious concept that continued to exist in many forms, provided one of the most daunting challenges. For historical archaeology, specifically, race was a topic that could not be ignored for long.

When American historical archaeologists began to investigate plantation sites in the late 1960s, it was inevitable that they would have to confront the complexities of race in some fashion, especially since no sociohistorical analysis of the United States is truly complete without taking race into account (Fields 1982:143–144, 1983:21). American archaeology's confrontation with race was all the more inevitable because of the growing understanding of the differences between race and ethnicity. Whereas ethnicity has been viewed as a legitimate archaeological topic for many years (e.g., Jones 1997, 1999; Kelly and Kelly 1980; McGuire 1982; Praetzellis 1999), historical archaeologists have been slow to recognize a comparable examination of race. As they began to excavate plantation sites, however, they were forced to confront the present-day reality that African Americans are usually defined "racially"—based on one physiologic characteristic, usually skin color—while other peoples are defined "ethnically" (Beeghley 1989:261–262). Anthropologically trained archaeologists instituting research programs at plantations in the 1960s undoubtedly believed that the study of ethnics, as "cultures," was a respectable realm of inquiry, while the examination of race was "to enter a world of paradox, irony, and danger" (Omi and Winant 1986:xiii). Consequently, much of the research on African Americans in colonial and antebellum America has been conducted from a "culturalist" viewpoint (Orser 1990:122–129).

It was with an anthropological background that Charles Fairbanks began his archaeological testing at Kingsley Plantation in 1967, and his research was appropriately geared toward investigating "some aspects of slave lifestyle and of their cultural processes" (Fairbanks 1984:2; also see Fairbanks 1974: 62, 90–91, 1983:22–24; Walker 1988:156–157). His accompanying search for Africanisms—material reminders of Africa—was anthropologically relevant in light of the Herskovits (1958)/Frazier (1964) debate over the trans-Atlantic persistence of African culture. Within Fairbanks's avowed anthropological perspective, Africans in the New World were members of cultures who worked diligently in the most adverse conditions to create new lives for themselves. For Fairbanks (1984:9), as anthropological archaeologist, the task was "to deduce the behavior from... the discards of a culture" and to determine the dimensions of the cultural lives of slaves.

The overt anthropological interest in plantation culture was carried over into the investigation of Cannon's Point Plantation, Georgia, where Fairbanks and his students had the opportunity to excavate discrete slave, overseer, and planter settlement areas. Using the faunal remains found within the plantation's trash deposits, Fairbanks (1983:25) sought to reveal the "differences in life styles of the three groups." The way in which he modeled the precise social character of these "groups" is not necessarily clear. Nevertheless, Fairbanks and his students contributed a tremendous amount of research on African American cultural lifeways at plantation sites in the American South. The framework they used treated slaves as members of cultures who adapted to harsh conditions in the New World. Fairbanks, working within a well-established and anthropologically sound culturological framework, found no reason to refer to race in any substantive manner, even though he was well aware of the cruelty of slavery (see, for example, Ascher and Fairbanks 1971).

The word "race," however, was introduced into the archaeological lexicon because of Fairbanks's research program. One of Fairbanks's students, John Otto, in a paper provocatively titled "Race and Class on Antebellum Plantations" (1980), explicitly explored the impact of race at Cannon's Point Plantation. Otto (1980:8) argued that the three principal groups at the plantation—slaves, overseers, and planters—were arrayed along three distinct "statuses." A "social," or occupational, status served to divide plantation residents into three discrete segments: slaves as workers, overseers as supervisors, and planters as managers. An "elite/subordinate," or power, status divided the residents into only two groups: slaves and overseers as subordinates, and planters as elites. A third "status" was "racial/legal." This dimension divided the plantation into two groups based on legal standing: slaves were "unfree blacks," and overseers and planters were "free whites."

Otto's manner of conceptualizing the social nature of a past plantation site was important for several reasons. In a significant departure from the culturological framework of his mentor, Otto chose to distinguish the principal groups on a plantation in economic and historical terms rather than along cultural lines. His primary groups were "slaves, overseers, and planters" rather than, for instance, "African Americans," "Irish Americans," and "English Americans." His emphasis on plantation-based occupation further enhanced the idea that these groups, rather than constituting discrete cultural groupings, were archaeologically definable based on their place in plantation production. At the same time, however, he incorporated the notion of interaction within the social segmentation because there could be no slaves if there were no planters, and no planters without slaves. Further, Otto's (1980:8) use of the word "caste" to describe two social segments—one "white" and one "black"—though problematic and theoretically ill advised (Orser 1988a:738), drew dramatic attention to the seriousness of the racial divisions in American society (see Cox 1942, 1945, 1948; Myrdal 1944; Park 1928; Warner 1936, 1941), divisions which clearly remained, even after more than a hundred years since the War Between the States.

Otto's analysis demonstrated that his nod to the significance of economics at historic plantations contained an important insight but also a significant analytical problem. His failure to obtain unambiguous results from his artifact analysis overtly demonstrated the severe difficulties archaeologists would face when considering the material dimensions of race. The complexities of an archaeological research agenda that included race was made even more clear by another archaeologist writing in the same collection in which Otto's paper appeared. Vernon Baker's (1980) analysis of the ceramics from a site in Massachusetts known as "Black Lucy's Garden" was even more problematic.

Lucy Foster had lived as a freed slave in Massachusetts until 1845, when she died at the age of eighty-eight. Adelaide and Ripley Bullen (1945) excavated her home site in 1943, and Baker (1978, 1980) reanalyzed the ceramics in an effort to discover "patterns of material culture distinctive of Afro-American behavior" (Baker 1980:29). Baker thus cast his study in the anthropological framework outlined and pursued by Fairbanks, and expected that his analysis would reveal the archaeological nature of African American culture. His results, however, were not so straightforward, and Baker (1980:35) faced a significant problem with his interpretation: he could not decide whether the ceramic collection represented poverty—Foster had been indigent at the time of her death—or an African American presence. Simply put, did Foster create the ceramic collection because of economics or culture? Baker had framed his study in purely cultural terms, but he connected his conclusion—for those who wished to think about it—clearly with race, because "Only research on sites of poor whites, however, will substantiate fully the interpretive value" of the data (Baker 1980:36). In other words, holding the economic position constant—poverty—and changing the racial category of the residents of a different site would allow Baker to learn what dimension structured the ceramic distribution at the Foster site: race or economics.

Baker's conclusion about the difficulty of being able to present an unambiguous interpretation of the social meanings of the ceramics from the Lucy Foster site was more important than he may have realized. What he was saying, in essence, was that historical archaeologists cannot determine the primacy of race over economics *until* such time as they excavate a site occupied by *whites*. Only a comparison based on race would yield significant results. The subtext of his analysis is that race—as a perceived categorization—could not be separated from economics, especially in the United States (Orser 1991:114, 1998b: 664). Attempts to disentangle race from class, or class from race, have occupied American sociologists and anthropologists for many decades, and a complete catalog of their ideas and analytical findings would fill many pages. What emerges from the literature, however, is a clear declaration that any attempt to *remove* race from the analysis of American society is bound to be overly simplistic (Ransford 1977:45–59). The same holds true for archaeologists attempting to investigate the socioeconomic dimensions of ceramic collections from the United States, however they may wish to pursue this line of inquiry (Orser 1988a; Monks 1999).

Baker's analysis is also significant for his use of the word "white" in a manner that is both recognizable and readily understood by American historical archaeologists. Recent research has demonstrated, though, that the concept of "whiteness" is just as much a historical creation as is the concept of "blackness" (e.g., Allen 1994; Ignatiev 1995; Roediger 1991; Williams 1990). Baker portrays the naivete of historical archaeology when he postulates that the excavation of a site related to "whites" can be used as a baseline to compare the findings from a site associated with "blacks." It is as if we will all understand the "white" site, at least enough to help us interpret the "black" site.

Historical archaeologists became more willing to mention racism and to explore race beginning in the 1990s, and they published a number of pioneering studies in this regard (e.g., Babson 1990; Epperson 1990a; Fitts 1996; Franklin 1997b; Garman 1998; La Roche and Blakey 1997; Mullins 1999a). The chapters in this volume, when added to these investigations, begin to build a body of archaeological literature specifically focused on the difficult issues surrounding race.

THE DANGER OF IGNORING RACE IN AMERICAN HISTORICAL ARCHAEOLOGY

The growing literature about race and racism currently being created by American historical archaeologists does not necessarily mean that race and racism will become central topics within the discipline. It remains possible that the significance of race will continue to be marginalized by historical archaeologists who perceive the topic as too controversial to be addressed by "impartial" scientists, or by those who mistakenly view race as unimportant within archaeological inquiry. Some may believe that too strong a focus on race may tend to skew the research (e.g., McKee 1995: 4–5), not acknowledging, or perhaps merely not being able to admit, that the research has been skewed for years away from race (La Roche and Blakey 1997:92–93). We must remember in this context that American historical archaeology was created, and is maintained in some quarters, as a politically conservative field, originally intended to provide legitimizing physical support for the national ideology through the excavation of sites associated with the rich and the famous in American history (Orser and Fagan 1995: 25–26; Orser 1999:274–277). It is no accident that archaeologists at Jefferson's Monticello spent years scratching around the yards before they discovered the slave quarters in a sequence of research that represents the status quo of much American historical archaeology. We must note, though, that even the excavation of slave quarters does not necessarily mean that considerations of race will be included within the analysis.

Given the general conservative affinities of American historical archaeology, it is relatively easy to imagine its practitioners overlooking or ignoring race as a legitimate topic of investigation. The contributors to the present volume believe, to the contrary, that American historical archaeologists should not—and, in fact, in many cases cannot—overlook race and racism in their investigations, and that to do so can have analytically dangerous consequences. One of my reasons for writing *A Historical Archaeology of the Modern World* (Orser 1996) was to argue that historical archaeology has a strong and lasting contribution to make to understanding post-Columbian history, which is in truth a history that we are all in the process of making every day. The study of race fits squarely within this examination, though I was then remiss in not giving it more weight.

To explore the potential dangers of ignoring race as a topic within historical archaeology, I wish to focus on one of the most egregious examples I have encountered in the recent literature. My reaction to the study in question was so strong at first reading that it convinced me of the need for the roundtable, and of the necessity for historical archaeologists to reexamine the nature and goals of their field's ultimate project. The most basic question facing today's historical archaeologist is simply this: What do we wish our field to be?

The article in question is "A Future After Freedom" by Lu Ann De Cunzo (1998), originally delivered in 1997 as part of a symposium dedicated to the idea of "archaeologists as storytellers." Organized by Mary Praetzellis, the session posed the nagging question of how archaeologists can make their raw data —their numbers, measurements, and soil colors—"live" for non-archaeologists. How can archaeologists find interesting ways in which to portray how men and women actually lived in the past? This question, although not new, has long-lasting importance for the discipline because the underlying idea is that archaeologists should do more than simply write for one another. The issue of how to present archaeology is a serious one, and those excavators engaged in interpretive archaeology, or archaeology as storytelling, have created inventive ways to imbue life to now-deceased men and women, using stories, drama, and imagined exchanges between archaeologists and their dead subjects.

Most practicing archaeologists would agree that archaeology should be as interesting to as many people as possible, but interpretive archaeology is controversial because, like all humanistic work, it is unclear who speaks for whom. When an archaeologist puts words in the mouth of an eighteenth-century farmer or a Civil War soldier, it is reasonable to ask whether we are hearing ghostly voices from the past or merely the imaginative words of the archaeologist. Unless our archaeologist can unequivocally prove some kind of psychic experience or make us believe in some sort of psychic unity with the past, we are forced to conclude that we are only hearing, at best, the educated guesses of the modern-day archaeologist. The relevant question then becomes: Are we willing to believe what we are being told? We are not even necessarily asked to consider whether the story approximates past reality, but only whether it is plausible.

Fortunately, archaeologists who engage in storytelling do not take themselves too seriously, choosing to regard what they do as playful practice (Praetzellis 1998:2). In this manner, interpretive archaeology is much like postmodern literature that constantly and sometimes confusingly glides between past and present and from scene to scene. Archaeology conceived as storytelling has the potential to increase public awareness of archaeology, but it also contains hidden dangers. Is it possible that archaeological tale-spinning could have a negative impact on the discipline by showing non-archaeologists that exacting archaeological research is largely boring? Most people on a busy city street, when asked whether they would rather read *Gone With the Wind* or a serious report about excavations at an antebellum plantation in Georgia, would undoubtedly choose the novel. Their response would be understandable. But beyond this simplistic and somewhat unfair comparison between these two genres, archaeology as storytelling contains more serious potential dangers, particularly when associated with complex, emotionally charged issues such as race and racism. A perfect example appears in De Cunzo's (1998) paper for the storytelling symposium.

I selected De Cunzo's (1998) fanciful tale for illustration specifically because race and racism figure prominently in her story. Unfortunately, the account she creates tends to say more about the current state of American historical archaeology vis-à-vis race and racism than it does about the individuals whose daily lives she attempts to humanize in her story.

De Cunzo's story, which she confidently calls a "narrative" (De Cunzo 1998:52), is based on the excavation of house lots in northern Delaware once inhabited by two African American families, the Stumps and the Walmsleys, from the 1870s to the 1920s. The foundation for De Cunzo's story line is that "the Stumps and Walmsleys drew on their pasts and looked to the future as they created a distinctive cultural style framed by racism and constrained opportunity" (De Cunzo 1998:42). Her story is thus based on the culturological understanding of much African American archaeology—which envisions African Americans as members of a distinct culture—but with a wrinkle, because the Stumps and the Walmsleys find their ability to reach a bright future constrained by racism. She openly acknowledges that the story is based on her "imagination" (De Cunzo 1998:43)—she did not actually conduct the archaeological investigations at the sites—and continues, "The stories also highlight ambivalence toward identities grounded in materialism, and to a lesser extent, racism—lesser not because it did not define these families' lives in important ways, but because its influence and injustices have received heightened attention in archaeologists' stories about African Americans in recent years. These stories of racism had in part shaped my own inaccurate image of families like the Stumps and Walmsleys. I wanted to highlight other images."

My survey of the archaeological literature certainly does not substantiate the idea that (1) large numbers of historical archaeologists have taken up race and racism as topics, or (2) that having taken them up, that the insights they have obtained are largely exhausted or at least played out enough that "other images" can be explored to the exclusion of race. This is not to argue that De Cunzo's story cannot be presented, only that it is based on a faulty reading of the literature. She further states that her reading of historical and historical archaeological literature "on African Americans and the ravages of racism had shaped my expectations of the material signatures I would find inscribed in the archaeological sites of families like the Stumps and the Walmsleys" (De Cunzo 1998:52). Significantly, however, the average publication date of the four historical studies she cites is 1967, and of the two historical archaeology studies, 1985. My reading of the historical archaeological literature indicates that a serious commitment to the study of race did not begin until the 1990s. Given this chronology, it is surprising that De Cunzo's understanding of race and racism was not at least partially shaped by her having grown up in a nation in which race has paramount importance. Her conclusion is that her "expectations" (De Cunzo 1998:52) of how the archaeological remains should "look" were shaped by her reading, not by her own lived experience. The underlying notion here has profound significance for historical archaeology because it proposes that non-African American archaeologists do not "know" about race and racism unless they read about it. The authors of this volume would tend to argue that all Americans, regardless of racial categorization, are involved on a daily basis with issues of race and racism, albeit in different ways and to different degrees.

Be this as it may, De Cunzo argues that her "stereotyped" image of the effects of racism on African Americans indeed shaped her understanding of past African American life, and that she was only released from the inherent misunderstandings of this course of thought when she paused to consider the "cultural" side of African American life. So, De Cunzo—a middle-class, non-African American archaeologist born in the twentieth century—has written a story that claims to speak for late nineteenth-century and early twentieth-century African Americans. And, just as one might expect given these circumstances, unfortunate stereotypes invade her story, especially in the context of racism: a cotton dress is worn partly because it represents the cotton Rachel Stump's ancestors picked "down South"; the men wore watch fobs that resemble military medals "to memorialize the bravery of their ancestors"; and the men and women of the story enact prescribed, caricatured gender roles (for example, the women are bossy, and the men grumble to themselves about it) (De Cunzo 1998: 47–50).

By far the most troubling part of the entire account, however, is when De Cunzo instills her African American characters with their own racist attitudes. When she has one of her characters ponder "those dirty, worthless Irish men" (De Cunzo 1998:45), she perpetuates a long-standing American prejudice against Irish immigrants (see Orser 1998b: 664–665) and replays a tired stereotypic image of Irish versus African American. In perceiving the Irish as an ethnic group, structurally unlike her racially defined African American actors, De Cunzo clearly misunderstands the mutable nature of race in American history and reifies whiteness in the "dirty" Irish. In the zero-sum society De Cunzo visualizes, African Americans can only be employed as domestics once the Irish have failed in the same occupations. Thus confronted by a story about the past that seeks to develop a nonracist storyline, but woefully does not do so, we must ask ourselves as historical archaeologists interested in race and identity: Is this the kind of story we wish to tell?

De Cunzo's tale of African American life in historic Delaware amply illustrates that historical archaeologists have a long way to go when it comes to interpreting race and racism through archaeological collections, especially when the interpretations are fabricated as stories. It is perhaps fitting that the unofficial motto of the original storytelling session (as attributed to James Deetz) was: "I'd rather be wrong in an interesting way, than right and boring" (Praetzellis 1998:2). When it comes to race, De Cunzo's story clearly shows that historical archaeologists cannot afford to be wrong in an interesting way when the tale perpetuates unfortunate stereotypes and racist attitudes.

NEW PERSPECTIVES ON RACE, MATERIAL CULTURE, AND THE ARCHAEOLOGY OF IDENTITY

The contributors to this volume collectively and courageously attempt to develop a new dialogue in American historical archaeology about race and racism, and their relations to material culture. The topics range in time from colonial history to the early twentieth century, and geographically from Jamaica to northern Michigan. The men and women investigated include frontier fur traders and Victorian city dwellers. Careful readers may discern subtle disagreements between the authors in their different ways of examining race and racism. We celebrate this intellectual variation—though single-minded purpose—as these archaeologists, the discipline's most thoughtful practitioners, turn their substantial interpretive talents to the archaeological study of race and racism.

In the next chapter, Elizabeth Scott takes us to Fort Michilimackinac, a military outpost built by the French but inhabited by the British from 1761 to 1781. Much of the previous research at the fort focused on the acceptance by the area's indigenous peoples of the French and British material culture, and on their acculturation to the Europeans' ways of doing things. Other archaeological studies have concentrated on the different adaptations the two European powers made to the environment of the northern Great Lakes. In this chapter, however, we discover that Fort Michilimackinac was a multicultural place inhabited by men and women who were considered to represent different "races," including German Jews, French Canadians, Native Americans, African Americans, and Métis. By giving us this new view of life at the fort, Scott teaches us to develop new perspectives about the role of race in the colonial enterprise.

Ywone Edwards-Ingram, in chapter 3, takes us to another colonial place that was infused with racial designations: seventeenth- through nineteenth-century Virginia. Here we see race from a different angle, one that encompasses medicinal practices. We learn that these practices exposed racism because they helped to define the social relations enacted on plantations. In Virginia's slave society, healthcare practices as basic to humanity as those associated with motherhood and child rearing were circumscribed by racist beliefs that women perceived as white provided the heirs of an estate, while the women categorized as black provided the laborers. We also learn that slaves used material things in medicinal rituals that were intended only for themselves.

In chapter 4, the setting remains in colonial Virginia, but Terrence Epperson introduces us to critical race theory, a field that addresses the legal foundations that surround the construction and perpetuation of race. Critical race theorists embrace the idea that race is a social rather than a biological creation, but they argue that race is nonetheless all too real. Living men and women experience racial identification and prejudice regardless of how that may actually conceptualize race. Epperson's careful analysis shows that the application of critical race theory to historical archaeology provides a strong challenge to archaeological orthodoxy.

Christopher Matthews, in the next chapter, moves into the eighteenth century and provides a comparative examination of two urban centers: Annapolis, Maryland, and New Orleans, Louisiana. Using a framework from political economy, Matthews explores how race becomes identity by investigating the sociohistorical contexts within which men and women defined their self-identities. This analysis necessarily includes concepts of slavery and freedom, with each word being defined somewhat differently in Annapolis and New Orleans. In both locales, however, race helped individuals conceive their social place and identity.

In chapter 6, Maria Franklin takes us back to colonial Virginia and shows us how foodways can be used as a vehicle for racial and cultural identity, and how foods can serve to construct and maintain group boundaries. Food can serve to authenticate and realize identity, and can be charged with symbolism and ideology. While the African Americans Franklin investigates were enslaved on plantations—with their foodways system thus existing within an environment of oppression and enforced poverty—they were still able to pool their knowledge and resources to produce foodways practices that demonstrated some measure of autonomous cultural production.

In chapter 7, Laurie Wilkie takes us to another plantation, this one in Louisiana and inhabited by African Americans from slavery to freedom. Wilkie uses Habermas's theory of communicative action, reinforced with personal accounts, to demonstrate how race, racism, ethnicity, gender, and class are forever intertwined. This perception of interlinkage makes it virtually impossible for archaeologists—or anyone else for that matter—to privilege any one of them when considering identity. Her findings have obvious and serious implications for any archaeology of race and identity, especially since everyday action constructs and reconstructs identity as an ongoing process.

In chapter 8, Robert Paynter moves us out the American South and into New England, a region most Americans perhaps may not immediately associate with race and racism. The assumption people often make is that the construction of identity in New England was free of the virulent prejudices associated with the master-slave relations of the antebellum South. Giving this understanding, the construction of whiteness in New England is taken as a given. To demonstrate the fallacy of this position, Paynter establishes the presence of African and Native American identities in colonial New England, and argues for the construction of an alternative archaeology that is equipped to recognize and examine the dynamics of identity formation in the American North. Individuals termed "white" in New England did not obtain this designation within a social vacuum, but only in relation to the designations "black" and "red."

Mark Leone and Gladys-Marie Fry take a different tack toward race and racism in chapter 9. Using the archaeology at Annapolis, Maryland, as a jumping-off point, Leone and Fry institute a survey of the slave narratives compiled during the early twentieth century. Using this material, they forcefully demonstrate that much of the material culture archaeologists find associated with African American deposits was probably associated with the management of spirits for both harm and good. They establish the African character of these practices from the eighteenth to the twentieth century, and as is the case with foodways (addressed by Maria Franklin in chapter 6), these patterns of behavior were racialized into characteristics of identity that carried substantive meanings with them.

Paul Mullins continues to explore African American identity in the next chapter, but moves the discussion into America's late Victorian period and adds the often ambiguous creation of Irish identity as well. Focusing on bric-a-brac, a class of object that many investigators would slough off as insignificant, Mullins demonstrates that it is charged with subtle meaning. As part of popular culture, bric-a-brac permitted consumers to evoke images, not necessarily of what they were, but rather of what they wished to be. In an in-depth exploration, Mullins illustrates how bric-a-brac was ambiguous and complex in its ability to be infused with many messages at once and in various ways. These simple objects could proclaim freedom and racial prejudice at the same time, depending upon how and when their consumers chose to contextualize them.

In chapter 11, James Delle takes us outside the boundaries of the United States to the Caribbean island of Jamaica. Using spatial analysis as a guiding thread, he demonstrates how early nineteenth-century missionaries on the island worked to create racial hierarchies as the island's legal authority moved from slavery to freedom. Delle shows how the social discourse of the island provided complex meanings of "freedom," and illustrates how members of different classes and different "races" living within racist societies can internalize very different understandings of what it means to be free.

In the final chapter, Theresa Singleton considers race, class, and identity in personal terms and delves into the archaeology of free blacks. She amply demonstrates the many issues involved in the terms "free" and "black" as legal categories. In the course of her exploration, she cogently argues that it is impossible fully to comprehend slavery unless archaeologists also comprehend freedom. The imposition of an invisible yet very real color line limited social access and freedom of movement to free men and women judged to be black both in a slave-based society and in the one we now occupy.

One of the profound messages that emerges when these individual chapters are taken together is that the archaeological study of race is not merely about the past. As individual American archaeologists—including the authors of this volume—struggle with race and racism in their own lives, they use what they know and what they have experienced to help them conceptualize the central issues that beg analysis in the contexts of the past. Every author represented in this book has encountered race and identity in various forms, and has sought to untangle their intricacies and contradictions in the past sociohistorical contexts they have chosen to study.

The project to understand race and racism will certainly not end with this volume. We hope instead that this book charts a course to a sustained dialogue within the often-conservative confines of American historical archaeology, and from here to the rest of the world. The connections of race to economics, the creation and maintenance of institutionalized poverty, the role of race in structuring and guiding intercultural connections and allegiances, the importance of race in creating space, and myriad other topics involving expressions of material culture are legitimate concerns for historical archaeologists, and each topic requires detailed and long-term research. Historical archaeologists contemplating the study of race and racism should not be affected by claims that we already know enough about race or that a topic as potentially controversial as race has no place in serious archaeological research. This book seeks to show conclusively that cries for the intellectual detachment of historical archaeology are inappropriate and ultimately harmful to a field of inquiry that has so much to offer to the understanding of our human condition.

2

"An Indolent Slothfull Set of Vagabonds": Ethnicity and Race in a Colonial Fur-Trading Community

Elizabeth M. Scott

I began writing this chapter while the United States was strafing Serbia and Kosovo, and thousands of Kosovar Albanians were fleeing into the hills or being marched out by Serbian troops or packed into railroad cars and rolled out. Images of the Nazi annihilation of Jews and other "undesirable" European groups came easily to mind. Europe is tribal if it is anything (Asad et al. 1997; Dietler 1994; Gran 1994), and the depth and strength of racist feelings there are often difficult for those of us living elsewhere to grasp. We are conditioned to think of racism as existing primarily between those of different skin color, yet it is not so long ago that Irish and Jewish members of U.S. society were not considered "white" (Brodkin 1998; Metress 1997; Orser 1998b:664–665; Roediger 1991; Sacks 1994; Smedley 1998:694). Traditional historical archaeology has rarely attempted to lay bare the social and political complexity of the North American colonies, rooted as they were in centuries of European rivalry and animosity.

This chapter looks at the ways in which, in the context of what I am calling "secondary colonization," ethnic hostilities between European groups and their differing attitudes toward American Indians and African Americans seem to have created a racist society. In particular, it looks at Fort Michilimackinac in northern Michigan during the period of British hegemony, from 1761 to 1781. This is "secondary colonization" because, as victors in the French and Indian War (or Seven Years' War, as it was known in Europe), the British in 1761 occupied and colonized what had been, for nearly fifty years, a French colonial settlement. British and French Canadian cultures clashed on economic, political, religious, and social levels; they also coexisted, albeit unequally, for twenty years.

Archaeological research at Michilimackinac has revealed numerous examples of the assertion of cultural differences by men and women in this heterogeneous fur-trading community. Documentary evidence conveys the animosity between British, French Canadian, and German-Jewish residents, and their differing attitudes toward local American Indian groups, Métis individuals (offspring of Europeans and American Indians), and the small enslaved population at the fort (American Indian and African American).

This chapter also examines how archaeologists might talk about ethnic differences—that is, those identified by a group for itself—and racism—that is, racial designations made by one group of people about another, based on perceived physical and cultural characteristics (religion, language, dress, diet, architecture). Although most historical archaeologies of race have dealt with European and Euro-American interaction with peoples of color, the colonial situation at Michilimackinac demands that we also deal with racism among peoples of the same skin color.

Race and racism have received renewed attention within anthropology in recent years, in the refutation of biological "race" (e.g., Cartmill 1998; Templeton 1998) and the investigation of culturally constructed "race" and racism (e.g., Gregory and Sanjek 1994; Harrison 1998; Hill 1998; Mukhopadhyay and Moses 1997; Orser 1998b; Smedley 1998). Recent studies of Euro-Americans have shown the importance of economic class in the determination of "racial" whiteness in U.S. society (e.g., Brodkin 1998b; Hartigan 1997a, 1997b; Krause 1998; Roedigger 1991; Zimmer-Tamakoshi 1997). Other scholars have shown that there are different kinds of racism, and that they operate in different kinds of nation-states or hegemonies (Gran 1994); that perceptions of the same indigenous group differed among various colonizing groups and how, through time, a colonizing group could change its perceptions of the skin color of the indigenous peoples it was colonizing (Gailey 1994); and that African American ethnographers are confronted with assumptions about skin color, gender, and class in their interactions with Afro-Jamaicans (Harrison 1991).

Such scholarship illuminates the complexity of interpreting race and racism in the modern (post-1400) world and in capitalist societies. My argument in this chapter is that, over a twenty-year period in one fur-trading community, cultural constructions of race were drawn between Europeans of different nationalities, religions, and cultures as well as between Europeans and Native Americans and African Americans. These constructions may be explained by specific historical, political, economic, and social factors.

In the 1300s, the English colonized Ireland, as they had done previously in Scotland and Wales, with "implantations" of English culture, a term later shortened to "plantations" (Bumsted 1982; Orser 1996:89–106, 144–158, 1998b:664–665). The English viewed the Irish as "savage," "uncivilized," and inferior, especially when they failed to accept English domination (Orser 1998b:664–665; Smedley 1998:694). Thus, a cultural template for classifying people, for categorizing the Other, was part and parcel of English (and British) culture nearly three hundred years later when Britain began its "implantations" in the Americas and Africa. Although it is true that the particular forms that racism took in the New World and Africa were the result of a coming together of specific political, economic, and social factors, a racist hierarchy was indeed already in place (ready to be filled in with Native Americans, Africans, and other Europeans) and accompanied the British to North America.

Given this, and given the fact that the British had had roughly 150 years' experience colonizing North America by the time they came to Michilimackinac in 1761, it is not difficult to accept that they classified the Native Americans and African Americans there in racist terms. However, political and economic events, specifically the recent wars with France (1744–1748, 1754–1763) resulting in Britain's ultimate conquest of France's New World colonies, made it likely that the British would include French Canadians and Métis in this racial hierarchy as well, especially (as with the Irish) when they resisted British domination. In addition to using skin color, the British racialized French Canadians and Métis as "non-white" using cultural differences: religion, language, dress, architecture, diet, and attitudes toward native peoples.

Besides approaching colonization differently than the British, as will be discussed below, the French brought a strong Celtic identity with them to North America. This identity was used throughout French history to distinguish first between the Gauls and invading Romans, then between Gallo-Romans and Franks (Germanic), and later between Breton (Brittany) and Frankish-Roman France; most recently a Celtic identity has been used in an attempt to establish a long history of union in what is now the European Community (Dietler 1994). Since the 1970s, political groups advocating a secession of Quebec from Canada have drawn on this identity and used the image of French Canadians as colonized peoples in their campaign for separation (Roosens 1989:79–83). For their origins, the Parti Québecois (PQ) point to the French as the initial occupiers of Canada, the forebears who spread to the Rockies and to Mexico. The PQ does not, however, point out that those French forebears colonized Native Americans; the French community is portrayed not as colonizer, but as colonized. In their view, the colonizers have been the English since 1760, and the recent separatist movement claims to be merely trying to end that colonization (Roosens 1989:81–82).

Looking back, then, we see that the stage was set in 1761 for a collision of cultures: British, French Canadian, Métis, Native American, and African American. In the immediate postwar climate, ethnic and racial distinctions were drawn upon to rearrange the balance of power and division of labor in the fur-trade economy at Michilimackinac.

THE SOCIAL AND POLITICAL CONTEXT

When the British army arrived at Michilimackinac in the summer of 1761, they encountered an important fur-trading village evidently changed little by France's recent defeat in the French and Indian War. Indeed, when France capitulated, the residents at Michilimackinac secured quite favorable terms of surrender: "In short, the terms preserve to them all the free exercise of their religion, and leaves them in possession of their goods, furniture, real estate and peltries. They have also reserved to them a free commerce, the same as is enjoyed by the proper subjects of the king of Great Britain" (WHC 1855–1931, 8:216). Thus life proceeded as usual there when the British army arrived to take control in September 1761.

These new colonists disembarked at a large and well-established trading town. Earlier, in the seventeenth century (1672), the French had established a fort and mission on the north shore of the Straits of Mackinac, in what is today St. Ignace, Michigan. Around 1715, French settlers, most of whom had been born in New France and migrated westward, built Michilimackinac on the south shore of the straits. Over the next fifty years this settlement grew from a Jesuit mission and small, palisaded compound to a large, well-planned, fortified trading town with several streets, rowhouses, and a parish church (Heldman 1984, 1999; Heldman and Grange 1981:15–29). In the late summer or early fall of 1761, before many of the British arrived, the trader Alexander Henry estimated that there were about 30 families living inside the palisades (Quaife 1921:40), probably between 150 and 200 people.

Although many groups of Indians, some from as far west as the Mississippi River valley, periodically visited Michilimackinac to trade or conclude treaties, the two indigenous groups residing in northern Michigan between 1761 and 1781 were the Ojibwa and the Odawa. French Canadian traders and voyageurs at Michilimackinac married both French Canadian and American Indian women. The offspring of American Indian and European marriages became known as Métis, usually defined by Europeans as "half-breeds" (McDermott 1941:103) or "mixed bloods" (Gérin-Lajoie 1976:9). All of these people had lived within the palisades during the period of French control. French men also lived with Indian peoples away from the settlement. Voyageurs and sometimes traders spent their winters living with Indian groups and accumulating their cache of furs to be traded for goods at Michilimackinac in the spring.

The French colonial regime had incorporated American Indian societies in a series of economic and military alliances that required neither "cultural absorption" nor "armed conquest" (Milner 1981:137). Thus, when the British military and settlers arrived at Michilimackinac, French Canadians, Métis, and Indians were residing in the houses the peace treaty allowed them to keep and practicing Catholicism in the church they continued to own. They were involved in reciprocal relationships, both consanguineal and affinal, with which the British were completely unfamiliar. In business and family matters French Canadians were closely tied to local Indian peoples.

These connections caused problems for

the British early in their occupation of the fort. After the Seven Years' War, in which various Indian groups had allied themselves with the French or the British, these groups could no longer play one empire against the other. Combined with the "no gift-giving" policies of British traders and military officers, the loss of their balance-of-power position led to widespread resistance by Indian peoples in the Great Lakes region. In 1763, in a series of coordinated attacks known as Pontiac's War, Indian groups successfully revolted against the British.

At Michilimackinac, the local Ojibwa attacked the fort without having consulted with the local Odawa. This led the Odawa to protect some of the British as prisoners, later releasing or ransoming them. The Ojibwa did not attack the French Canadians at the fort, who, significantly, did virtually nothing to assist the British during the attack, and remained there afterwards to share control with the Ojibwa and Odawa. Most of the British military at Michilimackinac, as well as one British trader, were killed. Ezekiel Solomon, who will be discussed in more detail below, was one of the traders kept prisoner and later ransomed at Montreal (Quaife 1921:105). A year later, in the summer of 1764, representatives from the local Ojibwa answered a request from Sir William Johnson, the superintendent of Indian affairs in the Northern Department, to go to Fort Niagara in New York and conclude a peace treaty (Quaife 1921:158–159). Alexander Henry accompanied them, and they returned to Michilimackinac with the British military, French Canadian "volunteers," and several allies from various Indian groups. The local Ojibwa and Odawa agreed to peace and the reestablishment of the post at Michilimackinac (Quaife 1921:166–180; Johnson 1921–1965, 4:512).

Some British traders and merchants had preceded the 1761 occupation of the fort, among them John Askin and Alexander Henry. They were among the first to establish the relationships with French Canadians, Métis, and Indian groups that they would need to succeed in the fur trade. Peddlers, or sutlers, to the British army, including Ezekiel Solomon, also preceded the troops. They supplied the army with necessities and later became fur traders themselves.

However, it wasn't until after the 1764 peace agreement that civilians migrated in significant numbers to Michilimackinac and the Upper Great Lakes. Aside from the fact that peace had just been concluded with local Indian groups, 1764 was also when civilian government was reestablished in Canada. From 1760 to 1764, military rule had been imposed on the colony by the British victors, and until the Treaty of Paris was signed in 1763, there was still hope among the French Canadian population that New France might be returned to France (Igartua 1974:45). Thus, it was after British civilian government was established that the largest influx of new settlers came to Michilimackinac.

These immigrants included men, women, and children who came from other colonies in the New World and from Great Britain itself, as was true for Canada generally (Scott 1933:107). During and especially after the Seven Years' War, people left Scotland for the New World, settling primarily in Canada and parts of the southern colonies (Bumsted 1982). John Askin, a man of Scottish descent, came to the New World from Ireland in 1759, and came to Michilimackinac very soon thereafter (Quaife 1928:4–6). Among the immigrants also were persons from countries other than Great Britain who chose to come to recently acquired British lands. Ezekiel Solomon, originally from Germany, came to Canada along with the British army and later became a fur trader, as did several other Jewish peddlers, or sutlers, from Germany and Britain (Marcus 1970:381–388). Some settlers came from Dutch or other European communities in the eastern seaboard colonies. Arent Schuyler DePeyster, a commanding officer at Michilimackinac in the 1770s, was part of an aristocratic Dutch family in New York City; his wife was Scottish (Armour and Widder 1978:8).

Because no census or other governmental

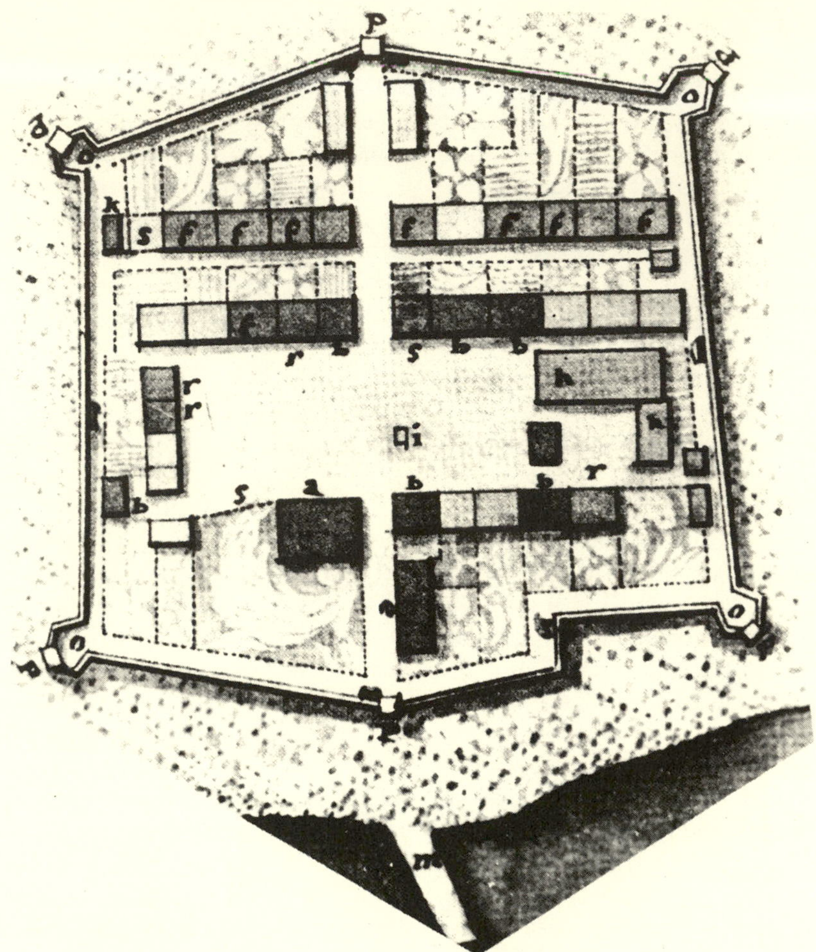

Figure 2.1. Lt. Perkins Magra's 1766 map of Fort Michilimackinac. Magra's legend identified: (a) the commanding officer's house, (b) inhabitants' [French Canadians] houses occupied by the officers, (e) provision store, (f) houses occupied by the soldiers, (r) English traders' houses, (h) chapel and priest's house, (i) a well, (k) a [powder] magazine, (s) king's lots. Those houses not labeled presumably had French Canadian or other non-British residents. (Courtesy of the William L. Clements Library, University of Michigan)

record of population exists for Michilimackinac between 1761 and 1781, it is only possible to estimate the number of people, using church, military, and personal records (Scott 1991b:36). The estimate of 150 to 200 French Canadian and Métis residents in 1761 was mentioned earlier. Lt. Perkins Magra's sketch of Michilimackinac in 1766 (Figure 2.1) and information from Armour and Widder (1978:11) suggest a conservative estimate of 75 British residents inside the fort at that time. However, by the late 1770s, the "suburbs" outside had grown to contain a hundred houses (Williams and Shapiro 1982), and a conservative estimate of 200 to 400 people might have inhabited them, likely including people of all the ethnic groups present in the settlement.

During the twenty years examined here, not only did the population residing at Michilimackinac increase from roughly 150 to 500 (a conservative estimate), it also fluctuated greatly in the course of a year. Some people lived in houses at the settlement only during the spring, summer, and fall. Throughout the spring and summer, hundreds more people gathered there, perhaps for only a few weeks, to exchange their winter's furs for goods and food, to collect supplies for trading ventures farther west, and to meet with government officials. Consequently, these population estimates are likely lower than was the case, especially given the large influx of people to Michilimackinac in the summers.

THE ECONOMY

British colonists joined an existing economic system at Michilimackinac based on the fur trade and tied to the rest of the world economy of the eighteenth century. The trade in furs had been common in Europe for several centuries (Serjeantson 1989a:129–131; Wolf 1982:158–159), and furs were the resource to be extracted from the Great Lakes region in both the French and British colonial regimes. Furs were produced primarily for the manufacture of felt hats. Beaver fur was most highly valued because the barbed hairs of the inner layer of fur could be pressed or "felted" together more closely than the fur of other animals, thereby making a more durable hat (Wolf 1982:159–160). Beavers had become extinct in England and Wales in the Middle Ages (Serjeantson 1989a:131).

A Clash of Capitalisms

Colonists and government officials at Michilimackinac and elsewhere in Canada used furs as currency (Quaife 1921:55–56; Johnson 1921–1965, 4:489–491, 893–896), and this is reflected archaeologically in the dearth of coins recovered at Michilimackinac (Heldman 1980). In many ways this was a barter economy, with furs, foodstuffs, and material goods used as payments for services and in exchange. In addition, the isolation caused by frozen or impassable lakes for half the year contributed to the self-sufficient nature of the community at Michilimackinac. This was similar to the frontier exchange economy of France's lower Mississippi Valley colony (Nobles 1989; Usner 1987, 1992).

The fur trade was based on credit, and thus face-to-face relationships were crucial to the system. Traders had to "purchase" material goods and foodstuffs on credit and then trade them to Indian groups or other traders for furs, repaying the merchant with the furs at the end of the year, when the trader would receive more goods on credit for the next year. Debts often were carried for months and sometimes years, and the parties involved knew each other personally. These kinds of economic relations were known also in other colonies prior to the American Revolution (Breen 1988:76; Briggs 1990; Isaac 1982:29, 120; Nobles 1989; Usner 1987:166–167).

Although this general characterization holds true for both groups, there were important differences between French and British approaches to the fur trade. The French fur trade was carried out according to tradition, personal honor between parties, and government regulation of "fair prices" for the "common welfare" (Igartua 1974:142–144, 177–178). Indeed, prior to 1760, the French Compagnie des Indes held the export monopoly for beaver and was bound to buy beaver in the colony at fixed prices (Igartua 1974:131). José Igartua has characterized this traditional approach as the conjunction of two distinct forces: (1) Indian attitudes toward trade that were not concerned with market mechanisms of supply and demand, and which were not separated from political, military, and religious activities, and (2) the French government's paternalism, which restricted the supply of furs by limiting the number of traders and regulating fur prices on the French market (Igartua 1974:245–246).

The British, however, viewed trading simply as a matter of price competition, and beaver prices therefore were subject to market fluctuations in price and demand (Igartua 1974:142–144). In 1763, the British established a licensing system in which all traders were required to bond their expeditions for double the value of their trade goods (Miquelon 1966:42). By 1767, a British domination of the fur trade began to emerge, with French Canadians conducting the trading ventures, but British merchants supplying the financial backing (Igartua 1974:255–256). British traders gained a further advantage from the British military's distrust of French Canadians and were able to increase their control over the fur trade and its wealth. French Canadians simply did not change their traditional way of conducting business and so were not "competitive" according to British rules of the game (Igartua 1974:148, 259–265).

Political and military decisions after the conquest also had much to do with these changes in the fur trade. At the end of the Seven Years' War, the British decided not to follow what they considered to be the extravagant French gift-giving policy with Indian groups (Igartua 1974:54–55). This led to widespread revolt in the Upper Great Lakes, which led in turn, once peace was restored in 1764, to the British government's attempt to restrict the trade to the posts themselves (Igartua 1974:62–63). Traders, both British and French Canadian, decried these restrictions, which did not allow them to winter with Indian groups and thereby go out and get the furs; by 1768, the regulations were somewhat loosened (Igartua 1974:70–74).

The Quebec Act and the Quebec Revenue Act, both passed in 1774, had widespread ramifications for the colony. In the fur trade, these acts increased the advantage of British merchants to the detriment of merchants in the American seaboard colonies; import duties were set on liquors coming from the American colonies such that British imports were cheaper (Igartua 1974:74–76; Miquelon 1966:144). Concerning social relations in general in Canada, these acts allowed French laws to be maintained and allowed Catholicism to be, essentially, the established religion of the province (Igartua 1974:74–76).

These acts were merely the formal recognition of conditions that had existed in Canada from 1760 onward. In 1765, there were at least 70,000 Catholics in Canada and fewer than 1,000 Protestants (Igartua 1974:60). French Canadians had continued to follow French law and custom in legal and commercial matters (Igartua 1974:148; Scott 1933). French notaries, although unlicensed by the new British government, continued to draw up deeds, marriage contracts, and wills for French Canadians (Scott 1933:151, 214, 290; Igartua 1974:159). Criminal law was English, but French Canadians could practice law in any of the courts in Canada, and exceptions to English law were made in civil courts: French Canadians could be tried in civil cases by French Canadian jurors, British colonists by British jurors, and in cases pitting British colonists against French Canadians, the juries were to be half British and half French Canadian (Scott 1933:185).

This quite remarkable arrangement attests to the strength of French resistance to British colonization in Canada. In Great Britain at this time, Catholics were barred from holding office in local or national government and were excluded from the legal profession (Scott 1933:92). While this ban held for positions in the colony's governing council (Igartua 1974:60), it did not hold for civil law in Canada. Thus, French Canadians were allowed their own representation and juries in the majority of legal issues affecting commerce and business. They also maintained their own property and inheritance laws, primarily through notaries.

Although the British became the dominant force politically, militarily, and economically in Canada, British and French Canadian cultural traditions, or "ways of doing things," coexisted, albeit unequally. It was this character of the colony, and its very real dependence on American Indian peoples for furs, that set it apart from the eastern seaboard colonies. This is clearly seen in the years preceding and during the American Revolution. British colonists in Canada remained just that—colonists—and had no desire to break with Great Britain. Unlike the American rebels, the British at Michilimackinac did not protest taxes and non-representation, and therefore did not boycott British goods (compare Breen 1988 for the seaboard colony boycotts). During and after the American Revolution, Loyalists fled to many parts of Canada, including Michilimackinac (Phyn and Ellice 1767–1776, 3:173; Norton 1976:399, 402; MPHC 1874–1929, 9:575–576).

Division of Labor: Who Did What for Whom?

Historic documents for Michilimackinac reveal a division of labor by class, gender, and ethnicity. It was a society politically and economically dominated by British men. The commanding officer held both military and civilian authority, and continued to do so even after military rule had been lifted in Canada in 1764. The troops, usually numbering around sixty men, were stationed there to maintain physical control of the area for Great Britain (Armour and Widder 1978: 11; Dunnigan 1973:13–17). Fur trading was dominated by men as well, at least on the European side. Virtually all men at Michilimackinac, no matter their primary occupation, also were involved in the fur trade.

There was a great degree of economic interdependence between cultural groups at Michilimackinac. European merchants and traders depended on other groups to provide the furs and to transport goods and furs. American Indians and French Canadian hunters and trappers (*coureurs des bois*) actually procured the fur-bearing animals. In the summer of 1716, approximately six hundred *coureurs des bois* gathered at Michilimackinac with their winter's furs (Ayer map of 1717). Merchandise was brought up the lakes, and furs taken back down, by men who formed the canoe crews, usually French Canadians, Métis, or American Indians. Interpreters in this community were French Canadian or Métis men; they were an absolute necessity in the fur trade and in maintaining good relations between Europeans and Indian groups.

Although European fur trading was dominated by men, at least three women were involved with their husbands in the fur trade. Alexander Henry identified one such woman, Madame Cadotte, as Ojibwa (Quaife 1921: 154–155). However, we do not know the ethnicity of the other two women, Mrs. Ainsee and Madame Chaboillez, who were identified in the documents only by their husbands' French Canadian names. During the nineteenth century, the women at Mackinac who engaged with their husbands in the fur trade were either Native American or Métis (McDowell 1978; Peterson 1981; Van Kirk 1980; Widder 1999, 1987). It is possible that this was the case in the eighteenth century as well.

The British military and Indian Department obtained foodstuffs from British men, French Canadian men and women, and Indian men and women. This food was primarily corn, used mainly for provisioning canoe crews, but French Canadians also supplied wheat, and American Indians supplied meat and maple sugar. British troops also maintained vegetable gardens and livestock at the fort for their own use.

French Canadian and Indian men were considered by the British as surplus troops to be called on during war. "Hired men" in this community were usually French Canadian or Indian. All of the servants identified in the historic documents were men; the military hired mostly British servants, and British traders hired mostly French Canadian servants. No women were specifically noted as servants in the historic documents examined here, although it seems likely that women servants were present.

American Indians and African Americans comprised the small enslaved population at Michilimackinac, numbering probably no more than fifteen. They were primarily house slaves, although one African American man enslaved by John Askin transported Askin's goods and furs by sailing ship between Michilimackinac and Sault Ste. Marie to the north. British, French Canadian, and Métis residents owned Native American slaves. These men and women were frequently identified in the documents as "paunis" and "paunisse," using the French masculine and feminine forms. The name may have originated with the trading or selling of Pawnee Indians who lived farther west (Armour and Widder 1978:36), for these slaves do not seem to have been from local Indian groups. By the last quarter of the eighteenth century, "panis" seems to have been a generic term used by the British and French Canadians for Indian slaves. African American men and one mulatto woman were owned by wealthy

British colonists in the settlement, and one African American man was enslaved by the priests of the Church of Ste. Anne. In addition, enslaved Africans or African Americans were included in the merchandise accounts of several British merchants and traders and two Jewish traders at Michilimackinac, although those slaves may or may not have resided there.

Within this division of labor we see other examples of the interdependence among various ethnic groups at Michilimackinac. It is significant that, in the written records examined here, the British were never interpreters, canoe crewmen, or "hired men," and they depended to a great degree on French Canadians to do much of the face-to-face trading with Indian groups. These were all positions that were crucial to the maintenance of the fur-trade economy at Michilimackinac, the raison d'être for British presence there.

The documents also indicate a rather general division of labor by gender. Men's work at Michilimackinac took place predominantly outside their homes, whether it involved trading goods for furs, paddling canoes, blacksmithing, carpentry, farming, hunting, fishing, or military duties. When men did engage in activities inside the household, such as the lead shot manufacture and metalwork carried out by Ezekiel Solomon and Gershon Levy (Halchin 1985), the products of that work often were used in business, such as fur trading. The exceptions to this were men who were servants or slaves in other men's houses. Their work was largely confined to the household, although John Askin's African American slave Pompey, who sailed his ships, was an exception even to this. The kinds of work that male servants and slaves did in the household likely depended on whether or not female servants and slaves worked in the same house as well.

French Canadian and British women were engaged most often in maintaining households. They worked in their own and in others' households, the wealthier women overseeing work performed by servants and slaves. This work included preparing food and drink, sewing, washing clothes, and child care. French Canadian and Métis women did engage in maple sugar production, which took place outside the fort. In addition, there were the three women who were partners in their husbands' fur-trading businesses, and who were American Indian and French Canadian or Métis.

Thus, there seem to have been four broadly defined economic groups in the settlement at Michilimackinac under British control. For analytical purposes I will call these classes, based on the degree of wealth and control over the products of one's labor or the labor of others. The upper class was self-employed or employed by the British government: the military officers, merchants, wealthier traders, and their families. The middle class was partly self-employed and partly employed by the upper class: middle-class fur traders, noncommissioned officers, soldiers, clerks, interpreters, and their families. The lower class worked for the middle and upper classes: poorer traders, hunters and trappers, artisans and laborers, canoe crewmen, "hired men," servants, and their families. Enslaved men and women had little if any political or economic power in the society.

Those in political control, the British, referred to these groups of people in class terms, but they combined ethnic, racial, and economic prejudices in their system of categorization. The British saw themselves as superior, even when their degree of wealth and occupation were the same as or lower than those of French Canadians or Métis. Although this view is the most evident to researchers, it was only one perspective of social organization in the community. The French Canadians, Métis, and American Indians who were dominated by the British politically and, to a large extent, economically, certainly viewed the situation differently. These groups likely used their own strategies for resisting this domination. Such perspectives, however, are more difficult to discern through the written and archaeological records than is the perspective of the dominant group, or what Peter Worsley (1981:

111) has called the "sub-culture of those who dominate."

OTHER CLASHES: ATTITUDES ABOUT ETHNICITY, RACE, AND RELIGION

British and French Canadians

The British saw themselves as distinctly different from, and superior to, French Canadian, Jewish, American Indian, and African American residents at the fort. Eighteenth-century British colonists referred to the French Canadians of what had been New France as Canadians and to themselves as English. It was not until sometime in the nineteenth century that the descendants of British colonists in Canada began to call themselves Canadians (Pacquet and Wallot 1987).

The British resented the trading ties and alliances already existing between French Canadians and Indian groups. These sentiments are clearly evident in the remarks of Maj. Robert Rogers, commanding officer at Michilimackinac in 1767:

> Since it is in fact true / and can be reported By a Multitude of Witnesses / that the French at Michilimackinac, St. Josephs the Green Bay, St. Mary's and other places in this Country where they are lurking & walking up and down, are an Indolent Slothfull Set of vagabonds, ill disposed to the English and having great influence over the Savages are continualy exciting their Jealosys, and Stiring up their hatred and Revenge against us, Ought they not therefore as Speedily as possible to be removed out of this Country for the better Security of British Subjects and British Trade? (Clements 1918:270–271)

Although Rogers's proposal was not carried out, the sentiments he expressed must have remained.

The British military were concerned throughout the period under study that the French would ally themselves with Indian groups and attack them as they had done in the Seven Years' War. During the American Revolution they feared that this alliance would extend to the American rebels as well. In 1778 the French residents, as well as some British traders, at Michilimackinac petitioned for a Catholic priest to be sent to the community, which had had only occasional itinerant priests since 1765 (Donnelly 1971: 39–59, 98–99). Arent Schuyler DePeyster, the commanding officer at the time, initially approved of this, but worried that "in case of a French War" it might be dangerous "to allow so many Ignorant Canoe men and Savages to have free access to the Church as it at present stands within the Fort. Were it removed into the Village, which is now become a Considerable place, it would obviate all objections I can possibly have" (MPHC 1874–1929, 9: 367).

Elsewhere in Canada, for example at Montreal and Three Rivers, the records of Protestant churches reveal that roughly half of the marriages prior to 1775 were between British and French Canadians (Scott 1933: 109–110). There was no Protestant church at Michilimackinac, and priests probably would not have performed marriages unless both parties were Catholic (Scott 1933:110). Although a few civil ceremonies performed by British commanding officers and justices of the peace were recorded in the Catholic church register, those records are understandably biased toward French Canadian Catholic marriages. To my knowledge, these are the only available records of marriages at Michilimackinac.

Indications of British-French intermarriage at Michilimackinac are slight indeed. In 1772, the wealthy merchant John Askin married Archange Barthe, a French Canadian woman from a Detroit trading family, after which Askin became closely associated with Archange's brothers and father in the fur trade (Quaife 1928:65–164). Between 1760 and 1781, twelve marriages were recorded in the register of the Catholic church at Michilimackinac (WHC 1855–1931, 18:485–490). Eleven of these were between French Canadian men and women, and one was between a British woman and man.

American Indians and Métis

There was in the eighteenth century a marked difference between French Canadian and British attitudes toward the native peoples they colonized. While both European groups saw American Indians as Other and as racially different, French Canadians allowed for their integration in society through marriage and religion, whereas the British generally did not. Indeed, the British viewed the French as inferior partly because of their willingness to "mix" with native groups.

Missionizing and conversion to Catholicism were key elements in French colonization (Axtell 1981; Zuckerman 1987). The French began the settlement at Michilimackinac as a Jesuit mission to convert local Indian groups and as a small fur-trading compound for themselves. They allowed people of any "race" to be converted, such that once local Indians were converted, or at least baptized, they were acceptable marriage partners and had a place in the community. Conversion led the way to civilizing, or becoming French.

The British view was markedly different. No British missionaries came to Michilimackinac, and conversion of local Indians is not discussed in the documents. The British believed it was necessary to "civilize" American Indians first, before converting them to Protestantism, or at least to do both at the same time (Rothenberg 1980; Zuckerman 1987:147, 149). Becoming British was a prerequisite for becoming Protestant. Although the British attempted to convert Indians in their eastern seaboard colonies (Axtell 1981; Rothenberg 1980; Zuckerman 1987), they did not do so in Canada. This perhaps was related to the "secondary colonization" of Canada and the continuing presence of French Canadians and Catholicism.

The British belief that American Indians were racially inferior is quite clear at Michilimackinac, as it was in other British colonies (Sheehan 1980). One year after the successful Indian revolt in the Upper Great Lakes, Thomas Gage wrote Sir William Johnson that the Ojibwa at Michilimackinac were "the worst People and greatest Thieves that Inhabit the Lakes" (Johnson 1921–1965, 4: 484). Robert Rogers, commanding officer at Michilimackinac in 1767, referred to Indians, as did most British colonists, as "Savages" (Clements 1918:263–264). In 1779, another commanding officer, Patrick Sinclair, expressed the view that the British should keep American Indians dependent on them for necessities, but not allow them to accumulate too many goods: "The Indians from Montreal, some of them of little note, & other dispicable receive a profusion of Presents. I met some young men with four guns each, their clothing was too good & in too great quantity, but endeavor, I beseech you, to bring about an attention to the necessity of keeping them dependant upon us for arms, & as much so for everything else as possible" (MPHC 1874–1929, 9:526–527).

Sinclair also expressed a denigrating attitude toward European men (mostly French Canadians) who had married Indian women or who lived with Indian groups. When the local Ojibwa ceded Mackinac Island to the British in 1780, Sinclair told them that "all of the White People who were married amongst them were called in & would have lotts of land on the Island. They send them in daily now & I hope we shall be able to clear the Country of such Destructive Members and make them usefull to themselves & to the Post" (MPHC 1874–1929, 9:579). Michael Zuckerman (1987:145) has described for other North American colonies this British attitude toward "men who mixed with the natives or embraced their ways in any measure." He contrasts Britain's unwillingness to accept American Indians with the willingness of France, Spain, and Portugal to incorporate the Indian "to one degree or another" in their colonial cultures (Zuckerman 1987:145).

The clearest indication of marriages or unions between French Canadian men and Indian women at Michilimackinac is found in the baptismal records of the Catholic Church of Ste. Anne (WHC 1855-1931, 19:59–78). When they were known, the priests identified the baptized individual by his or her parents' names. The records of fifty-four baptisms between 1760 and 1781 reveal forty-three marriages or unions. Nineteen of these (44.2 percent) were between men and women who were both French Canadian; eight (17.6 percent) were between French Canadian men and Indian or Métis women. Another five (11.6 percent) of the unions were between French Canadian men and slave women, presumably Indian slaves. There is no indication that African American women lived at Michilimackinac for any length of time during this period. The one mulatto woman mentioned as a slave seems to have lived there only briefly (Quaife 1928:105–107). Thus, I assume that the mothers identified in the baptismal records as "slaves" were Native Americans.

In spite of the problem of identifying ethnicity based on names alone, the documents examined here do reveal a marked difference in British and French Canadian intermarriage with Indian women. The British were much less willing to formalize unions with Indian women, either by marriage or by baptism of the children from those unions. No marriages between British men and Indian or Métis women were recorded in the church register for this period, and no baptisms for children with British fathers and Indian or Métis mothers.

Although there is no indication that British men married Indian women at Michilimackinac, sexual relations between them were common. Prior to his marriage to the French Canadian Archange Barthe, John Askin lived for several years with an Indian woman, possibly a slave, and they had several children who continued to live with Askin after his marriage (Askin 1766; Quaife 1928:12–13). When John Long visited Michilimackinac in 1779, he noted that because of the successful revolt in 1763, no Indian was allowed to "enter the fort with firearms, nor any squaw or Indian woman allowed to sleep within the walls of the garrison on any pretense whatever" (Quaife 1922:177–180). When Long tried to sneak some Indian women inside the fort despite the order, he was caught. However, the commanding officer's joking reprimand suggests that the order was concerned not with forbidding such relations, only with regulating where they might or might not take place (Quaife 1922:177–180).

Several songs and poems composed by Arent Schuyler DePeyster, one of the commanding officers at Michilimackinac, concern these relationships between British men and Indian women. In 1779, as he was leaving with the troops during the American Revolution, he wrote as part of a song, "We soldiers bid adieu, / An leave each squa a child on back, / Nay some are left with two" (DePeyster 1813:95–97). In a poem about maple sugaring he described the Indian "kept-mistresses" of British men (DePeyster 1813: 90–92).

Attitudes of Indian women toward relationships with European men is much more difficult to ascertain from the available documents. During the nineteenth century, unions between Indian or Métis women and Euro-American fur traders and merchants were important in establishing and maintaining business relationships. The unions, and especially formal marriages, joined both sides in reciprocal obligations and responsibilities (Brown 1980; Peterson 1981; Van Kirk 1980).

There is some indication at eighteenth-century Michilimackinac that Indian groups expected European men who were involved with Indian women to bear some economic responsibility for the women's relatives. When DePeyster described the Indian "kept-mistresses" of some of the British "gentlemen," he noted that their relatives were "very troublesome." It was, he said, "no less than keeping the whole family" (DePeyster 1813: 90–92). It is possible that, as in the nineteenth-century fur trade, these Indian women near Michilimackinac entered into relationships with European men in order to enhance the social and economic position of their families in a fur-trade society. The documentary evidence indicates that French Canadian men may have approached these unions with similar aims, since they often formalized them as marriages. However, British men at Michilimackinac seem to have had no such intentions for permanent relationships with Indian women.

Although sexual relations between British men and Native American women were not formalized or legalized, they apparently were common at Michilimackinac between 1761 and 1781. Zuckerman (1987) has described a very different situation for the eastern seaboard colonies in the seventeenth and eighteenth centuries, where British men largely abstained from sexual relations with Indian women. Later, in the nineteenth century in Canada, British and American men often formalized their relationships with Indian women. This occurred as Métis peoples formed a more cohesive and defined ethnic group within nineteenth-century Canadian society (Brown 1980; Peterson 1981; Peterson and Brown 1985; Van Kirk 1980).

"Métis" was not a term used by the eighteenth-century colonists at Michilimackinac. It is used here to discuss persons with Euro-American and Indian parents because after about 1815 these people in Canada began referring to themselves as Métis (Peterson 1981). They were, however, distinguished separately as early as 1749 by the Swedish naturalist Peter Kalm during his travels in lower New France (Benson 1987). He noted that "the Indian blood in Canada is very much mixed with European blood, and a large number of the Indians now living owe their origin to Europe" (Benson 1987:456–457). He further stated that these persons of mixed European-Indian heritage "dressed like the Indians and regulated all their affairs in their way. It is therefore difficult to distinguish them, except by their color, which is somewhat whiter than that of the Indians" (Benson 1987:456–457). Kalm also noted that there were "examples of some Frenchmen going amongst the Indians and following their mode of life" (Benson 1987:456–457).

There were Métis families at Michilimackinac as early as the 1730s. In his map and description of the settlement made in 1749, a French Canadian aristocrat named Michel Lotbinière noted that ten French families were living inside the fort, "among whom three are of mixed blood" (Gérin-Lajoie 1976:9). Fifteen years later, when he described the fort for the newly victorious British government, he noted again that some of the twelve to fifteen French families were of "mixed blood" (Lotbinière 1764). However, in none of the other documents written by colonists at Michilimackinac between 1761 and 1781 have I found such distinctions made. For example, John Askin never referred to his Métis children differently than he did the children from his later marriage to the French Canadian woman, Archange (Quaife 1928). British military correspondence likewise does not identify persons as part Indian or "mixed blood." Yet, through parental names, the baptismal records clearly show that Métis families, or at least Métis children, lived in the community during this time. It seems, then, that the particular families in which Métis people grew up—that is, the cultural contexts—were more important in shaping their perceptions of themselves and others' perceptions of them in this community than were any biological—that is, racial—distinctions. In other words, those who grew up in French Canadian homes considered themselves, and were considered by others, to be French Canadian. Those who grew up in both French Canadian and Indian settings were perceived as just that, people who were both French Canadian and Indian, or who moved back and forth between the two cultures. And those who grew up in British homes were considered to be British. This was a different situation than that of Métis peoples in Canada after 1815, when they began to think of themselves as a cohesive group set apart from others. Persons of mixed European-Indian heritage in the community at Michilimackinac in the middle to late eighteenth century were antecedent to the later group.

African Americans

The African American men and one mulatto woman who lived at Michilimackinac were enslaved, with one exception, by wealthy British colonists. British merchants and traders at Michilimackinac also occasionally bought and sold African American men and women as slaves; they were listed as merchandise and property on account ledgers and personal estate inventories (Pond et al. 1773–1775; Askin 1776–1779).

Little mention is made about enslaved persons in the documents, but we might be safe in assuming that they performed labor related to households and to the fur trade. John Askin enslaved two men, named Pompey and Jupiter, and entrusted Pompey, at least, with transporting goods and furs by sailing ship in the Upper Great Lakes. One African American man, about twenty years old, "belonging to" the Jesuit mission at the fort, was described as being "sufficiently instructed to even serve at the holy mass" following his baptism in 1762 (WHC 1855–1931, 19:64).

Except for this notation by the priests, there is no documentary evidence for French Canadian attitudes toward African American slaves at Michilimackinac. It is perhaps worth noting, however, that despite the trafficking in African American slaves carried out by British merchants and traders at Michilimackinac—that is, despite their availability—there is little indication that French Canadians owned them.

Jewish Traders

From 1765 until 1781, two Jewish traders, Ezekiel Solomon and Gershon Levy, lived in one of the houses at Michilimackinac that has been completely excavated (Halchin 1985; Heldman 1986). In order to understand their social and economic position in the community at Michilimackinac, it is necessary first to place them in the broader context of Jewish presence in Canada, and to understand French Canadian and British attitudes toward them.

Since the late seventeenth century, Jewish sutlers or purveyors had supplied English armies with foodstuffs and material necessities during its wars with Europe (Marcus 1970:707). Quartermaster or commissary work was a common Jewish occupation on the Continent in the eighteenth century (Marcus 1951:225). A sizable number of Anglo-German Jews accompanied the British troops to North America in 1759 and 1760, at the end of the French and Indian War, and remained in Canada afterward to become fur traders and merchants. Among these were Ezekiel Solomon, Levy Solomon, Chapman Abraham, Benjamin Lyon, and Gershon Levy (Marcus 1970:708).

These five Jewish traders formed a consortium during and immediately after the French and Indian War. They worked out of Montreal, Quebec, and Albany, obtaining merchandise from London and New York, and trading as far west as the western shore of Lake Superior (Marcus 1970:727–728). They divided up the area from Niagara to Michilimackinac with, for example, Chapman Abraham primarily at Detroit and Ezekiel Solomon at Michilimackinac and beyond (Marcus 1951:226). During the 1763 revolt in the upper posts, the consortium lost around £18,000 and were forced into bankruptcy (Marcus 1970:728; 1951:230–234). After this, the five traders seem to have gone their separate ways, forming partnerships with one or more of the original group but with other British traders as well.

Jacob Marcus (1970:387) has estimated that by 1780, there were perhaps thirty Jewish family heads or householders in Canada, most of whom were shopkeepers, fur traders, or merchants concentrated in Montreal. Although Jewish families were established there in the early 1760s, it was not until about 1775 that a formal community was present (Marcus 1970:382; 1953:436–437). Congregation Shearith Israel built its synagogue there in 1777 and adopted its constitution in 1778 (*Minute Book of Congregation Shearith Israel,* Marcus 1959:105). Ezekiel Solomon and Benjamin Lyon, the two Jewish traders most associated with Michilimackinac, were founding members of this congregation in Montreal.

During the period of British control at Michilimackinac, three Jewish traders resided there. Ezekiel Solomon was German, but we do not know the nationality of Gershon Levy or Benjamin Lyon. Solomon and Lyon were active in the community at Michilimackinac, pledging in 1778 along with many other merchants and traders to financially support a Catholic missionary there (MPHC 1874–1929, 10:288–290).

In general, the Jewish community in Canada allied itself with the British against an overwhelming French Catholic majority (Marcus 1970:387–388). Yet anti-semitism at Michilimackinac appears to have been stronger among the British than among the French Canadians. In the summer of 1776, Ezekiel Solomon arrived at Michilimackinac later in the season than usual only to find that one James Bannerman had sold Solomon's goods to someone else. Solomon demanded his goods, and Bannerman was forced to supply them, although he reacted to the situation by writing a friend, "Never had poor Devil more trouble than I have had with the Jews and their Contracts" (Wallace 1934:54–55). Ezekiel was identified by Sir William Johnsonn's aide in Caghnawagey, New York, as "Solomon the Jew from Michilic" (Johnson 1921–1965, 7:948–949).

French Canadian attitudes are less evident in the documents from the British period of control at Michilimackinac. However, one bit of evidence from the French royal notary's records is illuminating. Although the French refused to sell their houses to the British, choosing instead to make the British rent them, one French family, the Parants, sold their house to Ezekiel Solomon and Gershon Levy (Halchin 1985:38; Heldman 1999: 310). It thus seems that the French recognized Solomon and Levy as distinct from the British, either because of their Jewishness or their German-ness or both, and that they extended to the Anglo-German Jews preferential treatment compared to the British.

ARCHAEOLOGICAL EVIDENCE OF CULTURAL DIFFERENCES

The complexity of the political, economic, and social milieu in which the people at Michilimackinac lived and worked is apparent from the documentary evidence. The picture drawn from the archaeological records of their activities at the settlement both adds to and illuminates that complexity in material terms. I turn now to an archaeological overview of the settlement patterns and structures that have been identified at Michilimackinac, and interpretations made from them about socioeconomic position and cultural differences.

The results of forty-two consecutive years of excavation at Fort Michilimackinac have permitted archaeologists to identify four settlement patterns for the sixty-five-year European occupation of the site (Heldman 1984). The 1715 French settlement consisted of a small palisaded compound housing fur traders, missionaries, and a small number of French soldiers, with a Jesuit mission located outside the palisades on the west. Sometime in the early 1730s, the French greatly expanded the palisaded settlement, and the mission was enclosed within it. Seven rowhouses were built to accommodate the influx of French colonists engaged in an expanding fur trade. In 1744, for defensive reasons during the war with Britain, a second palisade was built around the fort, and a triangular earthwork constructed on the west. This was the settlement taken over by the British in 1761 (Lotbinière 1764), and when the British returned in 1764 after Pontiac's War, they began rebuilding and expanding it (see Figure 2.1). Over the next decade, they pushed out the north and south palisades to make room for provision stores, and used part of the central parade ground to build a soldier's barracks (Heldman and Grange 1981:39, 43). Beginning in 1765, many of the newly arriving British traders and merchants were ordered to build houses outside the fort on the east, in what became known as the "subarbs" (Williams and Shapiro 1982).

All of these occupational sequences have been identified archaeologically (Halchin 1985; Heldman 1977, 1978, 1984, 1999; Heldman and Grange 1981). Original construction of the rowhouses in the 1730s and their rebuilding around 1765 are clearly evident in the wall ditches. The French period deposits dating from the 1730s to 1761 are of a gray sandy loam, and the later British period deposits dating from 1761 to 1781 are of a brown sandy loam.

Once the British established military control at the fort, they also controlled the shipping routes and determined which goods were allowed into the settlement. British firms had a monopoly on shipping goods to this new colonial market, to the detriment of French firms. Thus, after 1761, few French commodities were available to the fort's residents; this is at least true for those materials most often depended upon by archaeologists: ceramics, bottles, and glassware. It therefore becomes difficult to determine from the artifacts which households may have been occupied by French Canadian or British civilian residents since, for example, the only ceramics available were British ones, or those obtained through British trade routes (such as Chinese export porcelain or German stoneware). Diet, revealed in the faunal remains, is one indicator of the cultural affiliation of a household's residents. In addition, architecture and clothing were also ways in which cultural differences were emphasized in the community, and which have salience archaeologically.

Architecture

Although the British did expand the palisades and add several buildings inside the fort, they changed the fort interior very little. Six of the seven French rowhouses and the church, priest's house, cemetery, and powder magazine remained in place from the 1730s until the fort's abandonment in 1781. In one rowhouse, that in the northeast section of the fort, all the houses but one were torn down, and that one was used as the British commanding officer's house. The other rowhouses continued to be owned by the French, and although rebuilt, they remained in the same locations. The British military and British traders and merchants rented these houses from the French Canadians, even after the barracks were built in 1769–1770 and after settlement began in the suburbs. Although there was economic variation among households along any of the streets inside the fort, the archaeological evidence suggests that the northwest portion of the town, that most protected from the prevailing cold, northwesterly winds, was the wealthiest, and that the southeast portion, more exposed to weather and also where the sometimes volatile powder magazine was located, was the poorest (Heldman 1984, 1986, 1999). Inside the palisades at Michilimackinac, the French Canadians, Métis, and later many of the British lived in similar houses, roughly twenty-three English feet (twenty French feet) square and attached to others in long rowhouses. They contained a half-story above, and some were divided into two rooms on the ground floor; some also had a root cellar under one of the rooms (Halchin 1985; Heldman 1977, 1978, 1986, 1999; Heldman and Grange 1981).

We know from archaeology at Michilimackinac, cited above, that the French Canadians did indeed continue rebuilding and repairing their houses in a post-in-the-ground (*poteaux-en-terre*) style, even after the British arrived. These structures were built of vertical posts set one against the other in a wall ditch, with clay chinking (called *bouzillage*) pressed into the interstices; some also had clapboards on the exterior. The only French structures built of horizontal beam construction (*pièce-sur-pièce*) were the church and the priest's house (Brown n.d.).

The British had not used post-in-the-ground architecture in more than a hundred years. Those who rented these houses from the French Canadian owners frequently complained about what they saw as exorbitant rents for dilapidated "hutts" (Heldman and Grange 1981:38). Daniel Morison noted in 1772 that during his four years as surgeon at Michilimackinac, he "was obliged to Lodge in old french Houses, not habitable, at a Vast Expense out of my Pay, by Plastering, thatching &c. to preserve myself from the Inclemency of the Winter Season" (May 1960: 45). Excavations in the southeast quarter of the fort revealed that British-period residents of these houses made exactly these kinds of changes to the interiors, suggesting cultural differences with the French.

Cultural differences are apparent even in something as mundane as the clay used to chink in spaces in the house walls. The *bouzillage* used by the French was a tan, yellow, or gray clay mixed with straw, animal hair, and even small animal bones. Found throughout the French occupation level at the site, *bouzillage* declines through time and is all but absent in the 1770s deposits (Heldman and Grange 1981:204–205). The British occupation levels contain instead pink clay chinking (with no inclusions or tempering), and pink clay was used in British-period hearth and chimney construction (Halchin 1985:92–93; Heldman 1977:21). Obviously different clay sources in the area were used, and the chinking made differently according to cultural preference. In addition, interior lath and wall plaster is found in several British-period house deposits but is virtually absent from the French-period deposits (Halchin 1985:91; Heldman 1977:21; Heldman and Grange 1981:198, 204). The proportions of window-pane glass and nails increase substantially in the artifact inventories of the British-period deposits (Heldman and Grange 1981:197–198). Finally, several British-period houses show evidence of flooring having been added with the 1760s rebuilding (Halchin 1985:98–101, 164; Heldman 1977:21–22, 43–44). The increase in nails may well reflect the increased use of floorboards as well as, perhaps, increased clapboarding on the exteriors. Thus far, no evidence of flooring has been recovered for French-period houses in this portion of the fort.

What seems apparent, then, is that although the French continued, for the most part, to own these houses, and had rebuilt them in the early 1760s following French architectural tradition, the British who rented them made as many modifications to them as they could so that the structures conformed more closely to British standards of a dwelling. They seem to have done what they could to change "hutts" into houses fit for British military and traders. In the few structures they were able to build inside the fort (the barracks and provision stores), the British used stone foundations and horizontal log or beam construction (Maxwell and Binford 1961:45–48, 70–77).

Clothing

Although very few remains of French ceramics, bottles, or glassware were found in the British occupation levels at Michilimackinac, there are some indications that French cloth and clothing were being imported by British merchants there. Some of the strongest evidence for this are the lead cloth seals that were attached to individual bolts of cloth. These are found archaeologically across the site and reveal that cloth from both French and British manufacturers was imported during the British period (Adams 1989). In addition, British merchants and traders continued to import French Canadian, Métis, and American Indian articles of clothing during the 1760s and 1770s. These included "Canadian Shoes," "Indian Shoes," "Mogizins," "Hatts for Chiefs," "Chief's coats," and large hooded greatcoats called "*capots*" (Scott 1991a). At the other end of the economic scale, British upper-class women insisted on keeping up with the latest styles and fashions, be they from London or Paris. The wealthy trader John Askin ordered shoes and clothes for his wife and daughter from Montreal and London merchants, including a wedding gown for his daughter Kitty: "Please have one made for her [in] the french fashion, of a light blue Sattin" (Quaife 1928:100–102).

Diet

Faunal analyses of several British-period households suggest that diets differed not only according to socioeconomic position but also according to cultural preferences. Although poorer traders and soldiers seem to have used wild species to a great degree (Shapiro 1978; Scott 1991b, 1997), the greater wealth of middle- and upper-class traders and officers allowed not only more use of domestic animals but also the choice of culturally preferred foods (Scott 1991b, 1996). Although all residents at the fort relied heavily on fish, given the settlement's location on the shore where Lakes Michigan and Huron meet, variations in other foods seem to reflect cultural food choices. This is seen in several households along the Rue de la Babillarde in the southeast, and generally poorer, section of the town.

In one household lived elite British officers only recently sent to Michilimackinac from Britain because of the threat of revolution in the American colonies. The diet of these officers, who lived in the house from the mid to late 1770s, is almost stereotypically British, judging by several cookbooks of the time. They ate beef, mutton, pork, and chicken. Besides fish, the only wild species eaten were hare, waterfowl (swan and ducks), and "game" birds (grouse and passenger pigeon). Swans had been associated with high-status households in Britain as early as the Middle Ages (Serjeantson 1989b:2).

In another household on the same street, the occupant, probably a fur trader of medium economic position, seems to have continued a diet similar to that of the French Canadians at the settlement for the preceding fifty years. There was relatively little use of domestic animals, only pork and a small amount of chicken, but a strong reliance on wild birds, mammals, and fish. Of the British-period households examined thus far, this one depended the most on wild mammals in the diet, primarily beavers. British distaste for beaver meat is clear in the documents, although small amounts of it were eaten by poorer traders and soldiers. The predominance of beaver in the diet for this household (13 percent of the estimated meat weight) suggests the residents were French Canadian, since beaver had been quite important in the earlier French-period diet at Michilimackinac (Scott 1985). It is possible that this greater consumption of beaver was for religious reasons. As early as 1749, Peter Kalm noted that the Pope had classified beavers with fish because the beaver "spends most of his time in the water" (Benson 1987:534). Thus, Catholics could eat beaver meat on fast days. Of course, this coincided neatly with the fact that beaver was the most important economic resource in the area. Such a classification certainly encouraged economical use of the entire animal—that is, for food as well as fur.

A third household is where Ezekiel Solomon lived, and, for a few years, Gershon Levy as well. They bought the house in 1765 from the French owners, the Parant family. After about 1767, Solomon seems to have lived there alone. In 1769, he married a French Protestant woman in Montreal and thereafter seems to have used the house at Michilimackinac only as a summer residence (Halchin 1985; Scott 1991b). In the 1760s, when he was a poorer trader newly arrived from Europe, his diet most resembled that of French Canadians at Michilimackinac, with some domestic meats but with a large proportion of his meat being from wild species. Later, in the 1770s, he had become successful in the fur trade and had become more involved with the Jewish community in Montreal. His increase in wealth seems to have allowed him to make a shift toward a more kosher diet: there is a dramatic decrease in his use of pork (from 27 percent of the meat weight to 9 percent) and virtual elimination of wild birds and mammals from his diet. Here we see how food might be used to emphasize or deemphasize one's cultural or religious differences from others in the community. In the 1760s, Solomon seems to have eaten as most of the fort's residents (French Canadians) did, in a way deemphasizing the aspect that most distinguished him from them, his Jewishness. But when wealth allowed him to choose not only the more expensive domestic meats but also the most expensive ceramics and glassware, he was able to emphasize his similarity with others in the community in those ways. He could afford to be "different" in his food habits without endangering his ability to be seen as successful in the community.

Anti-Semitism

In addition to the dietary information, there is also an indication of Solomon's cultural-religious identity in the "negative evidence" (Heldman 1986). For more than fifteen years, British soldiers and officers lived on either side of Ezekiel Solomon and across the street from him. Yet there was not one artifact of the British military found in his house or yard. In all other households that have been excavated along this street, even those lived in by traders, there is at least a button or two, military braid fragments, or something else to indicate some kind of interaction with the

British military in those houses and yards. But none at all with the Jewish trader living next door.

CONCLUSION: THE PAST IS PROLOGUE

And so we have archaeological and documentary evidence for assertions of identity by French Canadian, Métis, Jewish, and British residents at Michilimackinac. These could be viewed not only as different cultural traditions in coexistence, but also as political statements, made day in and day out. Against the backdrop of rivalry and animosity that had been in place for centuries in Europe, we see an eighteenth-century version being played out in the New World. Each of these groups used religion, language, dress, food, and house style to emphasize their cultural traditions. Using their language and alliances (kin and business) with local Indian groups, French Canadians and Métis enjoyed at least a degree of economic and social freedom from their British colonizers. French Canadian and Métis resentment toward the British was clear when they stood by and watched the Ojibwa massacre the British in 1763 during Pontiac's War. The British resentment toward all of these different groups is clear in the historic documents. It would seem Michilimackinac was a very tense place between 1761 and 1781.

In such a case, then, can we not see in the evidence both ethnicity and racism, both an identification with one group and a distancing from another? Merely following one's culturally preferred way of building a house could not be seen, in and of itself, as an assertion of identity in a racist society. Nor could one's choice of foods or clothing. But in the context of colonization, of being occupied by a colonizing group that you had just spent years trying to kill in a war, these normal daily actions might take on an "in your face" edge. And the same would be true for the colonizing group, reinforcing in its mind the inferior status of the groups being occupied and its own supposedly superior status. Such a combination of ethnic identity and racism toward the Other has been acknowledged in historical archaeology for what we might call primary colonization, that initial colonizing by a European group elsewhere in the world. It has been less acknowledged for settings of secondary colonization, in which the extra layer of a previous colonial society is present.

The situation probably would be similar in places like Louisiana and the Illinois country, France's colonies in the middle and lower Mississippi Valley. After the Seven Years' War, Spain received control of all land west of the Mississippi, and many French colonials moved west across the river, choosing Spanish rather than British rule. Spain did not, however, send troops and settlers in any great numbers to control the colony. The economic base there was agricultural, much different than in New France (Canada), and enslaved and free Africans formed a much larger part of the society. What we see in post-1760 Louisiana, however, is not a large-scale secondary colonization by Spain but a de facto secondary colonization by Anglo-American colonists moving west. This movement west increased substantially after the United States purchased the colony in 1803.

Even with a different economic base in the Mississippi Valley, however, the clash between French and British-Anglo ways of doing things, and then the coexistence of those traditions, would be similar to the situation in New France (Ekberg 1998). There would be, again, the differing attitudes between French and Anglos toward Africans and American Indians; different kinds of capitalisms; different systems of slavery; different religions, languages, dress, and foodways. It was probably even more complex in Louisiana because of the greater numbers of Africans who were part of society there. Similar clashes probably occurred in the seventeenth-century Northeast, where former Dutch colonies came under British control; in the early nineteenth-century Southeast, where former Spanish colonies came under U.S. control; and in the later nineteenth-century Southwest and West, where the United States defeated Spain in the Mexican War and then occupied those colonies.

In recent years, scholars have been admonished to keep their reconstructions of past societies grounded in particular political, economic, social, and historical contexts. That is what I have tried to do here, choosing to write not in broad, theoretical terms, but in what seem to be the more interesting and illustrative glimpses from a particular place and time. This *is* about capitalism, colonialism, race, ethnicity, class, and gender—and it is about *all* of them. To focus on one or two of these would be to leave the rest out of the picture. Only by trying to see them all in the workings of daily life can we do the most thorough archaeology possible.

Note

Much of this information is contained in my doctoral dissertation (Scott 1991b), which benefited greatly from discussions with Janet Spector, Christine Hastorf, William Rowe, Sara Evans, Allen Isaacman, Elizabeth Wing, and Keith Widder. The FAI Roundtable in Utah was a stimulating and thought-provoking two days, and I want to thank all of the participants for their lively discussion. Especially helpful in revising this chapter were suggestions and comments from Charles Orser, Robert Paynter, Paul Mullins, James Delle, Warren Perry, James Skibo, and an anonymous reviewer. Many of the ideas expressed here stem from myriad discussions with Donald Heldman over the last twenty years, and I am surely guilty of failing to attribute to him ideas that were initially his; he also provided helpful suggestions and comments on several drafts of this chapter. None of these persons, of course, is responsible for any lapses in logic, judgment, or fact that may remain. Finally, I would like to dedicate this chapter to the memory of Dr. Eugene T. Petersen, whose unwavering support was vital to the first three decades of archaeological research at the Straits of Mackinac.

3

African American Medicine and the Social Relations of Slavery

YWONE EDWARDS-INGRAM

Issues of race do not exist apart from or even alongside gender, class, and sexual norms; rather, these issues are articulated through one another.

(Stavney 1998:534)

She is a mother because motherhood was virtually unavoidable under slavery; she is outraged because of the intimacy of her oppression.

(Braxton 1989:19)

This chapter discusses the role of medicine in the social relationships between enslaved people of African descent and Anglo-Americans primarily in Virginia from the seventeenth through the nineteenth century. Examples from Jamaica, West Indies, are included for comparative purposes and to better illustrate practices on the American mainland. I review data from ethnography, archaeology, history, and literary and material culture studies. The primary focus, however, is on enslaved black women and medicinal practices relating to pregnancy, childbirth, child care, and the death of children. My study of medicinal rituals discusses diverse practices and beliefs that embodied social, cultural, biological, and religious dimensions of African American lifeways. Treating these as interconnected allows for a more comprehensive approach to medicinal practices and to notions of well-being.

I stress both the preventive and the curative dimensions of medicine as I look at the power of faith and traditions. Enslaved African Americans displayed remarkable creativity, adaptability, and a willingness to use diverse methods to prevent and cure illness. Prominent among the requisites for well-being were herbal remedies, taken internally or used externally on the body or within the cultural landscape, the use of power-endowed objects and kits, practices of mortuary rites, breastfeeding, and other healthcare practices of child care and motherhood (Edwards 1997; Gundaker 1993, 1998a, 1998b; La Roche 1994; McMillen 1985; Orser 1994; Savitt 1978, 1989; Thompson 1983, 1993; Wilkie 1997). My approach to enslaved Virginians' medicinal practices is also informed by Robert Grossinger's representation of medicine in *Planet Medicine* (Grossinger 1990). Grossinger treated healing as both a science (skills of surgery and pharmacy) and as an art (sympathy and intuition), which are not necessarily mutually exclusive approaches. Informed by a holistic and multifaceted definition of medicine, I examine the many ways enslaved women manipulated their identities as laborers, mothers, medicinal specialists, and nurturers.

Medicinal practices in colonial Virginia exposed racism and the "volatility of the experiences which collectively defined race" (Berlin 1998:1). Ira Berlin defines race as "the product of history" and notes that "it only exists on the contested social terrain in which men and women struggle to control their destinies" (Berlin 1998:1). Race is a historical and social construction based on perceptions of physical, cultural, and social differences among different groups of people. It can also be viewed as an institution and as an instituted ideology (Epperson 1997; Fields 1982). Ideologies founded on the superiority of whites and the inferiority of blacks, in different forms and under a variety of conditions, governed social interactions in slave societies. During slavery, whites used racist ideology and practices to "naturalize and rationalize" the enslavement of blacks (Berlin 1998; Epperson 1990a, 1990b, 1997; Morgan 1975).

The subordination and exploitation of one group of people to perpetuate the economic, social, and political rise of another is an essential aspect of racism. Terrence Epperson argues that racism "embodies contradictory tendencies of exclusion and incorporation, simultaneously providing a means of oppression and a locus of resistance" (Epperson 1990b:341). Exploring the intricacies of race relations as lived experiences and their manifestations in medicinal practices can partially reveal how people of African descent were simultaneously incorporated and excluded. Medicine was a key area in which enslaved Africans and African Americans negotiated, established, and changed their places in social relations. Widespread interest in treating illness and promoting health facilitated both the exchange and the withholding of knowledge and material and political resources.

RACE RELATIONS AND PLANTATION SLAVERY

The incorporation of Africans and their descendants into the labor system of Virginia in the seventeenth century evolved into racial slavery by the eighteenth century (Berlin 1998; Morgan 1975; Sobel 1987). They replaced white indentured servants as the main source of plantation labor. Slavery was now at the center of the economic system. Edmund Morgan (1975:316) explains that "the substitution of slaves for servants probably increased the productivity and almost certainly increased the profitability of the plantation system. But slavery required new methods of disciplining the labor force, methods that were linked to racial contempt." Whites legislated to control and degrade blacks, and at the same time elevate the status of the poorest and lowest-class white. Morgan (1975) declared that it became a matter of public policy in colonial Virginia to depict blacks as racially and socially inferior. Therefore, the law played a key "role in the institution of race and the naturalization of whiteness" (Epperson 1997:10). Marriage and miscegenation between whites and blacks, for example, were considered crimes (Sobel 1987). However, the relations between the slaveholder and the enslaved person influenced all other relations in slave society (Berlin 1998). These relations embodied both conflicts and cooperations. While slaveholders had considerable power over their enslaved people, these people were never powerless, but through overt and covert practices built a life for themselves and prepared their children for adulthood.

The health and procreation of enslaved people were major concerns for slaveholders, both for economic and humanitarian reasons. Ira Berlin noted that the nature of racial relations in slavery contributed to the intense interference of slaveholders as they concerned themselves with the most intimate parts of the lives of the enslaved. He referred to these practices as the "domestication of domination" (Berlin 1998:99). This intense interference in the lives of the enslaved was most evident in health care. The attitude of whites toward enslaved black people can be read in their actions.

In the eighteenth century, Virginian planter Landon Carter gave his enslaved people the harsh drug of rattlesnake powder (*Polygala senega*) for "bilious fever" (Erichsen-Brown 1989:359–362; Greene 1965). He observed that the drug worked well but had some side effects. Some of Carter's priorities are alluded to in his declaration, "I wish my own fears did not prevent my giving it to my Children" (Greene 1965:130–131). Illness, reproduction, breastfeeding, the weaning of infants, and other aspects of motherhood and child care were areas of contentions and negotiations between enslaved people and slaveholders. These activities and their various outcomes contributed to ambiguities in social relations. Decisions concerning motherhood and child care of enslaved blacks were enacted in an arena in which the power of slaveholders was never absolute, and relations continually changed; enslaved women and their families exerted contingent power.

Contradictions were deeply embedded in the social relationships of enslaved black women and white women in motherhood and child care. Elite planters and slaveholders passed laws that differentiated the children of white women from the children of enslaved black women. In 1662, legislators decided that the children of enslaved women should inherit the enslaved status of their mothers (Hening 1819). In *Reconstructing Womanhood: The Emergence of the Afro-American Woman Novelist,* Hazel V. Carby (1987:24) points out that "within the economic, political, and social system of slavery, women were at the nexus of its reproduction." She argued that the children of black women were property, the capital of the South. The offsprings of white women inherited this capital. These factors profoundly influenced perceptions about motherhood of black enslaved women and white women.

Opposing concepts of motherhood underlay and reinforced the hierarchical relationship of black women and white women. Enslaved women as "laborers and breeders" were linked to "illicit sexuality," while the "purity" of white women and their attainment of motherhood were glorified in varying degrees (Carby 1987; Stavney 1998). The ideologies concerning race and motherhood that evolved throughout slavery were developed and instituted to raise the respect and self-esteem of white women and simultaneously lower the social conditions of black women.

Though both subordinates of white men, white women and black women by law and racial practices were not considered equals. White women, however, did not seek any significant alignment with black women, and any disenchantment they harbored about white male dominance was not seen as any great threat to the social hierarchy of plantation society. In fact, some white women worked to uphold this hierarchy even when they had the economic base to challenge it (Anzilotti 1997). White women were placed in positions of power over black women. Elevating white women racially and legally over blacks helped to resolve some of the contradictions in the social relations between women in their subordination to white men (Carby 1987).

Carby insisted that social and racial practices during slavery impeded the sisterhood of white women and black women. She described the complex social structure in which these women interacted: "The barriers to the establishment of the bonding of sisterhood were built in the space between the different economic, political, and social positions that black women and white women occupied in the social formation of slavery. Their hierarchical relationship was determined through a racial, not gendered, categorization" (Carby 1987:55). Enslaved black women may have interacted frequently with white women as mistresses, planters' daughters, and overseers' wives, rather than as heads of households. Nevertheless, the social positions of white women were buttressed by economic power. Some white women with whom enslaved blacks contended were slaveholders, plantation owners, and managers (Anzilotti 1997). These positions provided white women with opportunities to exert tremendous influence in the lives of black women. The relationships between white and enslaved women during slavery involved acts of cruelty and betrayal as well as kindness and sympathy.

THE MEDICINAL PRACTICES OF ENSLAVED AFRO-VIRGINIANS

My survey of the literature on health and healing practices in Virginia suggests that studies have tended to focus on the nature of disease and illness, prevention and cure, and description of health practices (Bell 1957; Blanton 1931; Savitt 1978, 1989). This chapter shares some concerns with previous studies but differs in its explorations of the complex nature of social interactions within medicine. Folklorist Roger Abrahams found that the literary evidence about slavery includes racist and stereotypical accounts of the interactions between enslaved people and white people. Nevertheless, the reader of this literature should consider how it demonstrates clearly that "slaves had maintained their own ways and these were sufficiently attractive and productive that the plantation was able to accommodate and even encourage these differences" (Abrahams 1992:xxiii). Enslaved people had access to information and materials that they used in medicinal practices from the early years of the forced migration of Africans to the Americas. However, documentation of their experiences, from their perspectives, is available more for the nineteenth century. Slave narratives and interviews of former enslaved individuals, for example, offer more information from their viewpoints (Escott 1979; Perdue et al. 1976). When added to accounts of slavery written by whites, these sources broaden interpretations of medicinal practices.

Through an awareness of the biological and social causes of illness, enslaved individuals contributed to medical knowledge. However, as enslaved people interacted within the complex social networks of colonial Virginia, they were both socially and economically subordinated and elevated at different times, because whites often held contradictory attitudes toward the enslaved and their knowledge of healing and medicine. Sometimes they acknowledged this domain of knowledge, but at other times they denied its usefulness (Morgan 1998; Sobel 1987).

The laws of Virginia both proscribed and encouraged African American medicine. Colonial authorities legislated against Afro-Virginian medicine but made exceptions for practices that were undertaken without malice or with the consent of the legal owners of the enslaved. Thus, while acknowledging the potential danger to whites posed by enslaved people's medicine, particularly poisoning, Anglo-Virginians condoned African American medicinal practices (Hening 1819; Morgan 1998; Sobel 1987). One Virginian governor granted an enslaved man his freedom when the man revealed the roots and barks that he used to cure yaws (Sobel 1987). Many Afro-Virginians used their medical skills to help slaveholders to have a healthier enslaved population. Eighteenth-century planter Robert Carter of Nomini Hall had an enslaved coachman, called "Brother Tom," who was renowned as a doctor and was borrowed by neighboring planters to treat their slaves (Blanton 1931). Social interactions between whites and blacks constantly challenged legal and social definitions about the enslaved.

The conditions of health care and the qualifications, competencies, and availability of doctors were significant factors that contributed to or prevented interracial interactions in medicine (Bell 1957; Blanton 1931; Savitt 1978, 1989). In rural areas, many whites treated themselves, their families, and their slaves. The widespread practice of "private doctoring" in rural areas discouraged trained doctors from settling in these places. Urban areas such as Williamsburg in the eighteenth century had a large number of doctors. In addition to these doctors, apothecaries and merchants prescribed and dispensed medicine (Gill 1972). Some tradespeople such as barbers and blacksmiths as well as professionals like lawyers and ministers also practiced medicine. Enslaved people who were legally owned by or who interacted with medical practitioners were probably influenced in their approaches to medicine by such relationships.

THE MATERIAL CULTURE OF AFRICAN AMERICAN MEDICINAL PRACTICES

With the proliferation of studies on African Americans more information is available to study medicinal beliefs and practices. Scholars of the African diaspora have spent considerable time investigating behavioral practices, ideologies, and materials of the past world of slavery (Edwards 1997; Gundaker 1993, 1998a, 1998b; Orser 1994; Singleton 1991; Sobel 1987; Thompson 1983, 1993; Wilkie 1997). The scholarship has highlighted the multiple uses of objects and the landscape (Edwards 1998; Gundaker 1993, 1998a, 1998b; Sobel 1987; Thompson 1983, 1993). Several objects, including coins, shells, ceramics, beads, and tobacco pipes, and archaeological features such as root cellars and graves have been associated, from a multidisciplinary perspective, with medicinal practices and well-being (Edwards 1998; Edwards-Ingram 1997; Orser 1994; Wilkie 1997).

In the Americas, people of African descent had complex and dynamic relationships with both a mythical and a real Africa (Berlin 1998; Ferguson 1992; Gundaker 1998a, 1998b; Thompson 1983, 1993). Grey Gundaker (1998a:8) writes that "interaction between African, African American, and European-derived practices and knowledge systems also resists unilinear notions of transatlantic continuity—*not* because there are too few connections, although the forms connections take are quite diverse and often convoluted; rather . . . there is *too much* information on too many levels—and too much more to learn—to expect anything less than a wide-ranging network of connections and disjunctions between the old and the new."

Enslaved African Americans not only practiced European-derived medicinal traditions but also African-related customs, including using particular objects as charms, selecting specific colors, and enclosing disparate materials in containers as part of harmful or healing rituals. Tradition and adaptation embodying resistance and accommodation were important elements of African American cultural practices (Howson 1990).

Archaeological interpretations of American slavery have considered solidarity and individuality in African Americans' activities to combat racism. As enslaved blacks defined and redefined their identities, they manipulated material objects in cultural demarcations. The archaeological study of the material side of race and racism is a difficult, but not an unattainable, task (Orser 1998b). Already some archaeologists have interpreted diverse remains to expose how the material remains of slavery articulate race, class, and ethnicity (Ferguson 1992; Orser 1998b; Paynter and McGuire 1991).

Leland Ferguson (1992), for example, studied how enslaved African Americans used coarse earthenware pottery in culinary and medicinal practices that drew on African parallels or antecedents. These activities were mostly confined to the private sphere of slave life, separated culturally and mainly "invisible" to whites. They failed to threaten the social and political structure of plantation society in any significant way (Edwards-Ingram and Brown 1998). But in the face of racial oppression, these acts of "opposition" and "self-confirmation" may have inculcated and sustained solidarity among the enslaved community. Overall, the separatist cultural acts of enslaved African Americans benefited whites, too, because "they served more to contain the potential volatility of slave resistance than express it" (Edwards-Ingram and Brown 1998:7).

Enslaved African Americans may have felt empowered when they were able to be their own doctors or choose doctors from the black community. Both whites and blacks had faith in black medicinal practitioners (Blanton 1931; Edwards 1997; Morgan 1998; Savitt 1978, 1989; Sobel 1987). Many of these practitioners relied on herbal remedies. Some enslaved people preferred to use herbal medicine and the services of herbal doctors rather than expose themselves to the remedies of white doctors.

Changes surrounding birth, child care, and death in black families necessitated medicine incorporating knowledge and practices of Africa, European-derived pharmaceutical materials and medical systems, and American-evolved medicine. Archaeologists have recovered evidence of the multifaceted nature of medicine testifying to African Americans' resourcefulness and ability to seek multiple means to promote well-being. Investigation at a house site of an African American midwife in Mobile, Alabama, for example, found objects presumably associated with midwifery (Wilkie 1997). These materials include patent medicinal bottles, whiskey containers, animal bones, yellow sulfur, glass crystal, and flaked stones. The midwife likely mixed different medicinal knowledge and practices in her work. African American medicinal precautions during childbirth include the custom of placing a knife under the bed of a woman during childbirth in hopes that it would "cut" the pain. Children were required to wear necklaces made of pierced coins, animal teeth, and buttons to counteract illness in childhood and to ease pains during teething (Wilkie 1997:86–87).

In summer 1999, I conducted interviews in Jamaica on childcare traditions and practices. Both in the past and today, Jamaicans stressed the importance of protective rites. To guard against evil spirits and even friendly deceased family members, babies were dressed in red or made to wear red objects. Bibles were left opened above the babies' heads to take advantage of the power of the written words in protection. Scissors and measuring tapes were used in conjunction with or without the Bibles (Edwards-Ingram 1999; Rhoda Vassell, pers. comm., 1999). According to tradition, the dead feared the measuring tapes because on seeing these objects, their status as dead people would be emphasized. They would recall that they were measured so that they could be outfitted and provided with coffins for burial (Edwards-Ingram 1999). Another custom dictated that both mothers and newborn babies stay indoors for nine days. During this interval they would not be allowed any visitor except the midwife and immediate family members (Rhoda Vassell, pers. comm., 1999).

In the early nineteenth century, an enslaved midwife informed Matthew Lewis (1834:97), a slaveholder in Westmoreland Parish, Jamaica, that "Oh, massa, till nine days over, we *no hope* of them. " Lewis was concerned about the high number of infant deaths caused by tetanus, but his effort to institute measures to combat this illness was resisted by the mothers. He had ordered that immediately after birth, babies should be plunged into a "tub of cold water" (Lewis 1834:320–321). The mothers were so set against this order that it could not be enforced.

Practices of the Bakongo people, who traditionally occupied parts of southwestern and central Africa, perhaps show some light on the actions of these mothers. This group considers the dead as occupying a watery, upside-down, white world underneath the world of the living. The Bakongo cosmogram visually represents the idea that birth, life, death, and rebirth are connected. It is frequently depicted as a cross within a circle. Charms, usually of trashlike materials, helped the Bakongo to negotiate with the spiritual world (Gundaker 1993; Thompson 1983). Some Africans who were enslaved in the Americas were from the Bakongo. Drawing on practices of the Bakongo and Bakongo-influenced peoples, I tentatively suggest that these mothers may have been alarmed by this order because perhaps they considered immersing infants in water akin to reinforcing these children's connections to the realm of the dead. It is likely that medicinal activities were instituted during the first nine days to guard against this possibility. The children needed rituals to bring them into life fully—the world of the living—and not activities to reinforce ties with the world of the dead.

Enslaved people's beliefs about the interconnections and disjunctions between the world of the dead and the world of the living were alluded to in childcare practices. According to Jamaican traditions and practices, the ninth day after birth and death was significant, and these times were observed with appropriate rituals to promote well-being (Edwards-Ingram 1999; Rhoda Vassell, pers. comm., 1999). In the American South, nine was considered a lucky number and was important in ritual practices (Leone and Fry 1999). Mourning customs in Jamaica include nightly "set-up" gatherings with the family of the deceased, culminating with a special ceremony on the ninth night. This ceremony marks the final separation and "send off" for the dead (Edwards-Ingram 1999; Vassell 1999). "Set-ups" or "settin' ups" were also part of mourning customs in the American South (Nichols 1989). These all-night meetings at the home of the bereaved family allowed for friends and families to support each other. Spiritual songs and prayers along with recollections about the deceased were usually included in these meetings (Nichols 1989).

PLANTS AND WELL-BEING

Enslaved people asserted some control over their lives through different cultural practices surrounding plant use. They used plants for dietary and medicinal needs, and assigned medicinal, nutritional, symbolic, and magical properties to plants. Enslaved people included information from Africa and within the African diaspora to cultivate and gather plants for medicinal and nutritional purposes (Grimé 1979; Heath and Bennett 2000; Laguerre 1987; Mitchell 1978; Mrozowski and Driscoll 1997; Perdue et al. 1976; Raymer 1996). These enslaved laborers knew that the intake of plant substances could enhance health or cause illness. Plants were enlisted in preventive and curative medicine. They were used to make tea, for baths, and as ingredients in wrapped charms and other medicinal kits.

Hard work, poor diet, and unhealthy living conditions were primary factors that contributed to poor health among slaves. Other common illnesses included cold, fever, dysentery, and problems with worms—particularly for children. Many plant remedies were used in the treatment of colds and as worm medicine for children as well as adults (Grimé 1979; Groover and Baumann 1996). Some enslaved people were injured while engaged in everyday tasks. Some maladies were wounds that took a long time to heal. In South Carolina traditional home remedies, the blossoms of the okra plant were used alone or mixed with octagon soap and sugar to treat sores that were difficult to heal (Mitchell 1978:72).

Some slaveholders and plantation managers directly inflicted injuries upon enslaved people (Mintz 1999; Perdue et al. 1976). Some injuries may have related to the ordeals of enslaved women when they were forced to have children without their consent. Some enslaved women did not affirm life in ways that slaveholders considered rational. They refused to have children who, even before birth, were designated slaves and given to whites. Some of these women may have resorted to abortive practices to prevent further exploitations of their bodies. This exploitation was twofold because black women were productive as both laborers and procreators, providing slaveholders with an ongoing labor force (John 1999).

The documentary evidence suggests that some plants functioned as abortive and contraceptive materials (Grimé 1979; Groover and Baumann 1996; Mitchell 1978). Mark D. Groover and Timothy E. Baumann studied African American archaeological remains from the eighteenth and nineteenth centuries in South Carolina (Groover and Baumann 1996). They used the documentary evidence to help identify plants that may have been used for medicinal purposes. Cotton found both in the documentary and the archaeological records was identified as a plant that may have been used for contraceptives and for reproduction. The bark of the root of cotton was considered effective in inducing abortion (Mitchell 1978:42). Both Native Americans and European Americans used this plant to ease the pains of childbirth and in related areas of women care (Mitchell 1978:42). The okra also is associated with reproduction and contraceptives (Grimé 1979).

One writer describing eighteenth-century slave life in Guyana wrote that "the female slaves who intend to procure abortion, have found the advantage of previously lubricating the uterine passages, by a diet of these pods" (Grimé 1979:63). Okra is believed to be indigenous to Africa. In eighteenth-century Jamaica, a naturalist recorded that the plants "are very carefully planted by Europeans, as well as slaves in their gardens, and the unripe pods, which are in use, are common in markets" (Grimé 1979:64). Folk practices in modern Jamaica have associated the okra with miscarriage and abortion as well as childbirth (Rhoda Vassell, pers. comm., 1999). Consequently, pregnant women should refrain from eating okras in the early months of pregnancy. But nearing the time of delivery, this food is recommended as one that will help to smooth the process of birth.

Plants were incorporated in practices to harm as detailed in descriptions of conjuring (Perdue et al. 1976; Puckett 1969). It was necessary to consult black doctors particularly for illness caused by malevolent forces. White doctors and slaveholders would not have been interested or probably lacked knowledge to treat illness of such nature. Whites usually viewed slave medicine as superstitious and dangerous. Thomas Jefferson of Monticello, for instance, who owned about two hundred slaves during his life, had little patience for such practices. Jefferson's paper described the prescriptions of black doctors as poisons (Stanton 1993:43). Some slaves believed that they were actually poisoned or conjured by other slaves who used plant materials. Misfortunes could also result from violations of acceptable practices; for example, if the slave did not cultivate sweet potatoes to keep malaria away or failed to carry a certain root in his or her pocket (Perdue et al. 1976:278–279, 310).

Enslaved women treated many ill slaves with plant remedies on southern plantations. Planters recognized and used the skills of enslaved women as "doctors" and midwives (Blanton 1931; Greene 1965). Some planters' concerns about slave health were genuine and were not just measures to maintain a reliable workforce. At times, both factors were closely intertwined.

Slaveholders provided enslaved people with rations of corn, meat, occasionally vegetables, fruits, and milk. Overall, slaves were provided with inadequate food supplies. Whites sought to instill blacks with a sense of inferiority by withholding and limiting food items. These practices deprived slaves of some basic material things. Regulating the quantity and quality of enslaved people's food was definitely a deliberate practice to keep these individuals in a state of poverty and dependency. From the seventeenth century, Virginia was described as a place with abundant food, plants, and wildlife. Robert Beverley, a Virginia historian, named several plants growing in early Virginia. Counted among these are cherries, persimmons, chestnuts, hickory nuts, walnuts, grapes, various melons, peaches, potatoes, peas, beans, and maize (Beverley 1971 [1705]). Another Virginian, William Byrd III, boasted in the eighteenth century that the gardens in the colony had vegetables and herbs such as cucumber, radishes, asparagus, beet, broccoli, fennel, chives, garlic, rosemary, and turnips (Carson 1985).

Enslaved Virginians may have incorporated networks of food exchanges and sharing as strategies to change diets and to maintain health. The archaeological evidence has augmented historical descriptions of enslaved people's effort to fight the oppression of slavery and the exploitative practices of slaveholders. Archaeologists have found that enslaved Virginians exerted some control over the food they ate and their well-being by supplementing the plantations' usually meager rations through gardening, livestock production, hunting, fishing, and the gathering of wildlife (Atkins 1994; Edwards-Ingram 1999; Singleton 1991).

Some medicinal and nutritional plants were cultivated in gardens, while others were gathered from woodlands and byways. Historical and archaeological evidence confirms that enslaved people had gardens. The historical evidence includes plantation records, accounts listing the purchases made by or from slaves, and maps showing the layout of plantations (Gibbs 1999). Remains of plants, clues for fenced enclosures, irregular soil disturbances, and planting beds are among the evidence that archaeologists have used to interpret gardening activities (Brown and Samford 1991; Edwards-Ingram 1999; Heath and Bennett 2000). Archaeological collections from slave sites have examples of tools probably not owned by slaves, but used by them for their own gardening needs.

In 1732, a traveler found that slave gardens in Virginia contained "potatoes or (?) Indian pease and Cimnells [plants of the squash family]" (Stiverson and Butler 1977: 32). Sunday was the general day that slaves farmed their little gardens. In 1774, a Virginia teacher noted that "in several parts of the plantation they are digging up their small Lots of ground allow'd by their Master for Potatoes, peas &c; All such work for themselves they constantly do on Sundays, as they are otherwise employed on every other Day" (Farish 1957:96). Apparently, enslaved Virginians planted a variety of crops in their "little gardens." They may have practiced intercropping. Intercropping would have ensured some soil preservation and food crops at different times of the year. Plants such as pumpkin, watermelon, potatoes, and beans may have been planted between taller plants such as corn. Gourds grew on vines, probably on fences. Slaves may have planted other gardens in clearings in the woods or on marginal lands of plantations. Travelers would not have readily seen these areas, and therefore they usually described gardens at slave quarters.

Former enslaved blacks throughout the American South described various types of gardens associated with plantations. Willis Cofer of Georgia remembered that there was one big garden of four or five acres to feed both whites and blacks. The garden had "cabbage, collards, turnip greens, beans, corn, peas, onions, 'taters' [potatoes]" (Killion and Waller 1973:43). According to Cofer, the slaves were given lands to cultivate for their own purposes. They were allowed to work on these plots after they finished field work. Most of the slave plots were worked at night (Killion and Waller 1973:43–44).

Another former slave from Georgia described only one big garden: "They weren't no separate gardens. They didn't have no time to work no gardens of their own" (Killion and Waller 1973:50). A former Virginian slave remembered that enslaved people were permitted to have gardens, and this was one means to gain "many trifling conveniences. But these gardens were only allowed to some of the more industrious" (Duke 1995:32). Some enslaved laborers may have been too exhausted and ill at the end of the day or on weekends to engage in gardening for themselves. Yet the fact that many of them did spoke eloquently of their resilience and determination to have some control over their own lives and that of their families.

Archaeological studies support the documentary evidence that enslaved people used plants for medicinal and nutritional needs in motherhood (Groover and Baumann 1996). Archaeologists, however, have written more about plants as dietary supplements than plants for medicinal use among slaves. Recent research in Virginia suggests that cultivated staples, nuts, and a few wild species dominated the findings from slave sites (Heath and Bennett 2000; Higgins et al. 2000; Mrozowski and Driscoll 1997; Raymer 1996). The evidence overwhelmingly seems to support dietary and subsistence practices rather than medicine, usually defined narrowly for these studies. For example, the symbolic and spiritual aspects of plants largely have been ignored. Some studies identified plants used for firewood and for building slave cabins (Heath and Bennett 2000; Higgins et al. 2000; Raymer 1996). These broader interpretations provide more linkages for studying health and well-being.

PLANT USE AMONG AFRICAN VIRGINIANS

For this research, I used documentary and archaeological records, but I employ a broader definition of medicine and health to study plant use among African Virginians. This population used plants not only for dietary needs but also to prevent and cure illness, to control risks including the potential misfortunes of daily life, and in efforts to evoke and tap spiritual forces to work on their behalf. From this perspective, the archaeological data include seeds, cultivated plant remains, and charcoal wood remains that can be used to discuss practices that affected the well-being of enslaved people. By looking at the interrelated dimensions of the nutritional, medicinal, symbolic, and magical use of plants, a clearer picture emerges of their life-ways.

Archaeologists have recovered seed remains from slave quarters at Philip Ludwell III's Rich Neck Plantation in Williamsburg (Franklin 1997a; Mrozowski and Driscoll 1997), Thomas Jefferson's Poplar Forest Plantation in Bedford County (Heath and Bennett 2000; Raymer 1996), and William Randolph III's Wilton Plantation in Henrico County, Virginia (Higgins et al. 2000). Rich Neck was occupied from about 1740 to 1778, while the Poplar Forest site dates from 1790 to 1812. The Rich Neck slave quarters may have housed some of the 21 slaves listed on a 1767 inventory of the estate. Enslaved people lived and worked at Poplar Forest perhaps as early as the 1760s. By the 1790s, members of seven enslaved families, numbering fewer than one hundred, lived at Poplar Forest. The Wilton Plantation slave site was occupied from 1750 to 1840. The Randolphs had 105 slaves in 1783, but this number declined in the nineteenth century as slaves were sold to pay off debts or moved to another plantation.

Botanical remains were recovered mainly from root cellars, other sub-floor pits, postholes, and in trash pits associated with the living areas of enslaved people at these plantations. Only carbonized or charred seeds were used in these analyses to eliminate the uncertainty surrounding the origins of uncharred seeds at these sites. It is difficult for archaeologists to conclusively date uncharred seeds.

Evidence from Poplar Forest, Rich Neck, and Wilton Plantation indicates that plantation gardens and the adjacent woodlands provided cultivated and wild plants for enslaved people. The cultivated species include beans, melons, corn, wheat, cowpeas, squash, and peanuts. These plants were probably grown in gardens close to the slave quarters. Wild species gathered by slaves include edibles such as black walnuts and hickory. Slaves also made beverages for relaxation and as tonics (Duke 1995; Perdue et al. 1976), perhaps using persimmons (found at Poplar Forest) and honey locust (from Rich Neck). Traditionally, blacks in South Carolina used persimmons for babies' teething pains (Groover and Baumann 1996). An 1802 traveler's account indicated that persimmons were used as a worm medicine to treat blacks. Apparently white children were also given the same medicine (Grimé 1979:116–117).

At Poplar Forest, there is evidence of planting beds and traces of chemical indicating the use of fertilizer near the slave quarters. It is uncertain whether this was an estate garden or a slave garden. However, there is a strong possibility that enslaved laborers farmed this garden. The gardens at Rich Neck and Wilton may have been house-yard gardens or common plantation gardens although both types may have been present.

Enslaved people grew starchy grains as plantation products. They were also supplied with these grains from plantation purchases. Some of these grains and other plants were stored at the slave quarters and served as nourishment to enslaved people. Former slave Booker T. Washington suggested one form of food storage. Washington (1993:5) wrote that his cabin had a dirt floor, and in the center of it "there was a large, deep opening covered with boards, which was used as a place to store sweet potatoes during the winter." Most plant remains on slave sites have been recovered from sub-floor cellar features.

When slaves cultivated plants on their own time, it served as a source of money used to procure other goods that they needed in their daily lives. Both males and females actively engaged in planting and foraging for plants. At Monticello, Thomas Jefferson regularly purchased agricultural products, including seeds, from slaves (Bear and Stanton 1997; Gruber 1990). He had many transactions with particular slaves but did not own some of them, for on several occasions he gave the money to their masters to pay them. The Jefferson household's purchases included clover seeds, watermelon, hominy, beans, corn, potatoes, gourds, grass seeds, hops, cotton, melons, cucumber, and cherries (Bear and Stanton 1997; Gruber 1990).

It is obvious that Virginian planters encouraged the commercial activities of their slaves. Planter Landon Carter wrote, "My people always made and raised things to sell" (Greene 1965:484). These activities may have helped to ameliorate conditions in the enslaved community, but they also relieved planters of some of the responsibility for providing for their slaves. Consequently, enslaved Virginians were thrust into consumer relationships that hinted at equality, but as legal property they were excluded from becoming "meaningful" proprietors.

It is not surprising that enslaved people knew about plants and plant use. After all, they were mainly agricultural workers. Some of them were selected to be specialized gardeners and worked in orchard, kitchen, and ornamental gardens. White Virginians made frequent references to specific enslaved individuals as gardeners (Farish 1957; Greene 1965). Some of these black gardeners worked alongside white ones. The historical evidence implied that slaveholders selected males rather than females as estate gardeners, but women, men, and children farmed slave gardens, usually on Sundays or at nights.

Women were often skilled gardeners and combined these duties with other roles in motherhood and child care. Frederick Douglass described his grandmother Betsey Bailey as a good nurse, "a capital hand at making nets" for fishing, and a competent gardener (Douglass 1994 [1893]:476). She was known to have great success in keeping her seedling sweet potatoes viable through the winter. Grandmother Betsey was requested to help in the planting of potatoes by various individuals in her neighborhood, for it was believed that "her touch was needed to make them grow" (Douglass 1994 [1893]:476). She was usually rewarded with a share of the harvest, a rather advantageous situation for her and her descendants.

Slave gardens might not have been as carefully tended as those of the gentry because most skilled slave gardeners lacked the time. Archaeological evidence suggests that weeds were present among the cultivated plants in slave gardens, and some of these plants had medicinal and food values (Heath and Bennett 2000; Higgins et al. 2000; Raymer 1996). Slaves likely gathered weeds from agricultural fields, roadsides, or their yards. Finding weeds may not have been a problem for some slaves, for not all areas of slave yards were cleared, and some probably did not weed their gardens. A nineteenth-century description of a slave yard notes that "on every side grow rancorous weeds and grass interspersed with fruit trees, little patches of vegetables" (Breeden 1980:120). Some slaves probably tended their little patches and allowed the weeds and grass to grow freely elsewhere.

Weeds including knotweed, goosefoot, smartweed, and pokeweed have been identified in the botanical records from slave sites in Virginia and South Carolina (Raymer 1996; Groover and Baumann 1996; Higgins et al. 2000). Many of these plants were used for food, including pot herbs or greens, and also as medicine (Grimé 1979; Higgins et al. 2000; Raymer 1996). In Jamaica, for instance, slaves used pokeweed for greens (Grimé 1979:160).

Some plant staples had symbolic as well as nutritional value, and African heritage likely influenced their use among slaves. Traditionally and even today in Kenya, West Africa, beans have been associated with women and fertility (Robertson 1997). Among the Kikuyu people, *njahe,* "small round black beans with a white cap," have been significant to the transitional stage of the reproductive cycle of women. It is also a special food served during pregnancy and especially after childbirth for nursing mothers. Knowledge about this bean is important to female and to Kikuyu identity. Beans were probably linked to strength and fertility in the Americas. Enslaved people in Virginia may have tapped their symbolic values too. The cowpea, or black-eyed pea, for example, was prescribed by a former enslaved Virginian woman as a food that should be eaten on New Year's Day to have plenty of money throughout the year (Perdue et al. 1976:248).

Plants had magical and symbolic meanings in other ways. Traditionally in the American South, plants such as cedars were planted in graveyards, and because they are evergreen, they may have served as symbols of immortality (Puckett 1969:421–422). Former enslaved African Virginians insisted that different roots were applicable to different situations, for example, to keep money in your pocket and to get a job (Perdue et al. 1976:246, 310). Adam and Eve and Sweet William roots were named as plants that were useful in these areas. While relating his experiences as an enslaved person, George White described his knowledge of plants: "I just go an' get me some roots when ever I feel sick. I know master weed, peter's root, may apple, sweet william roots are good for a lot of things" (Perdue et al. 1976:310).

Some plants were linked to oppression because they were implicated in slave punishment and illness. Many slaves were seriously scarred and harmed, at times fatally, by flogging, and not even pregnant women were spared this punishment (Perdue et al. 1976). Such whippings allowed slaveholders to reduce slaves to the status of children, thereby increasing the degradations they faced. One Virginian slaveholder preferred cherry trees for meting out punishment; according to a former slave, this master "would always cut hisself a cherry sapling, cause a cherry sapling don't make no soar on a slave's back" (Perdue et al. 1976:27). A slave scarred by whipping had a lower resale value. Hickory switches were also favored for flogging slaves (Mintz 1999; Perdue et al. 1976).

It is obvious from looking at how plants were implicated in punishment and illness that enslaved people viewed some use of plants with disfavor. William Wells Brown, who escaped enslavement and later documented aspects of his life, described "the Virginia Play." This practice of white slaveholders involved tying up and whipping slaves, who were afterward smoked over a fire of tobacco stems (Mintz 1999:135).

Overall, plants and plant products were useful to slaves. One former slave recalled that "the wooden bowls what slave chillun ate out of was made out of sweetgum trees" (Killion and Waller 1973:57). Gourds grown in slave yards served as utensils and containers (Perdue et al. 1976:16) that also may have been used to mix and store medicine. Archaeological research has identified species of plants that were important as firewood and as structural materials in Virginia (Higgins et al. 2000; Raymer 1996). Oak, elm, hickory, and pine were among the main plants used as firewood. The primary building materials used for structures such as slave housing included oak and pine (Higgins et al. 2000; Raymer 1996). Housing slaves in adequately built quarters and providing them access to good firewood were significant factors that contributed to a healthy slave population.

In spite of the frequent occurrences of illness and death, factors further compounded by threats or actual events of forced separation by slaveholders, many enslaved people nurtured children and family life. Having access to proper food, adequate accommodations, and good medicine were important to slaves, and they did not just wait on slaveholders to provide these necessities. Enslaved people were proactive in providing for themselves and their families, and plants and plant use were implicated in their survival and their search for autonomy and freedom.

MORTUARY PRACTICES: SOLIDARITIES AND CONTENTIONS

Mortuary practice is a productive area of analysis for studying communal behavior, negotiations, disputes, cooperation, racial tensions, creativity, persistence, and resistance (Costlin 1999; La Roche 1994; McCarthy 1993; Orser 1994; Perry 1997a). Apparently burials provided appropriate settings for planning resistances against slavery. In 1687, the colonial authorities in Virginia deliberated about the danger of slave funerals. From their account, it seems enslaved people were gathering on Saturdays and Sundays "in great Numbers in Makeing and holding Funeralls for Dead Negroes" (McIlwaine 1925:86). The council believed that these occasions were being used to plan insurrections. The governing body was reacting to the discovery of a slave conspiracy on the Northern Neck and found it necessary to issue a proclamation "requiring a Strickt observance of the Severall Laws of this Collony relateing to Negroes, and to require and Command all Masters of families haveing any Negro Slaves, not to permitt them to hold or make any Solemnity of Funeralls for any deced Negros" (McIlwaine 1925:86–87). Enslaved people had to obtain permission to hold funerals, and mourners from other plantations had to get the consent of their masters or mistresses to attend these gatherings (Walsh 1998).

Matthew Lewis (1834:227) reported on a conspiracy that was discovered at a child's funeral in Jamaica in 1816. The overseer at the plantation where the funeral was held had noticed a large number of strange black "mourners" at the cabin of the father of the deceased, who had roasted a hog for the occasion, and had eavesdropped on their conversations. The "mourners" had used the child's funeral as a swearing-in ceremony for the conspiracy.

Laws regulated funeral activities of enslaved people but did not obliterate ritual practices connecting to burials. Food and liquor were important at funerals and were usually provided by the family of the deceased to the mourners (Nichols 1989). In 1750, a South Carolina resident noted "payment of one pound, ten shillings for the making of a coffin and for rum and sugar at the burial of a slave child" (Morgan 1998:641). In the late eighteenth century, Virginian planter Robert Carter refused to sell Old Nat "brandy to bury his Granddaughter Lucy," but he offered him a dollar, "telling him that he might lay out his Annuity as he pleased" (Morgan 1998:641).

Africans and African Americans believed that proper burial was necessary to guarantee good health among the living (Nichols 1989; Thompson 1983). Enslaved people practiced different combinations of African-derived, American-made, and European-related burial rites. In the Americas, some Africans and their descendants believed that after death they would return to an African spiritual homeland, but some considered heaven to be the new meeting place (Sobel 1987). In 1762, a Virginian planter noted in his diary that "Frank, a daughter of Betsy and old Jack, died. A few hours before, she told her mother she was dying and hoped to see her in heaven" (Sobel 1987:186). The funeral of an enslaved boy in nineteenth-century Jamaica was described as conducted "that night according to African customs." It was "accompanied with dancing, singing, drinking, eating, and riot of all kinds" (Lewis 1834:327).

Incorporating rites from different religious traditions may have been one way to guarantee that all bases were covered in efforts to sustain well-being. Charles Orser (1994:36) noted that African Americans were perhaps willing to bury the dead with African-inspired objects mainly because these materials would be hidden. Perhaps these "grave goods" and their associated behavioral practices were not intended for the "white gaze" and thus represented blacks' efforts to exclude whites and potential conflict over burial practices.

Internal conflicts among African Americans probably influenced funeral customs and material objects associated with graves. At times, enslaved people may have disagreed about burial practices, particularly if African-related rituals were considered incompatible with other forms of religious beliefs such as Christianity. Contentions over funeral procedures and customs may have been resolved by allowing both conflicting and compatible practices within the same ceremony. These contentions were probably considered best surmounted for the sake of group solidarity in the face of a dominant oppressive culture.

While some aspects of death rituals are not amenable to archaeological studies, burials are visible and recognizable. Cathy Costlin (1999) suggested that objects found in graves represent intentional and meaningfully placed materials as parts of rituals for the living as well as for the dead. Investigations of the nineteenth-century cemetery of the First African Baptist Church in Philadelphia uncovered evidence suggesting African and African American burial rites, even when touched by the Baptist faith, included practices of placing objects such as shoes, coins, and ceramics in graves (McCarthy 1993). Many of the deceased may have practiced Christianity as Baptists, but the archaeological evidence shows that other religious traditions were also observed. Both the material and the performance aspects of mortuary rites brought together different people and religions.

Archaeological analysis of the colonial African Burial Ground in New York included the study of 427 burials (Perry 1997a). Children represented as much as 45 percent of the burials (La Roche 1994), a testimony to high infant mortality in colonial America. Warren Perry (1997a:3–4) describes "a double burial with a woman cradling an infant in her right arm suggesting death in childbirth or soon thereafter." In Africa, some graves are separated from others based on the circumstances surrounding death. Death by childbirth and suicide, for example, requires special funerary treatments (Perry 1997a). In colonial times, if blacks in New York were practicing such rituals, they may not have deemed it necessary or were unable to enforce any special treatment to segregate the remains of the woman and child from the other burials. Living under conditions of domination and with racial discrimination, including the involuntary separation of families, African Americans may have changed some of their burial traditions to suit their own perceptions of the reality of their existence. The African American community may have decided that this ritual of separating the dead had become inappropriate.

Some of the materials that were placed inside and on graves were associated with the deceased before death (Orser 1994; Thompson 1983). Other objects were included as provisions for the dead and as payment for passage to the spiritual world (La Roche 1994; Sobel 1987; Walsh 1998). Beads, coins, clay pipes, and ceramics are prominent among items that are frequently recovered from African American graves.

At the Utopia site near Williamsburg, Virginia, an African American cemetery with the eighteenth-century remains of thirteen adults and twelve infants or small children was uncovered (Fesler 1996; Walsh 1998). Three adults were interred with clay tobacco pipes under their arms, and an adolescent was buried with a necklace of "transparent multifaceted, amethyst-colored glass" beads (Fesler 1996; Walsh 1998). Lorena Walsh (1998: 125) suggests that it was "a cherished possession in life."

Burial practices indicated that African Americans had sought to live a life of dignity that they also conferred to the dead. They continued to engage in their own cultural practices in spite of different levels of material needs. The custom of placing valuable and usable objects in graves can be read as evidence of African Americans' efforts to perpetuate their notions of ideals, respect, and dignity, strengthening both individual and community.

Beads have been found with the remains of Africans and their descendants in the African Burial Ground in New York (La Roche 1994; Perry 1997a). Cheryl La Roche (1994) studied some of the burials and their associated artifacts, and found that both infants and adults were buried with beads. One child was buried with beads at the waist, while another was interred with beads around the neck. An adult female burial had about a hundred beads around the pelvis (La Roche 1994).

Beads protected African Americans in life and in death (La Roche 1994). Power or energy resided in these objects, which could be accessed for good or evil purposes. Christianity, Islam, and other religions influenced the use of beads by Africans and African Americans (Dublin 1987; Orser 1994). Beads associated with Christianity have been found in the burial of a black male, presumably an African, at a cemetery in New Orleans, Louisiana. The burial dates to the late eighteenth to early nineteenth century (Orser

1994). In Islamic cultures, children and women were identified as people in need of extra protection, and when they wore bead amulets, their protection was believed guaranteed (Dublin 1998). Beads, particularly blue ones, are common in contexts other than burials on African American sites, and archaeologists have associated their occurrence with medicinal practices, particularly as objects used to "ward off the evil eye" (Stine et al. 1996).

Ethnographic and ethnohistorical data support the archaeological evidence that beads were used, and are still used today, to protect children in Africa and the Americas. Beads have also been linked to procreation and fertility. Some enslaved women and men may have welcomed children, believing that children "ensured personal immortality through living memory" (La Roche 1994:14–15). Fertility and procreation likely were perceived as sacred functions, and enslaved women probably used beads, including waist beads, to influence activities in these areas. A raccoon baculum (penis bone) found with the archaeological remains from the living area of George Washington's enslaved population at Mount Vernon Plantation also has been linked to fertility ritual (Atkins 1994).

THE ENSLAVED WOMAN AND MOTHERHOOD

> Slavery severely tested the link between parent and child but never broke it.
>
> (Morgan 1998:548)

Joanne Braxton (1989:20) points out that "as laborers and producers of children for the market, slave women were objects of sexual desire as well as profitable commodities." The conditions of slavery both encouraged and hindered maternal desires and aspirations in enslaved women. The prospect of rearing children, defined legally and socially as slaves, may have caused many women to practice preventive measures against pregnancy, to commit abortion, to run away with their children, and even to engage in desperate measures such as killing their own children (Braxton 1989; Gilroy 1993; Morgan 1998). Some enslaved women became mothers without having any expressed desires for motherhood, yet others apparently encouraged motherhood and healthy children, never fully accepting that their children or themselves were property. Childbearing was also one way for and enslaved woman to express her individuality, as well as her attachment to the slave community (Gilroy 1993). Children were testimonies of enslaved people's determination to survive, of their faith as members of the slave community, and of their hope for a better life and freedom. Children were at the center of some women's struggles to establish and sustain well-being and respectability.

Motherhood and child care perhaps were more difficult and painful in slavery than under other conditions, but many women never gave up their responsibilities to protect enslaved children. Philip Morgan (1998:541) suggests that "although a measure of callousness and passivity was almost inherent in a parent-child relationship under slavery, most slave parents were loving and caring. They might well have been bitter, but not generally toward their children." Morgan cited several examples of caring relationships between parents and children in colonial Virginia and South Carolina, including that of one enslaved mother in South Carolina who carried her child on her back while she worked with a hoe and could not endure the cries of her child when the child was left at the end of the row (Morgan 1998:541). Lorena Walsh (1998) believed that the practice of carrying children may have been discouraged by whites because it was so different from whites' childcare traditions and practices. In addition, they likely believed that the practice would decrease female slaves' productivity.

Slaveholders did not encourage slaves to carry children around while they worked at the "big house." George Washington complained about the frequent visits of children from the quarters to the main house grounds. He had ordered against these activities, but they had not abated (Sobel 1987:143). Work at the "big house" fragmented enslaved families, forcing them to leave their children behind at the quarters, but apparently some slaves resisted and harbored children close to their work areas in defiance of orders against these practices (Sobel 1987). Such everyday activities of resistance in slavery were likely as important as outright acts of rebellion.

For many enslaved women, motherhood was not a call to be conservative; on the contrary, it was a time for radical action. Enslaved women confronted oppression by instigating measures to combat racist practices. They regulated their childbearing and even suppressed it when necessary, instituted their own schedule for breast-feeding, dictated and negotiated the appropriate time to wean children, and directed the allocation of specific food and medical care for themselves and their children (Braxton 1989; Mair 1986). Their activities often opposed plantation directives.

INCORPORATIONS AND EXCLUSIONS IN NURTURING

Although many white Virginians breast-fed their babies, some used black wet nurses. Apparently the custom was popular with the elites in the eighteenth century. Philip Fithian, a tutor to planter Robert Carter's children, noted in his diary that "the conversation at supper was on Nursing Children, I find it common here for people of Fortune to have their young Children suckled by the Negroes! Dr. Jones told us his first and only Child is now with such a Nurse; & Mrs Carter said that Wenches have suckled several of hers—Mrs Carter has had thirteen Children. She told us to night and she has nine now living" (Farish 1957:39). When black women nurtured white babies, some white women did not concede them any recognition of equality. Regarding enslaved people as extensions of slaveholders' will, whites simply accepted the services of enslaved black nurses as commonplace. Some whites, however, did note how helpful their enslaved nurses were with the white children (McMillen 1985).

Sally McMillen (1985) found abundant evidence to study motherhood and the experiences of literate middle- and upper-class white women between 1800 and 1860, but far less data about enslaved women. Nevertheless, she says that "there is nothing to indicate that using a black wet nurse aroused a southern woman's racial sensibilities" (McMillen 1985:352). Perhaps not, but the racial designation of black nurses may have mattered outside whites' homes—in the slave society of the American South.

Some advertisements in the Charleston *Courier* in the nineteenth century were for black nurses, but one blatantly stated, "Wet nurse wanted. A wet nurse to go traveling; none but a white need apply" (McMillen 1985:351). At times, the requirement for wet nurses was "available milk" (McMillen 1985:353); at other times, race was an important variable in the decision-making process. Breast-feeding crossed racial lines both ways in the relationship between whites and blacks. Some white women breast-fed black babies. Their reasons for undertaking this activity perhaps were far more complex and not best described as economic or altruistic. McMillen (1985:354) suggests that this "was one way some southern mothers arose above racial prejudice."

Child care provided the contexts for some female bonding between enslaved women and white women, but it also contributed to abuse. Some encounters were fraught with violence and spite (Braxton 1989; Carby 1987; Gilroy 1993). One former slave reported on the death of his cousin, who was killed by a white mistress. The cousin had fallen asleep while attending to the mistress's baby, and the cries of the baby had disturbed the mother's night rest. The angry mother used an oak stick to murder the girl (Gilroy 1993:67–68).

While some whites in Virginia rewarded enslaved child-care providers, some complained about them. Landon Carter bemoaned the fact that he had only enslaved people to take care of his children, and he was unhappy with the quality of care given by black nurturers (Greene 1965:194). Other slaveholders were more grateful. Virginia planter and later absentee owner Philip Ludwell III, who died in 1767, wrote in his will that "whereas I stand engaged by promises to give freedom to 2 of my slaves, named Jane & Sarah, daurs. of Cress, for her faithful and unwearied care in nursing my dear little orphans from the death of their mother & finally sacrificing her life in their service, Now I empower my daur. H.P.L. on my death & desire her to have them brought over to England & manumitted" (McGhan 1993:652). Black women who cared for white children were intimately associated with these families and often exacted concessions for such care and "acts of inclusion." Some black caregivers, for example, requested special favors for their own children, including freedom.

Perhaps some enslaved women had little choice about becoming nurturers to white children. As enslaved laborers they had few options for avoiding unwanted and exacting tasks. In 1858, when Ella Thomas of Georgia did not have enough milk to nurse her child, the problem was solved because "one of the women at the plantation had just lost a baby a week old, and Pa kindly offered us the use of her" (McMillen 1985:350). Perhaps this was one enslaved woman who was "forced to offer her service willingly." Other enslaved blacks may have willingly offered their services as wet nurses to save the lives of both enslaved and white children.

McMillen (1985) found that most white mothers breast-fed their babies, but she wondered about the acquiescence of enslaved women who had to serve as wet nurses to white babies: "It would be interesting to know how slave women reacted to the nurturing duty imposed on them by their owners. Whether they resented feeding a white baby, particularly if their own had just died, or whether their maternal needs caused them to welcome the substitute baby is unknown" (McMillen 1985:351). Marie Schwartz (1996) suggested an answer to these questions: "The need for a wet nurse by the white family put an additional strain on a breastfeeding mother, who might find herself nursing another child in addition to her own" (Schwartz 1996:248–249). Child care took enormous toll on enslaved mothers or caregivers who sometimes had to stay up nursing babies, thus reducing their own sleeping time. Nursing duties may have also hindered enslaved women's productivity as laborers on plantations. Their production may have been less than other women who had older children or were without children (Schwartz 1996).

Joanne Braxton's representation of enslaved women as "outraged mothers" weakens the premise that black women welcomed the care of babies, white or black. Braxton writes that the "outraged mother" operated with a full awareness of "the abuse of her people and her person" (Braxton 1989:21). These "outraged mothers" planned their own pregnancies, traveled far to visit their children, and "sacrificed and improvised" both to upheld and nurture "flesh and spirit" of children, self, and family. Lucille Mair (1986:11) believes that black motherhood during slavery became "a catalyst for much of women's subversive and aggressive strategies directed against the might of the plantation."

CONTENTIOUS ACCOMMODATIONS: THE EXERCISE OF SOCIAL POWER

Slaveholders had difficulty resolving their desire to accommodate the nutritional needs of infants while at the same time maximizing the labor of mothers and other women (Greene 1965; Morgan 1998; Schwartz 1996). The wishes of slaveholders and enslaved mothers both coincided and conflicted in this unstable arena of race and labor relations. Arrangements were adapted and discontinued as mothers used open means such as negotiations as well as covert measures to ensure children's well-being. Landon Carter, for example, had problems with his nursing enslaved mothers over how many times infants should be fed. He wanted to grant them three feeding periods, but the women wanted five (Greene 1965:496; Morgan 1998:544). Some planters allowed enslaved mothers to keep babies nearby or to work closer to their cabins (Schwartz 1996).

Many slaveholders used elderly women, older children, and ailing blacks in childcare and health services. In 1805, thirty-four females and seventeen males were chosen as medical attendants on ten Jamaican properties belonging to John Tharpe. About half of these enslaved attendants presided over births or cared for children. Most of them were weak, sick, or otherwise unsuitable for field work (Sheridan 1985:91–94). Some of the midwives were weak, while one of the children's cooks were described as having "incurable sores." These blacks in health care were, in monetary terms, among the least valued slaves.

The poor health and the advanced age of plantation caregivers and medicinal practitioners may have hindered children and mothers from getting adequate health care, but patients, children, and other recipients may have benefited from the knowledge and support of these people (Gundaker, pers. comm., 1999; Sheridan 1985). Children may have been prepared for adulthood by the lessons they learnt from grandmothers, mothers, uncles, and aunts, as well as unrelated individuals. Undoubtedly many medicinal specialists had their first lesson in health care from elderly relatives and other caregivers. The practice of using elderly women and older children in child care may not have been totally foreign to some enslaved blacks. Perhaps what was strange, and maybe alarming, was the weak and sick condition of these caretakers, most likely resulting from the abuse of slavery. In Africa, mothers were not the only nurturers of children; different relatives and other nonrelatives took an active role in child rearing, thus giving credence to the saying that "it takes a whole village to raise a child" (Gundaker 1999).

Chesapeake planters encouraged a naturally increasing slave population by importing more girls and women (Berlin 1998). By 1700 the majority of slaves in the Chesapeake were Africans, but that changed by the 1750s. By mid-century more than 80 percent of the enslaved population was creole, American born. The planters "delighted in the growth of an indigenous slave population, as it allowed them to transfer much of the cost of reproducing the workforce to the workers themselves" (Berlin 1998:127). For instance, Thomas Jefferson said, "A woman who brings a child every two years [is] more profitable than the best man on the farm [for] what she produces is an addition to the capital, while his labor disappears in mere consumption" (Berlin 1998:127). On purchasing two fifteen-year-old girls, another slaveholder remarked about the advantage of having "young breeding Negroes" (Berlin 1998:127).

Slaveholders tried different inducements to increase birth rates on their plantations, and instituted various incentives and indulgences to gain enslaved people's compliance with their own domination and oppression. In the early nineteenth century, Matthew Lewis instituted honors for mothers, including a "play day," for the enslaved people on his Jamaican plantation (Lewis 1834:125, 191–193). One honor allowed mothers to wear a "scarlet girdle" and to receive special attention and favors. Nevertheless, the birth rate remained low on his plantation, with only 12 to 13 children born each year to his enslaved people, who numbered above 330, with females outnumbering males (Lewis 1834:320–321). Lewis blamed illness as one factor contributing to high infant mortality.

Mortality from illness was very high among children in slave societies (Berlin 1998; Farish 1957; Lebsock 1987; Lewis 1834). Children died from illnesses such as dysentery, typhoid, smallpox, and malaria, and as children arrived and departed, family structures changed. One enslaved woman in Virginia lost seven children, all below the age of ten, alarming the rest of the enslaved population (Farish 1957). Enslaved and free women could expect to bear six to nine children although there are reports of women who bore as many as thirteen (Farish 1957; Lebsock 1987).

Most mothers were very attached to their children and used both human and spiritual aids to ensure their well-being (Lebsock 1987; McMillen 1985). Naming practices were also included in the requisites for well-being. Both whites and blacks participated in naming enslaved people, but researchers have shown that blacks attached special meanings to names (Morgan 1998). Examples from nineteenth-century Jamaica clearly show that enslaved people believed that names encoded powerful medicine. One father told Matthew

Lewis that he wanted to change his enslaved son's name to that of his dead grandfather because he believed that the child's ill health was caused by the grandfather's displeasure that the child had not been named after him (Lewis 1834:349). A mother with a sick child on the same plantation also requested a name change for her child because she was certain that the child would not prosper with a name such as "Lucia" (Lewis 1834:349).

CONTENTIOUS ACCOMMODATIONS: LIVING AREAS FOR ENSLAVED PEOPLE

The exercise of social power in slavery, evident in acts of domination and resistance, also had material visibility (Epperson 1990a; Paynter and McGuire 1991), and studies of the past cultural landscape of Virginia have revealed racist practices regarding African Americans. Slave dwellings, for example, were usually poorly constructed, although some were well made out of bricks. The arrangement of slave housing, usually close to work areas and not visible from the formal approaches to plantation manors can be read as evidence of how slaveholders ordered and shaped the landscape of slavery.

Enslaved people inserted their own concepts of space and approaches to the cultural landscape. Some requested certain locations for their cabins, and slaveholders conceded to some of these demands (Sobel 1987). Enslaved women promoted their own approaches to their environment, and some of their activities may have related to health concerns. In the 1720s, Virginia planter Robert "King" Carter argued about yard maintenance with his bonded women. The women had been sweeping the areas around their cabins and the paths to their gardens plots. Drawing on African American traditions, sweeping yards may have been one way to keep these areas free of things that might have been placed to harm the inhabitants. Carter was displeased over these swept yards but was unable to curtail this practice. Apparently, the swept yards contrasted unpleasantly with his nearby manicured lawn (Hudgins 1990:68).

Archaeologists have suggested that the need for surveillance and discipline, particularly the need to constantly remind enslaved people of their "inferior" status, influenced the location and the condition of slave quarters and yards (Epperson 1990a; McKee 1992). Plantations were, foremost, business enterprises, and slaveholders and managers prioritized efficient labor and time management strategies in matters of living arrangements. The reproduction and production of women counted in the spatial layout and social relations of the plantation. It could be argued that the construction and location of slave quarters were intricately connected to the need to indulge and reward reproductive women. Jefferson informed his overseer in Bedford County that "Maria having now a child, I promised her a house to be built this winter, be so good as to have it done" (Sobel 1987:111). Women used these concessions to their advantage in sustaining their communal and family ties. Maria's house was to be built next to that of her sister (Sobel 1987).

Archaeologists should consider the possibility that the location and condition of the quarters they study may have resulted from this need to accommodate the requests and requirements of nursing mothers and caretakers of children while maximizing labor productivity. Undoubtedly Thomas Jefferson considered these factors when he told his overseer to build black houses adjacent to each other so that "the fewer nurses may serve & that the children may be more easily attended to by the superannuated women" (Sobel 1987:111).

Whites may have included blacks as nurturers of their children, but they excluded them by representing them as people without self-respect and self-esteem. Whites often described blacks as filthy, and depicted slave quarters as untidy, trash-filled places (Edwards 1998; McKee 1992). Some slave quarters were crudely built and incorporated trashlike materials of stick and mud. To protect themselves from fever, cold, and other illness in drafty cabins, slaves also stuffed various objects between the logs of cabins, and their use of objects such as textiles and plant parts, may have resulted in multicolored trashlike displays (Edwards 1998). By intermixing particular colors as fillers, however, residents may have guaranteed extra spiritual protection for themselves and their children.

Concerns about sanitation and the health of enslaved people in the nineteenth century caused some slaveholders to insist that slave houses be raised above the ground, allowing for a crawl space beneath that could be kept free of trash. Archaeologists have found examples of pier-supported structures that may have resulted from these attempts to change slave living areas (Singleton 1991). Archaeological studies have found less evidence for pier-supported houses in eighteenth-century Virginia, where slave houses had remarkable numbers of root cellars and storage pits dug in the flooring. These pits became receptacles for trash during and after the occupation of these houses. Root cellars and trash pits have served as rich contexts for the recovery of materials used in medicinal practices. These materials include plant remains, pharmaceutical bottles, ceramic ointment jars and salve pots, other ceramics, shells, metals, and animal bones.

Studies of African American yards and gardens have documented the clutter of new, recycled, and found objects that have been used to decorate these places (Gundaker 1998a, 1998b). Some of these displays appeared to be "piles of junk," but studies have shown that African American spiritual beliefs and practices figured prominently in the making of these displays. They were not trash, but materials that articulated with beliefs and the presentation of self. These displays made vital statements about political, social, and economic factors affecting African Americans' well-being (Edwards 1998; Gundaker 1993, 1998a, 1998b).

CONCLUSION

Medicinal practices helped to define the complex nature of the social interactions between blacks and whites during slavery, and circumstances surrounding women's production and procreation contributed to practices of inclusion and exclusion in race relations. Racist practices dictated that white women supply the heirs and that black women supply the laborers of plantation society. Black women, however, worked to change the legal and social definitions and practices of enslavement. They employed medicinal practices on behalf of the living and ritual practices for the dead. This preliminary research shows the potential of using a multidisciplinary framework to address how race and racism were implicated with medicinal practices of motherhood and child care during slavery. Undoubtedly, more research will contribute significantly to scholarship regarding the interactions of black and white women and the nature of social interactions, culture change, and the practice of medicine in colonial Virginia.

Note

I would like to thank Gregory Brown of the Colonial Williamsburg Foundation for reading and commenting on an earlier version of this chapter. I would also like to commend the editor, fellow contributors, and others whose work made this volume possible.

4

"A Separate House for the Christian Slaves, One for the Negro Slaves": The Archaeology of Race and Identity in Late Seventeenth-Century Virginia

Terrence W. Epperson

DURAND DE DAUPHINÉ

"Christian Slaves" and "Negro Slaves"

For a period of slightly more than six months in 1686 and 1687, a Huguenot exile using the nom de plume "Durand de Dauphiné" traveled through much of Tidewater Virginia, providing a unique participant-observer's perspective on the young colony (Chinard 1934). As part of an effort to encourage Huguenot immigration to the New World, Durand's account was published in The Hague in July 1687 as *Voyages d'un françois exilé pour la religion avec une description de la Virgine & Marilan dans l'Amérique.* Although this account has been widely cited in discussions of plantation architecture and settlement patterns (e.g., Bogger et al. 1994; Deetz 1993:77; Mouer et al. 1999:91; Pickett 1996; Upton 1986:214; Wright 1940:193), Durand's narrative also offers valuable insight into the social construction of racial difference during the final decades of the seventeenth century. In this chapter, I supplement Durand's account with additional documentary analysis, particularly concerning the plantations of his primary host, Ralph Wormeley II (1650–1701). Drawing on this information, as well as recent and ongoing historical and archaeological research in the Chesapeake, I explore some of the archaeological ramifications and research possibilities for the further analysis of race and identity. After discussing "vulgar anti-essentialism" and the perils inherent in uncritical applications of social constructionist analysis, I offer suggestions for future research.

While the precise identity of Durand de Dauphiné has never been established, his account tells us he was a relatively prosperous native of Provence who fled France after Louis XIV's revocation of the Edict of Nantes in October 1685 unleashed a reign of terror against Protestants. After a series of misadventures, narrow escapes, and a very rough ocean passage, Durand arrived in Virginia on September 22, 1686. Before relating his travels in the colony, Durand devotes the next four chapters of his narrative to "Brief Description of America (Chapter VIII), On the Beauty and Fertility of America (Chapter IX), On Wild and Domestic Animals (Chapter X), and The Trees of Virginia (Chapter XI)."

Although he was accompanied by his French servant through his entire adventure, Durand consistently conflated the institutions of indentured servitude and slavery. In Chapter 8 he provided the following explanation of the distinctions he noted within the bound labor force: "A difference exists between the slaves that are bought, to wit: a Christian twenty years old or over, cannot be a slave for more than five years, whereas Negroes & other unbelievers are slaves all their lives" (Chinard 1934:110). This distinction between, on one hand, "Christians" and, on the other, "Negroes & other unbelievers" becomes especially important in his discussion of the plantation landscape in the following chapter:

> Some people in this country are comfortably housed; the farmers' houses are built entirely of wood, the roofs being made of small boards of chestnut, as are also the walls. Those who have some means, cover them inside with a coating of mortar in which they use oyster-shells for lime; it is as white as snow, so that although they look ugly from the outside, where only the wood can be seen, they are very pleasant inside, with convenient windows and openings. They have started making bricks in quantities, & I have seen several houses where the walls were entirely made of them. Whatever their rank, & I know not why, they build only two rooms with some closets on the ground floor, & two rooms in the attic above; but they build several like this, according to their means. They build also a separate kitchen, *a separate house for the Christian slaves, one for the Negro slaves,* & several to dry the tobacco, so that when you come to the home of a person of some means, you think you are entering a fairly large village. (Chinard 1934:119–120, emphasis added)

Durand's account clearly indicates the existence, at least on some plantations, of spatial segregation between indentured servants ("Christian slaves") and enslaved Africans ("Negro slaves"). However, at least from his outsider's perspective, this puzzling practice was not based upon racial prejudice, but rather upon religious distinctions. We might be tempted to attribute his anachronistic formulation to his obvious ignorance of Virginia law and social practices. After all, by the time of Durand's visit it was clear that baptism of enslaved persons would not result in their manumission and that the practice of perpetual, heritable enslavement was to be restricted to persons of African descent. However, the rationale for this distinction was not as clear as we might think.

"Any Christian not being Negro, mulatto, or Indian"

As it happens, Durand's sojourn occurred during a fundamentally crucial period in the formulation and implementation of "whiteness" in Virginia (Allen 1994, 1997; Epperson 1997, 1999a). Just seven years before, the Reverend Morgan Godwyn (1680), an Anglican cleric who had traveled in Virginia and Barbados, had published *The Negro's & Indians Advocate.* This book passionately advocated baptism of enslaved persons in the belief that Christianity would address the spiritual needs of both masters and slaves while simultaneously assuring a more loyal and less rebellious enslaved labor force. Godwyn lamented the fact that through "corrupt Custom and Partiality" the terms "*Negro* and *Christian, Englishman* and *Heathen*" had been "made *Opposites;* thereby as it were implying, that the one could not be *Christians,* nor the other *Infidels*" (Godwyn 1680:36).

Publication of *The Negro's & Indians Advocate* was an important factor in the establishment of the Society for the Propagation of the Gospel in Foreign Parts in 1701, although Anglican proselytizing among enslaved in Virginia met with limited success (Anesko 1985; Bond 1996; Gomez 1998:244–250). While Godwyn's work effectively undermined the Negro/Christian dichotomy, it was not immediately clear what rationale would be developed to supplant the religious justification for slavery. The term "white" does not appear in Virginia legislation until four years *after* Durand's departure, in a law designed to prevent "that abominable mixture and spurious issue" which would supposedly arise from intermarriage between any "English or other white man or woman being free" and "any Negroe, mulatto, or Indian man or woman bond or free" (Hening 1809:87).

Even when the term "white" is not used, we can follow the juridical construction of racial difference that was occurring at the time of Durand's visit. For example, note the differences between two statutes, the first enacted in 1680, and the second in 1705. The first law stipulates that "if any Negro or other slave shall presume to lift up his hand in opposition against any Christian, shall for every such offence...have and receive thirty lashes on his bare back well laid on" (Hening 1809, 2:481). The 1705 slave code repeated the provision, punishment, and general form of the earlier law, but quietly incorporated several significant alterations: "If any Negro, mulatto, or Indian, bond or free, shall at any time, lift his or her hand, in opposition against any Christian not being Negro, mulatto, or Indian, he or she so offending, shall...receive on his or her bare back, thirty lashes, well laid on" (Hening 1809, 3:459).

While the 1680 act applied only to enslaved people, the 1705 law was explicitly racial and applied to both enslaved and nonenslaved people of color. In 1680, "Christian" was an unproblematic category, but the later law recognized that a "Negro, mulatto, or Indian" could be baptized, hence they were specifically excluded from protection under this law. Significantly, the language of the act was also expanded to specifically criminalize acts of resistance committed by women of color.

Thus Durand's 1687 distinction between "Christian slaves" and "Negroes & other unbelievers" is not as peculiar as it might first seem. In fact, his account invites us to reverse the polarity of the typical explanation for spatial segregation. Rather than saying that planters housed indentured servants and African slaves in separate quarters because of their innate racial differences, we can say that a perception of "racial" difference between these two elements of the bound labor force is, at least in part, a *result* of disciplinary practices such as spatial segregation. While this maneuver is indeed instructive, the reversal of the dichotomy between racial difference and spatial definition can only serve as the first step in a genuinely dialectical analysis.

Returning to the travels and travails of our Huguenot exile, Chapter 8, entitled "Trip to Pianketant, Middlesex, Northumberland, Rappahannock and Stafford Counties and to Maryland," includes Durand's visits to the plantations of Ralph Wormeley II and William Fitzhugh. His desire to visit Monsieur Wormeley appears to have been prompted in part by the knowledge that Virginia's current governor, Francis Howard of Effingham, was in residence at Wormeley's plantation Rosegill. Durand arrived at Rosegill in mid-December 1686 and noted that "Monsieur Wormeley...owns twenty-six Negro slaves & twenty Christian. He holds the highest offices, and owns at least twenty houses in a lovely plain along the Rappahannock River. He has rented his most comfortable house to the Governor. When I reached his place I thought I was entering a rather large village, but was later told that it all belonged to him (Chinard 1934:142). The Frenchman was very appreciative of Virginian hospitality; the governor hosted the two o'clock meal every day, while all other meals were taken in Wormeley's house.

During the "five or six days" Durand lingered at Rosegill, he was able to observe sessions of the Governor's Council. One of the matters under discussion was a "ship from Guiana [Guinea?], loaded with Negroes" that had been confiscated by English men-of-war because of illegal operations.

After the council adjourned, Durand accompanied Wormeley on a visit to his Portobago plantations on the upper Rappahannock (near the present-day location of Fredericksburg). Durand describes a landscape only recently opened to European settlement. Along the north side of the Rappahannock he counted "eight or nine houses that Monsieur Wormeley has built on his estates or plantations.... I noticed also that about two-thirds of the lands were wooded, the other meadows which were, as I have already mentioned, the plantations that belonged to the savages five or six years ago" (Chinard 1934:151).

Durand expressed an interest in visiting a village inhabited by "savages" that was visible on the opposite (south) bank of the Rappahannock River. The next day the party entered the village, and Durand described the "savages" as having "rather pretty houses, the walls as well as the roofs ornamented with trees, & so securely fastened together with deer thongs that neither rain nor wind causes them inconvenience. These people are darker than the Egyptians we see in Europe. The men do nothing but hunt & fish, while the women plant Indian corn. The crop belongs to the community, each taking whatever he needs. The women also make pots, earthen vases & smoking pipes. The Christians buying these pots or vases fill them with Indian corn, which is the price of them" (Chinard 1934:153).

As parting presents, the Indians gave Wormeley "a dozen deerskins," while Durand and his companion Monsieur Parker were each given "a handful of pipes" (Chinard 1934:154). As they left the village, Wormeley offered to sell ten thousand acres of land on both sides of the river (presumably including the Indian village) to the prospective French settlers. The entourage of twenty then proceeded to the Potomac River plantation of William Fitzhugh in Stafford County. They passed the night with "a great deal of carousing," entertained by "three fiddlers, a jester, a tight-rope dancer, [and] an acrobat who tumbled around" (Chinard 1934:158). By Christmas Day, Wormeley and Durand had returned to Rosegill. Durand departed for England on March 15, 1697.

Like almost everyone else Durand met in Virginia, William Fitzhugh and his neighbor Nicholas Hayward had been very interested in selling vast expanses of real estate to the Huguenot exiles. Hayward's proposal, entitled "Propositions for Virginia," was appended to Durand's narrative when it was first published in 1687 (Chinard 1934:179–180). Hayworth may have actually facilitated the initial publication in hopes of attracting settlers. However, the response of the prospective buyers was apparently disappointing. On June 1, 1688, Fitzhugh wrote to Hayward, "I thank you in your kindness of Mr. Durand's book & must agree with you, as well as I can understand it, that it's a most weak unpolite piece, having neither the Rules of History, nor method of description, & taking it only as a private Gentleman's Journal, 'tis as barren & defective there too" (Davis 1963:245).

WORMELEY OF ROSEGILL
Cavalier Contradictions

"Barren & defective" though it may be, many details of Durand's account are corroborated by independent archaeological, architectural, and documentary analysis. In a study that would subsequently become a cornerstone of Jim Deetz's Flowerdew Hundred analysis (Deetz 1993; see also Emerson 1999; Mouer et al. 1999), Dell Upton (1982) examined seventeenth and early eighteenth-century room-by-room probate inventories and found that the number of rooms in planters' houses increased steadily until about 1680. After that date, however, the number of rooms per house dropped sharply, returning to the 1640 number by about 1720. Upton attributes the post-1680 drop in the number of rooms per house to increasing conflicts between masters and their bound labor force (including both servants and slaves) and the concomitant removal of bound laborers from the main plantation house to outbuildings or outlying quarters (see also Ameri 1997; Chappell 1982; Linebaugh 1994; Neiman 1993; Wells 1998).

Durand's 1686 description of relatively small planter homes surrounded by large numbers of outbuildings, including quarters for bound laborers, is certainly consistent with Upton's analysis. In many respects, Durand's account is also validated by archaeological studies of the "impermanent architecture" of the seventeenth-century Chesapeake (Carson et al. 1981). However, this classic study of earthfast architecture (structures based on post-in-the-ground or earth-laid sill techniques) is also challenged by Durand's statement that "they have started making bricks in quantities, & I have seen several houses where the walls were entirely made of them" (Chinard 1934:119). Recent historical and archaeological studies have also confirmed this aspect of the exile's account, highlighting the hitherto under-appreciated importance of brick domestic architecture in the seventeenth-century Chesapeake. For example, Dwayne Pickett (1996) attributes the florescence of brick domestic architecture in the third quarter of the century to the arrival and consolidation of a new ruling elite, the royalist exiles (the storied "Virginia Cavaliers") who fled England after the 1649 execution of Charles I. In his analysis of colonial Virginia churches, Upton (1986:102) addresses the contradictions inherent in elite architecture through his distinction between *style* and *mode.* While style represents the commonly understood elements that "assert a building's universality," mode serves "to articulate separations and distinctions among the people who used the building." The "quasi-domestic" style of colonial Virginia churches evoked a universally understood "house of God" metaphor, while the specific modes of construction mirrored the houses of the wealthiest gentry, making it clear that "the house of God was not a slave's house or a common planter's house; it was a gentleman's house" (Upton 1986:164). This use of elite architectural modes becomes especially apparent in the late seventeenth-century congruence between brick houses and churches (Pickett 1996). Therefore, the period when Anglican doctrine was becoming more inclusive with the publication of *The Negro's and Indians Advocate* (1680) coincided with a refinement of the architecturally expressed separations and distinctions.

Although the spatial separation between planters and their bound laborers, both enslaved and indentured, has received considerable attention, the spatial distinctions *within* the bound labor force—that is, the separate houses for "Christian slaves" and "Negro slaves" indicated by Durand's account—has received little archaeological analysis. Historians, however, have been a bit more attentive to this issue. The close contact between enslaved and indentured laborers in the years before Baconn's Rebellion in 1676–1677 was, of course, a fundamental element in Edmund Morgan's classic work *American Slavery/American Freedom* (Morgan 1975). Similarly, Lorena Walsh, in her recent study *From Calabar to Carter's Grove: The History of a Virginia Slave Community,* indicates that recently arrived enslaved Africans probably "shared dwellings and worked alongside white indentured servants (mostly young men)" through the early 1680s. Her analysis of a northern York County plantation indicates that "interracial work groups would have been common... into the 1680s but less frequent thereafter" (Walsh 1997:31). This issue is complicated by the fact that Durand's visit occurred during the period when Chesapeake planters were moving from indentured servants to slaves as their primary labor source (Menard 1977). However, within the Chesapeake there was a great deal of regional variation in the pace, timing, and magnitude of this transition (Kulikoff 1986).

Durand's 1686 account of the separations within the bound labor force is augmented by documentary analysis of the plantations of Ralph Wormeley and his Middlesex County neighbors. This analysis is enhanced by the fact that Middlesex has the most complete records of any Tidewater Virginia county, a factor that was fundamental in Darrett and Anita Rutman's selection of this area for their analysis of the period 1650–1750 (Rutman and Rutman 1984a, 1984b).

Christopher Wormeley, the uncle of Durand's host, served as governor of Tortuga in the early 1630s and came to Virginia soon after the Spanish capture of the island. He settled in York County, where he was soon joined by his brother, Ralph Wormeley I (DeBusk et al. 1982; Rutman and Rutman 1984a: 259). Christopher died in the early 1640s and his widow, Elizabeth, later married, in turn, Richard Kemp and Sir Thomas Lunsford, successive owners of Rich Neck Plantation in York County. In February 1650 the royalist émigré Henry Norwood provided the following account of Ralph I's hospitality: "It fell out at that time that Capt. Ralph Wormeley (of His Majesty's Council) had guests in his house feasting and carousing, that were lately come from England, and most of them my intimate acquaintance. Using the common freedom of the country, I thrust myself amongst Capt. Wormeley's guests, and had a kind reception from them all, which answered (if not exceeded) my expectations. Sir Thomas Lunsford, Sir Philip Honeywood, Sir Henry

Chicheley, and Col. Hammond were the persons I met there, and enjoyed that night very good cheer" (Force 1836).

At the time of the carousing Cavaliers' convocation, Wormeley, Lunsford, and Chicheley were all patenting large tracts on the Middle Peninsula between the Rappahannock and Piankatank Rivers, the area that would soon become Middlesex County. Ralph died later the same year, leaving widow Agatha and sons William and Ralph (II). Soon after, Agatha married Sir Henry Chicheley. The October 1653 list of tithables indicates that Chicheley controlled some 3,800 acres within the future bounds of Middlesex County. His land was worked by seventeen indentured servants; no enslaved laborers are noted. More than half of the heads of household listed in 1653 had previously lived in a cluster on the south bank of the York River (Rutman and Rutman 1984a:46, 48–49). Middlesex County was formed from a portion of Lancaster County in 1669.

Young Ralph's wealthy stepfather sent the lad to England for a proper education; he matriculated (but did not take a degree) at Oriel College, Oxford in 1665. Upon returning to Virginia he married his second cousin, Katherine Lunsford, daughter of Sir Thomas Lunsford and Ralph's cousin Elizabeth. In the words of a local history, "How strange and funny life could be. Katherine's great Aunt Agatha would now become her mother-in-law!" (DeBusk et al. 1982:27). Ralph and Elizabeth had two children, Elizabeth and Catherine. Following the death of his first wife in 1685, Ralph married Elizabeth Armistead of Gloucester, who bore him Ralph (III), John, and Judith. In 1690 Ralph Wormeley II became one of the founding trustees of the College of William and Mary. When his estate was appraised in 1701, his personal property was valued at £2,861, making him, by far, the wealthiest man in Middlesex County (Wright 1940:191).

Although none of the Rosegill buildings described by Durand are extant (Gray et al. 1978), and no archaeological work has been performed, the documentary record provides some clues regarding the interactions between enslaved and indentured laborers on the plantation. Records for early importations of indentured and enslaved laborers are sketchy. In June 1681 William Fitzhugh asked Wormeley to secure "five or six" slaves for him from ships reported to be arriving soon on the York River (Davis 1963:93, 175). Demographic analysis also indicates significant importations of enslaved workers in 1684 and 1696 (Rutman and Rutman 1984b: 191). At the time of Durand's visit to Rosegill, Africans (almost all of them enslaved) constituted only 8 percent of the county's population (Rutman and Rutman 1984a:166). Recall Durand's statement that Wormeley "owns twenty-six Negro slaves & twenty Christian." Rutman and Rutman (1984a) believe this is probably an accurate assessment. The relatively equal balance between enslaved (26) and indentured (20) laborers indicates that the transition from indentured servitude to slavery had only just begun. The situation would be far different by the time Wormeley's estate was inventoried in 1701. Although the statement regarding separate houses for "Christian" and "Negro" slaves did not refer to a specific plantation, Rosegill is the only plantation Durand describes in any detail, and it is reasonable to assume that the statement applies to Wormeley's holdings.

The primary mechanism for obtaining land in seventeenth-century Virginia was through the headright system. The right to patent fifty acres of land was granted to whoever paid the passage for an individual entering the colony, whether enslaved, indentured, or free. On December 2, 1689, Ralph Wormeley II received a certificate from the county court for the importation of eighty-one named individuals, presumably indentured servants (Middlesex County Orders 1680–1694:438). This transaction entitled Wormeley to patent an additional 4,050 acres. It is highly unlikely that Wormeley imported all of these servants for his own use. Most of the indentures were probably sold to other planters. However, at least two of the

Table 4.1. Inventory of the Estate of Ralph Wormeley, Esq., November 17, 1701

	£	s.	d.
[Day 1, Structure #1]			
parlor			
chamber			
chamber over said chamber			
chamber over said parlor			
stair head in the passage			
[Day 2, Structure #2]			
nursery			
old nursery			
the room over the Lady's Chamber			
Lady's Chamber			
entry			
closet			
closet			
the Pine Quarter	£	s.	d.
1 old Negro man named Jack & his wife Doll	20	—	—
1 Negro man named Will	35	—	—
1 Negro woman named Betty wife to the above Will	30	—	—
1 mullato named Randall	35	—	—
1 boy named Frank	25	—	—
1 boy named Billy	25	—	—
1 girl named Margaret	08	—	—
1 girl named Betty	08	—	—
1 girl named Hannah	08	—	—
1 sucking child named Samuel	02	—	—
1 Indian man	25	—	—
1 Negro woman named Margaret	30	—	—
1 woman named Sue	25	—	—
(14)			
the hog house quarter			
1 man named Jimmy	30	—	—
1 woman named Betty	25	—	—
1 man named Ralph	30	—	—
1 girl named Kate	25	—	—
1 suckling child named Jenny	02	—	—
1 Negro man named Gunner	25	—	—
1 Negro woman named Sarah	25	—	—
1 Negro woman named Martha	25	—	—
1 old Negro woman named Sarah	10	—	—

Table 4.1. Inventory of the Estate of Ralph Wormeley, Esq., November 17, 1701 continued

(9)			
At the home house			
Frank a Negro woman	30	—	—
1 Negro girl named Jersey als Arabella	30	—	—
1 Indian boy named Jack	16	—	—
(3)			
At the Quarter over the Creek			
1 Negro man named Caesar	30	—	—
1 Negro man named Harry	32	—	—
1 Old Negro man named Dick	15	—	—
1 boy named Jack	30	—	—
1 Negro woman Phillis	29	—	—
1 sucking child named Flora	02	—	—
1 boy named Abraham	07	—	—
1 boy named Jeffry	10	—	—
(8)			
At the home house			
[. . . .]			
In the Smith's Shop			
[. . . .]			
In the barne			
[. . . .]			
At the home house			
English Servants			
Thomas Reed 1 year & 9 months to serve	07	—	—
Samuel Low five months to serve	00	10	—
Richard Eastry the shoemaker two years two months to serve	14	—	—
Rowland Thomas the Taylor two years to serve	12	—	—
James White the miller six months to serve	00	10	—
Catherine Morrell two years to serve & 3 months to serve	06	—	—
Sarah Pitts two years to serve	06	—	—
John Mayo six months to serve	06	10	—
(8)			
In the Kitchen			
[. . . .]			
In the Gorat House			
[20 firearms]			
In the Chamber over the old Dary			
[. . . .]			

Table 4.1. Inventory of the Estate of Ralph Wormeley, Esq., November 17, 1701 continued

In the Little roome			
[. . . .]			
Negroes			
Jack the Carpenter	35	—	—
Robin the Cooper	35	—	—
Captaine [?]	35	—	—
(3)			
At Fleming Quarter			
Negroes			
1 man named Tom	26	—	—
1 woman named Sarah	25	—	—
1 girl named Sue	30	—	—
1 boy named Frank	30	—	—
1 girl named Margery	17	—	—
1 boy named Ben a natural foole of no value	—	—	—
1 girl named Christian	05	—	—
(7)			
At Robinsons Quarter			
Negroes			
1 man named Jo	32	—	—
1 man named Lawrence	33	—	—
1 man named Jack	33	—	—
1 boy named White	35	—	—
1 woman named Nora	30	—	—
1 woman named Rose	30	—	—
1 woman named Beck	30	—	—
1 girl named Ester	30	—	—
1 boy named Dick	25	—	—
1 girl named Bess	12	—	—
(10)			
At the Quarter called Whitakers			
Negroes			
1 man named Towerhill	30	—	—
1 man named Grasheer	33	—	—
1 young man named Fouly	35	—	—
1 mullato man named Tawney	35	—	—
1 woman named Beck	30	—	—
1 woman named Alice	28	—	—
1 young woman named Moll	30	—	—

Table 4.1. Inventory of the Estate of Ralph Wormeley, Esq., November 17, 1701 continued

1 boy named Peter	16	—	—
1 boy named Tawney	12	—	—
1 boy named Harry (sucking child)	02	—	—
Captain Harry a cooper an old man	15	—	—
(11)			
At the new Quarter			
Negroes			
1 man named Anthony	35	—	—
1 man named Tomboy	35	—	—
1 man named Johnne	35	—	—
1 young woman named Hannah	30	—	—
1 very old man named Toney	10	—	—
1 old woman named Sue	05	—	—
1 very old woman named Dinah	00	10	—
1 Negro girl named Jenny	22	—	—
(8)			
At old Crumwells			
Negroes			
1 old man named Crumwell	05	—	—
1 old man named Will	05	—	—
1 old woman named Franck	10	—	—
1 boy named Crumwell	10	—	—
(4)			
At Blackwalnut Quarter			
Negroes			
1 girl named Nanny	30	—	—
1 girl named Moll	06	—	—
1 sucking child named Sanco	02	—	—
1 Negro man named Ralph	35	—	—
1 man named Sanco	35	—	—
1 man named Kit	35	—	—
1 man named Red	35	—	—
1 man named Frank	35	—	—
1 old woman named Jenny	15	—	—
1 woman named Dinah	30	—	—
(10)			

Source: Middlesex County Will Book A, pp. 113–131.

Table 4.2. Inventory of the Estate of Maj. Robert Dudley, December 1, 1701

At the Dwelling plantation	£	s.	d.
One Negro boy named Jack	32	—	—
One Negro man named Jacob	30	—	—
One Negro man named Abraham	30	—	—
One Negro man named Isaac	31	—	—
One Negro woman named Jeny	29	—	—
One Negro woman named Maud	29	—	—
One Negro boy named Marcellus	06	—	—
One Negro boy named Letty	06	—	—
One Mallato boy named Fulston	02	—	—
One Irish boy William Raighu (?)	14	—	—
One Irish man Thomas Stapleton 4 years to serve	12	—	—
	221	—	—
[other room and building notations:]			
In the Inner Roome above			
In the Porch Chamber			
In the outer Chamber			
At the Quarter			
one mallato woman at 2 years to serve	02	—	—

Source: Middlesex County Will Book A, pp. 98–106.

individuals on the 1689 list appear in subsequent court records as troublesome Wormeley servants. On June 6, 1692, James Boile was sentenced to receive thirty-nine lashes on his bare back for running away (Middlesex County Orders 1680–1694:557). Similarly, Richard Wilkins was sentenced to serve as Ralph Wormeley's servant for an additional five years and twelve days because "he hath with a Negro and a Mulatto run away from his said master's service twenty eight months and fourteen days." Court records indicate that Richard Wilkins's confederates were "Lawrence, a Negro" and a "Mullatto slave named Mingoe." Having appropriated at least two guns, the trio was charged with causing "great disturbance and Terror of their Majesties good subjects." Lawrence was specifically charged with kicking in the locked door at Wormeley's Hog House quarter and taking "two shirts, one pair of breeches and a Gun." Mingoe received thirty-nine lashes (the same punishment servant James Boile received in his unrelated escapade), and Lawrence was dispatched to General Court in Williamsburg where his ultimate fate (quite possibly execution) is unknown (Middlesex County Orders 1680–1694:526–528, 535, 539, 546–548; Schwarz 1988:70).

Rosegill in 1701

At the time of Ralph Wormeley's death in 1701, Rosegill was an expansive tract, stretching for some four miles along the Rappahannock River and extending inland for more than a mile. In one area, Wormeley's holdings spanned the entire peninsula between the Rappahannock and Piankatank Rivers (Rutman and Rutman 1984a:153). In 1705 the Wormeley estate held 5,200 acres in Middlesex, by far the largest holding in the county (DeBusk et al. 1982:3). The estate also held large tracts in Rappahannock and York Counties. Unlike the nearly even spilt between indentured and enslaved laborers

Durand noted in 1686, Rosegill in 1701 was overwhelmingly dependent upon enslaved labor (see Table 4.1). Nevertheless, we can discern the residential distinctions within the bound labor force. The probate inventory of Wormeley's estate lists eighty-five enslaved "Negroes or Mulattos," two enslaved "Indians," and eight "English servants" (although one might question the "English" identity of someone named John Mayo). We note with interest a girl (her low valuation of £5 indicates she is quite young) at Fleming quarter named Christian and wonder if she had been baptized. At the time of his death Ralph Wormeley owned a copy of Morgan Godwyn's *Negro's and Indians Advocate* (Wright 1940:199).

Since a detailed room-by-room, building-by-building inventory was compiled for Wormeley's estate, we can trace the perambulations of the inventory takers in some detail (see Table 4.1). While most of the enslaved Africans lived in outlying quarters, three separate clusters of bound laborers were enumerated "at the home house," apparently referring to laborers housed in separate outbuildings near Wormeley's residence. Eight "English servants" (two women and six men) are listed. Three of the male servants are listed with occupations (shoemaker, tailor, and miller). The list of servants appears between the notations for the barn and the kitchen, indicating that they were all occupying the same outbuilding. They are clearly housed in different quarters than the enslaved workers. The inventory also indicates spatial segregation between skilled and unskilled enslaved workers. The notation for Jack the Carpenter, Robin the Cooper, and Captaine[?] places them "in the little roome," possibly in or above the old dairy. Although the labor situation had changed drastically since the time of Durand's visit, the probate inventory appears to confirm that his account of enslaved and indentured laborers living in separate quarters outside of the planter's dwelling. However, as indicated by the court records concerning Mingoe, Lawrence, and Richard Wilkins, "interracial" rebellious cooperation still occurred on occasion.

Close Quarters: The Dudley Estate in 1701

Wormeley's estate stands in stark contrast to that of his neighbor, Robert Dudley, whose inventory was taken less than a month later (Table 4.2). With his twelve bound laborers and 950 acres of land, Dudley was more typical of the Middlesex planter, although his wealth was still well above average (Rutman and Rutman 1984a:168). Only one laborer, an unnamed "mallato woman at 2 years to serve" resided at an outlying quarter. The low valuation and the notation "2 years to serve" indicate that she was an indentured servant and not a slave. All of the remaining laborers (nine enslaved "Negroes," one enslaved "Mallato," one "Irish boy," and one "Irish man") resided "at the Dwelling plantation." After listing the dwelling plantation laborers, the inventory proceeds immediately to "In the Inner Roome above." Apparently, all of the bound laborers were sharing the same living space within Dudley's dwelling. Additional research would certainly be required to verify this hypothesis and determine if it is a general pattern. However, the two inventories certainly indicate wide variations in the housing arrangements of bound laborers.

The Irish identity of two of Dudley's three indentured servants also raises intriguing questions, particularly for anyone who has read Noel Ignatiev's (1995) book *How the Irish Became White* (see also Allen 1994; Canny 1976). Writing two decades prior to the Wormeley and Dudley inventories, Morgan Godwyn attributed the following "petulant Taunt" to enslaved Africans: "If the Irishman's Country had first lighted in the Englishman's way, he might have gone no further to look for Negro's [*sic*]" (Godwyn 1680:35–36). While other inventories typically had separate lists for "Negroes" and "English servants," the Dudley inventory placed everyone on the same list, distinguishing whether each individual was "Negro," "Malatto," or "Irish." The Wormeley and Dudley estates also epitomize the bifurcation that characterized servant immigration to the Chesapeake at the end of the seventeenth century. On one hand, we find mature, relatively skilled English servants who were able to negotiate and seek enforcement of fairly favorable indentures. On the other, we note increasing numbers of impoverished, desperate Irish servants, particularly after the mid-1680s (Carr and Menard 1979:230). The defeat of the Catholic cause in the "Glorious Revolution" of 1688–1689 increased the flow of Irish servants, and by 1698, Francis Nicholson, then governor of Maryland, worried that the recently arriving Irish servants might "confederate with Negroes" (Allen 1997:119; Carr and Menard 1979:230, both citing CO 5/714, Nicholson letter to the Lords of Trade and Plantations, 20 August 1698; see also Webb 1966).

RESEARCH POTENTIAL
The Archaeology of Servitude and Slavery: Rich Neck and Utopia Quarter

The preliminary findings presented herein regarding spatial separations between enslaved and indentured laborers during the late seventeenth century could certainly be elaborated and tested archaeologically. Although the questions are not being addressed in the terms discussed in this chapter, two ongoing projects in the Williamsburg area demonstrate the potential for this research. Rich Neck was occupied by the late 1630s and was demolished c. 1700. Richard Kemp, the first owner to actually reside at Rich Neck, was purchasing significant numbers of enslaved Africans as early as 1638. Although these purchases indicate a very early involvement with chattel slavery, the extent to which he used indentured labor is not known. Ongoing archaeological fieldwork at Rich Neck has revealed two late seventeenth-century post-in-the-ground structures, apparently quarters for bound laborers. A coffin-less burial, tentatively identified as a young female of African descent, has recently been discovered between the quarters, and the potential definitely exists for discovering additional burials (McFaden et al. 1994; Muraca 1997, pers. comm., 1999).

A portion of the Utopia Quarter site was initially examined by William Kelso (1984). Subsequent fieldwork conducted by Garrett Fesler (1998a, 1998b, 1999) has revealed a site ideally suited to an examination of the changing Chesapeake labor force during the late seventeenth and eighteenth centuries. Four spatially and temporally distinct phases of quartering structures have been defined at Utopia, each corresponding with discrete periods of plantation ownership. Phase 1, the area examined by Kelso, dates to the ownership of Thomas Pettus II (1669–1691). Pettus's inventory lists five "Negro servants," one "indentured servant boy, and one Indian boy." With the information at hand, it is impossible to determine the precise status (whether enslaved or indentured) of the "Negro servants" and "Indian boy." Phase 2 coincides with the plantation ownership of James Bray II (c. 1700–1725). This period saw a significant influx of enslaved Africans; James's inventory lists twenty-eight slaves, although it is not known who lived at this particular quarter. Phase 3 (c. 1725–1750), the ownership of James Bray III, appears to coincide with a period of increasing demographic stability among the enslaved population. The 1750 inventory lists twenty-seven enslaved individuals, some of whom also appeared in the 1725 list. The final phase coincides with the ownership of Lewis Burwell IV (c. 1750–1780). No inventory survives for Burwell's estate.

In addition to the quarters and associated features, the Utopia site contains a burial ground dating to phases 2 and 3. A total of twenty-five individuals (twelve small children or infants and thirteen adults) have been recovered. One burial was not placed in a coffin; the rest were interred in wooden coffins (five hexagonal, the remainder rectangular). Three individuals were buried with white clay tobacco pipes, and one of the female sub-adults was buried with a blue glass bead necklace. To the limited extent that such a determination could be made, the individuals appear to be of African descent. A local advisory committee was formed to guide the research and reinterment of the burials. The committee is currently seeking scientific guidance and funding to conduct DNA research on the ancestral remains.

The fact that both Rich Neck and Utopia apparently contain burials of enslaved Africans raises a whole spectrum of research possibilities and community issues. In Virginia, as in New York City (Blakey 1998; Epperson 1999b; Perry 1997b), the burial of enslaved Africans was an intensely contested realm of cultural practice. Following the 1687 "discovery of a Negro Plot, formed in the Northern Neck for the destroying and killing His Majesty's subjects," the Virginia Council faulted masters for "permitting [their Negro slaves] to meet in great numbers in making and holding of funerals for dead Negroes" and issued a proclamation "requiring a strict observance of the Several Laws of this Colony relating to Negroes, and to require and command all Masters of families having any Negro slaves, not to permit them to hold or make any solemnity or funerals for any deceased Negroes" (McIlwaine 1925: 85–87).

The Right Questions/The Right Site

The hypothetical ideal archaeological site for addressing the issues raised in this chapter would contain at least three spatially and temporally distinct phases. During the earliest phase, bound laborers (enslaved and indentured) would be sharing living quarters with the planter's family in a situation similar to the early occupations at Flowerdew. During the second phase, the enslaved and indentured laborers would be sharing a compound well removed from the planter's house. During the final phase, the enslaved and indentured laborers would be occupying separate quarters, thereby enacting and reifying the emerging concept of racial difference. It is not clear that Utopia or Rich Neck (or any site, for that matter) could fulfill these precise requirements, but the information presented herein indicates that an archaeology of "race" in the early Chesapeake is an eminently plausible undertaking.

Deetz (1993:88) *almost* got it right when he wrote, "The full establishment of slavery as an institution based solidly and solely on race did not take place in Virginia until after 1680." He correctly identifies a crucial transition. It is not, however, as he would have us believe, an instance where the preexisting category of race suddenly became more important in defining and justifying slavery. Rather, something much more interesting was occurring—the actual construction of racial difference. In our research we need to remember that race is a social construction, a mark of difference that was imposed, resisted, and transformed. These processes should be visible in the archaeological record if we ask the right questions.

RESEARCH PERIL

Archaeology and Critical Race Theory

When I began my dissertation research some years ago, my use of the phrase "social construction of race" generally elicited reactions ranging from skepticism through noncomprehension to outright hostility (Epperson 1990b). However, things have changed a bit. As philosopher Ian Hacking (1999:35; see also Hacking 1997) writes, "The metaphor of social construction once had excellent shock value, but now it has become tired." Drawing primarily upon titles of books published during the past decade, Hacking (1999:1) begins his book *The Social Construction of What?* with an "A" (authorship) to "Z" (Zulu nationalism) list of things that are said to be socially constructed. Other topics about which "The Social Construction of _______" tomes have been penned include the feeble mind; masculinity; white collar crime; serial killers; the child viewer of television; the Landsat Satellite System; and, of course, race. At the urging of the American Anthropological Association and others, the federal government has even signed on, at least in theory. The "Office of Management and Budget Standards for the Classification of Federal Data on Race and Ethnicity" released in 1995 states: "Public testimony and research indicate that race and ethnicity are subjective concepts and inherently ambiguous. For purposes of collecting data in the United States, race and ethnicity are cultural concepts and social constructs" (OMB 1995: 44, 677). While the apparent movement away from the biogenetic concept of race has been encouraging, there is a real danger that social constructionist analysis can be deployed to undermine the legitimate concerns and interests of minority descendant communities.

The emerging field of critical race theory (CRT) addressed this issue very effectively, posing a challenge and possible paradigm for the development of a critically engaged archaeology of race and identity. As an outgrowth of the critical legal studies movement, CRT acknowledges, analyzes, and challenges the fundamental role of the law in the construction of racial difference and the perpetuation of racial oppression in American society. As a movement comprised primarily, but not exclusively, of scholars and activists of color, critical race theorists, known as "race-crits" to distinguish them from the "crits" and the "fem-crits," also believe that personal experiences of racial prejudice inform and strengthen theoretical analyses. They are therefore particularly interested in fostering and supporting the distinctive work and voices of minority scholars and insist—quite reasonably—that the victims of racial oppression should play a fundamental role in the analysis of that oppression.

The introduction to the 1995 anthology *Critical Race Theory: The Key Writings That Formed the Movement* uses the term "vulgar anti-essentialism" to critique "the claims made by some critical theorists that since racial categories are not 'real' or 'natural' but instead socially constructed, it is theoretically and politically absurd to center race as a category of analysis or as a basis for political action" (Crenshaw et al. 1995:xxvi). While most race-crits emphatically reject the concept of biologically distinct races and embrace the premise that race is, indeed, socially constructed, they nonetheless argue that race is "real" "in the sense that there is a dimension and weight to the experience of being 'raced' in American society, a materiality sustained by law" (Crenshaw et al. 1995:xxvi; see also Mukhopadhyay and Moses 1997; Harrison 1995).

Two recent CRT studies demonstrate the pervasive effects of debates regarding the social construction of race. In a wide-ranging discussion of Supreme Court rulings, Donald Braman (1999) discusses how marginalized groups, particularly gays and lesbians, have —quite appropriately—sought heightened scrutiny of discriminatory classifications under the Fourteenth Amendment. Since this amendment refers specifically to race, the marginalized groups seeking equal protection must, in some fashion, "analogize to race." Therefore, the nature of this category "race" becomes an important factor in determining who is, and is not, entitled to Fourteenth Amendment protections. The Court further confused matters in the 1973 *Frontiero v. Richardson* ruling (411 U.S. 677 [1973]), in which it held that "sex, like race and national origin, is an immutable characteristic determined solely by accident of birth." Braman argues that a fundamental misapprehension of race as an immutable biogenetic category has led many gay and lesbian activists to reject social constructionist theories of sexuality and embrace research purporting to show a genetic basis for homosexual proclivities. While Braman overstates the extent to which the Court has embraced social constructionist theories of race, he is certainly correct in his finding that debates over the nature and meaning of "race" can have unexpected and far-reaching consequences.

A paradigmatic example of "vulgar anti-essentialism" is provided by Marta Rose's (1996) analysis of "race obliviousness" in the U.S. Supreme Court decision that invalidated the minority-majority Eleventh Congressional District in Georgia (*Miller v. Johnson,* 115 U.S. 900 [1995]). Rose (1996:1569) views race obliviousness as a natural consequence of white privilege and notes that the "erasure of race, the invisibility of whiteness, makes a great deal of sense to those whose race privileges them in the social, political, and economic realms." For most Euro-Americans, whiteness is taken as the unquestioned norm; therefore, race is either invisible or is thought to be synonymous with ethnicity. In the *Miller* decision, the Court majority appropriated the rhetoric of the Civil Rights movement to advance a construction of race that is antithetical to the experiences and interests of most black Americans. While recognizing that "respect for . . . communities defined by actual shared interests" can be a legitimate concern in congressional redistricting, the Court asserted that "race" can never serve as "an actual shared interest" for African Americans. In the Court's construction, race is entirely discrete from "political, social, and economic interests"; therefore, the idea that blacks might organize politically around race is "an offensive and demeaning assumption" which "embod[ies] stereotypes that treat individuals as the product of their race" (Rose 1996:1566). While African Americans have certainly been in the forefront of struggles to create a political system where race is not an impediment, the Court appropriates the moral force of the Civil Rights movement to advance the proposition that "if race *should* not matter in our ideal world, then it *cannot* matter now" (Rose 1996:1567).

Archaeology and Race Obliviousness

Within historical archaeology, a recent example relevant to the discussion of vulgar anti-essentialism and race obliviousness is provided by M. Drake Patten's paper on the politics surrounding excavation of the Foster Homesite in Charlottesville, Virginia. I am somewhat sympathetic with her position; I agree historical archaeologists need to do a better job "in our public education about race and gender as cultural constructions" (Patten 1997:138). On more than one occasion I have also tried to explain (somewhat unconvincingly) that "race may not be real, but racism is" (Patten 1997:138). However, I part company with Patten when she deploys a social constructionist analysis to defuse criticism regarding the initial excavation and analysis of the site by an all-white crew. Catherine Foster, who purchased the property in 1833 and died in 1863, was enumerated as a "mulatto" on census forms. Following the Civil War the neighborhood that developed on and around the Foster property was known as "Canada," probably in reference to the haven for escaped slaves. In describing the controversy arising from excavation of the site, Patten challenges the present-day definition of Foster as an "African American" and decries the manner in which Catherine Foster was "utterly appropriated by the local community, however they might be characterized." Patten (1997:135) also regrets the use of the T-shirt slogan "Ask me about African American archaeology in Charlottesville." However, as Theresa Singleton (1997:149) has noted, someone identified on nineteenth-century census forms as "mulatto" would probably self-identify today as "African American" or "multiracial." Contrary to Patten's implication, the fact that Foster's living descendants are identified as "white" negates neither the concerns of the African descent community nor the importance of this site for African American archaeology.

One of the fundamental tenets of critical race theory is the insistence that we, collectively, must allow ourselves "to know what we know" (Matsuda 1989). A common example is the issue of hate speech. We know that a white person's use of that most vicious of racist epithets is not the equivalent of a black person yelling "stupid cracker." This knowledge of social reality should be admitted and reflected in legal analysis. Therefore, a seemingly neutral law or campus code that punishes the use of all racial epithets equally, regardless of context, will, in fact, be inherently biased because it refuses to acknowledge the structural inequalities arising from racism. Therefore, it is particularly problematic when Patten (1997:137) asserts an equivalency between the racial identities ascribed to her and to Catherine Foster: "When the *[Washington] Post* condemned our project, the focus was not on the questions it raised, nor even on Catherine, but on me, on my racial identity as white. There is a certain irony to this: both Catherine Foster and I had become subject to the same external application of a category, even as our lives were temporally separated." Although it was a temporary inconvenience in the context of the project, Patten's identity as a "white" person is one that confers status, privilege and power. The same cannot be said for the categories "Mulatto" or "African American."

CONCLUSIONS: DECONSTRUCTING WHITENESS

In 1686–1687, participant-observer Durand de Dauphiné unwittingly offered a perplexed yet insightful account of how the Virginia plantation landscape was being refashioned in a process we can now recognize as the construction of racial difference. Although this was a profoundly material transformation, we can also trace concomitant developments in such disparate realms as law, Anglican theology, and empiricist epistemology (Epperson 1994). Durand's account is consistent with archaeological and documentary research conducted on late seventeenth-century Chesapeake plantations. Although no archaeological research has been conducted at Rosegill, the plantation of Durand's primary host, Ralph Wormeley II (1650–1701), documentary research presented herein (see Table 4.1) supports the Huguenot exile's account of the emerging spatial separations of the plantation landscape. However, the counterexample of Wormeley's friend and neighbor Robert Dudley, whose estate was inventoried less than a month later (see Table 4.2), reminds us that these spatial separations were not consistent or universal. The fact that Dudley was sharing living space with both African and Irish bound laborers also reminds us that who would be counted as "white" was not merely a matter of pigmentation.

Recent research and antiracist activism have, for the most part, taken us far beyond Winthrop Jordan's conception that "races are incipient species" (Jordan 1968:584). The realization that race is a socially constructed category and not a biogenetic essence is gaining widespread acceptance. However, this paradigm shift carries its own risks, and I would concur with Ian Hacking's (1999:35) observation that "an all-encompassing constructionist approach has become rather dull—in both senses of that word, boring and blunted." Furthermore, as we have seen, uncritical application of constructionist analysis raises the specter of "vulgar anti-essentialism" and the possibility that our research could be deployed for uses that are antithetical to the interests and concerns of minority descendant communities.

One possible resolution of this dilemma is to shift the focus of historic archaeological analysis from "the construction of race" to "the invention of whiteness" (e.g., Allen 1994, 1997; Brodkin 1998a; Fields 1990; Harrison 1995; Ignatiev 1995; Paynter, this volume; Roediger 1991). This maneuver is comparable to Fernando Coronil's (1996) analysis of "Occidentalism," which he sees as "not the reverse of Orientalism but its condition of possibility, its dark side (as in a mirror)." Similarly, critical race theorist Jerome Culp writes that as a social construction, "race is only skin deep, but white supremacy runs to the bone" (Culp 1999:1638–1639). In this spirit, "whiteness" is seen as the "condition of possibility" for the construction of racial difference. By foregrounding the issue of whiteness, we emphasize the inherent asymmetry in the process of racial identity formation and minimize the possibility that our work will be used against the strategic essentialism that is inherent in many analyses of African American cultural identity.

I would like to close with a plea that we be wary of the dangers of race obliviousness and naive assertions of colorblindness. Although it is valid and important, the analysis of race as a social construction should not be deployed to deny the "reality" of race, particularly for the victims of racism, nor should it be used to belittle the concerns of minority descendant communities. The Supreme Court notwithstanding, race can indeed serve as "an actual shared interest" for African Americans and other minority communities. In response to the challenge posed by critical race theorists, we must be certain that the archaeological analysis of race and identity is simultaneously race-conscious and anti-essentialist. The way will not be easy, but the task is crucial.

5

Political Economy and Race: Comparative Archaeologies of Annapolis and New Orleans in the Eighteenth Century

Christopher N. Matthews

The central effort in this chapter is to understand how race becomes identity, and how this process may be illuminated archaeologically. Within any given social formation there exist means of self- and Other-definition which are used to situate individuals in social roles or identities. The making of racial identities occurs when individual physical characteristics are invested with meaning so that they appear representative of social and cultural inclinations. The contributors to this volume and I would presume the majority of its readers likely agree that the making of racial identities is a suspicious project associated with prejudice, racism, and social inequality. Nevertheless, I believe that much of the historical archaeology of race has failed to adequately conceptualize this point, relying too heavily instead on established social differences rather than exploring how those differences originated and were reproduced through time. In this chapter I offer political economy as an alternative approach in historical archaeology that conceives of actors, agency, and structure existing in deeply embedded contexts of social discourse. The relevance of the contexts employed need to be determined for each case, so I illustrate the approach with a comparative study of the archaeology of race and identity in Annapolis and New Orleans in the early eighteenth century. The focus in these cases will be on exchange as a mode of social interaction that established relations and worked to create new cultures. To begin I want to briefly consider the practice of the archaeology of race to explore how difference is generally conceived in historical archaeology.

EXOTIC ESSENCES

Following Marx (1967, 1970) and others (Butler 1990; de Certeau 1984; Foucault 1979; Gramsci 1971; Harvey 2000; Roseberry 1989; Wolf 1999), I begin with an understanding that social forms do not develop consensually but are the result of contest and conflict in which all elements of life, including identity, are employed as strategies for success. An important part of what is at stake in social formations is the ability to develop and sustain a discourse that sets agendas, determines legitimacy, and creates the various sorts of boundaries that define the group. In any situation where such a group encompasses multiple voices, there will be ways that different voices are made coherent but remain distinct, and thus are simultaneously included and excluded in the social process. For the majority of subjects considered in historical archaeology, race is very much one of these ways.

I see this approach to social formation as a critique of a habit in historical archaeology to exoticize its subjects (see also Cohn 1996; di Leonardo 1998; Fabian 1983; Ryan 1981; Sider 1986). Especially in the case of the archaeology of minority and indigenous groups, past people are too often identified with particular artifacts and/or artifact patterns. One strong impulse in this work is to identify, for example, Africanisms and other African American distinctions from the dominant European norm. While I strongly believe that this work has brought new and critical insights to the field and has clearly established that a tradition of Eurocentrism has been a taken-for-granted element of the discipline, I caution that there is a fine line between recognizing and reifying difference. Archaeologists must be critical of the place they set for race in social analysis: are we studying "people of race" or "people with race"? Choosing the latter, I believe race is a route toward (rather than from) a strategically formed and performed identity, and thus a tactic employed in the struggle to form the contours and content of social discourse. Though people are regularly raced (by both others and themselves) in this process, this does not mean that we can therefore subsume racial identity to social subjectivity. In fact, doing so essentializes difference, making racial identity a precursive rather than recursive artifact of the social formation and thus something that stands apart from and is immune to social critique. In this way we cannot assume that racialization is always a matter of subjugation. It is, perhaps, more productive to see it as a means of forming difference in the political struggle to establish the trajectories of social discourse.

POLITICAL ECONOMY

The rich terrain of the social that is being promoted here is what I believe a strong reading of political economy reaches toward. I want now to step back a bit in order to lay the groundwork for what political economy is as a way to define some of the archaeologically feasible signatures of political economic processes. To date, political economy lacks any established meaning in historical archaeology (cf. Leone 1995; Leone and Potter 1999; Paynter 1988; Paynter and McGuire 1991). One pernicious cause for this is the association of political economy with Marxism. Many in historical archaeology have treated Marxism poorly, even fearing that its use is representative of a latent communism of its practitioners (Moore 1995). At a more practical level I believe a problem with political economy is that it appears to mix traditional divisions of social scientific research, which divides the world along lines of economy, society, politics, and ideology with roles, usually externally conceived, for the environment and culture also included. Dividing the world in this way, however, has been determined to be part of the Cartesian project which has essayed to make the separation of the material and the ideal seem natural (see, for example, Butler 1990; Thomas 1996). There are two essential problems with this practice. The first is that the divisions employed are heuristic: useful indeed for research but not actually practiced in the real world. The second is that these divisions, as they are typically employed, tend to be overly determined and inflexible, leaving many aspects of life bouncing from one concept or regime to the other, hopelessly placeless, and potentially lost in the model's interstices.

An example of the confusion of heuristic and real-life categories in historical archaeology is presented in Parker Potter's (1991) critique of standard plantation archaeology. Potter argues that many plantation archaeologists rely on essentialist categories to produce interpretations of social life that place the economic status of slaves along the same continuum as their owners and other white neighbors. The status continuum was believed useful because the price-quality of slaves' artifacts, from an *economic* point of view, suggested a greater worth than would be expected given the *social* status of slaves. Potter demonstrates that the construction of a status continuum is inappropriate. The status of slaves—as a legal, moral, social, and political phenomenon—makes the use of a merely economic continuum inadequate and misleading. Being mere subjects of an economy, slaves, by definition, were not part of the same economy as their owners (see also Fields 1985). This example of the misuse of the heuristic breakdown of the world shows how when these notions are employed, they tend to act as rigid, objective points from which to understand evidence. The plantation archaeologists critiqued by Potter (1991) employed a notion of an economy that stood apart from its subjects and was seemingly able to assess them against an objective pole. Slaves and even slave owners, that is, were set on a continuum against which they could be judged, but which in fact they had very little to do with. Merely a construction of archaeologists, the "economy" employed was a fiction.

To improve these studies we need to better conceive of past people as agents fully immersed in and engaged with the cultures in which they lived. The relative status of the subjects needs to be established in terms more true to the lived life of the people being studied. Because social status is always relative, the price of ceramics cannot by itself establish social standing, only prices understood in the social context of their use. What, for example, if all ceramics, even the most expensive, were priced at a level that left no one unable to obtain them? To improve this work, archaeologists need to pay more attention to culture. However, this is not an appeal to rescind economic scaling in favor of the mind and its templates. Slaves and slave owners indeed came from different backgrounds, but can it be assumed that cultural backgrounds determine the meanings and uses (Shackel and Little 1992) of the recovered ceramics? Instead, this call for culture begs that we see past economies, for example, as part of the social discourse that influences, and is influenced by, the political relations (that is, power and standing) developing within a given group.

To better define social discourse, archaeologists might adopt the Marxian notion of the social relations of production, or the relations that exist among people associated with the production of their society. In this view, actors, not artifacts, are examined first. It is important, also, to understand that we need to explicitly define whom we are studying both in terms of individual identities and how those identities are employed in the struggle to establish and alter social discourse. Doing so, we can conceive of the social relations of production formed not just through types of people economically interlocked, but through real people vying for advantage, heeding and subverting customs, and making their world as they do so. Rather than an abstract economic system or a social economy of agents, a political economy is a real-life analytical process that focuses on the motivations and strategies of social beings striving to sustain and improve their positions within a given cultural understanding of society and status (see Marx 1967, 1970; Roseberry 1988, 1989; Wolf 1982, 1999). It is a process that we can use, but even more, it is a process that our subjects used in the first place. Part of the archaeology of agency in the perspective of political economy, therefore, is the understanding that all people *struggle* to understand who they are and what that means.

Political economy in this sense is a way of approaching and arranging social scientific evidence that places the focus on the everyday struggles of social and cultural production (Lüdtke 1995; Medick 1995; Sider and Smith 1997). These struggles may be as commonplace as poor wages or long commutes, or as structurally significant as the construction and performance of gendered roles and identities. It is not the level of action (economy, society, politics, and so on) that is determinative, but the everyday struggle to reproduce or transform social discourse which employs these levels as mediated nodes of discourse. The example of exchange, an important part of the archaeological illustrations to follow, demonstrates how political economy allows the everyday significance of culture and economy to be realized in a coherent unison.

Exchange in Economy and Culture

The study of exchange in economics and anthropology has traditionally taken two paths toward interpreting market activity or other incidents of trade. Formalists prefer to study and model the structure, or form, of the economy. This means identifying who trades what, with whom, where, and when. The output of the research tends to be models that appropriately characterize all the dimensions of an economy of trade. The point is to evaluate the efficiency of the structure, which will allow an understanding of not only the movement of goods but exactly how smoothly that movement goes. Formal modeling allows for systems to be analyzed and improved.

Some basic assumptions made in formal models have been shown to limit their effectiveness. Most generally, critics accuse formal models of overlooking the agents acting out the processes being modeled. At a deeper level, formal models also neglect the determinative power of cultural perspective. Marketing efforts in modern capitalism, for example, fail to realize the meaning of commodities to potential consumers because the envisioned subjects are understood only as beings committed to efficiency, profit, and consumerism in the same terms as corporate capitalist culture. Even when supposedly accounting for cultural differences, these efforts misconstrue difference by not recognizing that its source is in the competing cultural schemes that exist alongside (not within) corporate capitalism.

To breach these limitations, economic anthropologists proposed substantive approaches to economic analysis focusing on culture in the analysis of exchange (Dalton 1969, 1982; Polanyi 1957; Sahlins 1965). Substantivists argue that the economy is embedded in social relations whose meaning takes precedent over any economy of exchange. A principal issue in substantive economic research is the role that exchange might play in the construction of social status. Through mechanisms such as reciprocity, redistribution, and market systems, social orders are identified and formed, and individuals within those orders cast in place. These advances were presented as a way that economic analyses could break loose of the Eurocentric and overdetermined perspective of formalism. Unfortunately, these models do little to understand the notion of culture. Instead, reified cultural tropes are frequently used to establish the meaning of exchange. Groups, for example, are understood to either resist hierarchical development through reciprocal exchange and obligation, or to preserve hierarchy through redistribution. The trouble with the way substantivist approaches have been employed is their assumption that the social whole takes precedence over its everyday construction.

Both the formalist and substantivist schools rely on flawed notions of the social world. Formalists place too much emphasis on the behavior of self-interested individuals in an abstract economy. Substantivists, leaning the other way toward a social understanding of exchange, tend to assume group-interested behavior that reproduces social wholes through everyday activity. While the cultural emphasis of the substantivists provides an important alternative to market-minded formalism, it largely overdetermines the behavior of the sorts of exchange carried out everyday by insisting on their relevance to a structured norm. To develop a culturally focused understanding of exchange and economy that allows for at least a tempered individual creativity is the task.

In archaeology, Ian Hodder (1982) argues that paying attention to the symbolism and contextual significance of the goods being exchanged moves in this direction. One method is to record the particular biographical aspects of exchanged goods. Where they are found, what they look like and are made of, and how they may have been used are all symbolic and contextual aspects of material things that have a bearing on the meaning of their exchange. Clearly, to be able to determine these aspects and meanings is an important step beyond the formalist-substantivist divide, but meanings must also be couched in terms of strategies. What was at stake, or what was being done, in the exchange? Hodder (1982:209) believes that "the exchange of appropriate items *forms* social obligations, status, and power, but it also *legitimates* as it forms." Thus, in the process of exchange, agents are making something as they go. It is this something (for example, social status, identity within a group, and/or ethnic/racial boundaries between groups) that makes exchange not only social, but also a powerful medium in which the particular meanings of the social are illustrated and can be challenged or reproduced. To illustrate these points, I now turn to the archaeological studies.

Exchange and the Archaeology of Identity

The following examples draw from my work in both Annapolis and New Orleans. As I finished up the former study (Matthews 1998, n.d.) and began the latter (Matthews 1999), I began to see distinctions in the colonization process and the sorts of local communities European colonization formed during the eighteenth century. My goal recently has been to bridge the many patterns of divergence I encountered. The point here is to contrast the local communities of Annapolis and New Orleans as they faced and constructed aspects of a capitalist political economy. At the very least I hope to demonstrate that these two places followed divergent paths which make evident the contingency of colonization and its relationship to the developmental social processes of modernity. At a deeper level I hope this analysis shows how race developed as a contingent social fact.

To draw the archaeological data of Annapolis and New Orleans into a comparable set that reflects their independent steps toward mature capitalism, I adopt an approach to exchange developed by Lewis Hyde (1979). Drawing broadly from the study of traditional and modern economies, Hyde (1979:61) opposes "gift" and "commodity" exchange. The basis to the theory is the way in which exchange works with social boundaries: "A gift, when it moves across the boundary, either stops being a gift or else abolishes the boundary. A commodity can cross the line without any change in its nature; moreover, its exchange will often establish a boundary where none previously existed (as for example, in the sale of a necessity to a friend). *Logos*-trade draws the boundary, *eros*-trade erases it."

Hyde (1979:xiv) defines *logos* as "reason and logic in general, the principle of differentiation in particular." The action of *logos*-trade is the production of a logical order through the separation of exchange into its constituent parts. *Eros,* the root of "erotic," is "the principle of attraction, union, [and] involvement which binds together" (Hyde 1979:xiv). Through gifts, discrete persons and groups may come together through the medium of the exchange. They find in one another attributes that are binding, as aspects of the donor are retained in the gift as it passes to the receiver. Gift-giving in this way is erotic. Commodity exchange separates these social aspects so goods transfer hands without the binds of social obligation or interrelation playing a role. Rather than assuming gift or commodity exchange as normal, Hyde regards them as expressions of social patterns that are realized through a recursive exchange process. In the following discussion, I argue that these forms of exchange played a critical role in the formation of new cultures during the colonization of North America in the eighteenth century. In particular, the exchange of goods materialized strategically formed racial identities that were the keys to social reformation.

Annapolis: Toward a Modern Identity

An archaeology of exchange in early eighteenth-century Annapolis permits an exploration of how the modern political economy of capitalism found footing in one context. Because exchange in this case was based in the commodity, we can explore how aspects of life (the social, political, and economic) became segregated from each other and within themselves. To make this argument, I review the historic formation of a class society around the turn of the eighteenth century in the Chesapeake. Class formation involved aspects relevant to identity and race in particular as slavery and the plantation mode of production came to dominate the region. Slavery affected the scope of production by permitting slave owners to outproduce their non-slave-owning neighbors. Additionally, as African slavery replaced European indentured servitude, the formation of a class society established not only a wealthy upper stratum of slaveholders but, through race, a disenfranchised working class. The point is that racial slavery removed from the political arena the poorest group as it segregated the social whole into two distinct categories: free and slave.

Slavery and race are essential to understanding class formation in the Chesapeake because of their basis in commodity exchange. Certainly, the person of the slave was understood as a commodity that could be bought and sold. It must be questioned, however, whether any slave owner ever truly denied the human essence of their slave; did any slaveholder fully equate their human property with their land, animals, and crops? I submit that this never was the case, but I say so without meaning to deny the power of the slaveholder over the slave and the racism endemic to their relationship. Rather, the humanity of the slave allowed the authority of wealthy planters to successfully forge the class they did. Defining slavery along the lines of race and the belief in the inherent inferiority of non-whites, wealthy planters established at the core of social discourse a distinction within every individual between their self and their racial identity. This segregation into supposed constituent parts is exactly what a culture based in commodity exchange does.

An archaeology of this cultural development can take many forms, but to fully appreciate the power of commodity exchange relations, I believe we need to look at how wealthy white planters established class standing within their own race. Equating slavery with blackness, the wealthy used race to subordinate the working class. This process, however, simultaneously equated freedom with whiteness. The social discourse of freedom is informative about the way culture and class in Chesapeake formed. Freedom in one sense meant freedom *from* chattel slavery, but exactly what freedom allowed one to move *toward* was not made clear. This ambiguity in meaning was seized by wealthy planters to establish their position.

Class formation in the Chesapeake can be set at the end of a long era of social development which, because of profit-minded colonists and harsh environmental conditions, only slowly matured. The desire of early settlers was tobacco. The commodity promised riches, leading many people to plant it to the exclusion of other activities. Tobacco cultivation, however, was hard labor requiring the attention of as many hands as could be had, so indentured servitude was adopted by European planters. The influx of new people allowed tobacco cultivation to take hold, but the limited ability of people to survive, or plants to endure, stunted the growth of the Chesapeake colonies and occasionally threatened their very viability (Tate and Ammerman 1979; Main 1982; Middleton 1953; Morgan 1975).

A principal effect of the harsh tobacco economy was the slow formation of families and, with them, the creation of family wealth. Without stable families the native-born fared little better than immigrants since, with parents dying young, children failed to inherit the needed capital to advance beyond the baseline economic status of newcomers. Because the natives had little in the way of a stable local social structure, immigrants found they stood on not only the same economic ground, but on the same political ground as well (Jordan 1979). It was the rare exception when a family survived with both parents living long enough and being productive enough that they had something of value to pass along as inheritance. Inheritance, however, proved to be the key to social advancement. Probate records show, for example, that in six Maryland counties at the end of the seventeenth century the average wealth of the decedent correlated directly with the status of their family: those men who were married with adult children held more than seven times the wealth of single men at death (Main 1982:268).

The beneficiaries of this wealth were distinct in three particular ways. First, they were natives and thus had a connection to the Chesapeake distinct from immigrants. Second, because they inherited wealth, they began adult life holding the necessary capital to be established planters in the region. This position was markedly different not only from that of immigrants, but also that of their parents, who had turned meager beginnings into fortunes. Thus, thirdly, while in many cases their parents had labored in the fields alongside servants and slaves, the native sons of inherited wealth knew little of the toil of tobacco cultivation. The most prosperous among them, freed from the worries of everyday survival, were educated as children and focused their attentions on law, politics, commerce, and establishing in the Chesapeake what they believed was an adequate representation of English gentry culture.

The elaboration of the advantages of inheritance allowed the new gentry to establish their power in many arenas. Marriages that followed class lines created alliances among wealthy families and formed localized cadres of authority that turned formerly more fluid social orders into webbed familial relations of siblings, cousins, and in-laws (Jordan 1979:267–270; Kulikoff 1986:240–259). These alliances supported the persistence of elite men in local assemblies, a continuity that made their way of legislating standard, and their reelection secure (Jordan 1979:253–263). The Chesapeake gentry also used inherited wealth to purchase enslaved African labor. One estimate shows that the number of slaves, as the percentage of tithables in independent households, more than doubled from 1674 to 1700 (Morgan 1975:326). Slavery was symbolically important because the cost of slaves was more than all but the very wealthy could afford. This advantage was seized by the native elite, who found the extra cost of a slave compensated in the lifetime of labor that the slave provided compared to the four or so years of work of indentured servants. This in turn allowed the wealthy to purchase more slaves, adding to their capacity to outperform their neighbors. This pattern is illustrated in the one Maryland study by the fact that estates with ten or more slaves steadily rose to claim two-thirds of all slaves by 1719. The same study also found that even though the number of slaves grew through time, the percentage of households without servants at all grew from 60 to 67 percent (Main 1982:260). The privileges of slave owning not only advanced the wealthy, but also indirectly affected the ability of others to afford servant labor at all.

The resources that the native elite used to purchase slaves and secure political authority also allowed them to consolidate power by creating debt relations with their neighbors. Having superior resources in the Chesapeake largely meant having farther-reaching credit in England. With credit for tobacco acting as currency, planters could obtain the goods they desired and used to make the colony seem more like the homeland. Because this was a general desire among settlers, wealthy planters became merchants, brokering their poorer neighbors' tobacco to supply these people with material goods (Morgan 1975:366).

Through marriage, political authority, slaveholding, and merchanting, the native elite consolidated and expanded their wealth and privilege. These processes, however, had dimensions of social discourse that need to be better understood to fully appreciate how the rising class established its authority. The use of slavery by wealthy planters was part of an effort to redefine the order of things in the colonies. For every plantation that grew through slavery, those that did not found themselves evaluated against a new norm that placed substantial symbolic value on property ownership and the production of wealth. Through this reformation, slavery and freedom came to define the very essence of being in the Chesapeake (see especially Isaac 1982; Morgan 1975).

This belief was codified, for example, in a 1669 Virginia law that protected the right of a master to kill his slave and remain free from the charge of murder "since it cannot be presumed that prepensed malice (which alone makes murther Felony) should induce any man to destroy his own estate" (cited in Morgan 1975:312). The racial basis of slavery was also clarified to serve these ends. For example, the power to determine life or death was linked to the racialization of the slave owner and the slave in a 1682 law dissolving the legal difference between Native American and African slaves, making a slave of either

Figure 5.1. South face of east wing foundation, Bordley-Randall House, Annapolis, Maryland. (Photo by the author)

race bound for life. As well, miscegenation laws passed around 1700 established that a white woman bearing a child by a black or mulatto father was to be fined, and the child, though legally free, to be put into service for the benefit of the parish of its birth for thirty years (Morgan 1975:336).

Disenfranchising non-whites through slavery was essential to the authority of the native elite, but resolving class tensions within white society was another issue. Slavery and racial identity, however, were employed to establish a coalition among whites that aimed to resolve the political economic contradictions within the white society. Establishing the meaning of freedom both legally and symbolically as the opposite of slavery allowed the wealthy to build a racial bridge between themselves and their poorer neighbors. The point was not that poor whites could be reduced to slavery; the racial basis of slavery made that impossible. The point was that white people should strive for freedom, no matter how it was defined. Even if different definitions served contradictory purposes, the *search* for freedom itself was how whites came to define themselves.

I illustrate this process by turning to evidence from the archaeological record of the Thomas Bordley House site in Annapolis. A slaveholder and merchant, Bordley helped establish the foundations of commodity exchange in Annapolis. He immigrated from Yorkshire, England, to Kent County on Maryland's eastern shore (Morton 1969: 2–3). In 1694, he left Kent for Annapolis to study and then practice law in the colonial capital. Through a shrewd marriage to Rachel Beard, widow of the well-placed proprietary surveyor, and a successful legal practice, Bordley rapidly rose to the upper levels of the political and economic structure.

Bordley obtained the five lots of ground for his house in Annapolis in the 1710s. Excavation adjacent to the still-standing structure determined that most of it was built by 1726 (Matthews 1996). More than just dating the house, the archaeological evidence speaks to the cultural processes that led Bordley to build in the manner he did.

Specifically, I focus on the foundation of the house's one-story east wing, which was exposed in excavation along its three exterior sides (Figure 5.1). On the south (front) side a substantial four-foot deep foundation was revealed. Excavations adjacent to the east and north walls of the foundation showed that these sections were rougher in appearance and much shallower. A rising south to north stratum associated with the early eighteenth-century occupation suggests that the wing was built into a slight rise. The uneven depths of the foundation on its various sides are thus believed to be the result of this slope; however, the smoothly faced south wall and the character of the stratigraphic sequence surrounding the entire wing suggest that at least the upper part of the front wall was exposed to view after it was built.

The sloping stratum abutting the wall was a rich midden dating to between 1700 and 1748. This level was buried by a fill episode associated with the building of a garden terrace between 1748 and 1763. It is believed, then, that prior to the construction of the terrace, the south wall was exposed to no less than three feet below the current grade. This means a small set of steps would have been required to reach the door to the wing. Evidence for this stairway was found in a concentration of large debris within the early occupational level in front of the wing representing the covered area under the stairway, while an area around the concentration lacking such debris represents the formerly exposed ground surface around the stairway.

To understand the significance of the foundation, the Bordley House may be put in the architectural context of its time and place. In the 1710s, most Chesapeake houses were impermanent post-in-ground structures (Carson et al. 1981), and the same was true for the small city of Annapolis (Shackel 1994; Yentsch 1994). The shift to brick and stone construction using substantial foundations is thus a material transition possibly indicative of social change. Paul Shackel (1994, 1998) has explored the shift to more-permanent construction methods in the first decades of the eighteenth century and has demonstrated the temporal correlation of this architectural transition with the episode of class formation described above. Much of this social transition—notably the shift to slavery and the elaboration of debt—undermined poorer whites. We must assume that in order for this inequality within the white population to have persisted, the wealthy deflected challenges made by their weakened neighbors. The shift to permanent architecture is an example of one important means employed to do just this.

The earlier post-in-ground buildings had inculcated certain social relations. With their main support posts placed directly into the ground, these structures required frequent upkeep and repair to last more than a decade or so. Over the seventeenth century, these needs formed "maintenance relationships" in which owners sought "periodic contractual obligations with a local worker capable of mending the product" (Shackel 1994:92, citing St. George 1983:2). With the maturing social order, these relations proved to hinder more than help eager young elites as they sought to escape customary ways of doing business that bound them to working people. Houses built on stone foundations, though they required more investment at the start, required less upkeep over the long-term and thus released the elite from customary maintenance relations. In place of informal long-term care which bound working people and property owners, the gentry established relations with their neighbors that segregated the social relationship of the property owner and the working person from the economic transaction that accompanied the building of the house. The new order portrayed a certain equality among the parties based on their individuality as clients (that is, property owner and laborer). These new one-to-one relations, based on the seemingly concrete medium of economic remuneration for services rendered, rationalized the more abstract reciprocal social obligations exemplified by maintenance relations.

The stone foundation of Thomas Bordley's

house fits this model thoroughly. Personally, Bordley was emblematic of the new order. In addition to his Annapolis law practice, he owned plantations in Anne Arundel and in Kent Counties, and at his death he passed nineteen slaves to his eldest son. He was also a merchant, running a store out of his Annapolis house. Finally, he was a landlord, who, along with only three other men, owned more than half of Annapolis (Baker 1986; Matthews 1998:136–151). Certainly, in these aspects of his life and the relations they formed, Bordley faced the meaning of the new order everyday. Being a wealthy planter and operating a store out of his town house, many Annapolitans were in debt to Bordley, relying on his credit for the various goods they sought. His leaseholds also made his tenants dependent on him for their homes. Such debts and rents extended the individualist relations highlighted by Shackel to almost every arena of life in Annapolis, for to live in the city at this time meant most likely that one was involved through one or another essentially economic relation with a man like Thomas Bordley.

For Bordley, these relations were mitigated through the rationality of commodity exchange. We can be fairly certain that gifts rarely passed between Bordley and his debtors and tenants. This order, however, was segmented. Only applying to the free people of the city, it was a discourse restricted to whites. Though in this case freedom became defined by the right to hold debt and owe rent, through these relations with their wealthy neighbors, free whites continued to escape the bonds of slavery. From the other perspective, relations formed between individuals allowed the wealthy to disguise the appearance of class stratification within white society. All whites were conceived as freedom-loving individuals, so customary traditions such as maintenance relations were identified as archaic ways of living that hindered the search for freedom essential to the new identity of whites.

It is in this way that the foundation wall of the Bordley House is a materialization of race and identity. As the wall broke the traditions of maintenance relations, it materialized the order of commodity exchange and individual freedom. Because that order was couched in the attempt by the wealthy to disenfranchise the working class through racial slavery, individuals in the society were defined in racial terms. Thus, in the making of the Bordley foundation, the racialized identity in society was confirmed. As was noted above, the house foundation was built to be visible to onlookers. To leave the foundation exposed illuminated the new social order to the neighborhood, and emphasized that the order was represented in the whiteness and authority of the dweller within.

New Orleans: Toward a Creole Identity

The contrasts between Annapolis and New Orleans in the eighteenth century can in part be summarized in that the former was a more mature capitalist society than the latter. Though both places were established on similar grounds within profit-seeking plantation colonies, the Louisiana settlement stumbled and "devolved" over the course of the eighteenth century (Berlin 1998:77–92, 195–215; see also Clark 1970; Ingersoll 1990; McGowen 1976; Taylor 1984). This poor start led residents of the Louisiana colony to adopt new ways of living that accommodated the limitations and advantages presented on the frontier. In this context the mode of commodity exchange brought by Europeans across the Atlantic was disassembled as settlers encountered indigenous people who employed the tactics of gift exchange. As these two modes intersected, a new form, which may be called Creole exchange, was born. Creole exchange arises when the different modes of gift and commodity exchange encounter one another, yet fail to resolve their differences, allowing each to survive but to also breed a new form where the two become mixed. I argue here that it is through Creole exchange that a Creole identity was formed.

This approach challenges interpretations made to date in archaeology of colonial intercultural exchange (e.g., Deagan 1983; King 1984; McEwan 1986; Rogers 1990; Vernon 1988; Waselkov 1993; Wilson and Rogers

1993). Typically, the perspectives of European, Native American, and African people are represented so that each group is believed to behave in simple economic terms (even if substantivist), gaining whatever advantage they may from the encounter. The perspective adopted here employs a more membered meaning of exchange, balancing the economic with the political and the social. It is possible from historic documents and the archaeological record to understand that the exchange of goods between groups in colonial New Orleans was not just for survival, but also for the creation of a new culture supportive of the diverse perspectives of inhabitants that shared the responsibilities of living at this edge of the early modern world.

The founding of the Louisiana colony was originally for political purposes. With the development of prosperous English colonies along the North American Atlantic seaboard and the Spanish control of Florida and Mexico, France sought to secure its control of the North American mid-continent. This was especially the case after La Salle navigated the length of the Mississippi River in 1682, demonstrating that a vast colonial territory could be had that connected French Canada with the Gulf of Mexico. To this end the first French settlements in Louisiana were established along the Gulf coast near present-day Mobile, Alabama, and Biloxi, Mississippi. These outposts were envisioned to be building blocks for the population growth and agricultural development needed for permanent settlement in the lower Mississippi Valley.

In spite of these plans, the early settlements consisted only of a handful of soldiers, sailors, and traders under the authority of the two native Canadian Le Moyne brothers, Iberville and Bienville. These settlers had little interest in agricultural work and, with the infrequency of shipments from the homeland, found themselves dependent for survival on nearby native people. It was common for soldiers to be dispersed among the tribes when the garrison supplies fell short, and a few firsthand accounts tell of the rather favorable alternative that living with Indians presented. Pénicaut, while staying with the Natchez, recorded that "we almost forgot the orders of M. de Bienville for the pleasures we were having" (McWilliams 1953). Similarly, Cadillac, who was sent from Canada to bring order to the Louisiana colony in 1714, "found all the garrison in the woods among the Indians.... [T]he officers are no better off...they came to ask [him] for permission to go and seek their living from among the Indians" (cited in McGowen 1976:37). These encounters brought settlers into frequent contact with native peoples and native ways of living—including dress, architecture, diet, and medicinal traditions. Additionally, these encounters demonstrated to settlers that the best way to live as Europeans in Louisiana was not as farmers but as traders among the Indians. Native people eagerly exchanged deerskins, bear oil, and other goods, including food, for European manufactures, arms, and ammunition. This pattern of exchange ultimately challenged the practical function of the colony as colonial administrators abandoned their original plans to develop "measures to prevent their own people from completely succumbing to the Indian way of life" (McGowen 1976:12). At stake was the capacity of the French authority to maintain the basis of commodity production and exchange in the face of a powerful and attractive indigenous habit of gift exchange.

The intercultural relations among settlers and Indians, however, had developed into a way of life that took more than a century to uproot. Exchange benefited all parties. Partners gained not only profit but also the erotic bonds (see Hyde 1979) that spread the social order across the cultural and racial barriers that were believed fixed in the conception of the colony along the lines of commodity exchange. Exchange forced these barriers to be relaxed because from the native point of view, exchange occurred through the notion of the gift rather than the commodity.

Gift exchange was an important aspect of Native American culture since it was through such exchange that cultural groups identified their allies and enemies. As historian Daniel Usner (1992:26) observes: "They trade among themselves, and...with Europeans, not only to acquire scarce products or ritual items, but, as importantly, to demonstrate a willingness to maintain peaceful political relations." The exchange of goods as gifts rather than merely things or commodities allowed partners to assert a sovereign political standing. Having abundance enough to give and receive gifts implies a state of independence between, and equality among, partners in a competitive situation. Over the course of the eighteenth century, Indians in the lower Mississippi Valley recognized attempts by Europeans to create dependency relationships (White 1983), and through the tradition of gift exchange were able to resist these efforts. The French explorer La Salle noted that in dealing with Native people, "presents are so necessary...that if words are not accompanied by gifts and not related to them, they are considered meaningless" (cited in Allain 1988:76). Identifying trade goods as gifts and receiving them in politically charged situations rather than informal everyday trades asserted the integrity of Indian culture in the face of European mercantile exchange (Usner 1992, 1998; White 1983). These cultural habits helped establish native nations in the Southeast as a dominant force, ensuring that it was only through alliances with native groups that Europeans could successfully extend their economies inland and increase their profits.

Contending European powers used material goods to build allegiances with the large interior native nations of the Southeast. By the early 1700s, English settlers in the Carolina colony had expanded their reach inland through trade with the Chickasaw, an alliance that allowed English traders safe passage all the way to the Mississippi River. To counter, the French cultivated an alliance with the Choctaw, adversaries of the Chickasaw, who agreed to help keep English traders at bay. With this alliance established, the French founded the New Orleans settlement on the Mississippi River and pronounced their exclusive claim to the bounty of the territory. As on the Gulf coast, the French authority envisioned an agricultural colony along the banks of the Mississippi. However, because the Indian trade was so essential to the political success of the French authority, its practice in the colony was sanctioned, and trading proliferated at the expense of the hoped-for agricultural economy. An official of the Company of the Indies in New Orleans complained in 1724 that the settlement's population consisted mostly of "common people who were engaged in a commerce detrimental to the Colony and even to the interests of the Company" (Cruzat 1929: 125). Whenever a ship landed at the levee, "'common people' petitioned the Superior Council for the orders needed to obtain merchandise from the company warehouse, quickly emptied it of all kinds of goods, and resold them at much higher prices" (Usner 1992:42).

It must be noted that various factors have been presented to explain the poor start of the Louisiana colony. The colony did, indeed, lack the financial support of other French settlements, especially those in the Caribbean. Furthermore, with supplies running short on a regular basis, colonists were at times literally starving. Finally, poor political planning by the French monarchy, both in Europe and the Americas, has been cited to have distracted them from the colonization of Louisiana (Allain 1988; Taylor 1984). Each of these explanations, however, misses the mark because they all assume a trajectory of colonial development like that of the English colonies of the eastern seaboard. In this comparison Louisiana was obviously a failure, but this judgment sets Louisiana on an inappropriate scale. Even though the original plans for Louisiana were forged in emulation of the tobacco colonies of Chesapeake (McGowen 1976), the political economy of the lower Mississippi Valley failed to organize under this prime motivation. In fact, it can be said that no central political economy developed in Louisiana at all throughout the French regime (up to 1763) and only barely grew under the Spanish (1763–1803), and then largely through a supply trade with Cuba (Clark 1970; Taylor 1984). As such, the factors listed above should be seen more as effects than causes for the failure of the Louisiana colony. Without the stability of commodity exchange, royal and other investors, suppliers, and policymakers could only regard Louisiana as a marginal settlement that promised little in return. From this homeland perspective, New Orleans remained insignificant and only worth sustaining to maintain a French presence on the lower Mississippi.

I suggest that the failure of the French to thrive was primarily due to the ability of indigenous people, predominantly through gift exchange, to resist the political economic incursions of Europeans. Native people controlled many of the resources necessary for colonial survival, including food and transportation (as guides and rowers [Usner 1992: 227–234]). Even more, native people only very late in the game came to recognize Europeans as rivals. It was more the case that Europeans in the lower Mississippi Valley were seen as good allies for native groups who sought to expand their power over other native groups. From the native point of view, Europeans were useful but not necessarily threatening (see Usner 1992:13–14). This fact was made exceptionally clear in 1729 when the Natchez Indians, in alliance with the Africans living at the settlement, slaughtered the French village at White Apple, killing the 235 white settlers, one-eighth of the white population living on the Mississippi at the time (McGowen 1976:98).

Certainly after the Natchez attack, if not before, European settlers on the Mississippi came to understand their position. They did not hold the upper hand, but only one among the many hands which together allowed the colony to survive. Settlers acknowledged their relations with Indians (and at the same time with Africans) in terms that made racialized identities collapse. Instead, each group came toward each other shedding expectations and adopting new ways of living in the region that forged a Creole identity. In contrast to the process in the Chesapeake, where identity was constructed through racialization, the Creole identity in Louisiana was framed through intercultural exchange that minimized racial difference in favor of the freedom that doing so allowed.

What then is an archaeological signature of Louisiana's Creole identity? The research done to answer this question began with the recovery from several colonial period sites in New Orleans of a variety of Native American ceramics. (Sites include The Cabildo [Yakubik and Franks 1997], Durel Cottage [Jill Yakubik, pers. comm.], Madame John's Legacy [Dawdy 1998], and the Tremé Plantation [Matthews 1999].) Vessel forms show these ceramics were not "copy-wares" (Vernon 1988) and were likely used for food preparation and storage rather than service. Because of Deagan's (1983, 1995) work in Florida and the Caribbean, it was not immediately surprising to find Native American ceramics at colonial sites in New Orleans. However, Deagan (1991:105) has claimed that the presence of native material culture in European settings was peculiar to Spanish sites:

> Some of the most striking, recent results of archaeological investigations into American colonial society concern the overwhelming dominance of European material culture in Euro-American sites occupied by northern Europeans groups, and the contrasts between Euro-American sites of different origins. One of the only ways in which the French, Dutch, and English colonial sites were similar was in the *complete absence . . . of Native American influence in the material world.* This is in striking contrast to the Spanish colonies, where Native American items comprise an overwhelming majority of the material assemblages in households where only Spaniards were known to be living. (emphasis added)

Clearly, the recovery of Native American ceramics from French sites in New Orleans presents something new if not something different. What exactly was different has been part of the story of this section to this point. With these ceramics we can thus conclude the argument.

Two notable characteristics of the native ceramics from New Orleans contribute to

Table 5.1. Percentage of Aboriginal Ceramics at Colonial-Era New Orleans Sites

Site	Number of Aboriginal Ceramics	Number of European Ceramics	Total	Aboriginal Ceramics as Percentage of Total Ceramics
Cabildo	20	509	529	3.8
Madame John's Legacy	36	479	515	7.0
Tremé Plantation	234	1,434	1,668	14.0
TOTAL	290	2,422	2,712	10.7

Sources: For the Cabildo, Yakubik and Franks 1997: app. 1; for Madame John's Legacy, Dawdy 1998: app. C; and for Tremé Plantation, Matthews 1999.

Table 5.2. Comparison of Aboriginal and European Ceramics at New Orleans and Spanish Sites

Site	Number of Aboriginal Ceramics	Number of European Ceramics	Total	Aboriginal Ceramics as Percentage of Total Ceramics
St. Augustine, Florida	13,302	9,390	22,692	58.7
Puerto Real, Haiti	25,303	27,975	53,278	48.4
New Orleans	290	2,422	2,712	10.7

Sources: For St. Augustine, Hoffman 1997: Table 2; for Puerto Real, Deagan 1995: Table 13.3; for New Orleans, see Table 5.1.

our understanding of their role in the creation of the Creole identity. First is their relative proportion to European ceramics. As Deagan has shown, native materials represent a majority of the artifacts recovered from Spanish colonial sites, while in New Orleans they are relatively scarce (Tables 5.1 and 5.2). One reason for these proportions may be the fact that there is no evidence of Indians living at these sites. Indian slavery did exist in Louisiana, but no Indian slaves were ever counted by census takers at these particular sites (Hall 1992; Maduell 1972). It is believed, therefore, that the presence of native ceramics was the result of exchange.

The second peculiar characteristic of the native ceramics from New Orleans is their variety. No one particular type was clearly dominant at any of the sites. Rather, the ceramics represent a variety of traditions from the lower Mississippi Valley and Gulf coast, and some may even be from the Gulf coast of Mexico. This finding also provides another contrast to Spanish sites, where aboriginal ceramics tend to be dominated by only one or two local types (Avery 1995; Deagan 1983; King 1984; McEwan 1986; Vernon 1988). There are two likely explanations for this variety. The first is the documented fact that many Spanish sites were mixed households where Spanish and native people lived together. Deagan suggests that the presence of Native American materials at Spanish sites could be explained in part because resident Indians were using them. The lack of Indians at these New Orleans sites perhaps means that the non-Indian consumers of the pots were not as particular about what types they were. The second factor relates to the way of life at most Spanish sites. Unlike New Orleans, North American Spanish settlements were typically military and/or missionary outposts. These primary concerns limited the development of intercultural exchange in favor of establishing communities based on the authority of the Spanish Crown and its influence over everyday life. St. Augustine, Florida, is an exception to these site types, being a much more established urban enclave. However, even there, European supplies were still strictly controlled and distributed by the royal military, thus making for an economy formally organized by the state.

This formalization failed to develop in Louisiana since the state trusted its colonies to monopoly companies who cared less about the expansion of royal prerogative than turning a profit on their investors' backing (Giraud 1987). Without an established political/economic structure in Louisiana, the companies looked the other way when merchant ships under their authority bound originally for New Orleans stopped instead in the Caribbean or on the Mexican Gulf coast (Clark 1970; Hall 1992). As a result New Orleans was barely provisioned at all, but more than just starving the inhabitants, the loose policy of the monopoly companies permitted New Orleanians to pursue whatever means they could to provision their households. Settlers in the small city thus turned to the surrounding native people to gain some measure of security, if not profit. It is believed that the variety of ceramic types recovered in New Orleans represents the efforts of settlers there to build connections with a broad base of native groups. Because the exchange of goods with Indians was based in the formation of alliances, it makes sense that New Orleanians would seek to create alliances with as many of their neighbors as possible. Security on the frontier provided for both subsistence and defense. This was perhaps especially the case after the Natchez attack.

In this view the ceramics are a materialization of the intercultural alliances that formed the basis of early New Orleans society. We cannot know all of the aspects of Indian culture being used in colonial households, but it is known that certain aspects of Creole cuisine, many of which are still used today, were introduced in the first generation of colonization. Maize was obviously an essential staple, and *sagamite,* a lumpy corn porridge, preserved the lives of settlers in the early days (McGowen 1976:11). Additionally, one of the most well known local herbs, sassafras, was being sold by Choctaw women as filé for gumbo in the New Orleans market as late as the 1890s (Usner 1998:136). The fact that gumbo is likewise made with okra shows the presence also of an African cultigen in the Creole diet.

I believe this argument allows us to see that intercultural exchange brought the three groups of the region together in their common pursuit of life on the frontier. I do not hesitate to propose that the mixing of blood across racial lines which led to the creation of a large group of free people of color in New Orleans found its beginnings and rationalization in these same circumstances. It took the formalization of the political economy *after* the rise of sugar and cotton planting for this particular group to face the racial discrimination that defined its existence in the nineteenth century (Bell 1997; Hanger 1997). White Creoles faced their own form of discrimination in the nineteenth century as Americans organized and modernized the plantation economy (Tregle 1991). It was also only after the rise of the developed planting economy that the presence of native ceramics at New Orleans sites tailed off (Dawdy 1998; Matthews 1999).

Thus, for the first two or three generations of the Louisiana colony, a context supportive of the formation of the Creole identity was in place. From the collection of native ceramics recovered at the Tremé Plantation site, one sherd perhaps best illustrates the merging of cultures and races in the colonial New Orleans household and the creation of the new Creole culture that this process represents (Figure 5.2). This small, red-slipped rim sherd was inscribed with the letters *X* and *Y* (or perhaps *W*) after it was fired. It is believed that the rest of the European alphabet was inscribed along the rim of this bowl, perhaps as a way of learning and teaching the letters. Whatever its purpose, on an Indian pot a European conception of the world was inscribed. In this way the pot crossed the cultural barrier between Europeans and Indians through exchange. Its use as a template for writing and learning European culture suggests that the pot was a taken-for-granted part of the material culture of the settler

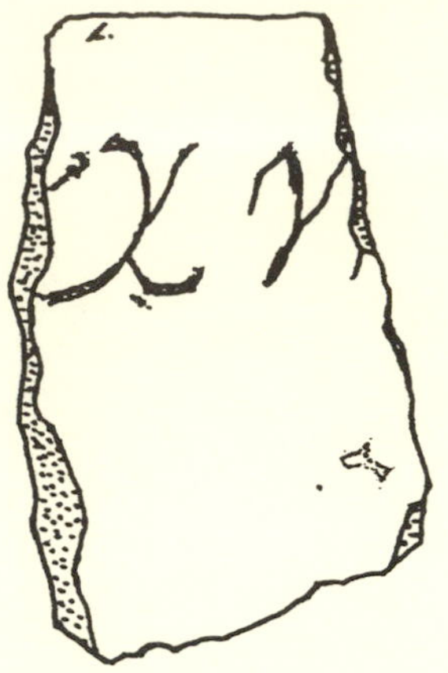

Figure 5.2. Inscribed aboriginal sherd, Tremé Plantation site, New Orleans, Louisiana. (Drawn by Don Graff)

household. It is this status, when the artifacts are no longer exotic but merely part of the everyday, that we can recognize evidence of the formation of a Creole identity in the archaeological record.

DISCUSSION

The examples of Annapolis and New Orleans illustrate how the formation of identities in history might be recognized in the archaeological record. The point has been to highlight the historical and thus contingent basis to identity by tying identity formation to the everyday conception of the self as set in given political economic contexts. My use of political economy, more so than a smothering cultural heritage or socioeconomic standing, made use of the reconstruction of the contexts which framed the choices people had and made as they defined who they were. It was shown how in their material life people like Thomas Bordley and the residents of colonial New Orleans found a means to mediate their conception of the social world with their places in it. Instances demonstrative of the manner that whites, in particular, employed cultural strategies to transform social identities in reference to race were highlighted. In Annapolis, the racialization of social identity was a significant emergent practice bound to class formation and the construction of a modern world, while in New Orleans race was minimized as culture creolized in an intercultural frontier exchange setting.

Key issues for both societies were the social and symbolic experiences of slavery and freedom. With slaves beholden to their master's will, the restriction of individual freedom was a basis to slavery and thus part of the social discourse in both places. For those not enslaved, however, the meaning of freedom was more ambiguous. In the Chesapeake, slave owners elaborated a meaning that secured a freedom *from* customary social relations and recast such relations in terms of commodity exchange. Social action enclosed the individual within the discourse of the wealthy by segregating facets of social life into independent spheres (that is, economic relations were believed to be independent of social relations in the process of cultural production). Freedom was thus established in support of the elite perspective, and the search for freedom defined in their terms.

In Louisiana freedom found another expression. The strength of native cultures and their persistent use of a gift-exchange economy deflated attempts by Louisiana slave owners and the French authority to acquire the political economic power to form the social order along the lines of commodity exchange. Freedom was defined by settlers more on their own terms. Missionary Paul Du Ru recognized this habit: "It is hard to get our people together. Some go fishing at daybreak, others hunting. French customs mean little to the Canadians, and they are more lawless than the others.... But what makes them most difficult to control is *the spirit of freedom* which they acquire in the forest where they have no master over them and they follow their own caprice" (Butler 1934: 37, emphasis added). Freedom in colonial Louisiana was not found in the social construct of individuality, but against that construct as settlers went to the forest to forge intercultural relations with Indians through the exchange of material goods. As in the Chesapeake, the freedom sought out in Louisiana broke the bonds of custom, but rather than finding freedom in the new contracts of debt and rent, freedom was realized in the self-determination experienced in the Indian trade.

These differences in the meaning of freedom in Annapolis and New Orleans reflect the variation in the centralization of political economic authority. In Annapolis freedom meant the right to participate in the dominant modern economy, while in New Orleans freedom meant the capacity to evade the modern order as settlers forged alternatives in part through the creation of alliances with Native Americans. Though in both cases race helped people conceive of their place and thus their identity, only in the modern political economy did race circumscribe the possibility for political economic freedom.

Note

This chapter benefited from the very helpful advice of the round-table discussants and the Snowbird seminar, especially Maria Franklin, whose prepared response was insightful and rewarding. I want to thank Chuck Orser, too, for the invitation to attend this excellent seminar. I also thank James Skibo, an anonymous reviewer, and Zoë Burkholder for their challenging commentary. My research in Annapolis benefited from the support of the University of Maryland, College Park, and my superb colleagues and friends at the Archaeology in Annapolis project. My research in New Orleans benefited from the support of the College of Urban and Public Affairs at the University of New Orleans and was funded by the Louisiana Endowment for the Humanities, the New Orleans Jazz and Heritage Foundation, and the Louisiana Archaeological Conservancy.

6

The Archaeological Dimensions of Soul Food: Interpreting Race, Culture, and Afro-Virginian Identity

Maria Franklin

In 1997, Tiger Woods clinched the Masters' Tournament and walked away with the coveted green jacket. A mere twenty-one years old, Woods had achieved superstardom and demonstrated his ability to excel in an overwhelmingly white dominated sport. Yet if Woods had seemingly broken through the color barrier, fellow golfer Fuzzy Zoeller was there to put him in place with a remark that probably made as many headlines as Woods's spectacular Masters' win. Tradition has it that the winner selects the menu for the awards dinner the following year. On the day of Woods's victory, Zoeller commented to CNN (Golf Magazine Online 1997): "That little boy is driving well and he's putting well. He's doing everything it takes to win. So, you know what you guys do when he gets in here? You pat him on the back and say, 'congratulations' and 'enjoy it' and tell him not to serve fried chicken next year. Got it? Or collard greens or whatever the hell they serve."

Zoeller's blatantly racist remarks served as yet another public reminder that denigrating racial stereotypes remain prevalent in American society. His statement required no reading between the lines. In plantation-era fashion, Zoeller first emasculated Woods by snidely referring to him as "that little boy." He then revealed his contempt for Woods, and African Americans in general, by concocting an image of him as a "fried chicken and greens eatin'" black who might be too ignorant to realize that dignified whites could not be expected to eat such lowly black fare. It mattered none that Woods, whose mother is from Thailand, does not self-identify solely as African American (referring to himself as "Cablanasian," or a mix of "Caucasian, black, and Asian"), nor that he went to Stanford and remains more bankable than Zoeller.

Zoeller's outrageous remarks serve as a point of departure for this chapter by foregrounding issues regarding the construction of race and identity, and the ways in which white racist ideology essentializes cultural practices in order to reinforce negative black stereotypes, and to reinvent the bounds of whiteness. Further, the incident underscores the metaphorical power we bestow upon foodways in negotiating identity and drawing group boundaries (Beoku-Betts 1994; Brown and Mussell 1984a; Gutierrez 1984; Kalcik 1984; Moore 1984; Zafar 1999). This chapter touches upon all of these issues from an archaeological perspective that focuses on identity formation among enslaved Virginians, and the ways in which foodways served as a cultural means to position themselves within colonial society. To state the obvious, we eat to survive, but what and how we consume—and further, the meaning and symbolism we tie to food—are altogether embedded in cultural mores, social relationships, and in our performance of identity (Kalcik 1984). The discussion that follows first situates this study within

African diaspora scholarship, which foregrounds race analysis and issues of identity formation. I then argue that eighteenth-century enslaved Virginians responded to the conditions and constrictions of their enslavement (including poverty, plantation food rationing, and surveillance of their activities) through active collaboration in forging a system of foodways that demonstrated self-sufficiency, creativity, and careful strategizing in creating this cultural institution.

My interpretations are further supported by considering the parallel development of Anglo-Virginian foodways. Anglo-Virginians recognized the emergence and form of black foodways, and in constructing themselves as racially different and superior, particular foods associated with black consumption were stigmatized. Evidence suggests that white Virginians made both conscious and unconscious efforts to physically and symbolically distance themselves from foods they perceived as fit only for the enslaved (see Kalcik 1984 for more contemporary case studies of this phenomenon). Eventually, however, the foodway practices of enslaved peoples would come to greatly define the substance of southern cooking for all.

THE AFRICAN DIASPORA, RACE, AND IDENTITY FORMATION

Scholars typically use the term "African diaspora" when referring to Africans or African-descended peoples dispersed through forced migration and enslavement to the Americas and the Caribbean, and their descendants (e.g., Gordon 1998; Lemelle and Kelley 1994; Orser 1998a; Singleton and Bograd 1995; Skinner 1993). The African diaspora further encompasses the post-emancipation immigration of Afro-Latino and Caribbean groups to the United States in particular. Thus, the African diaspora is typically understood to incorporate groups of people who, though geographically dispersed, are variously related through history, culture, and racialization.[1] Scholars of the African diaspora have largely produced a body of work where they attempt to define a series of traits that diasporic groups are thought to possess (see Clifford 1994:315–321; Shepperson 1993). One key characteristic is that such groups profess a black racial identity as a result of white racial oppression. Yet some current researchers contest these etic, largely static, and essentialist interpretations (e.g., Gilroy 1993; Gordon 1998; Gordon and Anderson 1999). While not denying the centrality of racial hierarchies and white racial ideology in African diasporic identity formation and cultural production, these scholars propose that researchers refrain from imposing a priori assumptions onto groups or individuals whom they define as "black" and therefore as members of the African diaspora. Instead, they suggest that self-ascribed identities be foregrounded. Further, rather than focus on the features that members of the diaspora should or must possess, Edmund Gordon and Mark Anderson (1999:284), for example, argue that "the various processes through which communities and individuals identify with one another, highlighting the central importance of race—racial constructions, racial oppressions, racial identification—and culture in the making and remaking of diaspora" must assume primary importance. This requires a shift from a descriptive to an interpretive approach in studying African Diasporic groups.

Gordon and Anderson's (1999) research on Afro-Creole populations testifies to the complex, unbounded ways in which people position themselves both culturally and racially. Further, their work highlights the fact that these fluid identities are situational. For example, Afro-Nicaraguans alternatively shift between identities privileging indigenous, African, or English origin and heritage depending on the social and political moment. Yet Afro-Nicaraguans are phenotypically "black" and African-descended, and as such they recognize that they are victimized by dominant racial constructions. In opposing white racial hegemony, they have allied themselves with blacks elsewhere by unifying into political interest groups under a banner of blackness in recognition of their shared plight (Gordon 1998; Gordon and Anderson 1999:293–294).

In a similar vein, Garifuna youth stylize themselves culturally in the symbols associated with black urban youth in the United States (Gordon and Anderson 1999:290–293). In their own words, this is a demonstration of "black power," of forging alliances with blacks elsewhere who are subject to the same or similar racial subjugation and marginalization. Gordon and Anderson (1999:289) clarify, however, that "this does not imply that Black identities are derived from dominant racial constructions but they necessarily engage them in the effort to imagine a discrete sense of peoplehood." It is in the spirit of forming a sense of "peoplehood," where individuals can pool their knowledge and resources, that racial affiliation with other African diasporic groups potentially becomes an empowering strategic move. Thus, while dominant racial ideology has served the political, economic, and social interests of whites (e.g., see Paynter this volume), it has in turn served as an impetus for group formation among peoples of the African diaspora in furthering their own interests across space and time (e.g., Epperson 1997, 1999a:172, this volume; Franklin 1998; Gilroy 1993; Gomez 1998; Hull, Scott, and Smith 1982; La Roche and Blakey 1997; Mullins 1999a, 1999b; Smith 1983; Thomas 1998).

While this chapter deals specifically with how enslaved individuals produced a collective Afro-Virginian identity, I recognize that these same individuals were not solely defined by this group construct. Alternative subject positions were undoubtedly crucial in negotiating the cultural and social terrain encountered during their lifetimes. Still, given the inextricable tie between race and enslavement, and the overwhelming influence of these twin oppressions in the lives of most Afro-Virginians, I find it necessary to foreground these factors here. Further, since race, as a social construct, possesses no fixed meaning, I do not intend that the experiences of the Afro-Virginians I discuss here are necessarily equivalent to those who came before or after. Finally, identity is situational, dynamic, and highly dependent upon the particular context within which it is defined and lived. I therefore locate my research within the Tidewater region of Virginia during the third quarter of the eighteenth century, when racism and plantation slavery were ubiquitous in the Chesapeake.

SOCIAL AND HISTORICAL LOCATION

Africans and American-born blacks were present in Virginia throughout most of the seventeenth century, yet they constituted no more than 7 percent of the entire population of the Chesapeake during most of this period (Walsh 1997:25). Little is known about their lifeways from the archaeological record because seventeenth-century sites are rarely investigated from the perspective that enslaved, indentured, or free Africans were present (see Miller 1996) or, alternatively, could have left physical evidence that can be conclusively linked to them.[2] Although these individuals acquired a range of identities based on birthright, religion, gender, and their status as free, enslaved, or indentured servants (Billings 1975:155–173; Morgan 1975; Rose 1976:15–27), their ability to reposition themselves within the existing social hierarchy, though precarious, was still possible (Berlin 1998:29–46; Breen and Innes 1980; Epperson 1999a). With the displacement of white indentured laborers by an enslaved African workforce toward the end of the century (Galenson 1986; Morgan 1975) and the construction of racial difference fully realized (Allen 1997:240; Epperson 1999a; Smedley 1999), enslaved Africans entering Virginia found themselves shackled to a system resolved to keep them and their descendants subjugated for life.

Between 1700 and 1740, Virginia's enslaved population escalated to the point where Africans constituted half of the total population, and more than 60 percent in some counties (Kulikoff 1986:37–38, 64–69, 319–345; Minchinton et al. 1984). This was largely due to the British control of the Atlantic slave trade, which doubled the numbers of Africans in North America every twenty years between 1700 and 1780 (Gomez 1998:19). Aggressive slave trading brought

Africans from Senegambia, Sierra Leone, the Gold Coast, Bight of Biafra, Bight of Benin, and the west coast of Central Africa (Gomez 1998:17–37; Morgan 1998:63; Walsh 1997: 55) to the Tidewater, where they mixed with American-born blacks, mulattos, and black Indians. Most would come into contact on plantations where they were commonly forced to work as field hands.

Alienation, disparity, exploitation, and terror marked the experiences of newly arrived Africans as white planters sought to dehumanize their human property through enslavement. Their sanity was further tested as they acclimated to a foreign environment and learned to interact with strangers often vastly different from themselves (e.g., Berlin 1998: 128–129). The imposition of a black racial identity and the English language were additional demoralizing tactics meant to control the enslaved population by erasing their tribal and language affiliations (Gomez 1998: 169–181).

By the 1740s, tobacco plantations were a common feature of the Tidewater landscape. Most enslaved Africans and blacks belonged to wealthy planters who dispersed their large workforce among a number of quartering sites (Walsh 1993). Although enslaved Virginians began to form families (Berlin 1998; Blassingame 1972; Gutman 1976a; Kulikoff 1986; Sobel 1987; Walsh 1997), and the subsequent number of American-born blacks rose, during the 1740s there still existed culturally heterogeneous enslaved communities that included the African-born (Berlin 1998: 110–111; Gomez 1998; Walsh 1997). Racism and enslavement together, however, served to underscore their shared plights within an otherwise sea of divergent experiences and backgrounds. For most, race was an unfamiliar social category. It was within this context that people exchanged and transformed cultural knowledge and practices as they engaged with their imposed identity of "enslaved black." Foodways no doubt served as one of the earliest vehicles for the expression of culture and identity.

Although what follows draws together evidence from a number of historical sources and archaeological sites, I will focus on one particular site, the data for which spans the period of 1740 to 1778. Thus, the site dates from the time when cultural and social heterogeneity among the enslaved population was likely at its peak, to the time when the number of Africans entering the Chesapeake declined and native-born blacks prevailed. The central case study concerns an enslaved community that once lived in the Tidewater on an outlying tobacco plantation known historically as Rich Neck. The remains of their occupation, particularly the faunal assemblage, comprise the main body of evidence for foodways.

Rich Neck Plantation, Williamsburg

Over the past twelve years, Colonial Williamsburg archaeologists have surveyed and excavated Rich Neck Plantation (Site 44WB 52; Franklin 1997a; McFaden et al. 1999; Samford 1991). Located approximately one mile from what was once the colonial capital of Williamsburg, Rich Neck Plantation lies two and a half miles north of the James River. Archaeological and historical research affirms the presence of elite slave owners, white indentured servants, and enslaved Virginians, all of whom variously occupied the area from the 1630s through the nineteenth century. The prominent Ludwell family acquired Rich Neck in 1665 and owned portions of it well into the nineteenth century.

Following a survey that uncovered portions of what appeared to be the remains of a slave dwelling, excavations in 1994–1995 exposed the footprint of a duplex consisting of fifteen root cellars and the brick foundations of a central chimney. The artifacts and primary sources together indicated that the dwelling was occupied between 1740 and 1778. Phillip Ludwell III was the absentee landowner of Rich Neck during this period and lived at Greenspring Plantation about five miles away. Thus Rich Neck operated as a satellite, or outlying, tobacco plantation. As one of the wealthiest Virginians of his time, Ludwell owned nine plantations and 235 enslaved blacks at his death in 1767 (VMHB 1913:395–413).

The occupation date range coincides with the peak of the trade in enslaved Africans in Virginia (c. 1740). By this time relatively stable enslaved families and communities had begun to form (Morgan 1998:503), and by the end of the eighteenth century most enslaved blacks were American-born. By 1767, Rich Neck's enslaved community was composed of twenty-one individuals: ten men, five women, three boys, and three girls (Franklin 1997:27–54). As many as five people (four men and one woman) were above the age of sixty. Importantly, two individuals may have been in their seventies. The remaining eight adults included women still in their childbearing years and five mature men. Along with the presence of six children, this suggests that the community consisted of mixed nuclear families, extended family groupings, and individuals who were single or had families on other plantations. It is likely that two family groupings, or roughly half of the Rich Neck slave quarter's population, occupied the two-room dwelling that was excavated.

The previous discussion regarding Virginia's slave trade suggests that by midcentury plantations were still the settings for cultural exchange between individuals with divergent backgrounds. Ludwell's probate inventory indicates further that this community did not simply vary along gender and age lines, for the presence of four elder men and a woman strongly suggests that at least some, if not all, of these individuals were born and raised in Africa.[3] Although the remaining populace was probably creole, or American-born, in all likelihood their parents or other close family members were African-born. Many creoles therefore received the skills and knowledge remembered from a homeland long gone but reproduced in Virginia through their African relations. As a result, Rich Neck's community was quite heterogeneous with a mixture of language skills, ages, genders, tribal origins, and the various worldviews, values, and cultural lifeways embodied in each individual. Such dynamic situations could be found on other Tidewater plantations, but their occurrence was mostly limited to the first half of the eighteenth century, coinciding with the astounding growth of the enslaved African population that consequently shifted the racial balance in colonial society. Thus, during the early years of Rich Neck's habitation (c. 1740s), the social and cultural scene of the slave quarter was highly dynamic, and rapidly transforming. Not only did these diverse individuals manage to form social institutions through kinship ties and codependence, but the archaeological evidence indicates that they endeavored to produce a unified cultural identity in line with their enslaved and racialized one. We can assess foodways as one example of this identity-in-the-making process.

CULINARY AND SUBSISTENCE PRACTICES AS MEANINGFUL AND MUNDANE

For Virginia's enslaved population, a number of factors variously influenced the form, content, and meaning of their foodways. Although interaction and the exchange of ideas fostered the development of a foodways system, plantation management, poverty, and the environment also played influential roles. With regard to cultural exchange, enslaved Africans likely expressed a strong inclination toward flavors remembered from home, and favored their particular ways of assembling, preparing, serving, and consuming meals. On Virginia plantations, these myriad traditions combined with those of American-born blacks, whites, and, either directly or indirectly, local Indians (Morgan 1998:477–485) to form a "cultural continuum" (Drummond 1980) of practices from which they could alternatively choose in transforming their subsistence practices. While some plants and animals indigenous to Africa were brought to Virginia (e.g., guinea hens, yams, cowpeas), enslaved Virginians had little available for consumption other than the native flora and fauna that the Indians had relied on for millennia, and the livestock and crops introduced from Europe (e.g., cattle, sheep, swine, wheat, and barley). The first half of the eighteenth century must have been a period of widespread experimentation with these new foodstuffs, using alien cooking and serving

Table 6.1 Taxa and Species Recovered from the Rich Neck Slave Quarters

Wild Mammal	Domestic Mammal	Fish
Opossum	Swine	Sheepshead
Raccoon	Cattle	Pumpkinseed
Eastern grey squirrel	Sheep/goat	White perch
Eastern fox squirrel		Redear sunfish
Red squirrel		Yellow perch
White-tailed deer		Atlantic herring
Rabbit		Alewife
		American shad
		Sucker
		Freshwater catfish
		White catfish
		Bluegill
		Gar
		Sturgeon
		Channel pickerel
Bird	**Reptile**	**Crustacean and Shellfish**
Chicken	Snapping turtle	Blue crab
Turkey	Slider/cooter	Oyster
Grouse/partridge	Red-bellied turtle	Clam
Canada goose		
Pigeon/dove		
Perching bird		

Note: Table does not include commensals.

instruments. To compound the challenge, enslaved Virginians would have had to develop cooking methods that coordinated well with their demanding workdays. Importantly, since planter provisions scarcely met their caloric needs, they needed to develop strategies for ensuring their own and their family's physical well-being. While the food provisioning system controlled by slave owners played a major role in slave diets, it neither ruled their palates nor dictated how they attached meaning to food.

Although the assessment of the Rich Neck slave quarter's faunal assemblage is still in progress, more than 27,000 bone fragments from five root cellars have been analyzed. To date, zooarchaeologists at the Department of Archaeological Research at Colonial Williamsburg have identified forty-five wild and domestic species (Andrews et al. 1997; Franklin 1997). Of these, Rich Neck's household consumed more than thirty species (Table 6.1), not including the shellfish recovered. With regard to the botanical remains, ethnobotanists identified sixteen families and species (Table 6.2; Mrozowski and Driscoll 1997).

My thesis is that Rich Neck's inhabitants during the 1740s were a mixed lot, with creole blacks and Africans forced to live and work together. During this community's life cycle, twenty years later, we can pinpoint twenty-one enslaved men, women, and children residents in 1767. This illustrates their success in forming families and suggests cooperation within a number of realms.

Table 6.2. Charred Seed Remains from the Rich Neck Slave Quarters

Latin Name	Common Name
Vigna sp.	bean
Vigna sinensis	cowpea
Phaseolus limensis	lima bean
Phaseolus vulgaris	common bean
Zea mays	corn
Zea hordeum	pearl barley
Triticum sp.	wheat
Secale sp.	rye
Cucurbita pepo	squash
Citrullus lanatus	melon
Prunus sp.	cherry
Rubus sp.	blackberry
Juglans nigra	black walnut
Quercus sp.	acorn
Gleditsia tricanthos	honey locust
Arachis	peanut
Galium sp.	bedstraw
Carex sp.	sedge

Source: Mrozowski and Driscoll 1997.

Shocker, Hester, and the remaining elderly individuals were probably present during the entire occupation of the dwelling remains in question (c. 1740–1778), serving as a source of cultural inspiration and familial continuity. As the entire community dealt with the reality of their enslavement and racialization, they built upon this foundation of commonality over time in forging a collective identity, the evidence for which should be recognizable in the archaeological record. Since I proposed that the cultural production of foodways played an important role in this transformation, it was necessary to be able to discern subsistence changes *over time* that might support this.

The faunal remains were recovered from two major episodes of backfilling: an early period between 1740 and 1765, and a late period from 1765 to 1778. It was therefore possible to delineate any potential changes in subsistence practices over time. I considered the evidence for food choices (particularly with regard to wild species), element distribution (specifically, meat cuts consumed from domestic species), and meal preparation methods, and found that during the forty years that the dwelling was occupied, Rich Neck's household endeavored to create a distinctive foodways style that was strongly associated, by themselves and others, with their collective identity as enslaved Afro-Virginians.

Livin' High off the Hog

Domestic livestock provided most of the meat protein consumed by the residents of Rich Neck. The evidence from faunal remains from other eighteenth- and nineteenth-century enslaved Virginian sites indicates that this held true for the enslaved belonging to most wealthy planters (Atkins 1994; Bowen 1993, 1995; Crader 1990; McKee 1987). At Rich Neck, the bulk of the bones came from cattle and swine, with sheep a distant third (Figure 6.1). Ludwell's probate inventory (VMHB 1913) shows that twenty-two head of cattle, four calves, ten hogs, and twenty-five sheep were being raised on the Rich Neck property, so it is fair to surmise that the enslaved household received their rations from these livestock.

We tend to assume that the enslaved were rationed only the poorest cuts of meat and innards, while slave owners and their families enjoyed the most tender and meatiest portions, such as hams and roasts. Joanne Bowen, however, argues that this is a modern assumption that has been uncritically imposed onto our interpretations of the past (Bowen 1993:39, 41–45, 1996:116). In fact, the faunal remains from Rich Neck (Franklin 1997a:196–199) and two contemporaneous slave sites—Mount Vernon's House for Families (Atkins 1994:57–58) and Monticello's building "o" (Crader 1990)—support her argument that blacks were commonly provisioned with whole animals. Moreover, evidence from Williamsburg's elite households indicates that the heads of calves and pigs

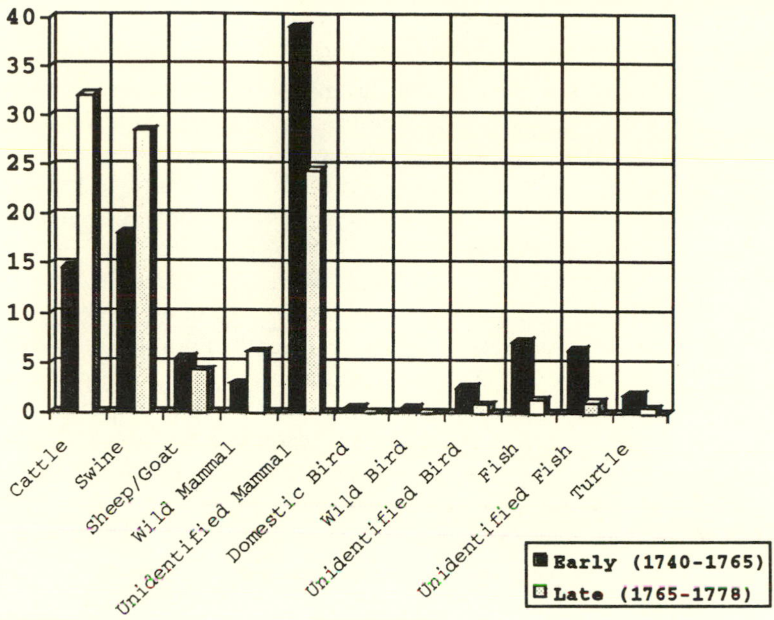

Figure 6.1. Percentage of total biomass, Rich Neck slave quarters, c. 1740–1778.

were commonly consumed by the wealthy (Walsh et al. 1997:162–173), and even the innards were not wasted (see Noël Hume 1978: 14–20). What we today would consider the cheapest, least desirable portions of an animal were consumed eagerly on a regular basis by even elite slave owning whites during the colonial period.

Ludwell's probate inventory also indicates that corn was both raised and stored at Rich Neck. Indian corn was regularly rationed to enslaved blacks throughout much of the plantation South (Hilliard 1972; McKee 1999; Moore 1989:72–73), and this was likely the case at Rich Neck. We also recovered pearl barley and rye (see Table 6.2), which were probably cultivated on any number of Ludwell's plantations. The rest of the charred seed remains came from garden variety fruits and vegetables, including cowpea (i.e., black-eyed pea), lima bean, squash, and melon (see Table 6.2). Although we found no evidence of garden plots in the form of fence lines close to the quarter, historical sources suggest that enslaved Virginians often kept personal garden plots (McKee 1999; Morgan 1998:140). Through gardening they supplemented their diets and seized the opportunity to earn money or goods through sale or barter of produce. Gardening also allowed them greater leverage in constructing their foodways (see also Joyner 1991:86). Likewise, enslaved Virginians raised fowl for their own use (McKee 1999:226; Morgan 1998: 139–140). At Rich Neck we recovered both immature and adult chicken bones along with egg shell fragments, lending further support for the conventionality of this household activity. While the faunal evidence demonstrates that Rich Neck's household members consumed both fowl and eggs on-site, it is highly probable that both were sold in town as well (Walsh et al. 1997:89). We found coinage at Rich Neck, and the quarter itself was a short distance from Williamsburg's marketplace.

Domestic livestock and grains, as well as cultivated fruits and vegetables, were important foodstuffs consumed by Rich Neck's household. Whether acquired through Ludwell's food rations or raised by themselves, domestic animal and plant species largely dominated the substance of their diets. Still, Rich Neck's household did not depend solely upon these foods, and individuals sought to diversify and supplement their diets by integrating wild plant and animal species into their foodways.

Searching Beyond the Bounds of the Quarter: Wild Plants and Animals

As did gardening and raising fowl, exploiting the environment for its natural resources also helped to shape black creole foodways (Atkins 1994; Crader 1990; Hilliard 1988; Jenkins 1999; Joyner 1991:85–86; McKee 1987, 1988; Reitz et al. 1985; Walsh 1997: 101–102; Yentsch 1994). The faunal and botanical evidence from Rich Neck intimates that this group was deeply familiar with the lay of the land. As historian Rhys Isaac (1982:52–55) posits, enslaved Africans lived within an "alternative territorial system" that contrasted with the heavily modified landscape preferred by elite whites (see also Upton 1988). Blacks understood the advantage of familiarizing themselves with their untamed surroundings—landscapes that remained wooded and natural—for they facilitated secrecy and anonymity. Before long, enslaved Virginians acquired an in-depth knowledge of their environment, and the flora and fauna sustained by it.

Successful subsistence strategies depended largely upon the Rich Neck household's familiarity with animal behavior and habitats, and the seasonality of a wide range of wild game (Reitz and Scarry 1985:81–83; e.g., Tuma 1999). Although some wild catch, most notably shellfish and turtle, may have been obtained through "opportunistic collecting" (McKee 1987:38), others required specialized skills such as the making of traps, fishing with hook and line or a net, and hunting with dogs or guns (e.g., Jenkins 1999). Africans may have been familiar with certain skills, fishing in particular, before coming to Virginia (Yentsch 1992). Finesse with firearms and traps may have been acquired initially through interactions with Anglo-Virginians and/or Indians, and then passed along through generations of black families. That one or more people from Rich Neck hunted with musket was confirmed by the discovery of gun flints, various-sized lead shot, and the remains of migratory bird species (Canada goose) and white-tailed deer. Some of the remaining bird species were likely trapped, snared, or netted (Reitz and Scarry 1985:81). Squirrel, raccoon, and possum were often caught by setting traps, downfalls, or snares (Atkins 1994:75). Ex-slave Peter Randolph (1969:29–31) related that slaves caught a variety of wild game with traps made of thin strips of white oak. The traps were checked at night and on Sundays, when there was time off from work. Thus, firearms were not required to catch most wild game, and some people alternatively caught possums by using dogs to track and run them up trees (Campbell 1994; Genovese 1972: 527; Killion and Waller 1973:59; Randolph 1969:29–30).

The fact that fifteen different species of fish were recovered from Rich Neck underscores the reliance on resources collected from the Chesapeake Bay's tributaries. Rich Neck is bordered by College Creek, a major waterway once navigable during the eighteenth century, that flows into the James River, itself only a few miles away. Thus, Rich Neck's household had easy access to prime fishing spots and did not have to travel far if traps needed to be checked. In addition to the use of traps, fishing was accomplished with hook and line or with nets or seines (we found one lead net weight from a root cellar). The remaining wild species included various aquatic and land turtles, oysters, and blue crabs. Shellfish were collected in shallow water habitats along beaches and tidal flats (White 1989). Folks from Rich Neck probably traveled to Archer's Hope, a neighboring Ludwell plantation on the James River, to gather crabs that migrated to shallow waters from the bay during the summer to molt.

The macrobotanical remains demonstrate that the individuals from Rich Neck not only actively participated in acquiring wild game and fish, but also foraged for black walnuts, acorns, blackberries, and chokecherries (see Table 6.2). We also found relatively large amounts of honey locust pods, which were used as a sweetener (Stiverson and Butler 1977:37); sugar was a luxury item that if provisioned by Ludwell was probably done so in scarce amounts. Locust pods were also brewed with persimmons to make beer (Killion and Waller 1973:40; Randolph 1969: 31). Enslaved blacks probably benefited from Indian knowledge of, and expertise with, edible and medicinal plants. The chokecherry seed was one likely example, as the local Powhatan were known to make teas with it to treat various illnesses.

To summarize thus far, between 1740 and 1778, Rich Neck's community relied primarily on cattle and swine for meat protein, provisioned grains (notably corn), and a greater variety of domestic and wild plant and animal species that they themselves grew or procured. Although newly enslaved Africans were initially unfamiliar with most of these species, Anne Yentsch (1994:202–203) suggests that many came from areas of West Africa where a bewildering array of animals was available at market. This may or may not at least partially explain a willingness to try new things. Their knowledge, however, of food preparation clearly influenced cooking methods within the slave quarter.

Slow Stews and Hasty Ash Cakes

While black victuals largely mirrored everyone else's in terms of content, they diverged from Anglo colonial foodways in terms of assemblage and preparation. And although all the members of a family or household variously engaged in the production of foodways, black women dominated when it came to conjuring up edibles (Fox-Genovese 1988: 159; Mitchell 1993:16; White 1991; Yentsch 1994:196–215; Zafar 1999:449–451). They were responsible for preparing meals within the slave quarter, and nearly all of the plantation household chefs were black females (e.g., White 1985:128–129, 1991:109, 119–120). This included Daphne, the Ludwell family cook who was listed in a 1774 probate inventory (Lee Family Papers, 1638–1867). The ex-slave narratives for Virginia underscore the enduring role that black women fulfilled over the years within the realm of foodways (Perdue et al. 1976:163–164, 181, 216, 311).

Both historical and archaeological evidence for black foodways throughout the South suggest that black women relied heavily on West African cooking methods such as stewing and baking (Ferguson 1992; Hall 1991; Hess 1992; McKee 1987:37; Mitchell 1993; Otto 1984; Walker 2000; WPA 1994: 227; Yentsch 1994:218).[4] Using a large iron pot (a common find on slave-related sites in the Chesapeake, including at Rich Neck [see also Ferguson 1992:102–103]), they created "one-pot meals" that were stewed slowly either in the fireplace or on an open fire in the yard. Archaeological evidence suggests that stewing was a widespread cooking method. Many of the mammal bones recovered from Rich Neck and other Virginia slave sites are highly fragmented, and some exhibit cut marks (e.g., Crader 1990; McKee 1987; see also Jenkins 1999). Both traits indicate that larger pieces of meat were butchered into smaller ones for boiling or stewing, and also to extract the marrow.

Black women may have chosen stewing over other cooking techniques for several reasons. Slow stewing, unlike roasting, required little supervision and could be tended from time to time when people were laboring in the fields. Also, tougher cuts of meat were tenderized by stewing (Bowen 1993:55, 1995:11). Finally, and importantly, enslaved women built upon their knowledge of African foodways by concocting nutritious meals starting with corn, rice, or vegetables as the foundation for stews to which pieces of meat were added for flavor and protein (Harris 2001: 15; Hess 1992; Yentsch 1994:218). In doing so, they reproduced this traditional practice, but transformed it with new ingredients.

Stewing wasn't the only cooking method used, as the preparation of corn shows. African-born slaves, such as the eldest members of Rich Neck's household, may have tasted corn for the first time in Virginia, but many of them were familiar with grains such as rice and millet, and with their preparation (see Hall 1991; Hess 1992). The mortar and pestle, central to a number of West African

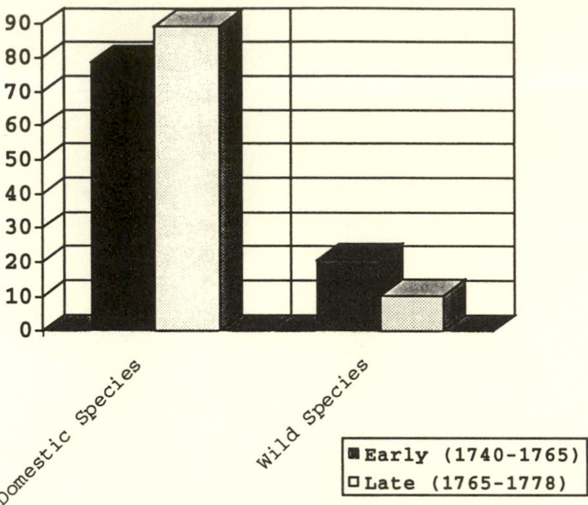

Figure 6.2. Total biomass, domestic versus wild species, Rich Neck slave quarters, c. 1740–1778.

peoples for separating grains from hulls, were also used in the Tidewater. An Englishman visiting Williamsburg in 1732 observed that corn was "the only support of the Negroes, who roast it in the ear, bake it for bread, boyl it when hulled, and like our buttered wheat, the children and better sort breakfast with it and make farmity. The first they call homeny, the latter mush. To hull it they beat it in a mortar as the scots doe their barley" (Stiverson and Butler 1977).

By using certain West African cooking techniques, enslaved women had at their disposal fairly uncomplicated meal preparations that coordinated well with the demands of forced labor. For example, they baked yams in hot ashes for a nutritious meal that even children learned to prepare (e.g., Hilliard 1988:319; Perdue et al. 1976:154, 163, 189; WPA 1994:78). The popular "hoe" or "ash" cake was prepared expediently by mixing corn meal with water, patting it into cakes, placing it on the blade of a hoe, and then into the fire, where it was covered with ashes and cooked for five minutes. Such filling meals were prepared and consumed hastily before leaving for the fields.

Enslaved women also appropriated European styles of cooking, and wild game was dry-roasted in much the way that the English preferred to cook fine cuts of meat. Opossum was regarded as a delicacy, and was fattened upon capture by feeding it persimmons. They were then roasted on a spit and often served with sweet potatoes (Hilliard 1988:317; Yetman 1970:96).

The women of Rich Neck excelled at "no-nonsense" cooking. Through their fundamental cooking routines, they not only delivered the culturally salient "one-pot meals" and baked foods, but also managed to integrate efficient preparation methods with the demand of their work cycles. While the discussion thus far has focused on how Rich Neck's community created a distinctive foodways system by redefining African-derived cooking methods, the evidence for changes over time in their diets reveals how the transformation of foodways may signify a concurrent move toward a shared group identity.

Disciplining Foodways

The major thrust of this chapter is that by the end of the third quarter of the eighteenth century, enslaved Virginians asserted a collective racial and cultural identity. As the enslaved residents of Rich Neck Plantation worked toward defining themselves as a group, we might expect to find a more stable and meaningful pattern emerging in their foodway

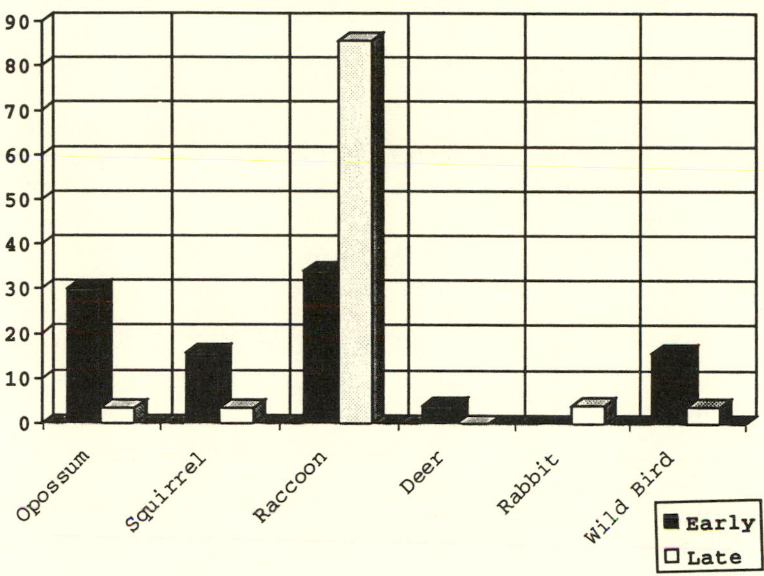

Figure 6.3. Percentage of biomass for wild mammals and birds, Rich Neck slave quarters, c. 1740–1778, in early and late deposits from root cellar contexts.

practices. Although, as stated previously, not all of the faunal remains from Rich Neck have been analyzed, there do appear to be some trends worth noting.

In comparing and contrasting the faunal assemblages from the early (1740–1765) and late (1765–1778) deposits, it is clear that domestic species—specifically cattle and swine—increased in the diet, while there was a related decline in wild species (Figure 6.2). A number of factors may explain the rise in domestic species consumption, including an increase in planter provisions or the independent raising of livestock by the enslaved household. With this shift there was also a decrease in the exploitation of wild species, but nonetheless a continued reliance upon them. For the later eighteenth and early nineteenth centuries, the analyses of faunal assemblages from Monticello (Crader 1990), Kingsmill (McKee 1987), Mount Vernon (Atkins 1994; Bowen 1993), and Flowerdew Hundred plantations (McKee 1988, 1999) likewise demonstrate that wild game continued to be central in the foodways of enslaved Virginians. Yet this is a broad generalization, and a closer look at the consumption of wild species from the Rich Neck assemblage discloses that this household may have relinquished certain animals from their diet while more actively pursuing others.

Figure 6.1 shows a spike in the use of wild mammals over time, and this was due to a nearly three-fold increase in the consumption of raccoon and the initial appearance of rabbit in the diet during the late period (Figure 6.3). Historical sources cite the wide appeal specifically of raccoon, squirrel, and opossum among enslaved blacks well into the nineteenth century (Campbell 1994:61; Genovese 1972:546–547; Yetman 1970:53). No firearms were needed to capture raccoon and opossum, and as nocturnal creatures they could be hunted at night when enslaved hunters were able to move about in secrecy. The marked decline in opossum consumption and the rise in raccoon consumption are difficult to explain at this point.[5] Raccoon meat may have been preferable, as ex-slave Anthony Dawson (Yetman 1970:96) recalled: "Sometimes de boys would go down in de woods and get a possum. I love possum and sweet-taters, but de coon meat more delicate and de hair don't stink up de meat." We recovered rabbit remains in only one root cellar, suggesting that rabbit was eaten no more so than squirrel or opossum during the late period.

It is worth noting that we found no deer remains for the late period, and a decline in wild birds as well, which may mean that firearms were no longer available for use at Rich Neck. This implies that Ludwell's plantation manager or overseer may have attempted to assert more control over the actions and movements of Rich Neck's community than in previous years (Ludwell was largely an absentee slave owner during this period). In response, Rich Neck's enslaved household turned to wild species that could be caught at night or trapped and then retrieved when the opportunity arose. But here, too, more research is needed. An alternative interpretation may be that white-tailed deer were scarce in the area due to overhunting, as well as to the introduction of grazing livestock, which damaged their native habitat (Manning-Sterling 1994:70–72; Walsh et al. 1997:28). As a result, Rich Neck's household would have shifted their subsistence strategies.

It is still possible to surmise, using the preliminary data from Rich Neck, that this group contrived a unique foodways system shaped by a number of factors. These included the influences of an array of cultural traditions, access to the Tidewater's natural resources, and Ludwell's provisioning system. Over time, domestic species consumption rose, although wild game and fish continued to be exploited. Importantly, Rich Neck's household went from experimenting with a wider variety of wild mammals to selecting for raccoon in particular. Similar comparisons of the types of fish species captured over time still require analysis. The dire poverty associated with enslavement and the likelihood that rations scarcely met the caloric or nutritive needs of the household further served as the catalysts to hunt, fish, trap, gather, and raise fowl and garden crops for sustenance.

Despite the number of variables that shaped Afro-Virginian foodways, what is significant remains the potential for foodways to serve as a meaningful signifier of identity, and to reinforce the cohesion and social ties of the enslaved community as its members participated in the multiple phases associated with food production, distribution, and consumption. The move toward group coalition and definition should be detectable in the archaeological record as patterns exhibiting increasing cultural homogeneity, and there do appear to be trends at Rich Neck that may be discovered at other enslaved-related sites. Still there is the question of uniqueness: Were these foodways exclusive to enslaved Virginians, thus signifying the performance of a group identity? This can be answered only by comparisons with the transformation of Anglo-Virginian foodways.

FOODWAYS ACROSS THE COLOR-LINE

One of the more striking features of slave-related faunal assemblages, in contrast to those collected from Anglo sites, is the diversity of wild game and fish species. The typical slave-related faunal assemblage from the Chesapeake region of Virginia consists of 5–20 percent wild taxa (Atkins 1994:21). Although beef and pork provided the bulk of meat protein for enslaved Virginians (Crader 1990: 691), over time the meat protein in their diet was quite varied, especially when compared with the diets of Anglo-Virginians. White colonists mainly consumed wild species under "frontier" conditions (Miller 1988; Watts-Roy 1996). Thus, faunal remains from the earliest seventeenth-century settlements along the James River contain high percentages of fish and deer in particular (e.g., Bowen 1996:97, 101).

Over time, whites exploited fewer wild species as areas became more settled and livestock had a chance to proliferate (Walsh et al. 1997:27). Using data compiled from an intensive study comparing rural and urban faunal assemblages from Chesapeake sites, Walsh, Martin, and Bowen (1997) state that wild species were never a significant factor in the colonial diet.[6] From their study of fifty-

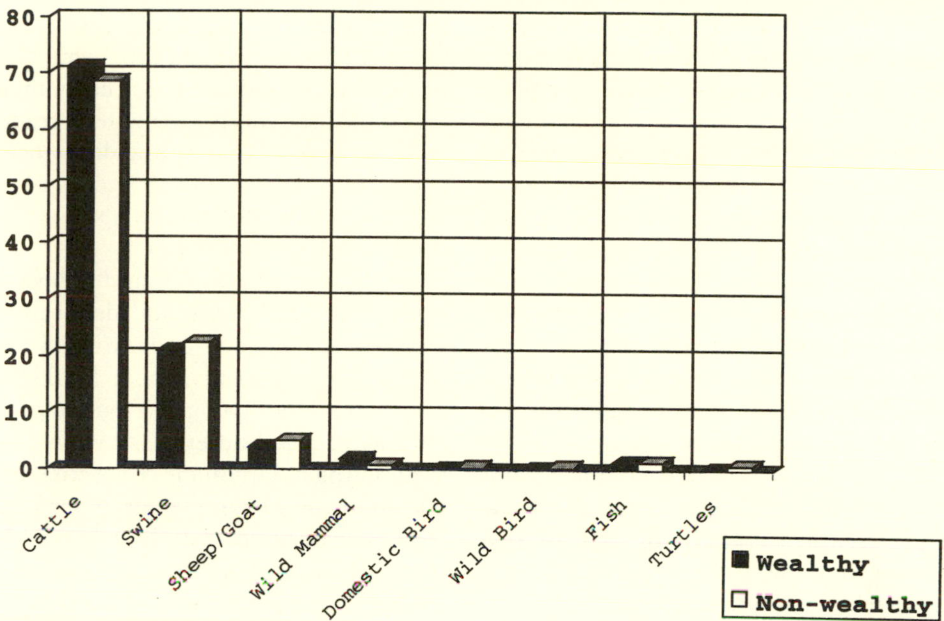

Figure 6.4. Percentage of biomass of identifiable domestic and wild species recovered from rural Anglo-Virginian sites (c. 1750–1800), including Curles Neck (wealthy planter; site 44HE388), the Boothe site (fairly wealthy planters; site 441W111), Ferry Farm (middling planters; site 44VB138), Gloucester-VIMS III (middling merchant; sites 44GL357, 44GL177), Gloucester Point (middling merchant; site 44GL197), and Hopewell (planters; site 44PG381). (From Walsh et al. 1997:243–251)

three sites, I have selected six rural Anglo-Virginian sites dating to between 1750 and 1800 in order to compare the dietary significance of wild species between these households with those of enslaved black households previously discussed (Figure 6.4). I chose rural sites in order to factor in the possibility that location within undeveloped areas coupled with less accessibility to town markets might result in a heavier reliance on wild species. Further, I chose two wealthy planter sites (Curles Neck and the Boothe site) and four "middling" planter and merchant sites in order to account for varying socioeconomic status. The very low percentages of wild mammal (>2 percent), bird (>.5 percent), and fish (>2 percent) consumed by these six households confirms that Anglo-Virginians—even in rural areas—overwhelmingly chose domestic livestock for their meat protein (see also Miller 1984:191–192).[7] Further research is needed, however, to account for the diets of poor whites, who may have had different subsistence practices that were perhaps more comparable to that of enslaved Virginians.

One of the more potent images of slave foodways is that of "pig's feet and chitlins" (the large intestines of the pig), even though during the eighteenth century, as previously stated, enslaved Virginians used various parts, including the meatiest portions. Although faunal research on later nineteenth-century slave-related sites in Virginia has yet to be done, it is probably safe to say that enslaved Virginians (especially on larger plantations) continued to receive whole animals as rations. This appeared to be the case in the Deep South on larger plantation holdings (Hilliard 1988:323; Jenkins 1999). In contrast, historical and archaeological sources demonstrate that by the end of the eighteenth century Anglo-Virginians were no longer consuming livestock head and feet.[8]

Following a trend that began in continental Europe, meat cuts were increasingly butchered and prepared so that by the nineteenth century, any telling evidence of an animal's original features were discarded by whites as waste (Yentsch 1994:234–235).[9] Market prices, which at first reflected age and species preference, eventually ranked body parts by price (Yentsch 1994:234–235). If slave owners fell under the influence of this foodways trend, the choicest meat cuts would likely have been saved for whites and the rest doled out to the enslaved population rather than tossed as refuse.

The foodways of enslaved Virginians contrasted with that of Anglo-Virginians by the later eighteenth century along at least two lines: wild game and fish were actively sought to supplement and add variety to their diets, and all of the elements from livestock continued to be incorporated. Marrinda Jane Singleton (Perdue et al. 1976:266), once enslaved in Norfolk, remarked of pigs, "You know, dar wasn't much to throw 'way 'cause you, ain't you never stopped to think 'bout hit? Kin use nearly every findin' in de hog, even what you find in de intels, dey use now dese new days for fertilizer." Fatback or bacon was added to vegetable greens for flavor and "substance" (Mitchell 1993:18). The less meatier cuts such as ham hocks and pig's feet were boiled, as they are now, until the meat was tender and falling off the bone.

Such foodway strategies were certainly in part due to economic deprivation, but not entirely. Ex-slave testimonies tell of the satisfaction in hunting and fishing, and the enjoyment in consuming the catch. Remarked one individual, "Oh! I was fond of 'possums, sprinkled with butter and pepper and baked down 'till de gravy was good and brown" (Killion and Waller 1973:79; see also White 1985:155–156). Further, oral recipes for "pig's feet," ham hocks, and chitterlings (or chitlins) were passed down and have come to be synonymous with southern cooking. Yet if foodways served as a cultural signifier for enslaved colonial Virginians, its symbolism worked both ways. Whites living within plantation societies were familiar with the eating habits of enslaved blacks. In their efforts to sustain domination, whites vilified black cultural traditions such as foodways by concocting stereotypes to perpetuate ideas regarding black inferiority and difference.

RACED FOODS AND RACIST STEREOTYPES

Foodways signal identity, and are used both to highlight difference and delineate group boundaries (Brown and Mussell 1984b; Mintz 1996; Thomas 2000; Walker 2000; Zafar 1999). For colonial Virginia, perceived notions of racial difference were manifested in how Anglo-Virginians conceptualized certain foods. For example, although Virginian colonists consumed fish, it was considered a mark of poverty in the Chesapeake (Noël Hume 1978:26–30; see also Randolph 1993:19), as well as in New England (Joanne Bowen, pers. comm.). Fish was commonly provisioned as a cheap and plentiful food source and was considered "slave food" (Atkins 1994; McKee 1999:224–226). Thomas Jefferson thought a diet of sheep, "diversified with rations of salted fish and molasses, both of them wholesome, agreeable and cheap articles of food," an enlightened alternative to corn and pork (Moore 1989:73). In Tidewater Virginia, the low price of fish (Walsh et al. 1997:95) and the decline in its consumption by white households toward the end of the eighteenth century (Miller 1988:190–191) may be related to its centrality in the diet of enslaved blacks. Whites had undoubtedly established the connection between fish and "blackness" given the role of enslaved blacks as major players in the selling of fish and oysters in Virginia markets (Walsh et al. 1997:88–91). Paul Mullins's (1999a) research on race and consumerism in nineteenth-century Annapolis confirms the racialization of fish consumption for parts of the Chesapeake. He states, "Among the most stigmatized of household-based consumption patterns was fishing. Many White writers reduced fishing to the archetypal diversion of lazy and content Black people" (Mullins 1999a:118).

The "fried chicken" comment made by

Fuzzy Zoeller after Tiger Woods won the Masters' reveals another historically racialized meal. Enslaved blacks were adept not only in catching fish, but also in raising domestic fowl. John Hatley Norton's inventory of his Virginian estate (c. 1782–1784; from Mullin 1972:49) reads:

> Fowls in the care of Old Betty:
> 10 guse, 6 fatning for Mrs. Norton's use
> 5 Turkies for breading
> 3 fatning for Mrs. Norton
> 5 Dungle hens
> 8 ducks

Unlike Norton's inventory, Ludwell's fails to mention domestic fowl along with other livestock, although archaeological evidence indicates they were raised on the property. This omission reveals that the fowl were considered the property of the enslaved household. As with fish, a wide variety of fowl were sold at Chesapeake markets, mainly by black women (Walsh et al. 1997:89). In Annapolis, white women dominated the sale of chicken and eggs until the late eighteenth century, when blacks assumed the role (Yentsch 1994:203–204). With this transition, the price of chicken decreased considerably.

These examples show that enslaved individuals were quite self-sufficient and actively created opportunities to provide for themselves and their families through judicious strategizing. For the enslaved, "leisure time" or "day off" is probably a misnomer, as they also labored during this time to produce foodstuffs that were then sold or bartered at local markets. In Virginia, their overwhelming presence on market days was so disturbing to white authorities that statutes were adopted to both curb and regulate their market activities (Walsh et al. 1997:89). In defiance, enslaved Virginians kept selling, and whites kept buying because such trade had become too important to the local economy. Likewise, hunting and fishing were often accomplished by "stealing away" from the slave quarter without the overseer's or slave owner's permission. Such actions were direct challenges to white domination. For whites, the prevailing image of the black hawker selling fish and fowl stirred and fueled sentiments of racial difference, which manifested themselves in racial stereotypes regarding black foodways. That degrading representations of blacks eating watermelon and fried chicken persist in the minds of white Americans underscores the symbolic power of foodways in projecting our notions of race, culture, and identity (see also Kalcik 1984: 51–52; Zafar 1999).

RECLAIMING THE ARTS: THE AFRICAN AMERICAN ROOTS OF SOUTHERN FOODWAYS

During my undergraduate years in Alabama, nostalgically referred to as the "Heart of Dixie" on its license plates, I could often smell cornbread baking in an iron skillet, greens simmering in a pot with bacon fat, and an assortment of other foods stewing or frying on the stovetop of the house I shared with three other women. Foods I had always associated with a black heritage were being prepared and consumed by one of my white female roommates with regularity and surprising finesse. My "black sensibilities" and, until then, uncontested beliefs that only African Americans privileged these dishes were suddenly challenged. Where was the "soul" in "soul food" if whites ate ham hocks and collard greens too? Having largely been raised in California, the only people I ever witnessed cooking chitlins were black, and not necessarily raised in the South. (I did at least know from my own family relations that "soul food" did originate in the South.) Soul food restaurants such as Mama's Home Cooking in my own hometown were both black-owned and serviced a black clientele. Yet my roommate's response to my puzzlement was simply that she had grown up in Selma eating this stuff too, and that it was simply what southern folks ate. Since then, I have come to better understand the ties between traditional African American cooking and southern foodways from my years spent in Alabama, Georgia, and Virginia. Likewise, as scholars and African American culinary experts (both the academic and nonacademic) have observed, the foodways of enslaved blacks provided the roots for much of what we refer to as southern cuisine (Beoku-Betts 1994; Genovese 1972:543; Hall 1991; Harris 1989, 2001; Hess 1992:xiv; Mitchell 1993; Moore 1989; Smart-Grosvenor 1992; Walker 2000). I proceed with my tentative interpretations about when and how this development may have occurred.

In Sam Hilliard's (1988) study of foodways in the antebellum Deep South (Mississippi, Georgia, and Alabama), he concludes that enslaved blacks and whites, in particular poor whites, shared similar diets. Stewed greens, cornbread, roasted opossum, baked sweet potatoes, wild game and pork characterized white diets as well as black. He concludes that for the most part, enslaved blacks assimilated white foodways: "Having the same basic foods with which to work and living under the close supervision of white masters, it was almost inevitable that slaves would develop similar cooking methods" (Hilliard 1988:324). Yet a counterargument can be leveled using the interpretations of enslaved Virginian foodways above. As early as the colonial period, enslaved Virginians baked potatoes, roasted game, relied heavily on pork, and raised vegetable greens in their garden plots. One-pot meals were the normal fare along with ash cakes, which were essentially the antecedents for greens cooked with pork and served with cornbread. So how did the foodways of the Upper South come to influence that of the Deep South? Considering the forced migration of slaves from Virginia to the Cotton Belt may help to resolve this query.

Unlike the plantations of Virginia and South Carolina (Morgan 1998), which grew tobacco and rice, plantations in Mississippi, Georgia and Alabama centered on cotton cultivation (Vlach 1991:33–37). America did not become a major exporter of cotton until the invention of the cotton gin in 1793. The gin separated seeds from the fiber, replacing the slow and tedious method previously done by hand. As would-be planters eagerly sought their fortunes in cotton, the demand for slave labor dramatically rose. In 1808, however, the U.S. ban of the Atlantic slave trade forced plantation owners to look elsewhere for enslaved labor. One major source was Virginia, where the peak of tobacco planting reached its height during the eighteenth century and then fell. Soils were exhausted by the nineteenth century, and as large plantation holdings folded, the need for enslaved labor diminished. Thousands of enslaved Virginians were sold south. As ex-slave Lorenzo L. Ivy (Perdue et al. 1976:153) remembered, "Dey sol' slaves heah an everywhere. I've seen droves of Negroes brought in heah on foot goin' Souf to be sol.' " In re-creating their worlds, these displaced individuals formed new families and social networks, and learned the language of cotton planting. They also shared their cultural knowledge within these fledgling plantation communities, thereby spreading the influence of Afro-Virginian foodways to the Cotton Belt. Again, factors such as the surrounding environment, plantation rations, and the influx of diverse European immigrant groups also tempered the form of emergent foodways. Nonetheless, the omnipresence of enslaved blacks in the Deep South and their frequent interactions with whites facilitated their impact on southern foodways even within the "big house."

The enslaved black woman chef's sphere of influence within the plantation kitchen provided opportune moments to control food preparation and thus the menu. Slave-owning families, at least to some extent, consumed victuals routinely eaten within the slave quarter (Moore 1989:81). Furthermore, white mistresses probably learned a thing or two about black food preparation while supervising domestic work. As a consequence, they left indelible evidence of their appropriation of black recipes in at least one early cookbook.

Mary Randolph published Virginia's first cookbook in 1824 (Randolph 1993). No ordinary woman, Randolph was born to a prominent slave-owning family at Tuckahoe Plantation in 1762. Randolph's marriage to a wealthy tobacco planter brought her to Moldavia mansion along the James River, where her husband owned forty enslaved blacks. The recipes in her cookbook suggest that some credit for Randolph's culinary experience and expertise is due her enslaved cooks. Take, for instance, her instructions for preparing "ochra soup" (okra is indigenous to Africa; Randolph 1993:17–18): "Get... young ochra... put it into a gallon of water... in an earthen pipkin, or very nice iron pot; it must be kept steadily simmering, but not boiling... add three young cimlins [squash], a fowl, or knuckle of veal, a bit of bacon or pork that has been boiled, and six tomatos.... Have rice boiled to eat with it." Randolph provides a litany of recipes for preparing every kind of dish, including meals that bear more than just a passing similarity to the foods of enslaved blacks. She succeeds in erasing the connection by her failure to mention it. Given the racial climate of the time, and the extreme rarity of early African American cookbooks (Harris 2001; Zafar 1999:451), black knowledge claims of southern culinary traditions could easily be dismissed. Meanwhile, the overwhelmingly popular *The Virginia Housewife or, Methodical Cook* was reprinted up until 1860.

Racial categories as social constructs must continually be reinvented in order to serve the purpose of maintaining structural inequality. The use of racial stereotypes is instrumental in defining difference, and works at both conscious and unconscious levels as "ideological justifications" for white privilege and black subjugation (Collins 1991:65). Their power of persuasion is undeniable. Offensive racial stereotypes implicating black cultural practices such as foodways, however, did not deter whites from absorbing and re-creating black culinary innovations. Nor did their appropriation of black cultural forms compel them to relinquish white racial ideology. Witness the immortalized "Mammy" figure imposed upon black women cooks who "ruled the back rooms with simpleminded power" and "could work culinary miracles day in and day out, but couldn't for the life of them tell anyone how they did it. Their most impressive dishes were described as 'accidental' rather than planned" (Egerton 1993 as cited in Zafar 1999:449). As Rafia Zafar (1999: 449) observes, "These buffoonish characters were the fictive counterparts of legions of unknown culinary workers, African Americans whose legacy and labor shaped much of what we eat to this day" (see also Collins 1991: 67–90; hooks 1981:84–85; Combahee River Collective 1982; White 1985:46–61).

CONCLUSION: THE BLACK IN BLACK-EYED PEAS

The mass exodus of African Americans during the Great Migrations of the first half of the twentieth century brought thousands from the rural South to cities in the north and west. Although blacks were unable to raise fowl or livestock or keep gardens in urban areas, grocery store purchases were still transformed into meals remembered from home. Outside of the South, soul food eateries still thrive in black neighborhoods. Importantly, their expertise of southern foodways continues to be passed down to younger generations (Medearis 1997; Pinderhughes 1990; Smart-Grosvenor 1992; Smith 1991; Walker 2000; Zafar1999), although most of us do not rely solely on traditional African American fare, nor necessarily possess the ability to prepare it. Yet for many, black-derived foodways outside of a southern context serve foremost as a signifier of blackness and of cultural identity and heritage. That is, contemporary African Americans also racialize foodways and use them to authenticate and realize black identity. Cultural practices are often strategically essentialized by blacks as a means of establishing common ground and to acknowledge and broadcast a collective identity. Thus, what are perceived as traditional black foods are often served at family reunions, during special occasions such as Kwanzaa, and within the public realm at African American cultural and social events. Foodways are highly charged with meaning and, in turn, possess profound symbolic dimensions. For instance, black-eyed peas (or cowpeas, indigenous to Africa) are still cooked and consumed in black households from California to New York on New Year's to ensure good luck in the coming year. While white Southerners are also known to partake in this ritual, one can simply point to this practice throughout the Afro-Caribbean as evidence for its African diasporic roots (Thomas 2000; Walker 2000).

In tracing the lineage of black foodways, one will discover regional differences and other characteristic nuances that challenge the notion of a unified African American culinary tradition. My objective, however, was not to provide a definitive statement on black foodways. Instead, I have attempted to demonstrate how race and enslavement served as the catalysts for group identity formation amongst enslaved Virginians, and that this process could be interpreted using archaeological evidence. Foodways seemed a promising candidate for the obvious reasons that food-related remains are common on slave-associated sites, and excavated materials from Rich Neck provided a case study where faunal data could be compared over time. Further, foodways are steeped in symbolism and are customarily used to project group identity and to reinforce boundaries of socially constructed differences (Brown and Mussell 1984b; Kalcik 1984:46). From the evidence considered, I have argued that by the end of the century, the mostly creole enslaved Virginian population possessed kinship ties with generational depth and enacted a group identity forged within a diasporic context as they struggled to survive. Their creation of a novel foodways system illustrates their ability to pool knowledge and resources, and to develop strategies for assuring some level of autonomy in their lives. It was perhaps an unintended consequence of racialization and enslavement that these should in turn serve Afro-Virginians as mobilizing forces for negotiating race and culture, and implementing their own within-group construct of identity.

Notes

I would like to thank Chuck Orser for taking the initiative to compose a volume on race and archaeology; it is direly needed, and I am grateful to be a part of this groundbreaking project. I must also extend my deepest appreciation to Elizabeth Scott, who provided an intensive and constructive critique of my very rough first draft. Each author who has contributed to this volume also voiced extremely useful and encouraging feedback in a roundtable discussion. I would especially like to thank Bob Paynter, Laurie Wilkie, Terry Epperson, Jim Skibo, and an anonymous reviewer. Their insights and comments are reflected in what I hope is a stronger piece of scholarship. This research was possible through the generosity of the Colonial Williamsburg Foundation's Department of Archaeological Research, and the cooperation and support of Marley R. Brown III, Anna Agbe-Davies, and Ywone Edwards-Ingram. Finally, and importantly, my interpretations are based on the rigorous analysis of faunal and botanical materials by my colleagues Joanne Bowen, Steve Atkins, Leslie Driscoll, and Steve Mrozowski. Any errors and missed opportunities here are, of course, due to my own shortcomings.

1. There have been recent attempts to redefine the concept of the African diaspora by recognizing both historic migrations within the continent of Africa (e.g., Larson 1999) and contemporary African immigration to the United States, Europe, and other parts of the globe (e.g., Pierre 1999).
2. The subject of Chesapeake pipes (commonly found on seventeenth-century Tidewater sites) and who was responsible for creating them is one exception, but there are currently competing interpretations as to whether Africans may have been involved (Deetz 1993; Emerson 1994; Mouer et al. 1999). Research regarding the transformation of architecture and space as a result of the construction of racial difference and slavery is the remaining example (Epperson this volume; Epperson 1999).
3. The birth dates for these five individuals fall roughly between 1697 and 1707, when Africans began to enter the colony in large numbers. More than likely, these individuals arrived as young adults.
4. Both stewing (in pottery vessels) and baking were food preparation methods used also by the Powhatan Indians (Roundtree 1989: 50–53). As the English colonists learned how to cultivate and prepare maize, fish, and hunt native fauna from the Powhatan (Roundtree 1989), their potential influence on enslaved foodways should be considered. The Powhatans' subsistence skills may have entered the slave quarter indirectly through Virginian colonists, or directly from interactions between blacks and Indians, some of whom were enslaved. Indians certainly were still present in the Williamsburg area during the eighteenth century (Kern 1999), but more research is needed regarding the nature of their interactions with enslaved Afro-Virginians. However, it must be kept in mind that enslaved Africans did arrive in Virginia possessing these skills.
5. Opossum may have been overexploited by enslaved Virginians, resulting in their decline.

However, I have not come upon any sources that indicate this.

6. Although the authors note that urban and rural households did not rely heavily on wild species during the eighteenth century, their calculations were made by including several enslaved sites (including the Rich Neck slave quarter) with a larger number of Anglo-Virginian sites of varying socioeconomic status. Their objective was to compare rural to urban sites, and not enslaved blacks to white colonists. Using the data compiled from a range of faunal assemblages (see Walsh et al. 1997:223–277), I have specifically selected Anglo sites to compare with enslaved sites.
7. Walsh et al. (1997) do not cite which specific wild species were recovered from the six Anglo-Virginian sites.
8. Elizabeth Scott's (1998) study of a nineteenth-century Louisiana plantation suggests that this may be a distinctly Anglo practice, as French planters were discovered to consume more pig's head and feet than their enslaved Africans.
9. The exceptions include the heads of hogs and calves (e.g., Randolph 1993), but these were served on holidays such as Christmas and were not everyday fare.

7

Race, Identity, and Habermas's Lifeworld

Laurie A. Wilkie

Discussions related to the concept of identity have often focused on distinct aspects of identity such as gender, race, class, religion, or ethnicity, privileging one particular facet of representation and presentation over others. The end result of such analyses is the oversimplification of complex webs of social relations that individuals are constrained by and which they must manipulate as they negotiate the paths of everyday life. Sherry Ortner (1991, 1998, 1999), Ruth Frankenberg (1993), bell hooks (1992, 1994), and Karen Brodkin (1998a), among many others, have demonstrated how constructs such as race, gender, and ethnicity are not independently constructed and can only be understood together. Not only are these intersections the spaces in which identity is performed, they are also the arenas in which ideologies of inequality are constructed and imposed—what Patricia Hill Collins (2000:69–71) has called "intersecting oppressions."

The targeting of one particular aspect of identity over another is not necessarily a result of researcher bias or preference, but can reflect the displacement of discourses from one arena of identity to another. Sherry Ortner (1991) provides examples of such displacements in her discussions of class and culture, observing that vocabularies of class in the United States often become enmeshed in discourses on gender, sexuality, ethnicity, and race. Ortner states that "such displacements are not without their costs. If class is displaced into other arenas of social life, then to that extent these other arenas must be carrying a burden of what might be called 'surplus antagonism,' over and above whatever historical and structural frictions they embody in their own terms." In the case of class, Ortner has argued that class operates in society as an identity constructed by individuals as well as a structure that is "real" within it. I would argue that race operates in a similar manner: as an identity imposed upon and contended with by individuals, but also as a larger societal structure. In this regard, I have found Karen Brodkin's (1998a) conceptualization of ethnoracial assignment and ethnoracial identity to be useful. Brodkin (1998a: 3) writes: "It is important to make a conceptual distinction between ethnoracial assignment and ethnoracial identity. Assignment is about popularly held classifications and their deployment by those with national power to make them matter economically, politically, and socially to the individuals classified. We construct ethnoracial identities ourselves, but we do it within the context of ethnoracial assignment. However, even though ethnoracial assignment and ethnoracial identity are conceptually distinct, they are also deeply interrelated.

The distinctions marked by Brodkin emphasize how identities are both created and imposed upon actors. In struggling to understand the social contexts that allowed for Jewish people to shift from being perceived as a "not-quite-white" race to one that is "bright white," Brodkin asked many of the same questions of interest to me, among them, how do generations maintain continuities between them while also allowing for fluidity in the construction of identity? Speaking of her own experiences, Brodkin recounts how her parents' generation consider themselves foremost to be Jews, she sees herself as Jewish and white, and her sons self-identify primarily as white. Although her sons acknowledge their Jewish heritage, they have never experienced the extreme anti-semitism that marked their grandparents' lives, and thus do not feel the same need to construct identities explicitly tied to the Jewish community. This observation is not unlike those of Thomas Eriksen (1993) and other anthropologists (e.g., Jones 1997; Romanucci-Ross and De Vos 1995) who have argued that ethnogenesis is a politicized process that occurs as a response to racism. Brodkin's (1998a:104) description of the negotiation of Jewish ethnoracial identities during the first half of the twentieth century could easily characterize the internal dynamics of any ethnic group:

> The Lower East Side of New York City, like eastern European Jewish neighborhoods in other industrial American cities, was a community of workers and bosses, shopkeepers and socialists, radicals and rabbis who were tied together in a mixture of forced and voluntary interdependence. There was no shortage of conflict over economics and politics. Interminable conflicts over meaning in general, and the meaning of Jewishness in particular, all took place within a context of intense interdependence where Jews were exploited and ghettoized by the larger society. In this context, ethnic identity meant identification with a community that was coping with anti-Semitism and inventing dreams of something better. People in these communities used their Jewish heritage on a daily basis to institutionalize and negotiate the meanings, values, and acceptable variants of American ethnic Jewishness.

I include this quotation from Brodkin because it embodies the fluidity and contestation that mark the negotiations of group identities within communal settings. Brodkin's analysis is not essentialistic, nor does she ignore, even in this short passage, the intersection of other aspects of identity into her consideration of the construction of Jewishness. Within historical archaeology, the permanence of the objects that we study often encourages interpretations that describe cultural practice in equally static frameworks, often losing the momentary and reflexive meanings associated with artifacts (Hodder 1997).

Within my research, I continue to grapple with how gender roles, occupation, race, cultural heritage, and so on provide individuals and communities with the means to construct a multitude of representations of self given particular situations and contexts. As part of this process, I am interested in how a group's perception of its heritage and sense of tradition informs its collective identity construction. I am particularly interested in the ways that individuals navigate the racialized landscapes of everyday life and cope with identities that have been imposed upon them. My work is articulated with the larger practice of historical archaeology in a number of ways, not least of which is a commitment to making my research relevant to the broader African American public through the process of community partnering.

Following the lead of social historians and historical anthropologists (e.g., Brodkin 1998; Collins 2000; Thompson 1963; Gutman 1976b; Mullings 1997; Ignatiev 1995) archaeologists are increasingly interested in understanding how racial differences come to be constructed, reproduced, contested, and in some cases, inverted (e.g., Epperson 1990a, 1999b; Orser 1998b). This scholarship accompanies a growing awareness among archaeologists of the necessity of constructing research problems shaped by the input of descendant communities/community partners so that the construction of research agendas can become decolonized (e.g., McDavid and Babson 1997; McKee 1995).

Community partnering is essential to African American archaeological praxis, particularly since so many of the practitioners are white. As the growing body of literature exploring the issue of "whiteness" has demonstrated (e.g., hooks 1992, 1994; Frankenberg 1993; Wray and Newitz 1997), white people may not always self-reflexively be able to identify the ways that the experiences of white privilege have shaped our understandings of race and racism. As such, community partnering forces white archaeologists to engage in a multitude of discursive relationships that serve to inform archaeologists of the concerns of the communities in which they work, while also challenging them to engage in critical self-reflection.

Particularly important to the discussion of community partnering has been the work of archaeologists advocating critical theory in archaeology. Leone's (1995) and Potter's (1991, 1994) work at Annapolis and Michael Blakey's (La Roche and Blakey 1997) and others' (e.g., Epperson 1999b) research at New York's African burial ground, and Maria Franklin's article "Power to the People" (1997a) are all excellent examples of the call for critical approaches. For those of us who incorporate community partnering into our research, we find that issues of continuing interest to the African American public include the cultural influences of Africa on black life, and the impacts of living with racism on African American families. These issues are important to communities of varying regional, socioeconomic, and political backgrounds. A growing Afro-tourism industry increasingly demands that the black experience and African American cultural history be presented to the public. For myself, I have found it impossible to turn from issues regarding the construction of cultural and ethnic identities precisely because these are issues of great concern to the people whose pasts' I study.

It is clear that many African Americans I work with in Louisiana and the Bahamas perceive themselves to be part of a cultural continuum with authentic roots in Africa. There are multiple ways that individuals see themselves as connected to their cultural past. In some instances, the connection is seen as linear and unbroken, with traditions passed directly from one generation to another. Others credit certain members of their communities as having preserved important cultural knowledge otherwise forgotten by the majority. These cultural conservators then were depended upon to teach what had been lost to the broader community. We can, of course, question the "authenticity" of these perceptions of cultural transmission, but to do so would distract us from my point, which is that a sense of shared cultural histories and experiences shapes modern constructions of African American identity. Any study of African American identities should consider how the actors are situated relative not only to their social historical context, but also to their understandings of their cultural heritage. For instance, when we see archaeological evidence of cultural practices that seem uniquely African American in origin, are these practices that were consciously participated in by individuals to construct corporate or communal identities, or were participants unconsciously following traditions? Although attributing intention to archaeological actors can be problematic, interpretive implications can be vastly different depending upon how individuals perceive the nature of their interactions with their cultural heritage. Individuals may be social actors engaged in maneuvers designed to enhance their status within society, but these actions are shaped by concerns outside of class ambitions and the constraints of racism. While we cannot ascribe singular intentions to actors, we must work to ensure that we consider the range of actions available to them.

Black feminist bell hooks sees the connection to the cultural past as necessary for the decolonization and affirmation of contemporary African Americans. She writes:

> Since so many black folks have succumbed to the post-1960s notion that material success is more important then personal integrity, struggles for black self-

> determination that emphasize decolonization, loving blackness, have had little impact. As long as black folks are taught that the only way we can gain any degree of economic self-sufficiency or be materially privileged is by first rejecting blackness, our history and culture, then there will always be a crisis in black identity. Internalized racism will continue to erode collective struggle for self-determination. (hooks 1992:18)

As such, I perceive the study of African American identity to be a politically situated endeavor. My research, however, is focused on the microscalar level. It is my contention that to best understand the social webs that enable and constrain the construction of identities and representations of self, we must study the interaction of individuals at the household or community level (Wilkie 2000a). At this level of analysis, we can use oral history, material culture, and documentary evidence to explore social relationships and their intersection with the perception, performance, contestation, and construction of identities between actors. This kind of particularistic, microscalar level of historical archaeological analysis has been aptly nicknamed "archaeobiography" (Clark 1996:14). In this chapter, I will demonstrate the strength of such an approach by drawing upon a historical archaeological case study from late nineteenth-century to early twentieth-century Louisiana following the relationships between two generations of the African American Freeman family and their white employers, the Matthews.

Theoretically, I have found myself attempting different approaches to understanding the relationships between individuals and society and materials. Of late, I have found the works of Jürgen Habermas to be useful, particularly his theory of communicative action, in which human agency is recognized as operating within and being shaped by a cultural sphere. Although not considered a member of the Frankfurt School of critical theory, Habermas is nonetheless an important philosopher of a social theory designed to critically engage and ultimately bring about emancipatory thought and action. As such, the theory of communicative action provides an outlet not only for interpreting the actions of past peoples, but also for situating their actions in a framework designed to be politically empowering. My use of Habermas, however, should in no way be expected to be orthodox. I use Habermas's theory of communicative action as a structuring foundation for my discussion and as a framework for the presentation of a critically self-reflexive analysis, but I also employ feminist and race theory to inform my interpretations.

HABERMAS'S CONCEPT OF THE LIFE WORLD

Individuals act within society as constrained agents, always creating, renewing and contesting the web of relations that situate them in their social context (Ortner 1991, 1998, 1999). Habermas uses the term *lebenswelt* (lifeworld) to describe this collection of behaviors, expectations, norms, and communicative acts that comprise daily life and serve to link individuals (Habermas 1984, 1987): "In coming to an understanding with one another about their situation, participants in interaction stand in a cultural tradition that they at once use and renew in coordinating their actions by way of intersubjectively recognizing criticizable validity claims. They are at once relying on membership in social groups and strengthening the integration of those same groups through participating in interactions with competently acting reference persons. The growing child internalizes the value orientations of his social group and acquires generalized capacity for action" (Habermas 1987:137).

In Habermas's view, individuals interpret their surroundings through the observation and analysis of social action. In any given social situation in which actors find themselves, they turn to their personal experiences to determine how they are to navigate through the social landscape. In any particular context, individuals engaged in communicative action have numerous options. Through these means, culture is constantly renewed and recreated. The nuances of symbolic communication are learned from infancy onward. Life experiences form the basis of a person's social vocabulary. Although Habermas specifically deals with linguistically conveyed communicative action, material culture is widely recognized as another medium through which meaning can be communicated (e.g., Bourdieu 1977; Giddens 1984; Hodder 1997; Thomas 1993), and I will be employing Habermas's ideas as relevant to the study of materials. Certainly material culture should not be seen as an equivalent to language (a point that has been made by other archaeologists, such as Hodder 1997), but it is similar to language in that it can be used to signify and convey a multitude of meanings and embedded subtexts. Like language, materials can be manipulated to communicate and contest social positions and ideologies in social discourse. Through daily experiences, the practices of the lifeworld become routine and normalized. This idea mirrors Giddens's (1984) "practical consciousness." Habermas's lifeworld has implications for our understanding of the impacts of race and racism as structuring agents in society. For black and white people, the lived experiences of racism, white supremacy, and the inequity of opportunities would be part of normalized experience of everyday life. The internalization of white supremacist views of black people by black people has been identified by bell hooks (1992, 1994) as one of the long-lasting impacts of living in a colonized society.

> Decolonized progressive black individuals are daily amazed by the extent to which masses of black people (all of whom would identify themselves as antiracist) hold to white supremacist ways of thinking, allowing this perspective to determine how they see themselves and other black people. Many black folks see us as "lacking": as inferior when compared to whites. The paucity of scholarly work looking at the issue of black self-hatred, examining the ways in which the colonization and exploitation of black people is reinforced by internalized racial hatred via white supremacist thinking, is awesome. Few black scholars have explored extensively black obsession with whiteness. (hooks 1992:11)

Just as hooks argues that African Americans internalized the white supremacist views of the society in which they lived, European Americans have learned to live unquestioningly with the trappings of white privilege (Frankenberg 1993). Patricia Hill Collins (2000:69) writes, "These controlling images [stereotypes] are designed to make racism, sexism, poverty, and other forms of social injustice appear to be natural, normal, and inevitable parts of everyday life."

Yet race is not the only facet of identity that individuals learn in their lifeworld; from the earliest days of childhood, a person learns through lived experience and encounters the expectations placed upon them by their families and communities for the performance of self, as well as through the desires, ambitions, frustrations, and fears that characterize their lifeworld. The advantage of the lifeworld concept is that it allows us to explore the relationships between individuals and different representations of race, gender, ethnicity, class, and so on that they may encounter, without essentializing any particular aspect of these representations. Keeping this concept of the lifeworld as a cultural historical context in which social action is embedded, I turn now to an example from Louisiana.

THE LIFEWORLD OF WEST FELICIANA, LOUISIANA, C. 1870–1940

West Feliciana Parish is nestled in a curve of the Mississippi River, just south of the Louisiana-Mississippi border. During the antebellum period, the parish was part of the lucrative Mississippi River cotton belt, home to more millionaires than anywhere else in the country. In many parts of the plantation South farms were characterized by small, if any, slaveholdings, but in West Feliciana, more than 8 percent of the planters owned fifty or more slaves (Wilkie 2000b). The commercial centers of the parish were the twin towns of St. Francisville and Bayou Sara, the former perched on a bluff above the Mississippi, the latter situated in the river's floodplain. Bayou Sara was a small but busy port town, sending out loads of cotton and receiving supplies and luxuries from the southern cities of Baton Rouge and New Orleans, until the infamous flood of 1929, when the town was destroyed by the raging river.

In 1890, African Americans comprised 84.9 percent of West Feliciana's population. By 1930, this figure had dropped to 76.4 percent, and in 1960, to 66.1 percent. In 1970, at least 50 percent of the parish population was still African American. Despite a demographic majority, African Americans have historically been politically, socially, and economically disenfranchised within the parish. This circumstance can be traced to the period following Reconstruction. The post-Reconstruction control of government by the Democratic Party stripped African Americans of the few social, economic, and political gains they had made during Emancipation. In West Feliciana, some of the plantations had begun to rebuild, and new industries, including timber and paper production, were developed. Agricultural and timber pursuits were both built primarily on underpaid African American labor (Wilkie 2000b).

Although West Feliciana never rebuilt its cotton industry to antebellum levels of production, cotton remained an important element of the economy. Plantations also came to place greater emphasis on the production of cattle, corn, and sweet potatoes, and greater numbers of individuals became involved in the timber industry. Cotton, despite its declining contribution to the parish's overall economy, continued to be farmed by African American sharecroppers through the 1950s. African Americans also turned to other means of employment, such as seasonal treks across the river to work loading cane and harvesting sweet potatoes. In 1964, West Feliciana parish produced fewer than 1,000 bales of cotton. In contrast, the top cotton-producing parishes in Louisiana at that time were producing more than 50,000 bales (Wilkie 2000b).

Today West Feliciana is reported to have one of the highest levels of poverty in the state. The area that was once part of the wealthy cotton belt is now a rural area dependent on a nuclear power station, the lumber industry, a paper mill, a cannery, and plantation home tourism for its livelihood. The high poverty level among African Americans in the parish is the legacy of the tenancy system, especially sharecropping, which was the primary form of employment for black Felicianians until the 1940s (Wilkie 2000b).

Although planters were first encouraged to employ freed-persons as wage laborers, tenancy and sharecropping became the standard labor arrangement during the postbellum period. Some planters viewed sharecropping as the means through which blacks and whites helped one another rebuild the South's agricultural industry. While the South's lack of abundant currency during Reconstruction may have encouraged the development of sharecropping systems, sharecropping ultimately became the new slavery, providing planters with maximum labor for minimum expenditure, and leaving African Americans trapped in poverty.

There were three primary forms of tenancy arrangements: cash tenancy, share tenancy, and sharecropping (see Orser 1988). Cash tenants owned their work animals and tools, could provide their own keep during the year, and paid only a flat fee for the use of a plot of land and house (Conrad 1965; S. Jones 1985). Being a cash tenant was perceived by African Americans as the best position in which to be, but also the most difficult to obtain. Share tenants were less independent than cash tenants. Share tenants owned most of their work animals, feed, and seed, and had the option to obtain cash credit. In return, they turned over a quarter to a third of their crop to the landowners. Under this labor arrangement it was still possible to earn a profit (Conrad 1965). The most infamous and common of the labor arrangements was sharecropping. Sharecroppers had only their labor to offer. Sharecropping families were both African American and European American in descent, but African Americans rarely were able to obtain renting or share-renting arrangements (Conrad 1965).

A sharecropping family was dependent on store credit to pay for household and agricultural supplies and goods until their crop was ready. At that time, they would pay half of their crop plus the portion of their share of the crop needed to pay their bills for the past year (Conrad 1965; S. Jones 1985). The "settle" (the annual balancing of the books) took place after the cotton had been harvested and the value of the crop calculated. The sharecropper's debts were then subtracted from their "share." Planters were notorious for underestimating the value of the tenant's crop and overestimating their debts. Such a system ensured that sharecropping families were kept in debt from year to year, unable to move from the plantation without somehow repaying the debt.

Sharecropping is said to have been established in the Felicianas as early as 1865 (Taylor 1974:374). Much has been written about the experiences of the sharecropper and the exploitative nature of this employment arrangement (e.g., Agee and Evans 1941; Conrad 1965; Gaines 1971; Maguire 1975; Orser 1987). Sharecropping under any managerial circumstances was a difficult way to earn a living, and almost impossible to escape from financially. Under unscrupulous management, sharecropping was often worse than slavery. Sharecroppers had no legal recourse when cheated by a planter. By overcharging croppers for the use of equipment, charging exorbitant interest rates on plantation store purchases, and lying outright, a white planter could ensure that a tenant family did not grow enough crops to pay their bills. Failure to pay one's bill required a family to stay on at that plantation for an additional year, or however long was necessary to repay the amount. In such a way, sharecropping became a means of creating a system of debt peonage. Families would sometimes trade everything they owned to pay a debt and escape from a particular plantation (Clayton 1990; Gaines 1971; S. Jones 1985; Maguire 1975). In at least one case in West Feliciana, tenants organized an effective boycott in the 1870s, when one European American planter, recognized by his peers as a good businessman, but a poor manager, was said to be unable to keep any African American tenants on his place (Wilkie 2000a). However, such displays of social disobedience could also have negative backlashes.

Planters thought African Americans, due to their temperament and physical attributes, to be best suited for hard farm labor. In a 1930 essay on agrarianism, Robert Penn Warren (1930:260–261) wrote, "In the past, the Southern Negro has always been a creature of the small town and farm. That is where he still chiefly belongs, by temperament and capacity; there he has less the character of a 'problem' and more the status of a human being who is likely to find in agricultural and domestic pursuits the happiness that his good nature and the easy ways incline him as an ordinary function of his being."

The white population of West Feliciana were unabashedly supremacist in their politics. In May 30, 1908, an editorial in the Bayou Sara *True Democrat* hailed the success of the poll tax first instituted in 1898 and admonished against repealing it. "In the prescriptions of this article is due the elimination of the Negro as a factor in politics in Louisiana. Only a few of the thousands of Negroes in Louisiana have paid or will pay their poll tax...to repeal this prerequisite to citizenship will encourage the Negroes to register and vote. It will be a menace to peace and order, it will be a threat to white supremacy." Another editorial, on March 21 of that year, reminded readers that no matter how discouraged they might be with the Democratic Party, not to vote Republican, for "so long as the Fifteenth Amendment remains part of the Constitution, the Republican party is a menace to Southern people." The right of African American men to vote had not become any less an issue over the nearly fifty years since the Civil War.

Not surprisingly, the racism of the political arena was only a reflection of the racism that tinted all interactions between the two races. In 1892, prisoners from the parish jail were used as laborers to repair crevasses in the levee. This was the first time such action had been taken, and it was applauded by the editors of the October 13, 1892 *True Democrat:* "If this course is continued, our jail will become a less favored resort. The average Negro's idea of bliss is plenty of meat and bread, and plenty of time to doze away the hours of the day, conditions currently met by our jails." The perceived natural laziness, lack of moral fortitude, and uncontrolled sexuality of the African American population were common themes expressed in the *True Democrat* and representative of Southern views in general (e.g., hooks 1992, 1994; Fox-Genovese 1988; Gaspar and Hine 1996; Lemann 1991; Terrill and Hirsch 1978). The black family was seen as volatile, unstable, and virtually nonexistent. On January 21, 1893, the *True Democrat* applauded what was perceived to be "a local movement among the colored population which is certainly a step in the right direction. An effort is being made in all the churches here to purge its members from transgressions of the seventh commandment, and as a consequence, there has been an increase in marrying and giving in marriage." In contrast, oral history interviews demonstrate that marriage was always a desired state in the African American community of West Feliciana. Most weddings took place within black Baptist churches. A review of marriage records for the parish, however, suggests that black couples, but not white couples, were charged fifty dollars to obtain a legal marriage. Most of them could not afford this fee and, as a result, were never legally married in the eyes of the parish.

Miscegenation was undoubtedly one of the most commonly used excuses for violence against black men. Whites perceived black men's sexual urges as being uncontrollable and thus a threat to white women's virtue, and this fear was used to justify segregation in the postbellum period (Litwack 1998; Lemann 1991:37; Roberts 1997). If the feelings of white Louisianans were not already clear on this issue, in 1894 the Louisiana legislators made interracial marriages illegal. White men argued that retribution was required against any black man who might insult the reputation or person of a white woman. The form of retribution was often swift and drastic. In 1892, an article in the *True Democrat* endorsed lynching, claiming, "Criminal assault by Negroes upon white women are of such frequent occurrence as to appear epidemic, and men are almost afraid to leave their homes when they are the least bit isolated. From all over the South come almost daily reports of these horrible crimes, and though usually vengeance is wrecked upon the transgressors, the vigorous measures often adopted seem to have slight influence in checking these brutal assaults. We are opposed to mob violence in most instances, yet we know of no surer, speedier or more effective mode of suppressing such crimes than by lynching the perpetrator."

Despite the emphasis on lynching as a justified tool for protecting the virtue of Southern white women, it is clear from newspaper articles through the 1890s that any perceived or actual crime could be considered punishable by lynching. From 1892 to 1896, one attempted and two successful lynchings were described in the *True Democrat.* Not surprisingly, miscegenation was not involved in any of the cases.

An 1894 lynching began as an attempt by a group of white men to whip Vincent Withers, who had been accused of burning a white man's barn. The *True Democrat* reported the story under the headline "An Unfortunate Event": "Withers was called out, but instead of answering the summons, opened fire on the party. He evidently had assistance, as fire was opened upon the assailants from the other side of the house. As a result, J. F. Roberts, Jr., of Laurel Hill fell dead, shot through the breast by Withers, and young Stevenson Reed, on the other side was shot in the left arm and side. After firing, Withers ran from the house when the party fired on him several times. The following morning he was found hanging to a tree."

In 1892, another African American, George Rucker, was shot and killed in a general store after being surrounded by a hostile crowd. The May 26, 1892, *True Democrat* reported in this case that there were rumors the crowd threatened to hang Rucker before gunfire began. Another group of white men went to the St. Francisville jail in 1893 in an attempt to lynch William Jackson, who had already been sentenced to fifteen years at the Baton Rouge penitentiary. The sheriff's refusal to release Jackson to the men was praised in the *True Democrat,* which stated that lynching was inappropriate in this case because the targeted victim had already been convicted to a reasonable sentence. Lynching, it was stated, "should only be done when the crime is so heinous instant justice is required." Violence characterized black and white communities alike in the postbellum South, but it is interracial violence that underscores the tension between the two groups and the inaccessibility of legal recourse to African Americans.

Access to justice under the law was not the only liberty denied to African Americans in West Feliciana Parish. The education of black students in the parish was well below the standards of that offered to the white population, although it is important to note that the availability of any education to African Americans was an improvement over the period of enslavement. Black public education was poorly funded in the Felicianas, and the local black communities had to pay their own teachers on a regular basis (Hall 1966). Until the 1950s, schooling for African Americans in West Feliciana was only available to the eighth grade. All but one of the African American schools in West Feliciana were run from churches until the mid-1900s (Hall 1966).

African Americans in West Feliciana did what they could to provide for the needs of their communities. On Star Hill Plantation, not far from Oakley Plantation, the Morning Star Society was founded. This society was said to have been organized in 1869 by Dr. Perkins, the owner of Star Hill, to help his ex-slaves learn to care for themselves, but such societies are well known throughout West Africa and were established throughout the New World (Lincoln and Mamiya 1990). The society was funded and maintained solely by the African American congregation. The society offered medical and burial benefits to its members at a cost of fifty cents per month. If a member missed a monthly meeting, that person was fined an additional fifty cents (Simmons 1942). The members of the Morning Star community also aided in the founding of similar organizations at other churches, including Mt. Pilgrim, the church attended by the tenants of Oakley (Simmons 1942:12).

ARCHAEOLOGICAL RESEARCH AT OAKLEY PLANTATION

Oakley Plantation was typical of many West Feliciana's plantations. During the antebellum period, the planter family of Oakley had owned as many as 250 enslaved people and produced hundreds of bales of cotton annually. The plantation was abandoned and fell into ruin during the Civil War, but was rebuilt by descendents of the first owners into a modest cotton-producing venture during the postbellum period, depending on the labor of twenty to thirty tenant families in any given year. Cotton production stopped at the plantation in 1949, when the land and surviving buildings were sold to the State of Louisiana to be preserved as a state park. Archaeological research took place at Oakley from 1991 to 1994, with large-scale excavations focusing on two African American house sites that collectively had been occupied from the 1840s to 1949. My discussion will focus on excavations at the Freeman house, the late nineteenth-century to early twentieth-century home of two generations of the Freeman family.

Discussions with former Oakley Plantation workers and their descendants were part of my archaeological research and revealed that this period of plantation life remains an important component of many African American families' narratives (Wilkie 2001). For many members of the descendant communities, as a university instructor, I was seen as a vehicle for educating younger generations of African Americans. Many individuals stressed how important it was for their children and grandchildren to understand how hard life had been and how much progress they had made.

Intimately tied to these narratives of success were stories about community strength: the importance of ethnic solidarity, mutual dependence, religious faith, and commitment to education (Wilkie 2000a). Community collaborators would tell about the efforts of any given tenant population to maintain and improve educational opportunities for their communities, and to support one another financially in times of hardship and illness. The proud stories of successful escape from an oppressive economic regime were always paired with nostalgia for the sense of community that had endured and, to their minds, was missing from contemporary society. A renewal of this sense of community was often suggested by community partners as a means of saving imperiled elements of African American society. The community clearly had an understanding of the factors that had contributed to their successful emancipation from the economic situation of the plantation, and wanted that understanding to be explored through the archaeology of plantation life.

It is important to note, at this juncture, that the incorporation of community partners into this kind of research is not so that descendants can have archaeologists write histories of their pasts that suit their current self-images or political needs. Instead, working with community partners allows researchers to recognize that certain issues and questions regarding the past that are important to descendants do not necessarily correspond to the intellectual fads of the academy. The discursive relationship between archaeologists and informants challenges not only the archaeologists, who have to consider different research avenues and interpretations, but also the descendants, who through the interpretive process self-reflect upon their understandings of their history.

While the community members' understanding of their past has been a vital part of interpreting archaeological remains for the broader public, their understandings have raised important questions to consider critically. How did the process of acquiring freedom from the plantation ultimately serve to extinguish the sense of community that had enabled this freedom in the first place? To use the words of Habermas, how did the African American lifeworld come to change so radically as to be unrecognizable to its inhabitants? This question shaped archaeological consideration of two generations of a single African American family whose members made the transition from tenancy to wage labor.

THE FREEMAN FAMILY

Silvia Freeman and her husband, Lewis, worked as sharecroppers throughout their marriage. Married in 1875, they had nine children, only five of whom lived beyond infancy. By the time Lewis died—sometime around 1885—the couple's oldest children, John and Joe, had entered their teens, accustomed to the lifeworld of the sharecropping community. A young widow with five children, Silvia Freeman seems to have caught the attention of the owner of Oakley Plantation, Isabelle Matthews. Silvia was promoted to the position of planter cook, and moved from the quarters to a house near the planter residence.

During her adult life, Silvia Freeman would experience the height of racial violence in Louisiana following the close of Reconstruction and lasting until the institution of Jim Crow laws. The opportunities for employment for African American workers in rural West Feliciana parish were limited to share-farming, the timber industry, and for the lucky few, service positions in the homes of white families. Essentialist racial notions held by the white community shaped the economic, educational, social, and political opportunities available to the African American community. Archaeological investigations of this house have allowed for new insights concerning this period of change in the life of

Silvia Freeman as she operated as a constrained individual living within a volatile racial landscape (Wilkie 2000a).

Silvia Freeman's occupational shift to cook represented an important economic advancement for her family. Silvia now worked for wages, not credit. In 1890, she was the highest paid wageworker at four dollars a month. The move also had significant implications for Silvia Freeman's time: domestic servants worked long hours, often at the beck and call of the planter family. This increased contact time with the planter placed domestics in the uncomfortable position of being seen as an information conduit connecting the tenants and planters. Relationships between black domestics and white employers were marked by a range of racial, gender, class, and power tensions that manifested themselves in a range of material expressions. In the case of the Freeman and Matthews families, the relationships between servant and employer consisted of an additional complex layer of social relationships between black and white women. Isabelle Matthews was Freeman's first employer, followed by her two spinster daughters, Lucy and Ida. Feminist scholars (e.g., Brodkin 1998a; hooks 1992, 1994; Frankenberg 1993) have demonstrated that there are dual images of womanhood in the United States: that of mothers for white woman, and that of workers for women of color. In contrast to white women, women of color have been traditionally represented as neglectful and unnatural mothers (Brodkin 1998a; Roberts 1997). As will be discussed below, tensions between these dual constructions of womanhood can be seen in the interactions between Freeman and the Matthews family.

Although domestics were paid in wages, their earnings were rarely sufficient to support themselves. Silvia Freeman was the highest paid of the Oakley wage earners with her salary of $4.00 a month in 1889–1891 (Oakley Collection 1817–1949). Other workers were paid $2.50 or $3.00 a month. Employers "supplemented" low wages with gifts of hand-me-down housewares. "Toting," a common practice that allowed servants to take home the remainders of the planter's meals, decreased their food expenses but also provided them less control over their families' diets. Interviews conducted by Susan Tucker (1988) with black domestics and white employers revealed the resentment that other types of "gifts" could inspire. Some women described being given ratty garments that they threw away as soon as they were out of sight of their employers' home, while others expressed the desire to have been compensated with higher wages instead. A few women, however, admitted being grateful for the gifts.

Charity in the form of used and ratty housewares would reinforce the power differential between the two parties while also reasserting the notion that black women were somehow incapable of properly caring for themselves or their children. Comparisons of the Matthews' and Freeman families' ceramic assemblages revealed that items and patterns found in the 1880s Matthews' assemblage were duplicated in the 1890s and 1900s assemblages of the Freemans. A comparison of faunal remains from the two sites revealed few differences between the species of meat being consumed by the two families, suggesting that the dietary preferences of the planter family shaped the diet of the Freemans through the practice of toting. Among the hand-me-down gifts provided to the Freemans were ceramic dolls and tea sets. Some of these items recovered from the Freeman residence were identical to those once belonging to the Matthews' children and now curated in the Oakley House. Not only did these white-faced porcelain dolls and numerous tea sets expose the Freeman children to the material trappings of the upper classes, but they also reinforced notions of white beauty and encouraged play revolving around skills of domesticity and service (Wilkie 1994, 2000b). These gifts could certainly be seen as an example of the planter family injecting their values and attitudes about race into the Freeman family.

While these relations between the Freeman

and the Matthews families were an important aspect of Silvia's new position, a striking feature of the archaeological assemblage associated with Silvia Freeman was the degree to which she maintained ties to the sharecropping community (Wilkie 2000a). Archaeological data clearly demonstrate that Freeman participated in bartering transactions with the sharecropping community, providing tenants who lived on credit with an alternative source of goods (Wilkie 2000a). Tenants and wageworkers alike had two means of procuring goods on credit at Oakley. The Matthews ran a small commissary in the back of their house that was stocked with some fresh meat, dairy products, a range of dry goods, and a limited number of other household supplies. The commissary was mainly used by wageworkers, who had their purchases deducted from their upcoming wages. For the broader tenant population, the Matthews maintained credit accounts with several general merchandisers and pharmacies in the towns of Bayou Sara and St. Francisville. Tenants could obtain goods at these locations, buying them against the Matthews' accounts. The Matthews were sent monthly bills. As a wage earner, Silvia was able to help sharecroppers minimize their debts to the planter family by purchasing goods they wanted and then trading them for home produce. Ledger entries show Freeman spent at least 25–40 percent of her income annually on tobacco, which she seems to have exchanged for fresh and home-canned fruits and vegetables that are evidenced archaeologically, but not in the documentary record. Also, Freeman is recorded in ledgers as withdrawing cash against her wages, suggesting that she also purchased goods or services outside of the commissary. Freeman does not appear as charging against any of the Matthews in-town store accounts. We can presume that the opportunity to spend her earnings in ways that could not be tracked by the planters must have been a welcome relief to someone who otherwise constantly negotiated her daily life in view of the great house. Freeman participated in the broader plantation community in other ways as well. Documentary evidence demonstrates that participation in the community church was important to Silvia, and that the church-run school educated her children.

Archaeological evidence also suggests that Freeman continued to rely on ethnically distinct medical and magical practices that served to tie her to the community (Wilkie 1996). These ethnomedical and spiritual practices reflected many different cultural and historical influences and processes. Oral history interviews have revealed that mass-produced products were often incorporated into medicinal and magical repertoires as a means of masking their uses in African American medicinal and spiritual practice. I would like to briefly discuss one specific example, since the purchase and use of this particular product can clearly be seen as communicating a number of different agendas and meanings.

Paul Mullins (1999b) has recently suggested that middle-class African American families in late nineteenth-century urban Annapolis selected for national brands over individual pharmacists' products as a strategy to ensure consistent quality and packaging. The rural community of Oakley seems to have adopted an alternative strategy. Ledgers and pharmacy receipts demonstrate that tenants were using pharmacists' goods in abundance as well as a number of national brands. Pharmacy bottles are not represented very well in the assemblages, but this factor is probably due to the levying of deposits on these bottles, designed to encourage their return. Other bottles at Oakley seem to have been reused, since they were recovered broken. The one exception to this trend was "Dr. Tichenor's Antiseptic," which was the most commonly recovered medicine from each of the postbellum assemblages at Oakley, and is well represented at other African American sites in Louisiana. The product is still immensely popular among black and white populations in Louisiana. Dr. Tichenor was a surgeon in the Confederate Army who decided to market his special antiseptic after the

Civil War. He first patented his product in 1883, working out of New Orleans (Fike 1987:123); however, historical evidence clearly demonstrates that the product was advertised and sold in Louisiana as early as 1872 (Gill 1997). The antiseptic was advertised as having the same benefits as many African herbal teas for treating internal and external medical complaints, including diarrhea, headaches, sore throats, colds, fevers, cuts, bumps, and bruises. Peppermint extract and alcohol were the two primary ingredients of Dr. Tichenor's Antiseptic. Mint, taken as a tea or a bath, is recognized by African Americans in the Caribbean and Louisiana as beneficial for curing chills, fevers, and diarrhea (Biben 1993; Jordan 1986). Peppermint tea was also popular as a handwash to bring good luck, or for washing bad luck away from a house's doorstep. All of these uses have been attributed to Dr. Tichenor's Antiseptic as well during oral history interviews. The product's popularity among African Americans at Oakley may be due to its similarity to the traditional remedy. Through the selection of consumer products that fit their ethnomedical expectations, African Americans were able to appropriate and reconstitute the meanings of these products within their community.

Just as the African American community's preferences for commercially produced medicine preferences reinforced a sense of a shared ethnomedical tradition, the selection of specific products could also be used to construct identities during negotiations with those beyond the limits of the plantation community. While Dr. Tichenor's Antiseptic is intriguing from the perspective of its potential ethnomedical significance, this product may have served as a symbol of multiple meanings in negotiations with general store owners. Reviews of ledgers reveal that the Oakley Plantation commissary never stocked this particular product. Families therefore had to obtain the product from general merchants in the towns of St. Francisville or Bayou Sara. Dr. Tichenor, as an advertising ploy to attract customers loyal to the Confederacy, used packaging that emphasized his status as a Confederate veteran. The box and bottle label of Dr. Tichenor's Antiseptic bore graphic imagery depicting a Confederate soldier killing a Union soldier with a bayonet. While the imagery of the label graphically suggested anti-Unionist sentiment, there is historical evidence that the product was also seen as promoting white supremacism. In 1872, shortly after the product was introduced, it was one of the products advertised by vans in the Rex Mardi Gras parade (Gill 1997:99). Rex, among other Mardi Gras Krewes, were explicitly white supremacist in their membership and focus. That such a product should be selected for so consistently by African American consumers was at first confusing to me. I first considered the possibility that the product was somehow forced upon African American consumers as a symbolic means of reinforcing the Southern racial hierarchy. Upon further consideration, however, I revisited this interpretation.

Unlike many other southern facilities, such as schools, churches, restaurants, and dance halls, stores were not racially segregated. All of the general merchants with whom the Matthews had accounts were white. Black and white patrons alike would come into contact in the store setting. African American authors such as Maya Angelou (1969), Ernest Gaines (1971, 1976, 1983) and Alice Walker (1973) have used general stores in their fiction as arenas for racial conflict and tension. As previously discussed, much of the racial violence in West Feliciana after emancipation took place in the town centers, and in at least two instances, immediately outside of general stores. The social discourse between black customers and white customers, as well as between the white proprietor and black customers, could be fraught with tension. By purchasing a product associated with white supremacy, as Dr. Tichenor's was in the ideology of its packaging, an African American consumer might have appeared to make a statement of accommodation to white individuals in the store. Therefore, the product served as a fluid symbol, used for one meaning in the public realm and for another within the home. It is interesting, then, to note that these bottles seem to have been discarded whole rather than being reused, even while other medicine bottles of equivalent size apparently were reused. Perhaps the packaging was distasteful enough to discourage reuse.

The children of Silvia and Lewis Freeman were ultimately all employed in some manner by the Matthews family. John worked as a yard hand until he married and moved back to Oakley Plantation as a sharecropper. Joe worked as the carriage driver until, following his brother's lead, he married and began to farm a plot of land. Thus, these brothers reentered the lifeworld of their parents, away from the economic advantages of life in the planter's house, in the community of their childhood. Whether this represented a conscious or willing choice on their parts is unclear.

This intersection of gender and race may have led to their banishment from the planter's house. Young black boys or elderly "uncles" were not a threat to white women, but young black men were. I introduced earlier Sherry Ortner's idea that those arenas of identity that are ignored discursively can produce tensions that are displaced into other arenas of social interaction, in turn amplifying tensions in those discourses. While Ortner uses class as her example, I would argue that hidden racial discourses produce the same tensions. A number of historical documents demonstrate that the Matthews sisters considered themselves to be broader minded than many of their contemporaries regarding race relations (Wilkie 2000a). Likewise, during oral history interviews, informants characterized both women as fair and honest with their tenants. In particular, one tenant remembered how Ida had requested that a number of her tenants, rather than family members, serve as her pallbearers, an action seen by the informant as evidence of her care, love, and open-mindedness. Yet, there is no evidence that any adult black man served in any capacity within their home. If any black men should have seemed "safe" to these women, it should have been Silvia Freeman's sons, who had gown up on their plantation, in the yard of their house. Racist anxieties could have been displaced into other arenas, such as the evaluation of job performance or other similar confrontations in the course of employer-employee relationships, culminating in termination or just enough strain that John and Joe Freeman found the life of sharecropping preferable to that of the house.

These brothers' lifestyles contrast with that of their sisters, Delphine and Eliza. During their childhood, Silvia Freeman's three youngest children, Eliza, Delphine, and Christine, also worked for the Matthews. As part of their interactions with the planter family, the Freemans received a variety of hand-me-downs. These younger daughters had not experienced the lifeworld of the sharecropping community for any memorable length of their lives. Instead, the lifeworld to which they belonged was a dual world of contrast between their mother's former life and the examples set before them by the planter family. The value orientations internalized by the younger Freeman children were drawn from these conflicting worlds.

Habermas (1987:169) has written that "on the basis of an increasingly sharp dichotomy between high and popular cultures, classes develop their own milieus, lifeworlds and value orientations specific to the various strata." For at least two of the Freeman daughters, Delphine and Eliza (Christine Freeman has not been traced further historically), the lifeworld of the household servant became their sole realm of experience. Following Silvia's death, Delphine and Eliza continued to live in their mother's house, working respectively as cook and house servant. Their occupations clearly placed them in a social class distinct from that of the farming families. The archaeological record shows less evidence than it did for their mother of the maintenance of ethnic practices that would have tied them to the broader community (Wilkie 2000a). The sisters placed greater emphasis on mass-produced medical goods. Little evidence exists for a continuation of their mother's spiritual practices, and there is no evidence of bartering with the tenant community. The tablewares, clothing, and dietary remains from the site demonstrate the sisters' increasing participation in the material world of the planter family. Delphine and Eliza even had access to such luxury items as a phonograph.

The sisters' upward mobility had consequences for the way that they were perceived within the broader African American community of the plantation. Several former Oakley tenants who had personally known Eliza and Delphine as well as John and Joe Freeman did not realize that the four were siblings (Wilkie 2000b). Oral history also indicates that the sisters' closest friend was the wife of another wageworker. Aside from this relationship, the sisters seem to have been relatively isolated from the rest of the African American community, not to mention the communicative acts that comprised this lifeworld. The structure of domestic service—its time demands as well as geographic isolation—limited the possibility for interactions, not only with sharecroppers, but also with other wageworkers. In the racially segregated world of the postbellum South, the sisters may have achieved greater financial autonomy than possible under sharecropping, but they did so at the expense of social relationships within the local community. As bell hooks (1992:19) observed, "One of the tragic ironies of contemporary black life is that individuals succeed in acquiring material privilege often by sacrificing their positive connection to black culture and black experience." The study of the Freemans would suggest the trade-off identified by bell hooks as a facet of contemporary black life can be seen at the last turn-of-the-century.

With their participation in the lifeworld of domestic service, the Freeman sisters accepted a labor arrangement not available to the sharecropping community. While sharecroppers were still largely involved in subsistence agriculture, domestic servants were selling their labor and, as a result, were severed from their former lifeworld. Habermas (1987:309) might characterize the experience of the Freemans as typical of individuals who become incorporated within capitalist organizations: "Organizations not only disconnect themselves from cultural commitments and from attitudes and orientations specific to given personalities; they also make themselves independent from lifeworld contexts by neutralizing the normative background of informal, customary, morally regulated contexts of action. The social is not absorbed as such by organized action systems; rather, it is split up into spheres of action constituted as the lifeworld and spheres neutralized against the lifeworld."

It can be argued that one cost of capitalism is the destruction of "traditional forms of life" (Habermas 1987:321). The Freeman sisters had options to a life of domestic service; their brothers provided them an entree into the tenant community. While reinforcing ties to lateral kinship networks and community, such an option would have also tied the sisters to an oppressive labor regime. The oppressive labor structures of the postbellum South forced families into a paradoxical situation: to take advantage of the economic improvements made possible by the lifeworld of their community, they had to contribute to the destruction of that lifeworld.

To understand the possible motives of individuals like the Freeman sisters, who seemingly abandoned their families and communities in exchange for the commodification of their labor, we must consider the other kinds of relationships that bound these women. Individuals willingly participate in capitalist systems, embracing an ideology that promises that hard work will be rewarded with social mobility and improvement in the quality of life. One means of evaluating social mobility is through a consideration of one's ascending and descending kinship relations. In part, the experiences of their mother, her elevation to the position of most trusted and highly paid servant on the plantation, would have served as authentication of ideology for the sisters. Sherry Ortner (1991:171) writes, "Because hegemonic American culture takes both the ideology of mobility and the ideology of individualism seriously, explanations for nonmobility not only focus on the failure of individuals (because they are said to be inherently lazy, or stupid or whatever), but shift the domain of discourse to arenas that are taken to be 'locked into' individuals—gender, race, ethnic origin, and so forth." As the Freeman sisters became immersed in American capitalist discourses and ideologies, their views of others would have been accordingly reshaped. The economic hardships of the sharecroppers and other tenants could have been seen as the end result of individual shortcomings, not the result of the structures of racism that had created the economic system. In such a way, the atomization of the individual, so prevalent under capitalist systems, would have served to mask the structures of racial inequality inherent in the economy of the South. As part of the ideology of capitalism, laborers also work under the belief that their children will be more successful than their parents. In this light, the transition to wage labor, even at the cost of weakened social and lateral kin relations, such as that with their brothers, served as an investment in the Freeman sisters' children. Although neither sister married, each had a daughter. Much as Eliza and Delphine had, their children grew up in the shadow of the great house, with all of the privileges and drawbacks that this lifeworld entailed. Archaeological evidence demonstrates that the Matthews continued to provide porcelain toys to the Freemans' children, suggesting the continuing influence of the planter family in the construction of racial identities in their families.

While the Freeman sisters specifically chose between farming and service, their choice was not very different from other sharecropping families who took advantage of circumstances that allowed them to enter the workforce as wage laborers. It is clear from the Freeman example, however, that the shift from one labor arrangement to another can lead to the alienation of the individual from the traditional lifeworld of their community. For the descendants of the wage laborers, the financial improvements in their lifestyle were tempered by their memories of the lifeworld left behind.

Ironically, even though sharecropping was a labor arrangement that led to the institution of a system of debt peonage, sharecropping families still maintained limited control over their production and were able to focus part of their household labor on subsistence goods that could be used to feed themselves or traded for other goods (Adams 1980; Adams and Smith 1985; Gaines 1971; Maguire 1975; Mandle 1983; Orser 1988b). Trade between households was a form of communicative action that aided in the re-creation of the lifeworld. Within sharecropping communities, certain individuals moved between a variety of occupations, serving as root doctors, preachers, teachers, midwives, or conjurers. The exchange of specialized services, such as ethnomedical and magical services or education, also served to create tighter webs of social relations between individuals and households (Wilkie 1994, 2000a). Improved educational opportunities provided a means for individuals to acquire wage-labor positions in towns and cities (Lemann 1991), but in selling their labor, families lost those limited opportunities for home production. As the archaeological materials from the Freeman family demonstrate, in these situations the social relations that had tied communities together became unwound. Families became economically more self-sufficient, but this self-sufficiency led to isolation of families and, ultimately, the breakdown of communal bonds.

Through recollections and impressions, descendants of the communities at Oakley Plantation conveyed a sense of the paradox in which their families had been entwined. As informed by these community partners, a critical archaeological interpretation of life at Oakley offers an understanding of the perceptions and choices that led to the destabilization of a lifeworld. Through this understanding, we can realize possible avenues for emancipatory action. The course of this research has led to an engaged understanding of the past processes that have shaped the present. The creation of a dialogue between community partners and the researcher resulted in new perspectives on the personal histories of individual families as well as their place within the larger context of postbellum change in the rural South.

Habermas's theory of communicative action as related to the lifeworld also provides an important interpretive tool for understanding the intertwining of race, racism, ethnicity, gender, and class without the need to essentialize or privilege any facet of identity over another. Individuals do not exist in social vacuums, but are defined and define themselves by the networks of social relationships that situate them within their community. Scholars have demonstrated convincingly how macroscalar studies of social relations between distinct communities of actors can be used to study the spread of capitalist systems on a global level (e.g., Orser 1996). Yet only through microscalar analyses of individuals and their families through the course of their lifetimes can we hope to illuminate these webs of social relations within communities. It is through everyday action and practice that racial, gender, and class identities are continuously constructed and reconstructed.

8

The Cult of Whiteness in Western New England

ROBERT PAYNTER

So that you may see that there was a Church of God in Egypt in Babylon and Ethiopia, who were Christians, as well as among white People, so called by the Blacks.
(George Fox [1676, reprinted 1701], "Gospel Family Order, Being a Short Discourse Concerning the Ordering of Families, Both of Whites, Blacks, and Indians," quoted in Epperson 1997:15)

Among the notions of identity prevalent in the United States today, racial identity is one of the most salient. Though the overwhelming majority of work done by historical archaeologists in North America is on Euro-Americans, the overwhelming majority of the work associated with the study of "race" considers African and African American settlements in the southeast United States and the plantation economies of the Caribbean. This work has added significantly to our understanding of the notions and practices creating "race" in North America. Singleton (1985b, 1988, 1990, 1995, 1999, 1995) has compiled and developed programmatic reviews of much of this work, and Orser (1998b) has recently summarized the intellectual and political forces shaping its study in historical archaeology and pointed out directions for change. Among the increasing numbers of monograph studies, Ferguson's (1991, 1992) analyses of colono-ware trace the impacts of differing forms of economic enslavement in the middle, lower, and Spanish South. Deetz (1993) has offered considerable insight into the materiality of the development of racial categories by tracing segregation in housing and the development of distinctive cultural markers in the seventeenth-century Tidewater. In very different settings, Orser (1988b) and Delle (1998) have investigated the impacts of emancipation on plantation production systems. And Mullins (1999a) and Yentsch (1994) have studied the lives of African-descent people in the urban context of Annapolis (see also Geismar 1982). Less has been said about the development of the red-white color-line and its interrelationship with the development of the black-white color-line (though see Feder 1994).

These studies have generally focused on the African-descent population in an effort to discover distinctively African American ways of life. The lifeways of the Euro-American population, when studied in the context of the color-line, are assumed to be normative and those of white people. One major exception is the work of Epperson (e.g., 1997, 1999a), who has insisted that we turn our attention to the origins of a distinctive sense and set of practices known as "Whiteness." He has traced this development in legal categories and material culture, noting the origin of "White" in southern legal and religious discourses and the reification of "Whiteness" in the materiality of southern plantations.

Building on these studies, but also marking a significant departure, is the work at the African Burial Ground in New York City, one of the most important projects in the historical archaeology of North America. Among numerous justifications for this claim, the study has successfully called to popular consciousness the presence of African-descent communities in the colonial American North in ways that have eluded other studies (e.g., Askins 1988; Baker 1980; Bower and Rushing 1980; Fitts 1996; Garman 1992; Geismar 1982; La Roche and Blakey 1997; Paynter et al. 1994; Schuyler 1980). For a period in the eighteenth century New York City had the largest slave population of any mainland English colony, and it remained among the largest throughout the eighteenth century (Berlin 1998:54). The biocultural analyses graphically demonstrate that the conditions of enslavement in the North were far from benign (La Roche and Blakey 1997); the archaeological studies give a sense of the diversity of the lives of African-descent people (Perry 1997a, 1997b).

The evidence from the African Burial Ground, and the other studies of African American life in the seventeenth- through nineteenth-century North, run counter to popular conceptions of the history of colonial North America. Most popular history narratives have the following elements. The colonial and early Republic North is posited as an economy based on the labor of freeholding whites working relatively small farms, connected to one another and to the world at large by merchants located in the few, relatively small but growing urban areas. This northern system of production based on small rural producers stands in contrast to the southern system based on plantations owned by whites and dependent on the enslaved labor of Africans for their profitability. Both rural systems tilled soil vacated by the indigenous red population, whose members had failed to use the land productively and were justifiably or tragically removed from the scene, either by government policy aimed at people who brutalized the English settlers or by disease that ravaged the "noble savages."

In these commonsense histories the identities of red, white, and black are usually taken as essential characteristics stemming from time immemorial. These identities clashed on the plantations of the South and on the plains of the West. But the presumed absence of African- and Native American–descent communities in the North made it immune to these conflicts. Thus, according to the popular conception, northern white identity developed free from the prejudices associated with the master-slave relations in the South and the conqueror-conquered relations of the West. In these accounts, the Whiteness of New England's European-descent population is not problematized, but rather assumed. The lack of a historical perspective on this construction results in a number of implications for today, among them the idea that northern racism is somehow more benign than southern white racism, that white Northerners were able to develop an untainted and benevolent attitude that led to the liberation of African people, and finally that Whiteness in this northern sense need not be a subject of social inquiry. Contrary to this last conclusion, Harrison (1995:63), among others, argues that anthropology needs to inquire into and work "against the convention of ignoring yet universalizing Whiteness as an unspoken but naturalized norm presumed to be unaffected by racism" (see also Epperson 1997:10). This chapter examines the popular and official histories of the rural North, and especially of rural western Massachusetts, reckoned to be one of the "Whitest" parts of the United States, and their implications for archaeologies of identity formation.

REPRESENTING RURAL NEW ENGLAND

The idea that New England is the historical enclave of the English and then other European immigrants, and only recently home to people of color—a generalization which in comparison to other regions has some truth to it—too easily glosses over the presence and persistence of communities of Native American– and African-descent people in this region. The simplistic image of New England has been presented in numerous places, including popular literature (e.g., McDowell and Madden 1969), the officially enshrined historical landscape (e.g., Paynter 1990), and in living-history museums that abound in the area. The overwhelming message, despite recent efforts to counter this misperception, is that the colonial history of New England is the history of Europeans.

One way that this perception makes its way into the collective consciousness of the region is through school curriculums. Massachusetts is currently struggling over what history should be taught in its public schools. The Department of Education has promulgated very specific curriculum guidelines for each grade. These contested guidelines provide a sense of what has been the practice in elementary and secondary schools, as well as a sense of what this state-sponsored collective memory will be in the future.

The official curriculum framework (Massachusetts Department of Education 1997) moves chronologically, highlighting key issues and indicating what level of detail should be known at what grade level. The section entitled "Beginnings to 1650" suggests that knowing something about the native peoples of North America—the Pueblo, Apache, Inuit, Cherokee, Iroquois, Huron, and the Wampanoag of Massachusetts—is desirable. So too, it suggests, is knowing about Columbus, Magellan, Cabot, Cartier, and Coronado, the "Discoverers." The section for the period 1600–1763 asks students to consider the coexistence and conflict between Euros and Native Americans. For New England this means learning about the cooperative relationship between the Wampanoag and the first group of European settlers (the Pilgrims), and then about the Pequot and King Philip's wars, the latter of which spells the demise of a native presence in New England. The rest of the story of the red-white color-line happens outside of Massachusetts, implying an absence of native people during the eighteenth, nineteenth, and twentieth centuries. The topics of the Indian removals and the Trail of Tears concern the people of the Southeast, and the topics of the wars of the nineteenth century involve European settlers and the native peoples of the Great Plains. With the close of these wars and the U.S. frontier in the 1890s, concern with native people drops from the curriculum guidelines altogether.

The story of the black-white color-line has a different trajectory, but the same message of absence from New England. African-descent people are mentioned in "Beginnings to 1650" through the introduction of African geography as a background for considering the Atlantic slave trade. A major goal of the African background section is to make clear that fellow Africans enslaved Africans. (There is no parallel suggestion for a consideration of slavery in European society as a background for understanding the European involvement in the Atlantic slave trade.) The guidelines mandate knowing that North American slavery had its inception in the period between 1600 and 1763, that some slaves were held in Massachusetts, and that Cripsus Attucks, an Afro–Native American man from Massachusetts, was a Revolutionary War martyr in the Boston Massacre.

The major point for this period is the difference between the northern economic system based on capital, industry, labor, and trade, and the southern economic system based on land, agriculture, slavery, and trade. This framework clearly leaves little room for an understanding of the African-descent population of Massachusetts during the eighteenth and nineteenth centuries. Brief mention of the heroic Civil War black troops from Massachusetts, the subjects of the movie *Glory,* closes the discussion of African American history in Massachusetts until the very recent controversies surrounding the desegregation of the schools in Boston. That Malcolm X lived in Boston and that W. E. B. Du Bois was from western Massachusetts are both ignored. The subtext is that the oppression of African-descent people happened elsewhere. And their liberation, led by Martin Luther King Jr., also happened elsewhere.

Professional history is more divided about the role of race in New England history. On one hand, many histories see the United States, and especially New England, as arising out of the dynamics of Europe and, in colonial periods, England in particular (e.g., Deetz 1977:28–43; Fischer 1989; Lemon 1984). Others do see English American identity formation, even in New England, as the result of the same processes that stole labor out of Africa, took land from the indigenous peoples of North America, and generated notions of racial difference (e.g., Drake 1987, 1990; Drinnon 1980; Horsman 1981; Nash 1982; Smedley 1993; Zuckerman 1987).

Melish (1998) has recently offered an important critique of the standard view of the racially white North. Paraphrasing her subtle argument, white New England was a deliberate and potent symbolic invention of the early 1800s, developed by regional elites in the midst of struggles between regions for hegemony in the new nation. In this "history," the North, in contrast to the slave-based South, is considered the paradigmatic way of freedom-loving life. This nineteenth-century moral society had a deep history, originating with the Anglo-Saxons in England and transmitted to New England in such founding documents as the Mayflower Compact. The problem with this vision was the fact of northern slavery during the seventeenth and eighteenth centuries. Though slaves were less numerous than in the South, Melish argues that slavery was an important economic institution, especially for the elites engaged in the developing capitalist economy. Justification for enslavement was based on the African-ness of the slaves, a "blaming the victim" argument. The religious assault on the institution of slavery took on a new potency when linked with the secular Enlightenment egalitarian principles of the revolutionary Republic in the late eighteenth century. However, the resulting gradual emancipation of slaves throughout New England made no provision for redressing the impoverishment that slavery had imposed on many of these people. Lacking a continuing significant place in the economy, African Americans were also written out of the possibilities of republican citizenship and scapegoated as disorderly people responsible for some of the confusion and distress of the times. Abolition meant the abolition of Africans from New England as well as the abolition of the institution of slavery. Practices to support this whitening of the region included symbolic degradation, legal and physical harassment, and proposals to extradite African-descent people to Africa. In the context of this anti-black assault, it became easy for northern elites to develop a story about the region that excluded blacks and slavery from its past in an attempt to take the moral high road as possessors of the inherently freedom-loving social system that should be adopted by the new nation.

Despite efforts along these lines, it is this early nineteenth-century invention of the whiteness and the justness of New England that still prevails. New England is seen—after an initial, brief, and for white identity, inconsequential period of native extermination—as a society and culture driven by processes endemic to a European and, in fact, English set of processes. Fostered in the popular imagination by state-sponsored educational systems, this perception amounts to an official, if incorrect, history.

TRIUMPHALIST AND ALTERNATIVE HISTORIES

Histories in which the present is presaged in the past, and the past unquestionably leads to the present, are parts of U.S. triumphalist ideology. Hu-DeHart (1995) and Wylie (1995: 260–262) note that such ideologies create a sense of the inevitability of the present by projecting essentialized cultural categories onto the past and by using erasure and disinformation to exclude any sort of social and cultural alternative. The results are dramas based on incipient versions of the present that detail how the present came into being, despite people and circumstances that stood in its way. Sometimes the obstacles were overcome because of superior cultural abilities, sometimes because of superior biological abilities, sometimes because of simple good fortune. Regardless, triumph over obstacles describes the arc of the past.

The official history of Massachusetts, as well as some professional perceptions of its past, contributes to a triumphalist history. As noted above, it is essentially a story about people of European descent. African Americans and Native Americans play diminished or nonexistent roles. The red-white color-line that was so crucial in shaping the white identity in the American West was eliminated early in New England. Moreover, the black-white color-line never became entrenched because the system of northern agricultural production was supposedly not based on slave labor. Any non-color-based racial line, such as that between the Irish and the English (Allen 1994, 1997; Ignatiev 1995; Orser 1998b), is ignored. The present African American population, in the common perception, has its origins in the twentieth-century migration out of the Jim Crow South. As a result, there is a long period, from the mid-1600s until the early 1900s, when a kind of whiteness by default developed in the North, one that simply reflected the population movement of people from northwest Europe, not the pernicious kind of the American South and West, where the white identity formed as the identity of the master and the conqueror, respectively. New England, in this story, represents a haven for refugee blacks and a region of ideas and practices that should be adopted throughout the country to overcome racial injustices.

Of course, triumphalist histories are contested. Schmidt and Patterson (1995) have edited a collection titled *Making Alternative Histories* advocating the construction of histories that tell the story from the point of view of those conquered during colonialism or subsumed during nation-state formation. Key aspects of such histories include "a past that forms the basis of an identity empowering [colonized peoples] to negotiate justice and to develop their communities in ways that overcome the ethnocide, displacement, and genocide caused by the slave trade, as well as the erasures of historical identity perpetrated by state collusion with international capitalism" (Schmidt and Patterson 1995:14). For Wylie (1995) alternative histories confront the generalizations and theories that undergird the dominant histories with data collected from many sources, including material, archaeological, and oral records, in addition to the familiar documentary sources of official history (Wylie 1995:266). These new sources of data will record the actions of ignored and marginalized peoples in the past, people whose interactions among themselves and with the dominant classes will be set in motion with theories of "the political-economic dynamic (especially of class struggle) by which the oppressive conditions of contemporary life came into being" (Wylie 1995:265). They also eschew characterizations of historical conflict "as an inevitable outcome of (essential) racial and ethnic difference" (Wylie 1995:265). By focusing on political-economic dynamics rather than racial statics, alternative histories avoid installing new, fixed structures of dehumanized domination (see also Blakey 1995) and as a result are "of relevance to contemporary people or their struggles" (Wylie 1995:265).

Among historical archaeological works of alternative history are those by Leone and Handsman (Handsman and Leone 1989; Leone 1981), which consider how museum exhibits structure a popular consciousness, and how they might be changed to present alternative positions. Parker Potter (1994) has demonstrated the utility of the ethnography of living communities as a key to uncovering dominant and alternative histories. And Leone and Silberman (1995) have written a full-blown alternative history in their remarkable book, *Invisible America*. For them, key points include bringing class variation and "racial" and national differences to the fore to counter the melting pot myth of the history of the United States.

An alternative history that studied the color-lines in New England would first of all take on the presumed absence of people of color from New England history. Such an examination would establish the presence and persistence of African- and native-descent peoples as well as those of European descent. Establishing presence and persistence amidst forces of exploitation and domination would then allow for the more complex task of interrogating all three regional "racial" identities.

ARCHAEOLOGIES OF PRESENCE AND PERSISTENCE

African Americans lived throughout New England in the colonial period, and traces of their presence can be found in the region's archaeological record. For instance, Deetz (1977) presents the case of Parting Ways, a cluster of homes of African American families who lived near Plymouth, Massachusetts, in the late eighteenth and early nineteenth centuries. Baker (1980), also looking at Massachusetts, has considered the economic condition of an African-descent woman based on an analysis of ceramic remains from her garden. And Bower (1991, n.d.; Bower and Rushing 1980) has conducted comprehensive studies of the African communities of Boston, one of the most important of which was centered on the African Meeting House in the center of the city.

A case of long-term residence by African Americans comes from supposedly lily-white western Massachusetts. In Great Barrington is the Boyhood Homesite of W. E. B. Du Bois, a home for members of the Burghardt family from the eighteenth century into the twentieth century. W. E. B. Du Bois was an African American scholar-activist, a cofounder of the NAACP, a moving force behind the pan-African movement, and a prolific author of scholarly and popular works on the state of the color-line in the United States and around the world (Du Bois 1968, 1984; Lewis 1993). Archaeological investigations conducted at the Boyhood Homesite (Paynter 1990, 1992, 1995; Paynter et al. 1994) were used to construct the phases of settlement by Du Bois's maternal relatives. Du Bois's ancestors first moved onto the site and built its house in the late eighteenth century. For the first two-thirds of the nineteenth century the Burghardts were farmers, housekeepers, and craftspeople. With the coming of industry and the decline of agriculture by midcentury, Burghardt men were increasingly engaged in farm laboring and domestic service, and the women in the family were housekeeping, engaging in domestic service, and taking in boarders. By the late nineteenth century, most of the Burghardts had left the region. Du Bois's relatives saw fit to sell the property of his maternal grandparents to a committee of admirers, who presented the property to Du Bois on his sixtieth birthday. He kept the property until economic circumstances led to its sale in the mid-twentieth century. The site was dedicated as a national landmark in the late 1960s at a ceremony attended by diplomats, nationally prominent members of the African American community, and white allies, as well as armed state police, rowdy hecklers, and FBI informers. Today the Commonwealth of Massachusetts owns the site, but insufficient funds have kept it an obscure referent on the historical landscape. These site-level evidences of the African American presence and persistence in New England is complemented by regional-scale studies. For instance, Figure 8.1 displays the settlement pattern of African Americans in the Connecticut River valley. The study area is the Connecticut River valley of western Massachusetts, today's Hampden, Hampshire, and Franklin Counties, an area also known before the 1810s as Hampshire County. Values for the African-descent population (as identified by federal census takers) of each of approximately sixty towns were plotted and graphed at town centers. Peaks indicate large numbers of people in that area (North 1908: 9, 11; Walker 1872:166; Wright 1887:68–71). The peaks, from south to north, are the Springfield, Northampton, and Deerfield areas, respectively. Despite the relatively low

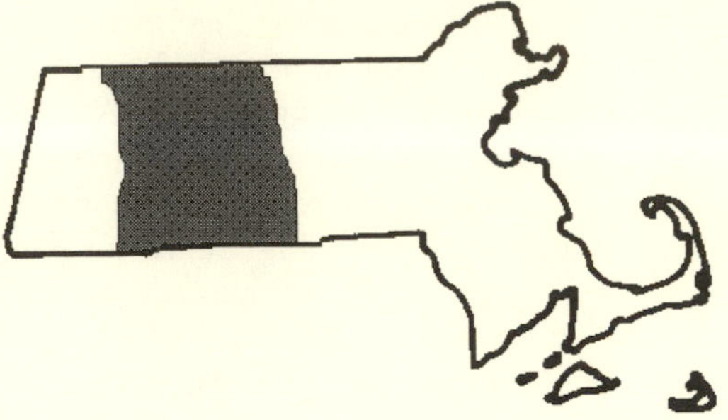

Figure 8.1. African American settlement patterns in the Connecticut River valley.

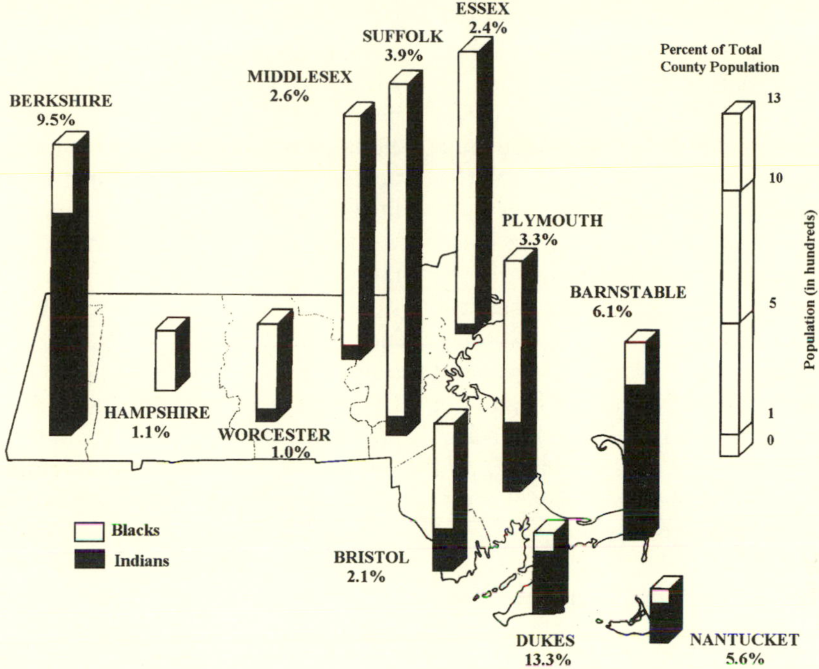

Figure 8.2. Blacks and Indians by county, 1765. (From Wilkie and Tager 1991:21)

totals (in the tens and hundreds, at a time when the European-descent population numbered in the hundreds and thousands), there is a widespread presence of African-descent people throughout the valley. Through time there is another trend: a marked centralization of the African-descent communities into fewer numbers of commercial towns.

Similar maps for native communities in historical western Massachusetts cannot be made. This is often taken as evidence of the truth of the common misconception that the native presence vanished from southern New England after King Philip's War. However, there is a telling reason for this silence, evident in Figure 8.2, a map of African- and native-descent people based on data collected in the mid-1760s (Wilkie and Tager 1991:21). Note that the Connecticut River valley region (then known as Hampshire County) is the only area within Massachusetts lacking any enumeration of native people. Contradicting this map are the material traces of native presence throughout the eighteenth and nineteenth centuries. Archaeological studies have yet to be focused on this issue, but numerous local museums contain the material evidence in the form of woodsplint baskets. These were sometimes incorrectly attributed to makers of European descent; however, studies by McMullen and Handsman (1987), among others, have enabled many of the baskets to be traced to native makers who lived in and traveled through the region throughout the nineteenth century.

Sites marking persistent communities of native people have been studied throughout other areas of rural New England. Many sites that had previously been written off as severely disturbed because of the mixing of European and native materials have recently been recognized as just such places of persistence. For instance, Savulis and Carlson (Savulis 1991, 1996; Savulis and Carlson 1989) have discovered that the Simons site on Cape Cod was occupied during historic periods when native people used both European and native manufactured items. Mrozowski (1999) has studied the extremely mixed assemblage of an eighteenth-century, native praying-town site. McBride (1993) has established a long history of native residence on the Pequot Reservation in southern Connecticut. Hood (Baron et al. 1996) has led archaeological investigations of the Croud site, the home of a farmer and miner, in central Massachusetts. Feder (1994) has investigated a refugee community of African-, Native American-, and European-descent people. And Carlson (1998) has completed the background documentary work for identifying historic-period native sites in the Connecticut River valley.

These archaeologies of persistence and presence, although only in the beginning stages, are testaments to cultural hybridity, with a mixture of artifacts, meanings, and histories. Some of the sites are of people marginal to the European power centers of society, as is the case with the Burghardt farms, the Simons site shell middens, and the Croud homestead. Others, such as that of the caterer who lived in the basement of the African Meeting House, were involved in setting the cultural tastes of the Euro-American elite. All reflect a negotiation of identity that comes from being in contact with people from differing classes and cultural backgrounds. These archaeological investigations are also having an impact on regional histories. For instance, McBride's studies figure importantly in the Mashentucket Pequot Nation's work on regional native histories. Hood's work, along with that of Marge Bruchac, has helped change the interpretive program at a major living-history museum, Old Sturbridge Village. And Krass and O'Connell (1992) present curricular material for use in western Massachusetts history classes that emphasizes the persistence of native communities.

Of course, material evidence is not the only evidence of the multicultural history of New England. Historians have assembled work on the subject of African-descent people and communities (e.g., Berlin 1998; Bower 1991; Cottrol 1982; Cromwell 1994; Curry 1981; Du Bois 1968, 1984; Greene 1942; Horton 1993; Horton and Horton 1979; Litwack 1961; Melish 1998; Piersen 1988; Propper 1997; Sheldon 1893) and native-descent communities (e.g., Brodeur 1985; Calloway 1997; Campisi 1991; Doughton 1997; Foster and Cowan 1998; Grumet 1996; Hauptman and Wherry 1990; Mills and Mann 1996; Noble 1997; O'Connell 1992; Simmons 1986) throughout the eighteenth and nineteenth centuries. African-descent people cleared, tilled and harvested fields, cared for their owner's children, worked with their owners to keep house, tanned hides, mined ore, sailed and provisioned ships, and ran commercial establishments, all under the constraints of the conditions of enslavement (e.g., Berlin 1998; Greene 1942; Piersen 1988). As Ira Berlin (1998:54) observes, "Slaves were neither an inconsequential element in northern economic development nor an insignificant portion of the northern population during the seventeenth and eighteenth centuries."

The presence and persistence of African and native communities contradict the notion that New England is exclusively European. And their presence and persistence raise the question of the effects that these different communities had on one another's identity. The triumphalist histories state that the small numbers of non-European people were assimilated into the European norm, their original cultures having had little impact on European cultural formation. The archaeologies of African- and native-descent sites suggest, instead, cultural hybridity, a mixing of cultural elements from many sources, in distinctive political economic situations. The repeated discovery of hybridity on archaeological sites has led other historical archaeologists to question the weight given to notions of assimilation (e.g., Beaudry et al. 1991; Orser 1996:58–62). The challenge is to understand how all these identities formed amidst negotiation and resistance.

IDENTITY AND ARCHAEOLOGY

Identity is a concept with much currency in contemporary archaeological and anthropological theory. Jones (1997), for instance, has recently reviewed the use of identity by archaeologists, especially regarding its relationship to ethnicity (see also Friedman 1992; Graves-Brown et al. 1996; Kohl 1998; Luedtke 1995; Rowlands 1994). Reviewing the history of archaeological uses of identity and ethnicity, and the theoretical positions of primordialists and interactionists, she seeks a usable notion in Bourdieu's concept of "habitus." Habitus, for Jones (1997:88), is "made up of durable dispositions towards certain perceptions and practices (such as those relating to the sexual division of labour, morality, tastes and so on), which become part of an individual's sense of self at an early age, and which can be transposed from one context to another." A matter-of-fact consciousness (doxa) is associated with a habitus. This only rises to the contemplation of difference (hetero or orthodoxy) when confronted by alternative ways of life. Colonialism is one, though not the only, social process that forces such confrontations and the growth of the awareness of ethnic identities. Difference persists as colonial social formations deliberately articulate various habituses poorly, resulting in an ongoing and fluid cultural process of the codification of self-conscious difference (Jones 1997:99–100).

Wolf (1982), with the concept of mode of production, provides insights into the forces that give shape to any particular habitus and to the interactions between them. He posits three well-known modes: the kin, tributary, and capitalist. Each requires specific social roles (among the many that may exist) for their realization: kin modes have husbands and wives, juniors and seniors, parents and children; tributary modes have givers and takers; capitalist modes have owners and workers.

These roles in concrete social situations are much more complex. For instance, husbands and wives can take on the multifarious meanings that abound in kinship studies. Tributary takers and givers can fracture into the many positions in elaborate bureaucracies and complex peasantries. Capitalist owners and workers can be subdivided into numerous technical positions in the division of labor. In addition, all these modal positions might be shared by any individual life; that is, wives can be workers and tribute givers serially or at the same time.

To complicate matters further, the cultural forms that make sense of these relations, and relations of relations, are not simply reflective mirrors of these practices. The cultural forms are taught in a variety of settings, by professors, by kin, by workmates, in schools, churches, mass media, homes, and businesses. They are applied by others to enforce relations, again in a variety of settings and to varying degrees of logical and functional coherence at different times and places. The cultural images have histories related to, but not identical with, the histories of the relations.

Identities arise from the complex flux of kin, tribute, and capitalist relations. Of significance for archaeology, the relations in these complex fields are about exchanges between the participants; they are material relations. Common practices have a materiality that comes to be read also as signs of strategic identities. For instance, accumulative material flows are based on the creation and manipulation of assemblages of material culture associated with their productive and transformative activities. These assemblages carry society's messages that mark or hide the relevant social agents in these interactions. The created piles of possessions and practices are manipulated to be recognizable, patterned assemblages signaling identities—positions, affiliations, and separations in the flows of power—readable through the use of cultural forms, by contemporaries as well as by observers from the future (Wobst 1977, 1999, 2000).

THE IDENTITY OF BEING WHITE

Recent research demonstrates quite convincingly that racial identities, as parts of social systems of oppression, are phenomena of our recent past and not a social principle extending back to time immemorial (e.g., Du Bois 1920; Williams 1944). For instance, St. Clair Drake's (1987, 1990) two-volume assessment of the relationship between color-prejudice, slavery, and racism from ancient Egypt through the ancient and medieval Judeo-Christian and Islamic worlds finds slavery, social differentiation, and associated prejudices, even color-prejudice. But what awaits the conjunction of slavery and African labor in the Western Hemisphere is the development of "systematic doctrines of racial inferiority and superiority" (Drake 1987:7); that is, racism. As Drake abundantly argues, these historical realities defeat the various theories of Atlantic world racial slavery that seek to fix racial antagonisms in deep, and universal psychological prejudices.

Smedley (1993) considers in more detail the development of the notion of race in North America. She argues that anti-black practices are rooted in the enslavement of Africans by the English throughout their mainland colonies; anti-red practices are rooted in the conquest of North America for English settlers. Conquest and, especially, enslavement created a particular contradiction for the emerging North American English capitalist society. On one hand, this society believed in and had practices associated with strong commitments to inalienable rights vested in any human being. On the other was the necessity to activate these rights through the ownership and accumulation of property. Somewhat familiar rationales involved heathenism and savagery (Patterson 1997) honed in the English conquest of Ireland and justified taking land from the native peoples of the continent. However, African slaves, whose labor was the source of much of the eighteenth-century wealth of the newly independent colonies, were paradoxically entitled to human rights and subject to property rights. This enormous dilemma was only resolved by the creation of a new way of thinking about human variation, one that imagined bounded biological groups who inherited essences that controlled their bodies, behaviors, and beliefs in an immutable, all-inclusive package. Membership in these mutually exclusive groups was signaled by skin color. This closed and immutable racial unit was filled with qualities that purported to establish natural black inferiority and white superiority. A great irony, noted by Smedley, is that considerable impetus for the crystallization of the notion of race arose in the late eighteenth and early nineteenth centuries as a defensive tactic among the advocates of slavery in response to the logical and moral assaults of the abolitionist movement and the promise held out by the cotton gin for even greater slave-based wealth (see also Allen 1994, 1997). Melish (1998:119–162) notes a related but distinct irony in the North of the same time, where the notion of race explained why freed African Americans remained in desperate conditions.

This notion of race fit well, too, with one of the great paradoxes of capitalism. Wolf (1982:389–390) points out that the equality posited by the market contradicts the realities of differences between workers and owners, and winners and losers, both endemic to capitalism. As Du Bois (1939) and Williams (1944) remind us, people who lost much under capitalism included the industrial working classes, the native people who lost their land, and the African people who lost their liberty in the name of profit. Capitalism had to comprehend the indigent worker, the bound African, and the dispossessed native. The hegemonic solution developed by eighteenth-century European capitalism was to measure the qualities of individuals, rather than the forces of accumulation, and explain the differences in social outcomes as a function of the differences in the qualities of people. Race, with its expectation of qualities fixed immutably in large groups of people, was exactly the kind of concept that could help resolve this contradiction on a mass scale.

Notions of whiteness gradually emerged along with the concept of race. Among archaeologists, Epperson (e.g., 1997, 1998, 1999a), more so than any other, has put the issue of the origin of the white identity on the research agenda. He has investigated the seventeenth-century uses of "white" in legal and religious writings about Virginia, and has detailed material aspects of the emergence of this distinct identity. "White" emerges in Virginia as the plantocracy sought to separate European from African servants, political economic dynamics laid out by Morgan (1975). Epperson notes that for much of the seventeenth century, people of European and African descent, when distinguished one from the other, were designated as Christians and Negroes. As chattel slavery became increasingly important and as some Africans converted to Christianity, the simple distinction of Christians and Negroes failed to contain the paradox that all Christians are equal before God but some Christians are subservient to other Christians. In a move that foreshadows the invention of race, this paradox was resolved by extending "Christian" to people of African as well as European descent. and inventing a new inversion for "Negro," namely that of "white" (Epperson 1997:13–17). In this new opposition, "white" is largely an empty term that designates a non-African Christian. The material practices at a number of Chesapeake plantations manifest the content of the whiteness as being not-African in the separation of white from the black people, the hiding of African housing from the sight of the white owners, and the enforcement of different spatial experiences on black and white people (Epperson 1999a:164–171; Deetz 1993; Upton 1985).

Whiteness as emptiness, or something that is only known in relation to another social identity, is still a characteristic of modern senses of being among many white people. Frankenberg (1995) identified it as one of the three themes of colonialist discourse emerging from nine relatively progressive U.S. white women. (The other themes are an explicit derogation of whiteness and an assertion of color-blindness.) The significant work of the empty category, as Frankenberg, among many others, points out, is the assumption of normativeness that accompanies it.

Whiteness also came to take on an explicit content. Smedley (1993:188–189) argues that Anglo-Saxonism was a crystallization of the idea of the white race that was rife with notions of white superiority. Anglo-Saxonism originated in sixteenth-century England. It conceives of a time before the Norman Conquest when the Anglo-Saxons of Britain lived in a world free of the inequities of the Roman Catholic Church and the feudal economic order. The political institutions of these free yeomen were figured as superior to any others in the world, and the revolutionary republicanism of the United States was considered a direct institutional descendant of these inventions by the mythical Anglo-Saxons. By the early nineteenth century, these political institutions had become linked to the emerging racial understandings in a variety of genres. For instance, Horsman (1981: 40–41) notes that the novels of Sir Walter Scott created a widespread popular imagination that could understand the superior U. S. political institutions as being linked to biologically inherited propensities for such behavior from earlier white people, the Anglo-Saxons. And part of this inheritance was a zeal to propagate these more just institutions, a racially based manifest destiny (Horsman 1981).

There is another hint in Epperson's study that a filled, rather than empty, category of white was in use, even in early colonial periods. Epperson cites Fox, the seventeenth-century Quaker and abolitionist proponent, alluding to a usage of "white" by contemporary Africans, "as well as among White People, so called by the Blacks" (see the chapter epigraph). What the meanings "white" held for seventeenth-century Africans in Virginia is a topic in need of further exploration. Part of this filled notion of white during slavery includes the understandings by African- and European-descent people of the contradictions of slaveholding. For whites the contradictions of citizen and property rights are a dilemma; for African-descent people, saying one thing and doing another amounts to hypocrisy. For instance, Patton and Stevens (1999) note in a recent review of the Thomas Jefferson–Sally Hemings paternity debate that slave narratives contain observations of hypocritical behavior as a characteristic of whites: "From the first introduction of the African to America, African descendants have been inundated with example after example of discrepancies between professed ideologies and civil conduct.... African Americans have now come to expect such hypocrisy on the part of the majority of Euro-Americans" (Patton and Stevens 1999:11).

White supremacy was one way that whites resolved slaveholding in the land of freedom (e.g., Jordan 1968; Morgan 1975; Omi and Winant 1986; Smedley 1993). Over the course of the eighteenth century, the sense of superiority associated with being white took on deep-seated psychological, as well as a social, dimension: it became a prejudice (Appiah 1990). For instance, in 1828 the Connecticut Colonization Society presented the nature of the color-line, attributing the lowly position of the African to prejudice: "In every part of the United States, there is a broad and impassible line of demarcation between every man who has one drop of African blood in his veins, and every other class in the community. The habits, the feelings, all the prejudices of society—prejudices which neither refinement, nor argument, nor education, nor religion itself can subdue—mark the people of colour, whether bond or free, as the subjects of a degradation inevitable and incurable. The African in this country belongs by birth to the lowest station in society; and from that station he can never rise, be his talents, his enterprise, his virtues what they may" (Ignatiev 1995:97).

Note the four ways one might try to defeat a prejudice: "religion," meaning all are equal before the Christian God; "education," meaning a credentialing of an ability to do the work; "argument," meaning the various political positions taken by the abolitionists; and "refinement," meaning a recognition of an ability to participate as a person of quality in society. In short, being white meant holding a deep-seated negative assessment of the quality of people of color.

The significance of being white in the nineteenth century can be seen in its implications for those groups, such as the Irish, whose racial status changed. As Ignatiev (1995:3) notes in his study of *How the Irish Became White,* attaining whiteness is about working-class and entrepreneurial Irish immigrants accessing and functioning within political and economic contexts: "it meant that they were citizens of a democratic republic, with the right to elect and be elected, to be tried by a jury of their peers, to live wherever they could afford, and to spend, without racially imposed restrictions, whatever money they managed to acquire." In other words, being white meant, for the Irish, engaging in the dominant institutions of society, from which they had been largely excluded in colonized Ireland. It meant, in Jones's (1997) terms, being well situated within the habitus of the dominant English-descent population. And it meant being able to do all the things from which blacks were excluded in the United States. Being white, a supposed mark of quality, conferred upon its holder a legitimacy and normalcy in entering into a wide range of social interactions. In this sense, being identified by others as "white" opened the way to social relations, especially power-laden social relations, in which control can be exerted. It functioned as cultural capital (Bourdieu 1984), and this is how it functions today.

Among an increasing number of studies on contemporary "whiteness" (e.g., Brodkin 1998a; Dyer 1997; Fine et al. 1997; Frankenberg 1995, 1997; Hale 1998; Roediger 1991, 1994, 1998; Sacks 1994), McIntosh's (1993: 211) early investigation clearly identifies how white skin color was "an asset for any move [she] was educated to want to make: "I could think of myself as belonging in major ways, and of making social systems work for me." Among the things her unearned cultural capital of being white gives her are that:

> —If I should need to move, I can be pretty sure of renting or purchasing housing in an area which I can afford and in which I would want to live....
>
> —I can be pretty sure that my neighbors in such a location will be neutral or pleasant to me....
>
> —I can go shopping alone most of the time, pretty well assured that I will not be followed or harassed....
>
> —I can go home from most meetings of organizations I belong to feeling somewhat tied in, rather than isolated, out-of-place, outnumbered, unheard, held at a distance, or feared....
>
> —I can remain oblivious of the language and customs of persons of color who constitute the world's majority without feeling in my culture any penalty for such oblivion. (McIntosh 1993:210–211)

People lacking the cultural capital of whiteness lack unconscious access to these supposed taken-for-granteds of life in the capitalist market secured by the liberal nation-state.

Whiteness is clearly a complex and historically fluid phenomenon. It began in the seventeenth century as an empty relational category: non-African and Christian. Developing during the second half of the seventeenth century, and becoming more influential as a way of thinking during the eighteenth century, it crystallized into a hegemonic ideology in the nineteenth century. Race became a novel way that the societies of the Atlantic economy understood the social world. This new sense of the basic divisions of humankind supplemented and, in some instances, overshadowed divisions based on the lines of class and religion. At root was a metaphor that distinctive biological groups passed propensities for culture from one generation to the next by means of biological inheritance. These groups were mutually exclusive, and the propensities fairly impervious to the effects of learning and the environment. These categories were hierarchically ordered, with white people of supposed Anglo-Saxon descent being at the top and black people of African descent at the bottom. Various and changing scientific theories were developed that supported measuring bodies as a means of measuring qualities. They ran afoul of the basic reality of biological interfertility and cultural adaptability, and secular and sacred beliefs in the unity of humankind. In developing a hegemonic pro-racial position, a mixed rhetoric of biological and behavioral differences developed as tests for group membership.

DEMONSTRATING WHITENESS

Demonstrating whiteness became, by the nineteenth century, a mixed rhetoric that relied on both biology and behavior. Distinguishing the quality of people became an obsession of philosophers, judges, clerics, and scientists (Baker and Patterson 1994a, 1994b; Patterson and Spencer 1994; Smedley 1993). Quality was marked not only by the color of one's skin, but also by the ability to participate in the practices of the superior parts of society. And material signs of quality—as argued by Leone (1988), Shackel (1992, 1993), and Bushman (1993)—was the ability to acquire and use the paraphernalia of the consumer revolution. Competencies in choice, taste, and performance were all hallmarks of being a person of quality. And this judgement of quality, along with phenotype, came to be merged as measures of racial identity.

This mixing is most clearly seen in legal decisions about racial identity. For instance, Melish (1998:35–37) describes an identity case from Connecticut in 1757 in which Jose Deming sued for freedom, contending that since he was not a "Negro," he could not have been lawfully enslaved. Deming specifically sought to convince the Connecticut General Assembly that "by my Countenance, by my Education, by my proficiency in reading and writing of the Portuguese Language, and by other Evidence, that I am no Slave or Native of Guinea" (Melish 1998:36). Witnesses also made use of a mixed rhetoric of performance and physique.

Gross (1998:159), considering cases from the antebellum South, chronicles the entanglement of phenotype and cultural performance. In the case of Joseph Nunez, the jury heard evidence on genealogy as well as about Nunez's and his father's social competencies: "his action and movements were as genteel as any man witnesses have known.... Witnesses well remember Jim Nunez's dancing, which was very graceful... [and that Nunez] dined with the Whites just the same as any gentlemen would have done." He was thought to be "a respectable Indian and white blooded man." Racial identity was also in question when women in New Orleans sued for their freedom on the basis of being unlawfully enslaved white women. Evidence presented to support these people's whiteness included a commentary on the general habits and possessions of differing races: "The Quartronne is idle, reckless and extravagant, this woman is industrious, careful and prudent—the Quartronne is fond of dress, of finery and display—this woman is neat in her person, simple in her array, and with no ornament upon her, not even a ring on her fingers" (Gross 1998:168).

Houses, architectural detail, furnishings, tableware, clothing, personal hygiene, and textiles were among the material aspects of life that became swept up in capitalist consumption, modern discipline, and the cultural codes of distinction. Many of the elements of this code are familiar to archaeologists as what Deetz (1977) refers to as the "Georgian": houses with symmetrical neoclassical façades, central hallways, and privacy for the owners; individual table settings of English cream and pearl wares; urn- and willow-decorated gravestones. Sweeney (1994) more recently has broken Deetz's sense of the Georgian into various sub-codes that reflect differential positioning in the emerging class structure of the Atlantic world (see also Johnson 1996). Leone and Shackel (Leone 1984, 1988, 1995, 1999; Leone et al. 1987, 1992; Shackel 1992, 1993) have linked elements of this code to the interpellation of modern capitalist discipline into the daily lives of its practitioners. Importantly, they have made the point that knowing how to use the material culture of the Georgian, the etiquette of it all, was as important as the possession of the objects.

Part of this code explicitly distinguished people of quality from people of different classes and color. For instance, Hall (1992), in a masterful study of South Africa, demonstrates how the architecture and foodways of the Georgian were part of a code for communication and competition used by the classes that owned people, and as such were part of the construction of white domination and black subordination. Epperson (1999a) details similar architectural and spatial properties used on nineteenth-century Chesapeake plantations to separate white from black.

Bushman's (1993) comprehensive study of the material cultural of the late eighteenth and early nineteenth century details the ways these elements were entangled with the cults of gentility and refinement in eastern North America. He argues that the etiquette and equipage of the former cult separated the late eighteenth-century elite classes from the middle and lower classes. Refinement describes the broader sets of practices made possible by the industrial-commercial revolution in the nineteenth century, used by the white middle class to distinguish itself from the white working class and people of color into the twentieth century. Evidence for racial policing of this marked boundary comes from Philadelphia. Even for the class of African American "barbers, carpenters, and other artisans, plus ministers and teachers who managed to accumulate property" (Bushman 1993:433), the practices of gentility were out of bounds. As Bushman (1993:434–440) details, middle-class blacks practicing the codes of gentility in antebellum Philadelphia were met with physical assault and vile caricature. White Philadelphians strove hard to make "manners, education, well furnished parlors, exclusive entertainments" (Bushman 1993: 438) and other genteel values and practices the preserve of the white republic (Ignatiev 1995). In a confused class analysis, Bushman (1993:438) attributes this reaction to a "middle-class sensitivity to invasions from below." But given the mass character of the attacks by whites and the class equivalency, if not superiority, of the African American targets, it is clearly a racial line that was drawn to limit the ability of one to pass in the North (see also Melish 1998:199–209). (No wonder that how consumption should be conducted and what it should mean was a perplexing subject for people in African American communities, a subject taken up by Mullins [1999b].)

Whiteness since the eighteenth century has been a mixture of the rhetoric of biology and the possession of and performance with the things of the Consumer Revolution. It has been cultural capital, key for access to major social institutions. This entwining of capitalism and racism is more readily recognized in the material assemblages and practices of the South and the West (Deetz 1993; Epperson 1990a, 1997, 1998, 1999a; Ferguson 1992); little has been made of the connection as it developed in the North. What follows are sketches of possible answers to these questions, drawn from archaeological, documentary, and architectural studies of Deerfield, Massachusetts. Though they lack the detail that has come from similar studies of the color-line in the South, they do point to the centrality of materiality as part of the process of being white.

TOWARD AN ARCHAEOLOGY OF NORTHERN WHITENESS

Deerfield Village in the Connecticut River valley of western Massachusetts is a mile-long street lined by homelots laid out during the first English settlement of the town in the 1660s (Epperson 1996; Garrison 1991, 1996; Hood 1996; McGowan and Miller 1996; Paynter et al. 1987; Reinke et al. 1987; Sweeney 1984, 1985). A cluster of homes at the northern end of the street is somewhat separated from the rest of the village by a cut and bluff, the result of an ancient course of the Deerfield River. In 1816, Hinsdale and Anna Williams bought a large homelot in this northern end that had been owned by an ancestor of Hinsdale, Ebeneezer Hinsdale.

During his life Hinsdale was among the wealthiest people in Franklin County, with investments in land, personal belongings, and financial notes. He was likely a practitioner of the lucrative trade in stall-feeding oxen, fattening them in valley towns in preparation for their journey to cattle markets in Boston (Garrison 1991:72). Anna made a well-appointed home for their two children.

The Williams home presented their social persona to themselves and to the village. Rather than tearing down the house of Hinsdale's ancestor, the Williamses had extensively remodeled the house to be in tune with the neoclassical code of their time (Sweeney 1994). The central chimney was taken out and replaced by a central hallway, so crucial to the senses and needs of privacy, separation, and circulation. The posts of the first floor were cut and raised so that the ceilings could be of a more fashionable height. An ell was added to include space for a pantry, buttery, modern kitchen, dining room, and office on the first floor; the second floor had rooms for family and hired help (Bill Flynt, pers. comm.).

External architectural details were used to set the scene. The front façade received touches of neoclassical decorative style, including a fan-light above the front door, a cornice, and delicate window casings. The ell was set flush to the south side of the main block, and the neoclassical façade was echoed on the south side of the ell, uniting the main block and the ell, and emphasizing the size of the structure (Bill Flynt, pers. comm.). The landscape surrounding the house was extensively leveled, with special attention paid to terracing the south lawn. A walkway of decorative red arkose stone on the south lawn led from the street to the rear of the house. Behind the house, and unattached, was a symbol of some of the Williams family's wealth: the barn. An observer standing on the bluff just a bit to the south would have had a remarkable view of a stylish house set upon an orderly landscape (Reinke 1985).

The view from the north side of the house, less visible from the street, is less concerned with announcing the stylish status of its owners. The plainly decorated ell was set back from the main block, and it received none of the neoclassical touches of its southerly counterpart. The windows in the ell were the reused eighteenth-century windows of the main block with their heavier and less stylish casings. The drive leading to the barn in the rear may have been covered with a crushed gray stone or may have just been bare ground. A detached privy that used to be on the north side had been filled with trash, most likely thrown out by the Williams family as they moved into their new home and a brick-lined privy was added to the rear of the attached summer kitchen (Bill Flynt, pers. comm.).

The interior was also furnished in a respectable style. The parlor, a prime space for formal entertaining, had eighteen chairs and a sofa to accommodate visitors. A Brussels carpet adorned its floor. The walls were covered with stylish French wallpaper depicting idealized circum-Mediterranean landscapes, and two paintings by their daughter. The most formal meals were served in the dining room on an extensive set of Chinese export porcelain, which had replaced the somewhat passé royal and scallop-edged creamware dining and pearlware tea service of their previous household (Bograd 1989:21–22). An essential part of the house of a respectable person such as Hinsdale Williams was a library, and the Williams had about 140 volumes, complete with 17 novels by Sir Walter Scott (Propper 1990).

At his death in 1838, Williams's (Anonymous 1838) obituary described him as "upright, devout, benevolent, industrious, temperate, and frugal—possessing incorruptible integrity." He was clearly a respectable man (Miller n.d.). The things with which he surrounded himself told him and all other social observers so.

Another code was in evidence at the north end of the village at just the time that the Williamses were moving in. The Ashley family lived across the street. Along with the Williams, Wells, Sheldon, Dickenson, and Hinsdale families, the Ashleys were among the leading farmers, merchants, and ministers of Deerfield, all of whom had enslaved Africans. (Indeed, owning Africans may have been another sign of gentility, along with owning the houses, furnishings, and clothing [Sweeney 1994:35].)

Jin Cole and her son Cato were living with the Ashleys in the early 1800s. Jin Cole had been kidnapped from Africa in the 1720s and sold to Parson Ashley as a teenager. She died in Deerfield in 1808. "She fully expected at death, or before, to be transported back to Guinea; and all her long life she was gathering, as treasures to take back to her mother land, all kinds of odds and ends, colored rags, bits of finery, worn out candlesticks, fragments of crockery or glassware, peculiar shaped stones, shells, buttons, beads, cones, —*anything* she could *string*" (Sheldon 1893: 55, emphasis in original). Though using some raw materials of European import, Jin Cole was mixing them with other possessions of little value to her respectable neighbors to create assemblages of great personal meaning. This was certainly not a Georgian assemblage, and looks more like the archaeologically recovered assemblages reported from Annapolis, Texas, and elsewhere throughout the South (Brown and Cooper 1990; Leone and Fry, this volume) and associated with African funerary, magic, and healing practices.

Cato carried on the practices of his mother. He "gathered trinkets to provide for his translation [*sic*], his most valued possessions being brass or copper buttons" (Sheldon 1893:55). Sheldon, who was a neighboring child while Cato was alive, also recalls Cato acting in ways that seemed less than genteel. For instance, Sheldon remarks on Cato "dunging out" with his hands rather than with a shovel. He also notes Cato's failed attempts to dance as well as the son of Parson Ashley. Cato and Jin accumulated different things and engaged in different practices from their neighbors and previous owners. And these practices led to an evaluation by these white people that they were different and less accomplished in the ways of the respectable.

In 1837, the year before Hinsdale Williams died, the village of Deerfield received a visit that drew another line on the social landscape. In late summer of that year, twenty-three "Indians" encamped three miles from the village. A number were descendants of Eunice Williams, the daughter of the Reverend John Williams, who along with around a hundred other villagers had been carried off to Canada in the attack of 1704 (Demos 1994; Haefeli and Sweeney 1995; Melvoin 1989:220–221; Sheldon 1972). Though most of these captives were redeemed, Eunice chose to live with the Mohawks and the Abenakis. Among the group of twenty-three was Eunice's eighty-year-old granddaughter, Eunice, who had desired to make the same journey her grandmother had made and pay respect at the graves of their ancestors (Fessenden 1837; Sadoques 1929).

These Indians were a curiosity to the Deerfielders, who entertained them, showed them relics of the attack, visited their encampment, and purchased woodsplint baskets. Reports from both sides were that the visit was amicable (Anonymous 1837; Demos 1994; Fessenden 1837; Haefeli and Sweeney 1995; Melvoin 1989; Sadoques 1929; Sheldon 1972). However, something must have been stirring in the minds of some of the villagers. On August 27, 1837, the Congregational minister, the Reverend John Fessenden, delivered a sermon about the visit. His text was from Acts 17:26: "And had made of one blood all nations of men for to dwell on the faces of the earth; and hath determined the times before appointed, and the bounds of their habitation." In the first half of the sermon he suggested that some people might not want to suppose that all humans were of one blood. He marshaled scientific, sacred, and common-sense arguments on behalf of the proposition of monogenesis, concluding: "There is in nature apparent but very little foundation for supposing that the various races of mankind, are any other than the different brands of the same parent sock. And the advantages of such an original appointment must be palpably evident to every reasonable mind, and it must be an occasion of the greatest satisfaction to have become firmly established in such a faith" (Fessenden 1837:9).

The need to make such an argument suggests that in Deerfield, as in the larger world, increasing numbers of people were coming under the sway of racial thinking, of understandings that rejected a commonality for all humankind. These inclinations were apparently given further support in Deerfield by the arrival in 1837 of people lacking many of the possessions and practices of respectable people: sedentary habits, substantial abodes, and an agricultural way of life.

The practices and possessions of people in Deerfield in the early 1800s marked society's divisions. In these examples from Deerfield, possessing and knowing how to use the things of the Consumer Revolution served to set one group off from two others. At least for some of the villagers, these material differences were not accompanied by an ideological understanding of immutable and fixed differences based on racial descent. However, Fessenden's and Sheldon's very acts of recording their observations suggest there were others who had adopted racial thinking and a biological sense of white supremacy. But even without an explicit racial philosophy, even among these sympathetic white observers there is a note of condescension. Fessenden (1837:13) refers to the Indians as "children of the forest"; Sheldon remarks on how Cato fails to measure up. As a result, there is a sense of cultural, if not biological, superiority. It is this cultural chauvinism, sometimes linked to biological reduction and sometimes not, that may be particularly crucial for understanding the history of whiteness in the rural North, a smugness that contributes to the evaluation of the region as the whitest part of the nation.

CONCLUSION

Hegemonic histories attribute New England and its global impacts to the dynamics of European-based cultures in European-descent communities. An alternative understanding is under development. In a clear contradiction to the dominant story, documents and material remains testify to the presence of African-descent peoples and the persistence of native-descent peoples, especially in rural New England. Needing greater study is the shifting nature of relations along these color-lines. Understandings developed of an interracial, rather than monoracial, context should result in a different picture of New England. They will need to encompass the role of material culture as possession and prop, as well as the role of biology, in signaling cultural difference. Archaeology has multiple roles in this enterprise. The tangibility of archaeological evidence can function as a corrective to biased documents, reminding us of ongoing and novel presences. On the sites of European-descent people, as well those of African- and native-descent people, the emergence of the culture of racism needs to be traced. Finally, archaeology's ability to create places on the public historical landscape can be used to reinterpret the history of this region for a broad, general public.

Note

A briefer version of this chapter was read at the 1999 World Archaeology Congress. Thanks to Terry Epperson and Kofi Agorsah for inviting my participation. Thanks also to Jim Delle, Jim Garman, Nancy Muller, and Paul Mullins, whose work on the color-line has honed my understandings. Marge Bruchac, Russ Handsman, Ron

Welburn, Jean Forward, Joyce Vincent, Art Keene, Neal Salisbury, Claire Carlson, Dena Dincauze, Liz Chilton, and Eric Johnson have taught me about Indian New England. Rita Reinke, Susan Hautaniemi, Ed Hood, Mark Bograd, and, more recently, Deb Rotman and Kerry Lynch have helped me rethink the Anglo community of Deerfield. David Samuels is helping me with symbols and semantics. Enoch Page's conversations and insights run throughout. Liz Scott's very pertinent questions may someday find the answers they deserve. Thanks to Dick Wilkie for permission to publish the map of Indians and blacks in Massachusetts from his fine historical atlas. Warren Perry has helped in countless ways to shape this chapter. Thanks especially to Ruth Mathis, even though all our hard work didn't make it into this version, and to Marge Bruchac, who has gifted me with the documents and frameworks to understand the significance of Eunice's visit to Deerfield. Bill Flynt has graciously shared his insights into the architectural and social world of the Williams family. Anne Laning, Ritchie Garrison, Kevin Sweeney, and especially Mimi Miller have helped me understand the Williams family and what is now the Williams site. Finally, thanks to Chuck Orser and the other participants in the "Race and the Archaeology of Identity" roundtable.

9

Spirit Management among Americans of African Descent

Mark P. Leone and Gladys-Marie Fry,
with assistance from Timothy Ruppel

The use of West African religious traditions among Americans of African descent in North America has been quite well established (Hall 1984, 1989; Herron and Bacon 1985; Hurston 1931; Hyatt 1970–1978; Joyner 1986; Levine 1977; Raboteau 1980; Rawick 1972–1979; Thompson 1983, 1993). However, there is much less information on the pattern of these religious traditions as practices, the items accompanying them, or the hoped-for effects. These are questions that could have clearer answers if archaeologists knew what combination of information would address them.

We have gathered a good deal of information to answer these questions, and first we will outline our assumptions in order to explain our results. We begin with the intellectual conditions we work with, as well as those we had to try to overcome.

We assume that the material remains on which we report, and the primary documents we cite, reflect the world of meaning of those who made and used them. The archaeological material is not random, and neither is the record of discussion of items left by former slaves. We also assume that the items used in the religious tradition we are rebuilding through archaeology and records played an active role in the functioning of the culture. In other words, the items helped make the tradition work.

This chapter is about Hoodoo. This is an important concession and a deliberate use of a name at this point because it was a secret religion. The pattern of religious practices called Hoodoo is a variant of Voodoo or Vodoun and centered on the existence of an all-pervasive spirit that was passive most of the time, but which could be directed by humans. West African Vodoun and Haitian Voodoo are tied, yet have separate histories, and North American Hoodoo was a set of practices derived from Africa but with a long history of development in eastern North America (Raboteau 1980; Thompson 1983). "Hoodoo" is itself a Southern folk term for an oral tradition practiced largely without professionals, without a named pantheon, and without an articulated theology.

We are leading to a description of Hoodoo, as well as a view of it as largely positive, a view normally taken in anthropology and folklore of any religion. Hoodoo depended for its efficacy on being kept secret from the objects of its magic, as well as from unbelievers of both the African American and European worlds. Therefore, reconstructing the patterns of the religion archaeologically requires us to present a large amount of numerical data that could never have been known to those who used and believed in Hoodoo. These patterns give us the time depth for the religious practices as well as their spatial extent.

To discover the time depth and spatial extent of the religion is a significant achievement, but it is one based on the assumption that patterns exist which believers were completely unaware of and did not comment on.

What we have had to overcome is much more compelling and makes our work much more important because it allows us to focus on those who doubt archaeology's ability to comment on religion. The nationally available printed opinions of two archaeologists encompass the reason for our preceding assumptions. Their opinions make our assumptions central to our work.

> John Seidel, a professor of anthropology at Washington College in Chestertown, Maryland, said scholars sometimes publish studies on the "caches" without explaining the context.
>
> "These objects are occasionally scattered all over a room, so it's hard to conclude that one group is a 'cache.' You can't label every crystal or piece of inscribed ceramic that you find as a cache," he said.
>
> Al Luckenbach, the archaeologist of Anne Arundel County in Maryland, said he is skeptical partly because he hasn't seen a photograph of a "cache" in its state as found.
>
> "If I found one of these caches, I would be photographing it and calling in people to look at it," he said.
>
> "In addition, in Charles Carroll's day, a man across the street from the house at the time was selling crystals in a newspaper advertisement," Luckenbach said.
>
> "We don't know for what purpose this guy was advertising crystals, but I doubt he was selling them to African Americans for ritual purposes." (Lucentini 2000:C3, C10)

These archaeological colleagues are making important points. What constitutes a "cache," and how does an archaeologist record one when it is found? And where do these materials come from? Within this second question is buried another: How is the meaning of the items determined? The first question is important, and we provide an initial answer here. The answer to the second is far more sophisticated and comes from establishing the meaning of the objects themselves. We also attempt an answer to that question.

We would like to report on an ongoing effort to deal with the material patterns produced by religious traditions derived from various areas in West Africa (Jones 1995). To establish a foundation, we begin with an event in local archaeology. In 1990 (Logan et al. 1992) in Annapolis, Leone and his colleagues excavated some materials that were unlike anything they had seen since beginning to excavate in the city in 1981: a group of a dozen rock crystals, perforated bone discs, a black river pebble, the broken pearlware base of a bowl with a blue asterisk on it, and two dated coins. The artifacts were found together in the corner of a room of an eighteenth-century house. The excavator, a skilled amateur, recovered them as a single entity; the artifacts did not come from different strata. They were removed before a photograph could be taken.

The find was publicized widely, including in the *New York Times*. One day after the piece describing the collection of fragments appeared in the *Times*, the curator of West African art of the Baltimore Museum of Art, Frederick Lamp, a former student of Robert Ferris Thompson, the well-known scholar of West African art at Yale University, called to tell Leone what he thought these items were. He said that these items were really one item, and that it was a cache related to West African spirit management. Leone has cited Frederick Lamp's identification of these materials ever since in scholarship and in the popular media. However, it remains important to establish a method that moves from episodic archaeological discovery accompanied by a serendipitous scientific identification to a general pattern. It is important to do this in order to respond to the other archaeologists who want to know what constitutes the remains of West African spirit management traditions and what does not. We attempt in this chapter to move from one successful identification in Annapolis to a pattern true for the North American South, and we aim to show how to use the existing literary material to reveal the pattern of practices originating in Africa and sustained by Americans of African descent.

Historical archaeology focuses on the spread of European culture and the interruption, destruction of, or response from those confronted by European colonization. Virtually any definition of culture stresses the wholeness or integrity of people's lives. People are assumed to strive for inner coherence in their society's customs and beliefs, and the basic assumption within the concept of culture is one of a self-understood, patterned, all-encompassing way of life that explains being and its consequences. To make use of these assumptions, historical archaeologists join the material remains they discover to documents that are often guides to colonialism's impact as well as to people's resistance to its effects.

When we generalize from our assumptions and circumstances, it is exhilarating to deal with the pattern of religion among Americans of African descent. Therefore, what was the cache discovered in Annapolis? Where else are similar remains found? How similar are the items to each other? How long were they used? Did their composition change over time? What did their makers and users say?

Annapolis itself provides a remarkable place to begin. Since 1990, Leone's project, Archaeology in Annapolis, has excavated seven major sites where Americans of African descent have lived. The sites date from the eighteenth to the twentieth centuries, are all in the heart of a tightly packed city, and are thus within short walks of each other. Each site was known to be associated with Americans of African descent before being excavated, but as the project's understanding of how to produce knowledge about Americans of African descent intensified, the focus on what was being discovered became much sharper.

The team composing Archaeology in Annapolis has dug four of the great eighteenth-century houses that represent the top of the city's social order. The four houses have been explored archaeologically since 1990 and are still occupied. One house was built by the Charles Carroll family and is now owned by the local Roman Catholic church; the Slayton House (Jones 2000) is a large row house across the street from the Carroll House; the Bordley Randall House is across the street from the Maryland Statehouse; and the Brice House is a few blocks from all the others. The major impact of our archaeological work has been to produce concrete evidence that Americans of African descent lived in them and used a very different pattern of material culture, one derived from Africa.

Archaeology in Annapolis also dug homes where free Americans of African descent had always lived. These included a turn-of-the century tenement, Gott's Court (Goodwin 1993; Warner 1990), which was built around 1906 and destroyed in 1950 for a downtown parking lot. The second site included many of the houses on Franklin Street (Aiello and Seidel 1994; Warner and Mullins 1993) that composed middle-class and tenement housing, all situated in a single block. These were built between 1850 and 1900 and were all torn down in the late 1950s and early 1960s for parking spaces. This multi-class block was faced with attached middle-class row houses that looked out to the streets and hid the tenements of poorer people built behind them. These, like the Gott's Court tenements, were alley dwellings.

The third environment was the Maynard Burgess House (Mullins and Warner 1993), built by a free black man in 1847, and owned and lived in by a succession of two African American families until the 1980s. The still extant house and yard were excavated extensively by Archaeology in Annapolis. All these domestic settings are within a short walk of each other, and all are directly associated with local African Americans, many of whom have family members living in or near Annapolis. The dated material from archaeology begins about 1790 at the Charles Carroll House, spans the nineteenth century, and continues into the twentieth century at many of the sites. The plentiful material from the twentieth century not only can be used to show a connection to earlier generations, but also serves as "sites of memory" for the reconstruction of a buried African American past (Fabre and O'Meally 1994).

Although these great houses were all built

in the eighteenth century, the material in them associated with Americans of African descent is from the nineteenth and twentieth centuries, with the exception of some late eighteenth-century material from the Carroll House. Materials were recovered from twelve caches of clustered and densely laid items forming what is left of bundles. One of these sets of materials contains hundreds of items from the east wing of the Brice House, believed by Leone and his team to be parts of a crossroads or cosmogram.

The contents commonly found in a cache in Annapolis are by now familiar and frequently include common pins or nails; perforated discs (buttons, coins, and shells); rings, sometimes too big to be worn on a finger; pieces of broken pottery; pebbles; pieces of glass; and crystals. All the objects are so juxtaposed and so closely placed that they cannot profitably be considered to occur accidentally. Three caches were discovered at Carroll House, as many as seven at Slayton House, and two at Brice House. But at Brice one of the two was actually an ensemble of four caches arranged so as to encompass the set of two rooms they were placed within.

As these caches were discovered, two lines of inquiry were followed simultaneously: one archaeological, one documentary. First, using the research design of Gladys-Marie Fry, a thorough exploration of the site reports (Leone and Fry 1999) on environments lived in by Americans of African descent in Virginia, North Carolina, and South Carolina was begun. All the site reports from Virginia and North Carolina were read that reported on slave cabins, urban settings in which Americans of African descent lived, rural homesteads belonging to tenant farmers, the Slave Pen in Alexandria, Virginia, and any similar place that merited attention. In addition, the site reports from coastal counties of South Carolina have been read, but not yet those from the whole state. Jane Cox read those from Virginia; Matthew Cochran read those from North Carolina and South Carolina.

There were thirty-six site reports on African American locales in Virginia, but

Table 9.1. All Items from African American Archaeological Deposits in Virginia, 1702–1920

ITEMS	FREQUENCY
beads	87
bottles	13
bones	93
broach	1
buckles	30
buttons	285
cameo	1
ceramics	10
chisel	1
circular frame	1
coins	19
comb	2
crystals	47
discs	48
gaming pieces	4
glass	11
hinge	1
hook	2
horse bit	1
horseshoe	3
jewelry	5
keys	2
knife blade	2
nails	49
necklace	1
needles	3
pendant	2
pins	625
rings	4
sinker	1
spring	1
stones	8
strainers	1
watch fob	2
wire	149
wood	1

Source: Leone and Fry 1999.

only seventeen with material collected and reported in such a way that it could be connected to our study. There were only seven useful site reports from North Carolina, and a dozen out of a total of seventy from coastal South Carolina. The ability of archaeologists to recognize caches or deposits of the kind found in Annapolis has been developed so recently that many earlier excavation techniques and descriptions failed to notice what now is clearly a pattern. Nonetheless, enough material, often of a truly coherent kind, was found and recorded by earlier archaeologists even though its meaning was unclear.

Archaeologically, there are many deposits composed of materials like those found in Annapolis. They can be identified in site reports because of a developing understanding not only of what to look for, but also of where to look. The first pattern that was becoming clear was the composition of deposits: nails, pins, bits of glass, buttons, bones, beads, coins—mostly pierced—and potsherds (Table 9.1). The second pattern that was becoming clear was placement. Caches were under chimney bases or hearths, under a room's northeast corner, and around doorways: under their sills, over the door, and by doorposts.

Table 9.1 lists the universe of items in Virginia's African American sites. It is fairly exhaustive and is derived from our joint survey, published in the *Journal of American Folklore* (Leone and Fry 1999). The table shows the counts for each item. Items are listed by site in the article. For our purposes the key comparison is with Table 9.2, a list of protective charms derived from the autobiographies. This list of items used in Hoodoo is twice as long as Table 9.1 and is filled with many items that perish when buried.

Table 9.1 lists the items that need an explanation for an archaeologist. Particularly, we want to know their use and meaning, which, if known, would show that they are the remains of Hoodoo practices. To explain the items in Table 9.1, we surveyed all the citations to "tobys," "hands," and "mojos" in the autobiographies. These synonymous terms refer to the ritual bundles by which Hoodoo works. It is quite unlikely that the names used in Table 9.1 denote the meaning of the item as it was originally used; that is, they do not convey metaphorical intent. In Hoodoo, coins, discs, and buttons represent the completeness of life or the circuit of the sun, and thus of life. Springs from a clock and water represent constant running. While these meanings come from the autobiographies, the true meaning or purpose of items is to be found only by exploring its combination with other items, joined to accomplish a task. None of those archaeological items ever occurs by itself; they are always found in combination. Thus, archaeological discovery tends to fragment sets intended for use as a whole.

The items listed in Table 9.1 have only modest overlap with those in Table 9.2. The most common items in Table 9.1 are beads, bones, buttons, crystals, discs, nails, pins, and wire. These are the most numerous items found archaeologically. Bones, buttons, and coins are the most frequently mentioned items in the autobiographies that could be found archaeologically. There is enough overlap to be convinced that we are dealing with material from the same set of practices, and yet enough differences to realize that we must look for an explanation for the discrepancies between the archaeology and the autobiographies.

The materials excavated throughout Virginia were similar to those being regularly recovered in Annapolis in the 1990s, as well as what was already known from Garrison Plantation (Klingelhofer 1987) near Baltimore. The material we surveyed from North Carolina was also similar. Other patterns emerged. The more material we uncovered in Annapolis, the more variation in distribution there appeared to be. But there was not more variation in the items found. In South Carolina and at the Levi Jordan Plantation in Texas, there were deposits that were much more elaborate and spread out than those known in Annapolis, but we did not notice this pattern until 1998, when we recovered a cosmogram in Annapolis (Cochran and Neuwirth 2000). A cosmogram is made up of

Table 9.2. Protective Charms

Charm (with key ingredient)	Function	Location
1. bag (toby)	prevent whipping	wear (unspecified)
8 dimes	protect from conjure	wear over heart
9 red ants	ease teething	around neck
asafetida (herb)	prevent smallpox	around neck
	prevent chills	around neck
	protect from conjure	around neck
	ease teething	around neck
devil's snuff	make friendly	under steps
lodestone	protect from conjure	around neck
powder	protect from conjure	around neck
salt	prevent palpitations	wear over heart
sand	avoid whipping	carry
sulfur	protect from conjure	knee: or shoe
wood ash	fix court case	carry
2. ball (silver)	protect from conjure	not given
3. band (red flannel)	gain strength	wrist
	prevent rheumatism	arm or leg
4. beads	prevent sickness	around neck
5. belt (snakeskin)	not given	wear
6. bone (black cat)	avoid whipping	pocket
	bring luck: with law	carry
	make disappear	not given
	avoid detection	carry
7. bones	not given	not given
8. brick (powdered)	protect from conjure	steps
9. broom	protect from witch	before door
10. buckeye	bring luck	carry
	prevent sickness	carry in pocket
		around neck
11. button	bring luck	carry
12. button (charm string)	bring luck	neck
6 white	bring luck/ease teething	neck
pearl	ease teething	neck
shiny	prevent sickness	wear
13. calf dropping	escape patrol	feet
14. claw (buzzard)	ease teething	neck
15. coin	protect from conjure	ankle, neck
	prevent rheumatism	ankle
	bring luck	carry
	prevent sickness	ankle
16. coin (brass)	avoid indigestion	neck
17. coin (dime)	not given	on string of beads
	protect from conjure	ankle
		swallow with tea
		shoe
	prevent cramps	neck

Table 9.2. Protective Charms continued

Charm (with key ingredient)	Function	Location
18. coin (penny)	prevent sickness protect from conjure avoid indigestion	ankle floor by door neck
19. coin (pierced dime)	prevent rheumatism	not given
20. corn shuck	protect from conjure	shoe
21. crab	make invincible	hold in mouth
22. feathers (bird)	protect from conjure	wear
23. flaxseed	protect from witch	around bed
24. fork	protect from witch	by bed
25. frog (dried)	ease teething	neck
26. graveyard dirt	escape patrol	feet
27. hand	control mistress	not given
28. hand (red flannel)	protect from witch bring luck protect from conjure	under armpit pocket neck
29. horseshoe	protect from spirits avoid whipping bring luck protect from spirits	over door over door over front door over door
30. jawbone (hog)	ease teething	not given
31. lead disc (with 9 holes)	prevent palpitations	around neck
32. matches	prevent headache protect from conjure	hair hair
33. mole foot	ease teething	neck
34. nails (5 new)	avoid whipping	in ground
35. needles (2)	protect from conjure	crossed in hat
36. newspaper (with red pepper)	protect from conjure	shoe
37. nutmeg	prevent rheumatism ease toothache prevent headache ease teething	neck neck neck neck
38. peace plant	protect from conjure	pocket or shoe
39. pins (in pincushion)	protect from witch	side of bed
40. rabbit foot	bring luck protect from witch avoid detection avoid whipping	carry wear carry neck
41. raccoon foot	protect from witches bring luck	wear carry
42. rattan	avoid whipping	wave in face
43. rattlesnake rattles	ease teething	neck
44. red pepper pod	protect from conjure	over door

Table 9.2. Protective Charms continued

Charm (with key ingredient)	Function	Location
45. ring (black)	bring luck	hand
46. ring (brass)	prevent croup	finger
	prevent heart pains	left hand
	prevent rheumatism	finger
47. root	avoid whipping	chew and spit
anjillico	prevent sickness	neck
devil's shoe string	bring luck	not given
	get money or job	chew
drink	protect from conjure	drink
five-finger grass	protect from conjure	over bed
John the Conqueror	protect from conjure	pocket
	bring luck	carry in pocket
rattle snake master	bring luck	not given
devil's shoestring	obtain favors	chew
	release from jail	spit in cell
	avoid whipping	tie around waist
48. salt	avoid ill will	footprints of guests
49. saltpeter	protect from conjure	shoe
50. shoe	protect from conjure	over door
old	protect from spirits	over door
51. sifter (flour)	protect from witch	by bed
52. silver	remove conjure	drink in whiskey
pieces	protect from conjure	boil and drink
53. snakeskin	protect from conjure	wear
54. stick	avoid pursuit	crossroads
	avoid whipping	under master's door
	avoid mistreatment	under master's door
55. string	protect from witch	on image
		in hair
	prevent sickness	neck
	prevent cramps	wrist and ankle
		wrist
	ease teething	neck
56. teeth (alligator)	ease teething	not given
57. turpentine	escape patrol	feet
58. urine	protect from conjure	back steps
59. urine and salt	protect from conjure	around door
60. yellow dust	avoid mistreatment	sprinkle

Note: Data collected from Rawick, *The American Slave: A Composite Autobiography* (1972–79). The Federal Writers Project, under the auspices of the Works Progress Administration, collected interviews from twenty-six states and the District of Columbia. Most of the interviews, however, focus on seven states in the Deep South: Texas (11 vols.); Mississippi (5 vols.); Georgia (4 vols.); Arkansas (4 vols.); and North Carolina, South Carolina, and Alabama, represented by two volumes apiece. This emphasis is also reflected in the numbers for informants with knowledge of conjuration items. Some states are represented by only a small number of interviews. These include Colorado, Kentucky, Minnesota, Oregon, Tennessee, Virginia, and Washington.

a set of bundles or caches arranged at the ends of the arms of a crossroads, a cross, or x-shaped axes. There is usually a cache at the center of the crossing as well as at the ends of the arms.

With all the discoveries, the first task of archaeologists working in Annapolis was to escape the claim that the discoveries were unique and uninterpretable (i.e., they were yard scatter or rubbish). Once a comparative search in Virginia, North Carolina, and South Carolina was started, the discovery of similar materials showed that the Annapolis material could be identified with a pattern of usage by Americans of African descent. Thus there was a general archaeological pattern. Further, because of ethnographic work in West Africa, the pattern of the circle of life or cosmogram, together with the use of crystals, ashes, and chalk for whiteness, had an African identity and was derived from West and Central West African religious practices. People in the autobiographies themselves said the practices came from Africa.

Our search involved sites occupied by Americans of African descent and the large amount of documentary information on slave life, particularly that collected in the 1930s from former slaves or their descendants. Our second line of inquiry, which involved the documentary records, began under Gladys-Marie Fry's direction. The part of this effort reported here has as its aim explaining the discoveries of archaeology. Timothy Ruppel made a virtually total survey of the primary literature compiled in the twentieth century from former slaves. Ruppel collected all mentions of Hoodoo's paraphernalia: bundles, hands, mojos, tobys, "fixings," doctor's kits, or "root work," which we have maintained in a database that is not fully published with this article. His words in Table 9.2 are the appropriate terms for the caches and deposits mentioned in the autobiographies but also discovered archaeologically. His was a search for citations of the material culture of Hoodoo that we knew of archaeologically.

The primary source of data on the lives of former slaves is the forty-one volumes edited by George P. Rawick and published between 1972 and 1979 under the title *The American Slave: A Composite Autobiography.* The autobiography was the outcome of the project sponsored by the Works Progress Administration Writers' Project, which set out to interview all living former slaves, especially in the southern states. Additional WPA data was found in individual volumes focused on Virginia, Louisiana, and coastal Georgia (Clayton 1990; Joyner 1986; Perdue et al. 1976). These, too, were read by Ruppel. The autobiographies produced thousands of pages of firsthand accounts of life in slavery, including information on religion and religious practices. This WPA project used a protocol: a set list of questions to be used in each interview. A second enormous volume of material was simultaneously collected by Harry Middleton Hyatt (1965, 1970–1978), and it concentrated on religious practices and beliefs that continued after slavery. Ruppel read this work completely. He also collected additional material from journals of folklore and the pioneering fieldwork of Newbell Niles Puckett and Zora Neal Hurston. In this chapter we cite only Rawick.

The WPA interviews address why bundles were made, how they were to be used, and what their hoped-for effects were. Such material allows for an initial effort to outline in greater detail the pattern revealed through archaeological finds. In the autobiographies edited by Rawick, there are 239 separate references to the use of specific material objects alluding to hands, mojos, bundles, and similar Hoodoo ritual objects. Standard to the analytical literature in folklore is the distinction that bundles were used for two different purposes: protection or retribution. Our data show that 75 percent of the intentions were to protect; 25 percent were to cause harm. Central to these beliefs was the understanding that good fortune and misfortune were the result of humans manipulating spirits.

In order to illuminate the archaeology, our analysis began with the material culture used for protection and how protection was to occur. This was productive but, in the long run, a misleading start, as will be clear. Given that protection from disease and harm was involved in making and using bundles, we asked for the sources of disease and what could alleviate these problems. Our report is quantitative (see Table 9.2) and shows the results of investigating the items associated with disease and curing. Before relating the numerical results which, like all quantitative data, tend to divorce patterns from people's life experiences, it is helpful to relay a narrative account of curing. This form of reporting is the only way the autobiographies have so far been used in folklore or historical archaeology. James Moore of Tin City, South Carolina, provided a clear description of conjure and healing. He told of a man who was conjured and began to swell up, and the local doctors couldn't tell what was wrong with him. A root man, known as the "Professor," was brought in to lift the spell. Upon being paid, the Professor found a little black sack in the stable and claimed that the sack contained the conjure. The root doctor then boiled mullen leaves and bathed the victim. In two weeks, the swelling went down, and the victim was cured (Joyner 1986).

After collecting and sorting all such episodes, Ruppel found 239 individual mentions of material objects in the WPA autobiographies edited by Rawick that were associated with magical items or the magical practices that cured diseases. The interviews that mention the range of materials and their uses involve more than 102 people from fourteen states, mostly in the Deep South, but also in Maryland and Indiana. Table 9.2 lists all items concerned with curing and protection (i.e., bag, hand) mentioned in *The American Slave: A Composite Autobiography* (Rawick 1972–1979) under the term "charm." Table 9.2 lists the malady or occurrence being dealt with and where the charm was to be placed or worn. The purpose of Table 9.2 is to provide evidence of the full range of variation of items used in Hoodoo for preventing disease, bringing luck, or providing protection. It is not our complete survey; it is a reduction that shows only one mention per item of, for example, a black cat bone used for avoiding whipping, when there were actually two in the autobiographies. Our point was to create an inventory of items that could be compared to Table 9.1. We have also recorded frequency of use as cited in the autobiographies. These are recorded in our text to make specific points, but not in Table 9.2.

By looking at our data, Ruppel found that protective charms worn on the body were used for two general purposes. One involved protection from sickness/disease. For example, a cord with nine knots around the leg prevented rheumatism; a brass charm around the neck prevented heart pains, as did a brass ring worn on the left hand. Charm beads around the neck protected against sickness, and a silver dime tied around the ankle turned black as a protective warning that conjure has been put down for the victim. Charms were limited to treating teething and toothaches, preventing heart pains, curing cramps and colic, relieving headaches, treating worms, and alleviating rheumatism. Generally, charms that were worn on the body were not to be buried in the ground or placed in a room.

The second general reason for wearing a protective charm was to bring good luck, to afford protection from disruptive occurrences, and to keep off conjure. Carrying a black cat bone in the pocket brought luck and prevented whippings. Wearing a string of buttons around the neck produced good luck. A rabbit's foot around the neck charmed the master. Corn shucks in the shoe, needles crossed in the hat, a sack containing lodestone, or a snake skin worn on the body all prevented conjure.

There was a well-defined set of medical problems and a generic set of damaging social conditions that charms cured or prevented. Wearing charms was not a common medical practice, nor a universal practice for all difficult circumstances. There were also distinct limitations; charms could not end slavery or racial segregation. However, charms did allow those using them to achieve some measure of control and coherence in a world of forced separations and economic injustice. In the course of his thorough reading, Ruppel realized that Hoodoo served as a survival tool, one that offered hope for an alternative to a regime of oppression and implied that these conditions were finite and ultimately surmountable.

If these were the limits of protection, then what was used to protect? Three items were employed predominately in healing and protecting, not an infinite variety. The three most frequently used were coins, small sacks called "hands," and animals' feet. There are other items mentioned as well (roots, horseshoes, buttons, string, rings) that help compose the universe. The most frequent items that appear archaeologically are pins, bones, buttons, and wire.

For the most part, items protect by being worn. Eighty-three percent (see Table 9.2) of occurrences say charms for protection were worn around the neck, carried in the pocket, or fastened around the ankle. These would not be available archaeologically in any recognizable way. Occasionally such items were worn in the hair, in a shoe, or under an armpit. A second class of protective charms appeared around doors or under the steps, and included horseshoes nailed over the door. The locations account for 17 percent of the total and would be available archaeologically.

At this point we know that there was a healing tradition that used metaphoric items to prevent a defined range of physical ailments as well as some socially imposed maladies. A protective charm was worn, usually visibly, or much less often placed around passages leading to the house. These practices identified medicine for physical and social ills and have been called a "sacred pharmacoepia" (Smith 1994). This community-oriented tradition of healing and protecting existed in a dialectical relationship with its counterpart, called "fixing" or "conjure." Any spell or disease could be counteracted by a more powerful and resourceful root doctor with the knowledge of the necessary antidotes.

Although we are attempting to reconstruct an aspect of Hoodoo that is unknown systematically—namely, its material culture—we find a discrepancy between the items in Table 9.2, identified through interviews, and the items in Table 9.1, found through archaeology. The most frequently found items archaeologically are pins (c. 625), buttons (c. 285), bones (c. 93), beads (c. 87), buckles, nails (c. 49), crystals (c. 47), and discs (c. 48). There is only overlap in terms of frequency of use with the counts from the autobiographies for coins (30), bones (21), and buttons, particularly if we think of buttons as discs (7). These are the items most frequently employed as charms that stand a chance of being found archaeologically.

There is only a 14.8 percent overlap with location when charms are compared to archaeological deposits. Because charms were worn 85 percent of the time, according to Table 9.2, and the rest of the time, as specified in the autobiographies (also in Table 9.2), they were used under steps, the floor by the door, over the door, or in the ground, and because this is where archaeological finds have generally been made, we claim quite limited coincidence between the location of charms and the location of archaeological items. If there is so little overlap between the archaeological record of Hoodoo and the directions in the autobiographies for making and using charms to control spirits, then is this a proper comparison? Perhaps John Seidel is correct when he says that "not every crystal is a cache," and perhaps Al Luckenbach is correct when he wonders whether there is a tie between crystals, African ritual traditions, and where they are found. Certainly, the tables derived from our survey of the autobiographies only begin to make the case for a connection between archaeological discoveries and the autobiographies. Our data do not prove a complete link; there is a discrepancy.

What can explain the weak tie between the bulk of citations on Hoodoo charms from the autobiographies and our intended use of them to explain the archaeological discoveries? Much, but not all, of the answer lies in the material reported in Tables 9.3, 9.4, and 9.5, devoted to malign conjure, better known as conjure and fixing. Of the items that stand a chance of being found archaeologically, the autobiographies show that bottles, needles, hair, and pins were used frequently in conjure. They are frequently found archaeologically. Bottles and hair were never used as charms. Further, only half of the items used for fixing were ever worn as charms. Table 9.5 shows that fixing items were frequently found under steps, in the fireplace, in the ground, or outside the house. These are also the places where conjure items are found archaeologically. Elements of malign conjure were rarely worn or eaten. Therefore, location begins to predict fixing. Further, the presence of bottles, needles, hair, or a poker is a highly reliable indicator of the use of malign conjure. Thus, we may have found a way to identify the known archaeological material and to predict the meaning of future materials.

These relationships raise the question of why conjure items would be found systematically in a person's home. We do not have the answer in this chapter. We can see through archaeology that the design of a room or set of rooms as a crossroads is never mentioned in the autobiographies and yet occurs archaeologically. Neither is the use of northeast corners or of crystals or quartz fragments. These archaeological occurrences may require that we look at and reread the autobiographies in a different way, with a new slant. That is as it should be, given the method (Binford 1983, 1987) we have employed.

Table 9.2 shows an overlap of about 50 percent in the items that could be used as charms or for fixing, so the items themselves, except for bottles, hair, and pokers, usually cannot be used to discriminate between the two parts of Hoodoo. Items plus location, however, do present a coherent picture. The autobiographies give the impression that charms were used continuously and constantly relied upon. Once made, they were not taken off. The impression from the autobiographies is the opposite for fixing. Fixing was done once, for a purpose, and then for-

Table 9.3. Items Used in Malign Conjure

Items	Frequency of Mention
1. dust (snake)	15
2. bags	14
3. hair (victim's)	12
4. bottles	7
5. needles	4
6. dust (lizard)	4
7. red flannel	4
8. dust (scorpion)	3
9. roots	3
10. pins	3
11. groundpuppy	3
12. little man	2
13. lodestone	2
14. fingernail (victim's)	2
15. bluestone	2
16. bone (black cat)	1
17. poker	1
18. foot track	1
19. stocking	1
20. underwear	1
21. beads	1
22. fluid	1
23. wood chip	1
24. blood (scorpion)	1
25. tack	1
26. insect	1
27. sulfur	1
28. penny	1
29. urine	1
30. water (clear)	1
31. clothing (victim's)	1
32. dust (frog)	1
33. snakeskin	1
34. horse hair	1
35. ashes	1
36. stone	1
37. feathers	1
38. rabbit foot	1

Table 9.3. Items Used in Malign Conjure continued

Items	Frequency of Mention
39. bone (dead man's)	1
40. nails (brass)	1
41. thimbles	1
42. bone (frog)	1
Total	107

Source: Rawick, *The American Slave.* There were sixty mentions of malign conjure in Rawick as reported in Tables 9.4 and 9.5, with a total of 107 items used for this purpose.

gotten because, presumably, the aim had been accomplished.

Because our data show that fixing could be done inside or outside the house, that it was done only once, and that there is considerable overlap of items used for charms and fixing, we are left with two questions: Why would people who lived in a house use fixing routinely? And, is our archaeological pattern really malign conjure (fixing)? These patterns have an explanation if a house contained long-term hostile relationships and if a community of African Americans was stable. We know both occurred frequently on plantations and in the big houses of Annapolis. Fixing thus may have been aimed at the master and at controlling the long-term subordination we know existed.

As shown in Table 9.4, conjure can cause harm, kill, inflict illness, drive someone crazy, or make a person restless. Thus we now understand the complete range of meanings of fixing or conjure.

Only at this point is it possible to see that we misled ourselves initially by searching the autobiographies for mentions of single items used for magical purposes. Such items are worn to bring luck and prevent illness, and are not likely to be found archaeologically in a recognizable context. When we forced ourselves to ask about the mismatch between the tables drawn from the autobiographies and those from the archaeology, we realized some part of the picture was missing. Only when we forced ourselves to listen to Seidel and Luckenbach did we realize there was more work to do. The extension of our work was to enter a domain suggested by the scholarly literature, but proscribed by prejudice: conjure. As it turns out, the pattern used to conjure is the one that is likely to be available for archaeological recovery. The items used and the locations favored generally match those which historical archaeologists have been finding for more than twenty years.

Table 9.4. Intentions in Malign Conjure

Intention	Frequency of Mention
Harm	13
Kill	9
Make sick	8
Make crazy	6
Not given	5
Control	4
Swelling	3
Poison	2
Cause rheumatism	2
Cause pain	2
Make restless	2
Make move	1
Cause maggots	1
Cripple	1
Make blind	1
Total	60

Source: Rawick, *American Slave.*

Our presentation should begin to solve the problem of identifying the densely packed collections of reused European and local items that were deliberately laid down in Annapolis from 1790 to 1920 under hearths, beneath thresholds, and in northeast corners of rooms. In our research into African American locales in Virginia, North Carolina, and South Carolina we demonstrated that material similar to that from Annapolis occurred in many other places. This element of our description has shown that the material occurred in domestic environments where Americans of African descent lived and worked, and that it was deliberately buried.

Table 9.5. Locations Used in Malign Conjure

Location	Frequency of Mention
Not given	25
Under steps	12
Tree	4
Drinking water	3
Alcohol	3
Running water	2
Hat	2
Food	1
Tea	1
Closet	1
Ground	1
Fireplace	1
Clothes	1
Bed	1
Hoe	1
Hair	1
Total	60

Source: Rawick, *American Slave.*

Further, the material included a rather narrow range of things.

Our parallel search of the narrative autobiographies involved reading all of Hyatt and all of Rawick, a remarkable task defined by Fry and accomplished by Ruppel. This chapter cites only Rawick. Our documentary work, the first quantitative analysis of these texts, helps to demonstrate that the deposits were made by Americans of African descent, were part of a religious practice called Hoodoo, and that the origins, as claimed by informants, were West African, and more particularly Central West African.

Because conjure was a set of extended metaphors, we acknowledge that our distinctions can never be precise. Nonetheless, a number of items can be given meaning based on similitude. Graveyard dirt appears only in malevolent conjure hands, and it was preferably from the grave of a murderer or an evil person. This dirt directed the spirit to do harm, such as causing the victim to be restless or to waste away and die. Powders made from snake dust (powdered, dried snake remains) caused blindness, swelling, or live snakes to inhabit the victim's body. Nearly half of the conjure hands intended to cause harm also contained items that embodied the intended victim's spirit. These items included hair, fingernails, foot tracks, underwear, and pieces of clothing, with the most commonly mentioned item being the victim's hair.

Hoodoo, sometimes called "conjure," could only work if its core principle was convincing: spirits existed and could be aimed. The aiming and deflection were achieved by the use of bundles, mojos, hands, and so forth, or the manipulation of a few other things that operated in the same way. Minimally, there were three parts to any bundle. Because a bundle was always made for a specific reason at a specific time, it contained something that stood for that time or need: a crab claw for tenacious strength, a bent pin or nail for an aching joint, a disc for the wholeness of life and thus to ward off disease. The disc, or a four-hole button, was the cosmogram, representing the wholeness of life that is not to be interrupted. Second, there had to be something from the person to be affected: hair, fingernails, pieces of clothing, string. Then there had to be something that contained, moved, and directed the spirits. This could be graveyard dirt, a crystal, broken glass or a mirror fragment, sulphur, red flannel, or loadstone. Finally, when combined and employed, the spirit cured someone's rheumatism, kept a violent master at bay, drew out a malevolent spirit, brought a desired mate, protected a child from harm, or drove someone away. The spirit was actually in the bundle, not just represented by it. And the spirit had to behave as the bundle directed. The spirit did not have a choice.

Spirits existed to be used, and "fixing" meant putting them to work for one's own good or against some other spirit or spirit user who had aimed at oneself. Because the dead wandered as spirits on their way back to the sea and traveled waterways in order to get there, the world was filled with them. The basic assumption was that their power could be controlled by having knowledge of what they responded to and how to evoke them. Contact with them had to be direct. They could be made to enter and exit a user's body, and when they did, they possessed it and made a person do things. This process of possession could be brought about by using mojos, hands, or tobys. Conversely, possession was cured, or warded off, by wearing protective charms.

How widely practiced was conjure? Because its effectiveness depended on belief in it by others, how widely acknowledged was it? To answer these questions, it was important to assume that there would be variation from one place to another, with stronger and more-coherent beliefs in Hoodoo where a community of Americans of African descent was coherent. In a place such as Annapolis, where the ability of whites to watch and supervise was enhanced because it was a densely built city, and where whites were dominant in virtually every sense, one might assume that Hoodoo would have been diminished because it was obviously not Christian. Our archaeological discoveries show the opposite to be true.

These questions suggested a third line of inquiry to Ruppel. Instead of looking only for evidence of material objects used to protect or to harm in the WPA autobiographies, Ruppel surveyed a range of magical practices and beliefs within clearly defined communities. Magical practices were defined as knowledge of or belief in divination, spirits, witches, protective charms, conjure, root workers, and magical powers. The WPA Georgia Writers' Project, which worked within a seventy-five-mile radius around Savannah, was used to construct our first answer. Project participants conducted 139 interviews with former slaves and their descendants from the Savannah area, including the coastal islands, in the 1930s. This material was published in *Drums and Shadows* (Joyner 1986). There were twenty communities surveyed. Less than a quarter of the informants expressed knowledge of root doctors, protective charms, the use of signs, or belief in witches. When asked another way, however, the result was very different. Half the interviewed population believed in spirits and had a knowledge of conjure, which they also called "fixing" or "root working," so conjure was widely understood.

In the twenty communities of Americans of African descent around Savannah, 74 percent of those interviewed had knowledge of these practices (Databank 2000). Even though the numbers may vary from community to community, it is out of patterns like these that we can see coherent practices using a defined set of items, for a clear set of aims, that were widespread in the North American Southeast for more than two and a half centuries.

To conclude, we have shown that Hoodoo was used to cure, protect, and occasionally to punish. We have shown the range of objects that was used to cure, to bring luck, and to prevent harm. When used to harm, the items were specific and are archaeologically visible. Thus it had already been established that there was a pattern of religious practices called Hoodoo, derived from Africa. It was a fragmentary belief system derived from Vodoun, and its rituals survived. We have shown that it was practiced from 1702 to 1920 throughout the American South, with specific objects, in specific places, whose purpose can been understood. This has been achieved through historical archaeology.

Note

The research in this paper was initiated by Professor Gladys-Marie Fry, Department of English, and was sponsored by the University of Maryland, College Park, through grants from Dean James Harris, College of and Humanities, Dean Irwin L. Goldstein, College of Behavioral and Social Science, and Acting Dean Charles Wellford, Graduate Studies and Research. All of the work on the autobiographies and the tables correlating the results was done by Dr. Timothy Ruppel. The essay was written by Professor Mark P. Leone, Department of Anthropology, who conceptualized the tables with assistance from Timothy Ruppel.

10

Racializing the Parlor: Race and Victorian Bric-a-Brac Consumption

PAUL R. MULLINS

In 1897, Charles Richmond Henderson (1897:37) was among a wave of Victorian thinkers who stressed the pivotal moral impact of apparently mundane goods. Henderson's analysis of the relationship between America's social woes and household material culture concluded that "our works and our surroundings corrupt or refine our souls. The dwellings, the walls, the windows, the furniture, the pictures, the ornaments, the dress, the fence or hedge—all act constantly upon the imagination and determine its contents." This soliloquy on the moral implications of sofas and lithographs seems somewhat overwrought in hindsight, yet from the mid-nineteenth century into the Depression, a wide range of Americans shared the conviction that material objects illustrated and forged their possessor's character and values (cf. Grier 1988:2). Henderson was simply one of many thinkers who assumed that even the most prosaic objects instilled, reflected, and reproduced powerful—albeit ill-defined—"moral values." Rather than reduce goods simply to passive reflections of style, culture, or wealth, genteel Victorians believed the material world actively created, shaped, and reproduced virtuous or degenerate values that either fashioned genteel discipline or bred Victorian society's most pressing dilemmas.

In many ways, Victorians' material moralism simply perpetuated longstanding apprehensions about the personal, communal, and spiritual tolls of material acquisitiveness and secular desire (cf. Horowitz 1985). Yet in the midst of a burgeoning consumer economy, dizzying social change, and quite stunning inequality, late nineteenth-century moralism assumed a quite distinctive tenor charged by racial ideology. Even the most commonplace household commodities were considered vessels of racial symbolism, and it was widely assumed that the dominant material symbolism was "white." "White" was a strategically ambiguous concept that concealed a tangle of class, gendered, and regional inequalities, yet racial ideologues argued quite successfully that this tacit white "norm" was the appropriate backdrop against which Victorians should interpret all social and material meaning.

The debate over material goods' racial symbolism extended to even the most innocuous objects. Perhaps the most commonplace class of commodities in Victorian homes was mass-produced bric-a-brac. "Bric-a-brac" is a somewhat inexact term referring to a range of primarily decorative objects that were common in American homes from about 1850 into the early twentieth century. Ornamental objects such as figurines, vases, statuary, and chromolithographs were produced in staggering quantities in the late nineteenth century, and they could be purchased in virtually any American market for a relatively modest cost. Mass-produced baubles depicted a vast range of motifs, including famous personalities (e.g., presidents, royalty), natural scenes (e.g., animals, landscapes), romanticized historical subjects (e.g., shepherds, aristocrats), and popular cultural motifs (e.g., classical art adaptations, colonized peoples).

Bric-a-brac's aesthetic diversity defies easy stylistic categorization, but these objects tended to feature exotic subjects, ambiguous motifs, or caricatures of everyday life that were "multivalent"—that is, the objects had a particularly rich (though still circumscribed) range of possible meanings. Bric-a-brac aesthetics and display were hotly contested among various ideologues who appreciated that its rich symbolism could be interpreted in a range of forms that could conceivably reproduce dominant ideology or resist those very ideologies. Consequently, bric-a-brac consumption was discussed extensively in household and domestic literature (cf. Mullins 1999a:155–157).

Late nineteenth-century racial ideology profoundly shaped all social experience and material symbolism, forging a fiction of universal opportunity and affluence that was radically contradicted in most Americans' lives by profound racist, class, and social barriers. Consequently, it is imprudent to believe racial ideology did not affect every single person in American public space, or that it is simply one "aspect" of identity (e.g., Wilkie, this volume). Race did end up having a quite complex range of effects that consumers negotiated in myriad ways, but we evade the sway of racial ideology if we champion the notion of identity as a fluid experiential juxtaposition of individual consciousness, ethnic history, generational wisdom, and whatever else we suppose gives us identity and makes us each individual. Bric-a-brac ultimately reveals racism in modern consumer culture as a complex lived experience that tactically maneuvers between dominant structural mechanisms, individual aspirations, and the overwhelming discrepancies between America's social possibilities and its concrete inequalities.

Despite bric-a-brac's prominence in turn-of-the-century homes and the heated debates over its appropriate consumption, few scholars have accorded these goods much significance. Archaeologically it is tempting to ignore these sorts of things because bric-a-brac is recovered in modest quantities, it was quite inexpensive, and these objects seem more whimsical than meaningful. Meaningfulness, though, often has little to do with exchange value, and the volume of period commentary on bric-a-brac suggests it had some social significance despite its affordable cost. Reducing these goods to frivolous ornaments disregards that even a seemingly "whimsical" object can harbor a penetrating, yet oblique, social commentary. Small quantities are often the very reason we focus on some goods, and in the case of bric-a-brac, careful curation and low breakage rates explain why it appears in modest archaeological quantities. It is telling that these objects often elicit considerable musing in the field and lab, but are usually buried in an artifact catalog. Our own curiosity is a strong clue that there is significant, albeit enigmatic symbolism lurking within these things.

This chapter probes how we can interpret such apparently mundane material goods as consequential mechanisms that reflected and shaped consumers' understandings of quite significant social issues, including racial ideology, nationalism, and affluence. Most of the material culture examined here came from thirty blocks of houses in West Oakland, California, excavated by the Sonoma State University Anthropological Studies Center (Praetzellis and Praetzellis 1999). The West Oakland project area had remarkable ethnic diversity: Europeans, Chinese, African Americans, and whites lived in the community, with most working at the Oakland railroad yards or in a supporting industry. These sites provided a stunning volume of material culture, including virtually every sort of bric-a-brac. Rather than reduce these objects to fascinating but ultimately trivial trinkets, we might instead wonder why so many consumers envisioned significant meaning in these baubles, and probe precisely what those meanings were.

THE AMBIGUITY OF BRIC-A-BRAC

Bric-a-brac was routinely produced and consumed with no absolutely clear sense of what an object or motif "communicated"; instead, these trinkets usually were not intended to represent anything particularly concrete (Mullins 1999a:165–166). Consequently, it is somewhat misguided to analyze bric-a-brac symbolism in a conventional stylistic analysis that defines what its historical motifs, recognizable personages, or depicted activities were intended to represent. Mass-produced baubles featured familiar popular symbols that were so vaguely or broadly defined that an object's consumer or viewer could interpret it in a reasonable range of ways. Bric-a-brac could evoke pleasant yet inchoate sentiments about a romanticized past, household class identity, Western cultural and racial roots, patriarchy, personal style, aristocratic behavior, or any number of things. It did not matter if a consumer could not clearly articulate the appeal of a given object; if anything, enigmatic motifs were among the most common in bric-a-brac.

This notion of ambiguous bric-a-brac symbolism is somewhat at odds with the standard premise that goods are consumed because they publicly display social identity and a dominant meaning stylistically "encoded" in the object. Thorstein Veblen's (1973) classic formulation of conspicuous materialism posited that things were consumed by a "leisure class" to publicly address society and exhibit social identity, so a good's "use value" rested on its capacity to display social prestige or some clearly defined social identity. In 1957, E. Franklin Frazier reduced "black bourgeoise" consumption to this sort of pretentious class display. Frazier (1957: 230–231) argued that the African American middle class was "constantly buying things.... Many of the furnishings and gadgets which they acquire are never used; nevertheless they continue to accumulate things. The homes of many middle-class Negroes have the appearance of museums for the exhibition of American manufactures and spurious art objects. The objects which they are constantly buying are always on display."

Obviously bric-a-brac was meant to be physically displayed, but it was not simply consumed so that its public exhibition would instrumentally "communicate" some distinct meaning about the consumer to others. Rather than assume its meaning to be public, self-evident, and defined by dominant stylistic mavens and viewers—which is how Veblen and many historical archaeologists tend to see goods—bric-a-brac's symbolism was equally abstract, contextual, and shaped by its consumer. Many consumers certainly did wish to impart their "style," "morality," or "status" with fashionable goods, but these terms were such malleable abstractions that they could entail many different things. Symbolically ambiguous objects allowed their parlor-making consumers to creatively daydream about their own identities and society, not simply to showcase who they were to others. Nevertheless, bric-a-brac symbolism was itself utterly ideological, so consumers did not individually fabricate bric-a-brac meanings that were disconnected to a broader social structure. Instead, material symbolism emerged from a complex tension between highly personal associations and broader systemic factors.

Bric-a-brac extended all material culture's flexible symbolism to its extremes by featuring ambiguous motifs that were primarily evocative mediums rather than straightforward representations. Consumers' attraction to bric-a-brac—and many ideologues' apprehension of the same trinkets—revolved around this ambiguous and evocative symbolism. For instance, a post-1889 cellar from an Annapolis, Maryland, home contained a figurine that was typical of late nineteenth-century bric-a-brac. The porcelain, overglaze-painted female figure's flowing hair, basket of flowers, and flowing dress are consistent with popular cultural idealizations of peasantry (Figure 10.1). We know relatively little about exactly how African Americans

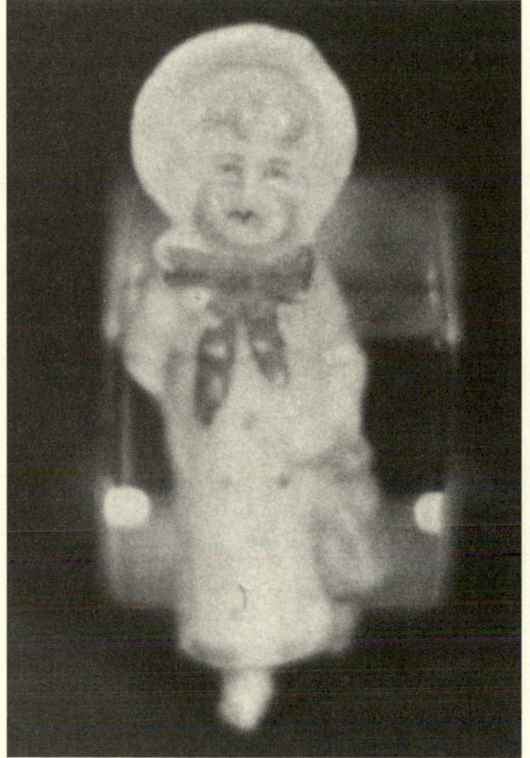

Figure 10.1. This porcelain figurine was recovered from a post-1889 cellar feature in Annapolis, Maryland. This motif was typical of late nineteenth-century designs that presented quixotic visions of bucolic, non-industrial subjects. This figurine had been discarded alongside a porcelain matchholder and a large household refuse assemblage in a feature that was filled by an African American family. (Photo by the author)

actually displayed such goods, but we can persuasively argue for how their symbolism would most likely be constructed across the color-line. This Annapolis object was one of many quixotic bric-a-brac depictions of a peaceful, non-industrial past, evoked in this figurine by the girl's happy and comforting pose. These sorts of nebulous motifs tacitly critiqued contemporary society by reference to idealized but ill-defined subjects: among the most common themes were bucolic and agrarian motifs that evaded (or at least glossed over) agricultural production's complications at the very moment traditional rural agriculture was disappearing from American society. The Annapolis figurine was discarded by an African American household whose members would seem particularly unlikely to ignore the harsh realities of agricultural life: some had been enslaved, and the others could not have ignored the profound underside of southern agriculture displayed on plantations all around Annapolis. In this home, as in most genteel parlors, the peasant figurine likely was consumed to symbolically "resolve" contemporary and historical realities by redefining them, providing a past that contrasted to the present, or naively posing agricultural life's utopian possibilities. Such peasant and agrarian motifs enjoyed widespread consumption among genteel Victorians because they provided a comforting ideological vision of America's agricultural heritage that contrasted radically to late nineteenth-century urbanization and social unrest.

Such motifs would seem problematic for many African Americans in the post-Reconstruction South, but this Annapolis household was headed by a middling social climber who was archetypal gentility in every way except for his African heritage. John Maynard had been born free in 1810, and he and his once-enslaved wife, Maria, purchased their house lot in 1847. Eventually they and their two sons' families became linked to Annapolitan African American elite in churches, fraternal organizations, and workplaces. While the Maynards never secured stunning wealth, John Maynard's 1876 probate inventory recorded a model Victorian parlor stocked with mahogany chairs, chromolithographs, and ornamental objects, including bric-a-brac. This assemblage underscored the household's fitness for citizen rights, if not its utter embrace of genteel discipline. However, this apparent endorsement of standard genteel discipline was noteworthy because black consumers were assumed to be racially incompatible with genteel privilege. The Maynards' home delivered a quite radical critique of whiteness by paradoxically embracing its genteel rules and commodity forms, thereby countering the white exclusivity associated with those rules and goods.

Bric-a-brac often featured quite familiar

Figure 10.2. Abraham Lincoln was one of the most popular characters in late nineteenth-century bric-a-brac, including chromolithographs as well as figurines like this one, recovered at 818 Linden Street in Oakland, California. This black-glazed redware figurine, discarded about 1887, originally had gilding on portions of the placard. Its design is typical of post-Reconstruction depictions of Lincoln, which focus on his role in preserving the Union and his ambiguous character traits rather than his role in emancipation. (Courtesy of the Anthropological Studies Center, Sonoma State University)

motifs, yet even the most prominent bric-a-brac personages and subjects had ambiguous meanings never far removed from race. In about 1887, for instance, a pair of neighboring households in West Oakland filled a shared privy with household refuse. Irish-born railroad collector Patrick Barry, his wife Ellen, and a daughter lived at 818 Linden Street in a flat adjoining their tenants, Norwegian mail carrier Ammend Dorisason and his Irish wife, Mary. Included in the Barry and Dorisason households' privy assemblage was a black-glazed redware figurine of Abraham Lincoln broken just above the knees (Figure 10.2). Lincoln assumed significant symbolic pertinence in the late nineteenth-century wake of the Civil War and emancipation, and he was among the most common characters reproduced in bric-a-brac ranging from chromolithographs to figurines to molds of his death mask (e.g., Castelvecchi 1885:6).

Lincoln was not consumed simply in the form of mass-produced goods: Kirk Savage's (1997:65) study of nineteenth-century public statuary recognizes that until the collapse of Reconstruction, Lincoln served as emancipation's public symbol. Statuary was public, permanent, monumental, and designed to provide a timeless pose and eternal symbolic resolution, so statues painted a somewhat more guarded picture of the president than the flood of Lincoln bric-a-brac. Nevertheless, figurine and statue aesthetics both were designed to impart ethereal personality attributes such as strength, wisdom, and achievement through devices such as gesture, expression, adornments, and physical pose. In the 1870s, for example, most representations of Lincoln smoothed out his gaunt frame and typically gave him more heroic garb than he wore in his lifetime. He often was posed with props such as a scroll or pen, alluding to his authorship of the Emancipation Proclamation, and sometimes they placed him standing over a once-enslaved African American freed by the Great Emancipator. This aesthetic reflected the firm link between Lincoln's post-assassination legacy and emancipation, and it underscored some Americans' optimism about the end of slavery.

The Linden Street figurine, in contrast, reflects a fresh post-Reconstruction vision of Lincoln. When Reconstruction collapsed, black-white racist relations rapidly reemerged as many Americans dispensed with the proposition that emancipation augured an antiracist society. This transformation in social and racial mood had an impact on subsequent Lincoln representations, which dispensed with African American figures and aesthetic devices such as scrolls; instead, Lincoln standing alone and unadorned became a symbol representing the Union's preservation, a wise moral compass who had healed the national rift (Savage 1997:122–124). Lincoln's role in emancipation quite quickly became subsumed to abstract personality features that evaded the resurgence of anti-black racism. The lost portions of the Oakland figurine may have had any number of gestures, poses, or accessories, but the modest remaining figure says a surprising amount about its symbolism. The space around Lincoln's feet is simply molded ground; the absence of a freed slave is consistent with shifts in post-Reconstruction Lincoln symbolism, and the remaining portions of the figurine do not refer to Lincoln's role in emancipation (e.g., scrolls). In the 1880s, aesthetic conventions stressed "realism" over idealized characterizations and contrived physical representations, and this figurine is not clothed in the flowing cloaks or classical garb favored in earlier postwar statuary. The Linden Street Lincoln is instead wearing modest trousers and boots, much as Lincoln himself actually wore. He stood before his viewer in relatively realistic rumpled clothing (apparently without accompanying aesthetic devices), his feet askance, and his gaze likely set forward, emphasizing his powerful personality and wisdom rather than his participation in particular historical events.

Post-Reconstruction bric-a-brac like the Linden Street figure rarely depicted African Americans. Conceding African Americans a material representation in public space or a parlor was akin to confirming their newly won citizenship or even implying their genuine rights, and no consumers devoted to white superiority were likely to make either concession willingly. Newly arrived immigrants who were themselves subject to racism and xenophobia were among the most likely parties to be troubled by public African American representations. For instance, in the 1880s a sculptor submitted a design for a New York statue that depicted a kneeling slave alongside Lincoln, but in 1890 the *New York Times* reported that the design had been rejected because "the figure of a negro in a public monument would arouse the resentment of the Irish citizens" (Savage 1997: 81–82). Of course, Irish immigrants were marginalized by racism themselves and often associated with highly stigmatized blackness. Consequently, depictions of African Americans would seem particularly unlikely motifs among Irish Americans like Patrick and Ellen Barry and tenant Mary Dorisason. Lincoln alone was a relatively "safe" and ambiguous symbol that could represent anything from political partisanship, to nationalist wisdom, to a consumer's embrace of American heritage. When depicted alongside an African American, though, the object posed complicated historical and racial symbolism. Most of the racial representation in bric-a-brac was equally oblique. While consumers could purchase virulent racist representations, most parlor ornamentation celebrated ideologies such as white supremacy, American industrial might, Christian superiority, Western domination, and patriarchy in quite symbolically elusive forms. Consequently, when we look to bric-a-brac for racial representation, it is critical to keep in mind that Victorians assumed that some dimension of racial symbolism was embedded in everything.

Figure 10.3. These two figurines were recovered in an early to mid-1890s feature at 1774 Atlantic Street in Oakland, California. (Courtesy of the Anthropological Studies Center, Sonoma State University)

CLASS AND CLUTTER: ASPIRATION AND ECLECTICISM IN THE VICTORIAN HOUSEHOLD

Like almost all bric-a-brac, the Linden Street Lincoln suggests more about aspirations than actual material wealth. The figurine was black-glazed redware, which by the 1880s was a passé medium for most ceramic production except flower pots. It certainly was less expensive and less desirable than refined earthenwares, porcelain, or Parian. Nevertheless, very little mass-produced bric-a-brac was particularly costly, and the complexities of Lincoln's symbolism remained, regardless of the medium.

Rather than focus on exchange value or the medium's symbolism, it makes more sense to examine how such objects accommodated so many consumers' aspirations for citizen privileges and personal security. In any context, bric-a-brac's symbolism was a situationally distinct fusion reflecting who its consumers consciously understood themselves to be, their objective position in social and class structure, and who they *wished* to be. Symbolically, bric-a-brac was a daydreaming commodity form which consumers mused over, idealizing who they were by dreaming about who they and their society *could* be. Especially for newly arrived immigrants and Americans subordinated by racism or poverty, apparently innocuous household goods provided a modest but significant mechanism that situated them in relation to the genteel mainstream and its genuine social and material benefits. These benefits and consumers' identities and aspirations were inextricably linked to race. For appropriately disciplined Americans who reproduced the genteel, tacitly white norm, race promised empowerment; in contrast, the champions of white superiority aspired to deny various Others the benefits of genteel identity. Consequently, there was fierce debate over what a seemingly objective object like a Lincoln figurine meant when displayed in an Irish American, African American, or white household, and whether citizen rights were conferred simply by consuming such goods.

"Aspiration" could entail many social and personal desires that took a wide range of material forms. For instance, some late nineteenth-century Americans implied their affluence and class aspirations through exotically cluttered Victorian parlors. An Oakland household at 1774 Atlantic Street had a quite visible material aesthetic that reflects one of the common forms taken by consumer aspiration. The residence was home to several African American families and one Irish immigrant's household over short successive periods, so the assemblage cannot be attributed to a specific household. Nevertheless, the African American men living in the home were all Pullman porters, and the Irish family was headed by a Southern Pacific laborer and a laundress, so these families at least shared comparable conditions. The early to mid-1890s assemblage includes a striking range of decorative goods: five vases (including two 4-inch matching blue glass bud vases), a lotus motif stoneware dish, and two porcelain figurines (one of a colonial figure and the other apparently a jester) were discarded into the privy (Figure 10.3). Like many post-Civil War assemblages, the Atlantic Street material culture was quite aesthetically striking and included a wide range of styles and motifs.

The styles, mediums, and colors of these aesthetically distinctive goods suggest a modest rendition of the archetypally colored, cluttered, and eclectic Victorian parlor, which stressed the power to consume over conformance to a clear decorative ideal. This aesthetic was championed by late nineteenth-century ideologues like the New York store Sypher and Company (1885:31–32), whose catalog concluded that "it is impossible that the old poverty of house-furnishing should ever come back. We shall no longer have rows of houses all alike inside.... Now we have individual tastes shown in our furniture, and they will be shown more and more as the means of gratifying them become more common." Before about 1900, such commentators envisioned the densely stocked, idiosyncratically decorated parlor as a material symbol of American affluence and genteel worldliness that was available on some scale to any sufficiently wealthy consumer.

Figure 10.4. The Mann privy included several examples of the popular decorative ceramic Parian, which often sat alongside stylish Victorian goods like this stemware. Objects like the vase in the center were marketed as art for genteel "middle-class" consumers, and their symbolism often borrowed from Classical art or more ambiguous and evocative motifs like this feminine hand. (Courtesy of the Anthropological Studies Center, Sonoma State University)

A circa-1885 privy at 654 Fifth Street in Oakland, California, provided a particularly ornate and eclectic example of this aesthetic focused on class aspiration and wealth. New Hampshire–born brothers Benjamin and Frederick Mann tried their hands at various ventures, including farming, mining, speculating, and banking. The 1880 census recorded the fifty-three-year-old Frederick as a miner, and his brother Benjamin as a "capitalist," suggesting their common entrepreneurial ambitions. The Mann privy contained a stylish assemblage of tablewares, including costly matching porcelains, decorated glassware, an earthenware candelabra, candlesticks, and specialized vessel forms such as spoonholders and gravy boats. The presence of a large table setting as well as coffee beans in the privy suggests that the household entertained guests for both meals and coffee. After eating at such a well-appointed dining assemblage, the family retired to a space decorated with Victorian bric-a-brac. The Manns' assemblage included a variety of cut, etched, and painted stemware, a distinctive cobalt blue candlestick holder with a dolphin-shaped pedestal, cut-glass lampshades, and several figurines and vases.

The Manns' bric-a-brac included three Parian objects, a decorative ceramic that was marketed as an affordable objet d'art evoking affluence rather than as an indifferent commodity curio. An 1846 English trade journal noted that the potteries "attach very great importance to this material, as offering a valuable medium for the multiplication of works of a high order of art, at a price which will render them generally available" (Briggs 1988:150). Art in Victorian homes implied wealth and aesthetic taste based on cultivation and education, but very few Americans could actually purchase or commission art for their parlors. Parian, though, blurred the boundary between art and commodity, and provided a mechanism for aspiring gentility to apprehend art symbolically, socially, and as a literal possession. The Manns' Parian included a striking eight-inch-tall vase molded in the form of a female hand grasping a lily flower (Figure 10.4). This was a relatively typical Parian design in the sense that the vessel did not reproduce a traditional high-art motif, but the medium itself may have been more symbolically significant than the objects' aesthetic designs. Parian was sufficiently expensive and uncommon that it would have been distinctive in most 1880s parlors.

The Mann and Atlantic Street assemblages' eclectic and cluttered aesthetic became the target of withering attack by 1900. In the 1880s and 1890s, a stream of style mavens became increasingly critical of parlors and objects like bric-a-brac that apparently stressed style over function. Decorative writer Clarence Cook (1878:100) was among the first observers to criticize the material glut in parlors, noting that the "New-York parlor of the kind called 'stylish,' where no merely useful thing is permitted, and where nothing can be used with comfort, is always overcrowded." In Victorian discourse, "eclectic" referred to interiors that evinced no clear decorative scheme, particularly spaces favoring decorative volume and texture over functional utility. Household decorator Clara Parker (1897:9) warned against such incongruous decorative volume when she concluded that "in all things—walls, carpets, chairs, sofa-pillows, bric-a-brac, fancywork—let there be not loud or startling effects, a jumble of striking combinations." Critics of eclecticism promoted decorative "harmony" and "rational" interior designs, which in American decorative codes hearkened back to spare, symmetrically balanced colonial precedents and rejected superfluous ornamentation (Brooks 1994:23–25).

Ideologues championing the new spare ideal clearly became concerned that the cluttered Victorian interior was available to almost any consumer by 1900. By the turn of the century, virtually all Americans could stock their front rooms with exotic mass-produced bric-a-brac, foreign-produced goods, and inexpensive furnishings, so the parlor's capacity to stress its consumer's distinctive individual taste and class power was undercut by the breadth of the aesthetic. Consequently, when ideologues found African American homes decorated with Victorian bric-a-brac, they often struggled to comprehend (and subsequently neutralize) the symbolism of those assemblages: such observers assumed that this density of stylistically charged exotic goods was a genteel aesthetic restricted to white people. In his study of New York City's "other half," Jacob Riis (1890:118) found many quite genteel African American households, yet he concluded that even genteel objects such as chromolithographs and parlor furniture failed to conceal the essential realities of poverty and race. Riis was surprised that "the poorest negro's room in New York is bright with gaily-colored prints of his beloved 'Abe Linkum,' General Grant, President Garfield, Mrs. Cleveland, and other national celebrities, and cheery with flowers and singing birds. In the art of putting his best foot foremost, of disguising his poverty by making a little go a long way, our negro has no equal. When a fair share of prosperity is his, he knows how to make life and home very pleasant to those about him. Pianos and parlor furniture abound in the uptown homes of colored tenants and give them a very prosperous air." Riis (1890:118) conceded that the African American was "loyal to the backbone, proud of being an American and of his new-found citizenship," but he could not resist reducing African American materialism to an artificial "air" that contradicted essential racial identity.

Long after Riis's analysis, white observers continued to be confounded by African Americans' reproduction of dominant, tacitly white material codes. In 1938 a Federal Writers Project interviewer visited an African American in New York City and noted that the "apartment was extravagantly furnished in studio fashion that would surprise many a downtown visitor. Any number of paintings and etchings adorned the walls, while a baby grand reposed [in] a corner of the living room in which much bric-a-brac were displayed" (Federal Writers Project 1938c). A pair of Federal Writers Project workers in North Carolina took a common approach to comprehending African American materialism when they denigrated the goods themselves. Describing a modest cash renter's home, the interviewers noted that "on the side table were a few china figures of the kind given away as pitch-penny prizes at the fair" (Harrison and Massengill 1939:52). A Virginia observer stigmatized such goods by observing that "salesmen also haunt Negro front doors with gaudy trinkets, Bibles, good luck charms, cardboard statuettes, and other trappings" (WPA 1940:338–339). By characterizing such goods as "gaudy" or "cheap" and stigmatizing their consumption context, these interviewers were attempting to neutralize symbolic value in what they considered to be African Americans' material insinuation of "white" symbolism.

Despite the move toward decorative "harmony," the families on Atlantic Street were among many Americans who remained attached to the notion that a cluttered, aesthetically prominent, and highly personalized assemblage was testimony to the household's affluence, taste, and style. The Atlantic Street households were working-class and of modest means, and as African Americans or Irish immigrants, they were certainly marginalized by racial ideology, so this was not an example of a truly affluent household demonstrating its wealth and social power. Instead, the assemblage suggests many marginalized peoples' persistent assumption that possessing unusual and striking material goods had ambiguous social cachet that was not dependent on the goods' narrow exchange value or dominant ideology. Marginalized consumers often have embraced a particularly visible material style that symbolically distances them from the conventional notion of penury, which often stresses that poverty is defined by an absence of material things. Stylistically visible assemblages and unusual goods, regardless of their cost, could confound what material marginalization literally looks like (cf. Mullins 1999a:164).

Race, Aspiration, and Household Material Aesthetics

Many West Oaklanders worked in elaborately decorated Pullman railroad cars that used West Oakland as a main West Coast station. Luxurious railroad cars had become quite common by the 1850s, providing well-appointed men's and women's parlors, and sleeping quarters adorned with stylish window curtains, paintings, upholstered chairs and benches, woodwork, and carpets (Grier 1988:47). George Pullman's Pullman Palace Car Company was founded in 1867, and Pullman and his fleet of well-appointed cars became symbols of American luxury, affluence, and monopolism. In 1897, English traveler George Steevens (1897:258) wrote that the American sleeping car is "a miracle of luxury. All the wood is mahogany—or looks like it—and all the cushions are velvet. It looks as rich and solid as the British dining-room of the old school." In the early 1890s Pullman himself suggested that the introduction of luxurious material culture to once-lowly rail cars was intended to have the same "civilizing" effect as domestic parlors: "Take the roughest man, a man whose lines have always brought him into coarsest and poorest surroundings, and the effect upon his bearings is immediate. The more artistic and refined the mere external surroundings, in other words, the better and more refined the man" (cited in Grier 1988:61).

Any well-appointed Victorian parlor had servants, and Pullman cars had a universally African American service staff that included many West Oakland residents. Porters received good pay in comparison to most working-class laborers, but the position consumed long hours, the work was difficult, and porters were subjected to standard anti-black racism (Spires 1994:207). Two Fifth Street households were headed by Central Pacific

Railroad porters. Between 1877 and 1882, porter Abraham Holland lived at 662 Fifth Street with widow Lucinda Tilghman, two of her children, and an African American domestic who, like Holland, was also boarding with the Tilghmans. Born about 1840 in Pennsylvania, Holland had served as a porter for the Central Pacific Railroad since at least 1874. Documentary evidence paints a convincing picture of Holland as aspiring African American gentility. Holland apparently was part of the African American–managed Sweet Vengeance Mine, which was active in Brown Valley between 1848 and 1854. A local newspaper reported that in one week of April 1852 the mine produced "rich dirt, we have taken $1,200," and less than a month later it yielded another $1,142 in a good week. The miners reportedly sent a significant share of these profits south to purchase the freedom of enslaved relatives.

Holland's personal and entrepreneurial ambitions were somewhat different from the social climbing that typified elite African Americans in the East (Gatewood 1990:138). Genteel African American circles in the East were highly structured hierarchies defined by factors such as ancestry, rigid behavioral codes, education, and skin color; wealth was simply one of many elements bearing on African American status in the East. In the West, though, family heritage counted for little because no family could make a claim to long-term community status; eastern color-lines had far less consequence in the West; and West Coast papers spent little ink on social life among the "upper tens" (Gatewood 1990:138). Instead, West Coast African American gentility focused more on individual initiative, entrepreneurialism, and personal wealth, which are stereotypical genteel values.

There still remained quite aristocratic social sentiments among African Americans in the West, though, and Holland likely entertained these. At the end of the Civil War, California was among the sixteen states with African American Masonic lodges, and by 1874 Holland had joined their number. Holland eventually ascended to the position of local Grand Master in 1878–1880, and he added to his Masonic membership a standard inventory of genteel African American social activities. In 1886, for instance, he was the president of Oakland's Literary and Aid Society. This likely was a typical African American "culture club" whose educational and social missions ranged from reading classical literature to promoting Republican candidates (Gatewood 1990:214). Holland also sent a son to college, which would have been routine among East Coast African American elite.

Abraham Holland certainly was prominent in his community, and Lucinda Tilghman was financially comfortable if not wealthy, but their early 1880s privy does not reflect the ostentatious materialism commonly associated with genteel Victorians. The privy does not contain any bric-a-brac with the exception of two flower pots. The household's genteel discipline is suggested by porcelain and white-bodied ceramics that were the height of 1870s table styles, as well as a host of grooming objects (e.g., combs, toothbrushes, and hair tonic bottles), a French porcelain brush holder, and several pieces of jewelry. At least fifty-seven glass chimney lamps were represented in the assemblage, as well as two porcelain candlesticks, a very high number of lighting artifacts among the Oakland assemblages. However, unlike the vastly more eclectic Mann privy at 654 Fifth Street or the small but eclectic Atlantic Street assemblage, the Tilghman/Holland assemblage did not have a preponderance of objects that are stylistically mismatched. Even the ceramics that were not purchased as parts of matching sets were the same color and basic shapes, so they could easily have been used together. The Mann and Atlantic Street assemblages presented a more eclectic appearance in colors, motifs, and shapes and likely contained more "clutter" of typical parlor goods.

Pullman Palace Car Company porter James William Carter lived nearby at 668 Fifth Street. Between 1889 and 1896, the

Carter household filled a 14-foot deep redwood-lined feature that likely had been a well. Like the Tilghman/Holland assemblage deposited roughly a decade earlier, the Carter assemblage also does not reflect particularly pretentious parlor materialism. The Carter assemblage contained a ceramic collection dominated by relatively inexpensive white-bodied earthenwares, a wide variety of decorated glass table vessels, and fifty saucers. While the assemblage included six redware flower pots, several vases, and a clock, it did not include any figurines. Like the Tilghman/Holland household, the Carter household apparently favored a somewhat spare and coordinated interior in keeping with genteel decorative ideology. West Coast African Americans were considered particularly individualistic and entrepreneurial, but at least these two assemblages suggest wealth and pretentious materialism were not key to African American social standing. In these cases, much as in the East, it is likely that a variety of social associations besides pure wealth contributed to African American social status.

RACE AND VICTORIAN EXOTICISM

"Exotic" motifs and objects were quite popular in Victorian material culture, but these exotics only vaguely referred to any specific people, place, or time; instead, they symbolized an abstract "Otherness" that reflected more about their consumers than various non-genteel peoples (Stewart 1993:148). Since the eighteenth century, collectors had accumulated goods from throughout the colonized and natural world, ranging from traditional handcrafted goods to items from nature. Such goods were rare and difficult to acquire, so their possession and display by an erudite collector was a powerful statement about elite collectors and the legitimacy of their class domination. Yet as the colonial world opened up over the nineteenth century, increasingly more exotic goods and non-Western aesthetic conventions reached Americans of modest means, and clever bric-a-brac manufacturers began producing a wide range of inexpensive goods that loosely interpreted non-Western peoples, styles, and subjects. By 1885, for instance, *Spelman's Fancy Goods Graphic* hawked a vast range of notions and reminded dealers that "everybody wants a collection" (Spelman 1885:137). The Spelman's catalog featured a typical range of exotic bric-a-brac from the colonial world (e.g., Japanese and French fans), distant lands (e.g., Egyptian princess ceramic wall plaques), nature (e.g., eighteen-inch decorated alligators), and the non-genteel present (e.g., African American figurines marketed as "Baskets of Darkies"). By the second half of the nineteenth century the consumption of exotic things was no longer the province of a small aristocratic elite: unique, mass-produced, and foreign-made exotics alike were quite common in the archetypally cluttered Victorian parlor.

Like all bric-a-brac, exotic goods were fundamentally a statement about their consumers, not about the place where they originated or the culture and time to which they ostensibly referred. Popular cultural descriptions of exotic peoples and places were predictably ambiguous, ideological, and racist: for example, American consumers' vision of "Turkish style" was re-created in numerous households' "Turkish corners," but that style had virtually nothing to do with Turkish history and culture (cf. Brooks 1994:20). Typical of such exoticized decorative ideology was a 1903 household manual describing an "Oriental Scheme for [a] Smoking Den" that included a "cozy corner [that] has a Moorish crown" (Barnard, Sumner, and Putnam Company 1903:30). Exoticism's appeal relied upon its invocation of racial ideology (especially the contrast of historical and cultural Others to the contemporary genteel West), its implication of worldliness and "taste," and the suggestion that exotic objects reflected material affluence.

The most striking shows of decorative material culture were utterly dependent on wealth, but even in these instances race and a tangle of genteel ideologies lurked within the symbolism. After the Paris Exposition of

Figure 10.5. When this photograph was taken in the late nineteenth century, the McDermott home in West Oakland was a model for formal front parlors. The room included oil paintings, French and Asian goods, a concert grand pianoforte, aesthetically elaborate fabrics and textures ranging from silk curtains to hand-painted ceilings, and a quite prominent golden eagle surveying the scene. (From the collection of Vernon J. Sappers)

1878, for instance, West Oakland's stunning McDermott estate added exhibition goods to a high-style Victorian interior. The August 10, 1878, *Oakland Times* reported that "the rooms are beautifully frescoed in oil colors, and have elegant French furniture. The windows all have elegant silk hangings with rich curtains to match. In the parlor may be seen a Watteau painting of great value... [and] bric a brac from the Paris Exposition.... In another room a pair of screens, Chinese work, embroidered on white silk... birds, nearly a hundred in number are represented flying about and at rest among flowers" (cited in Olmsted and Olmsted 1994:126–127).

The McDermotts' front parlor focused on recognizably foreign goods and styles to evoke, as the newspaper put it, "wealth, luxury, and taste" (Figure 10.5). The home's rear parlor, in contrast, was intended as the scene of family activities rather than socializing with guests and contained the Chinese silk frames as well as family pictures, books, needlework, rattan furniture, and more modest bric-a-brac than that in the front (Figure 10.6). The front parlor's foreign goods most clearly evoked the family's class power and worldliness, whereas the rear parlor's exotics represented the family's genteel domesticity.

Few household ideologues plumbed the complexities of Westerners' attraction to objects from other cultures and time, instead representing it as Americans' distinctive "curiosity." In 1885, Sypher and Company

Figure 10.6. The McDermotts' rear parlor was more clearly domestic than the high-style front parlor and contained fewer ostentatious material goods. Framed pictures—likely of family—are distributed throughout the room, and the parlor is graced by an assemblage of various handcrafted objects, dolls, Chinese rattan furniture, and collectibles, including plates over the fireplace and two rows of bric-a-brac on the desk shelves. (From the collection of Vernon J. Sappers)

(1885:8) rhapsodized that Victorians "take a very great interest in other peoples and in other countries, an interest so great that it has affected our whole way of living; not only our houses show it, but our pictures, our amusements, our books, our newspapers, and our dress. In our houses we give our love of adventure free play, and like to be reminded at every turn, of the fact that America, big as is her territory, is but a small part of the world."

Americans may well have had a "very great interest" in non-Western peoples, but little bric-a-brac contained substantially realistic references to contemporary colonized peoples. If anything, exotics from still-living cultures posed threats that an extinct, idealized, or utterly vanquished group (e.g., Native Americans) did not pose (cf. Stewart 1993:148). The hazard of the "Other" was neutralized by bric-a-brac that grossly caricatured or did not clearly refer to the realities of colonized peoples' lives—that is, bric-a-brac was intended to distance its consumer from such realities and verify what they already believed about themselves and genteel society. Most American consumers only "knew" bric-a-brac's foreign producers or non-genteel subjects through popular culture, so exotic bric-a-brac was unlikely to foster any genuine appreciation of the late nineteenth-century colonial world.

The traditional notion of an exotic good was one that was literally produced in another society using non-industrial techniques developed over centuries of craft production and aesthetic innovation. The most common West Coast exotics came from China and Japan, and the West Oakland assemblages included many Asian goods. Most Californians had some genuine exposure to Chinese immigrants, but popular ideologues painted a powerful racist caricature of the Chinese. Caricatures of groups such as the Irish or Chinese were sufficiently resilient, widely repeated, and so advantageous to other groups that they assumed the status of reality. Consequently, most Californians "knew" the Chinese and Japanese through popular culture and material style, and had no genuine comprehension of Asian cultures.

Some Chinese- and Japanese-manufactured objects probably were consumed for functionality or price as much as their unspoken capacity to summon forth various visions of the Orient. Yet many of these goods clearly were consumed for their decorative exoticism as much as for their utility or ready availability. Between 1892 and 1896, for instance, the family of Illinois-born paper hanger Harry Pierson Chapman lived at 828 Myrtle Street. The Chapman household discarded five Japanese porcelain vessels along with a Chinese porcelain vessel, an oriental motif vessel likely produced in an art pottery, and two porcelain figurines. Household writers often counseled home decorators to use Asian material goods such as these. For instance, Clarence Cook (1878:102) decreed just ten years after Japan was opened to foreign trade that "money is well spent on really good bits of Japanese workmanship.... A Japanese ivory-carving or wood-carving of the best kind,... one of their studies of animal life, or of the human figure, or of their playful, sociable divinities, pixie, or goblin, or monkey-man, has a great deal in it that lifts it above the notion of a toy." Cook's description reflected how many observers reduced non-Western aesthetics to whimsical artistic styles divorced of their cultural footing and easily integrated and reinterpreted within genteel homes. For most consumers, "the Orient" evoked splendor, art, wisdom, despotism, and sensuality, concepts whose meaning was based more on their tacit contrast to rational Western society than genuine understanding of the Far East (Said 1978). When Americans purchased Asian material goods, they were consuming an idea about the contrast of East and West that was suitable for display in a genteel parlor where rational people could make sense of the Orient.

Several of the Chapmans' Japanese vessels had no evident use-wear; for instance, one matching Kutani export cup and saucer show no clear saucer or cup base wear consistent with regular use. These Kutani vessels, produced in northwest Japan, have quite colorful depictions of birds passing over leaning reeds, a traditional aesthetic representation of seasonal change. This illumination of Japanese tradition probably escaped the Chapmans, who more likely displayed these oriental objects for their brilliant color, distinctive and exotic aesthetics, and insinuation of household worldliness. The bright Japanese palette would have been quite unlike the staid molding and overwhelmingly white-bodied ceramics favored by most period household ideologues. The Chapmans' Rose Canton bowl likely was also a decorative vessel since its elaborate overglaze scene is well-preserved, and even the household's English vessels are quite elaborately decorated. Cumulatively, the Chapmans' Asian ceramics, their bold but passé Rebekah at the Well Rockingham teapot, and decorated table glass suggest that this house was quite decoratively eclectic. A circa-1906 feature at 812 Market Street contained a similar swath of colorful and exotic goods. Deposited in the wake of the earthquake, the Market Street assemblage included colorful Victorian-style majolica, a Chinese celadon vessel, and two Japanese ceramic vessels. While the assemblage did not include any figurines and only three flower pots, it suggests a rich color palette and exotic styles similar to the Chapmans' assemblage.

The Chapmans, like most American consumers, may have been attracted to exotic aesthetics in general, with no articulate interest in whether any given object was actually produced in a foreign place, had a cultural or historical story to tell, was displayed alongside similar sorts of items (e.g., Asian goods), and so on. For instance, the household at 1774 Atlantic Street discarded a stoneware dish in a molded lotus flower form, a typical motif in Japanese aesthetics, but the vessel's base contains an unidentified mark that reflects the vessel's probable origins in a West Coast art pottery. This vessel apparently went unused and has hints of rim wear that may reflect its display on edge, so it was an ornamental item much like the Chapmans' bric-a-brac. In these cases, it would appear that some households were less concerned with acquiring a "genuine" Japanese artifact than with having an object that incorporated exotic symbolism.

The consumption of "real" exotic goods (or quality craft objects like the Atlantic Street lotus dish) was sometimes considered an antidote to the crudely executed flood of mass-produced goods. In 1898, for example, *The House Beautiful* (1898:61–62) noted that "if a poor man's taste demands a statuette, he is unable to purchase one of Rodin's marbles, and so attempts to satisfy his want by securing a [mass-produced] 'Rodgers group.' It would have been far better, for example, for him to have used an empty ginger jar for decoration." This comment augured the tone of many early twentieth-century critics of mass-produced commodities; *The House Beautiful*'s editors insinuated that the Chinese ginger vessel was more "artistic" because the Chinese craft producer was not divorced from the object in the way mass-produced goods were detached from living craftspeople. The Brady household at 812 Castro Street may well have taken *The House Beautiful*'s advice. Terrence and Annie Brady's circa-1889–1902 assemblage did not include any figurines, but it did include a Chinese ginger jar like that recommended by the magazine. The Bradys had a four-room house that included a formal parlor, and the "Japanese cabinet," twenty-three "pictures" (probably chromolithographs), and eighteen vases in Annie's 1917 probate inventory suggest the household still contained prototypical parlor furnishings long after parlors became antiquated.

The ultimate exotic was a unique object, and many Victorians collected objects from nature or antiquity to display alongside their mass-produced bric-a-brac. The best archaeological evidence for such consumption in West Oakland came from a privy deposited by the household of John and Katie Taylor. The 768 Fifth Street privy was filled in about 1884 with a relatively unremarkable assemblage of household refuse, but nine prehistoric groundstone net weights were recovered alongside the Taylors' domestic discards. Their recovery in a discrete deposit argues that the stones were discarded together during the formation of the privy fill and were likely collected by a household member. These net weights could have been collected in several local spots. In 1939, for instance, Oakland resident Fred D. Realey (1939:11) asked his readers of the *West of Market Boys' Journal* if they remembered "when Shell Mound Park was an ancient village and when excavations were made of the mound. There were discovered numerous bones of Indians, shells, arrow and spear heads and other objects of interest that had been owned by the Indian tribes of other days." The park in nearby Emeryville became a well-known amusement center, and it is likely that some West Oakland residents—perhaps including the Taylors—collected objects at this and other regional sites for their household assemblages.

Clarence Cook (1878:101) was among the household writers who advocated display of such objects. He noted that a Victorian

> cabinet might be made a museum for the preservation of all the curiosities and pretty things gathered in the family walks and travels. The bubble-bottle of old Roman glass stirred in walking by one's own foot in the ruined palace of the Caesars, and not bought in a shop; the Dutch drinking-glass, with the crest of William of Orange; the trilobites found in a

> Newburgh stone-wall, or the box of Indian arrow-heads, jasper, and feldspar, and quartz picked up in a Westchester County field; bits of nature's craft and man's, gathered in one of these pendant museums, may make a collection of what were else scattered and lost, and which, though of little intrinsic value, and of small regard to see to, will often find its use in a house of wide-awake children.

Cook's comments reflected that unique exotics from nature or history served as educational mechanisms as well as souvenirs that reminded their consumers of the collecting experience and the objects' interpretation by family members. All bric-a-bric potentially could be defined as a souvenir that referred to a specific personal experience. Cook's memory of "the box of Indian arrow-heads... picked up in a Westchester County field" indicates how otherwise mundane objects essentially became vehicles to remember experiences. This collecting practice certainly continued alongside mass-consumed bric-a-brac accumulation long into the twentieth century. In 1938, for instance, a Federal Writers Project worker in Nebraska reported on a "modest" African American home: "The rooms in the house although not elaborately furnished catch the attention of the eye because of the many wonderful paintings and pictures that are hung about the walls.... There are many relics in a cabinet that are very historical, as they have come from all over the world, being gifts from various friends" (Federal Writers Project 1938b). Several weeks earlier, the same interviewer had visited another African American who "has a lot of collections and relics that he proudly display[s]" (Federal Writers Project 1938a), and he described another African American neighbor's home as "well furnished with old style furniture, pictures, and relics" (Federal Writers Project 1938d).

Some goods were marketed expressly to commemorate a specific event. For instance, a circa-1930 African American deposit in Indianapolis, Indiana, contained an 1893 coin from the Chicago Columbian Exposition that depicted the Beaux-Arts style Mines and Mining Building. Inscribed "Coal Miner/ World Exposition Chicago," the coin certainly came from one of the Mines and Mining exhibitors, which included displays by diamond miners, a silver statue of actress Ada Rehan, and a Statue of Liberty made of salt (World's Columbian Exposition 1999:3). African Americans twenty-eight years removed from slavery were eager to participate in such a landmark event as the exposition, and Frederick Douglass, Booker T. Washington, Paul Lawrence Dunbar, Francis Watkins Harper, and George Washington Carver were among the parade of African American elite at the fair (Reed 1999). African Americans certainly experienced racism there, but many African Americans attended the exposition as lecturers, laborers, entertainers, and patrons. The exposition's significance is suggested by the Indianapolis household's reluctance to discard this souvenir medallion until the Depression. Leslie Stewart-Abernathy (1992) recovered a similar coin from the 1893 exposition on an Arkansas site, and Charles Orser (1988b:218–220) recovered a medallion inscribed "SOUVENIR OF THE 1887 ICE CARNIVAL" in a turn-of-the-century tenant farmer's cabin in South Carolina. The Minnesota Ice Carnival and the Chicago Exposition were sufficiently far removed from these consumers' lives to be exotic and invoke their worldliness. These objects contrasted to their consumers' prosaic everyday lives and provided a material representation of experiences that could not be represented in any other commodity form. They also formed a selective life narrative when assembled alongside objects drawn from personal experience, such as scrapbooks, natural objects (e.g., dried flowers from weddings), and postcards.

Objects collected from nature and antiquity nostalgically invoked the past, but they were fundamentally comments on the social world of the consumer; that is, they critiqued the present by lamenting some essential human experience lost by their consumer (Stewart 1993:139–140). Many West Oakland homes likely had objects like the Taylors' net weights displayed alongside shells, foreign exotics, and mass-produced bric-a-brac. The collection of goods produced by extinct "primitive" peoples provided their genteel consumers a readily displayable parlor lesson on the fate of cultures. The prehistoric peoples that once lived in Oakland had suffered the fate of cultures unable or unwilling to conform to capitalism and Western society, and they had been vanquished at least in part by a supposedly superior white, Western culture. These objects both verified Western superiority and delivered a warning that such a fate might befall the genteel West if it was not constantly vigilant.

CONCLUSION

In the 1880s Jacob Riis trekked through New York City documenting Gotham's impoverished masses of immigrants, people of color, and various other Americans forcefully excluded from affluence. Riis's subsequent account, *How the Other Half Lives,* had a spectacular impact on the once-untroubled Gilded Age elite, who consciously tolerated—if not condoned—profound poverty and marginalization in many places like New York. Yet, like many Victorians, even the morally indignant Riis was unable to subdue his own cultural xenophobia and racism and appreciate the complex aspirations that lurked beneath the surface of poverty. Riis was unable to comprehend that Victorian goods were genuinely significant to this "other half," much less that they could mean many things to various citizens. Nevertheless, such goods were often one of the mechanisms marginalized consumers used to secure some small but significant foothold into consumer abundance.

Like many subsequent commentators, Riis apparently could not fathom how consumers might project personally significant symbolism onto apparently inconsequential things. He seemed unable to even wonder why marginalized consumers would seek out goods that were intended for more lavish and ceremonial contexts than those in which they were eventually consumed. Others who did directly confront these questions, such as Thorstein Veblen, were prone to reduce it to "emulation" of the powerful by the powerless. Yet what bric-a-brac suggests is that such consumption is more complex than the instrumental copying of elite behavior. It is unlikely that many consumers were sufficiently naive to believe that their ceramic figurines or Victorian table settings would transform them into aristocrats. Victorian consumption instead makes a very powerful statement about the profound conviction many Americans had in affluence even when they were marginalized by that very society because of classism, patriarchy, racism, xenophobia, regional prejudices, and a host of other ideologies that always curtailed opportunity. Some thinkers reduce this apparent paradox to false consciousness, concluding that consumption is simply the masses' way of unwittingly participating in their own oppression. There is, indeed, a genuine measure of self-imposed oppression that is reproduced by consumption and its reproduction of wage labor. Yet it might just as well be argued that when consumers transform the meaning of mass-produced goods, they are using those goods as vehicles of social critique as much as self-inflicted oppression (cf. Hebdige 1979).

The reality, of course, lays somewhere in between. For instance, just as the Linden Street figure proclaimed its Irish American consumers' ambitions to citizenship, it also reproduced an anti-black historical vision and risked ignoring the similar prejudices inflicted on Irish arrivals. These contradictions were already in public space, but objects like this figurine evoked the complexities of riches, racism, and American identity that were difficult to otherwise articulate. For those scholars who hope objects will provide a clear reflection of nineteenth-century society's most pressing social dilemmas, bric-a-brac instead provides a fragmentary, selective, and distorted reflection: rather than delivering a resounding symbolic resolution of profound social quandaries, bric-a-brac in most cases evoked generally inchoate and idealized associations. Like most popular culture, bric-a-brac was a self-possessed reflection of American society that attempted to present back to consumers their deeply held preconceptions of themselves and others. Yet because its symbolism was so ambiguous, bric-a-brac inevitably had the potential to question and undermine those very preconceptions. The challenge is to identify what specific ambitions various consumers were most likely to connect to such symbols.

Bric-a-brac was, on one hand, an imaginative vehicle of personal and social ambition; on the other, none of these desires were simply hatched from consumers' imaginations and disconnected from dominant social structure. Bric-a-brac's material forms were not provided by producers who were intent upon fomenting revolution through the sale of household curios. Instead, householders selected goods that symbolically "situated" the consumer within the world by appearing to secure consumer culture's opportunities, but not threatening the social and ideological foundations upon which it stood. Because there was such a reasonably wide range of experiences of such ambition and ideology, it is not surprising that the meaning of household material culture would be so rich and complex.

Note

This essay would not have been possible without the assistance of the Sonoma State University Anthropological Studies Center. Adrian and Mary Praetzellis have been models for collegiality and intellectual support, plus they introduced me to artichokes. I have taken the McDermott photograph interpretations directly from them. Erica Gibson helped me organize myself in their collections and interpret the objects; Grace Ziesing discussed the assemblages and interpretations; and everyone on the staff was congenial and interested in the research. Thanks to Ginger Hellmann for taking the Oakland photographs. Thanks to the seminar members who commented on this chapter. Of course, none of them bear any responsibility for my interpretations or any errors of fact.

11

Race, Missionaries, and the Struggle to Free Jamaica

JAMES A. DELLE

Of all the contributions made by anthropology to the understanding of human societies, perhaps none is more significant than the proposition made by Ashley Montague, influenced by the earlier work of Franz Boas, that races are socially constructed categories, contextualized in specific historical moments. Writing in the aftermath of the Second World War, Montague argued that race was a concept used to reify existing social structures that bolstered a social hierarchy which perpetuated the existing systems of inequality that had emerged out of colonialism, imperialism, and slavery; racism was the social consequence (Montague 1964, 1974). If we agree with Montague's proposition, in order to overcome racism, we must understand the nature of social institutions that operate to perpetuate race-based inequality. As ironic as it may seem, one of the institutions that has historically worked to create racial hierarchies is the Christian mission. While a number of historical archaeologists have examined the material relationship between missionaries, colonialism, and Native Americans in California and the U.S. Southwest (e.g., Costello 1992), the U.S. Southeast (e.g., Saunders 1996; Thomas 1993), and Quebec, few have considered how Christian missionizing influenced the development of African diasporic cultures in the New World. This chapter seeks to open this topic through an analysis of the mission movement in early nineteenth-century Jamaica.

To understand how Christianity as practiced by missionaries influenced the development of Jamaican society, we must first acknowledge that missionaries in nineteenth-century Jamaica contributed to a wider social discourse on the meaning of freedom. As posed by the historian Thomas Holt (1992), freedom is a historical problem. At the heart of the problem of freedom is its nature as part of a dialectic; freedom exists in opposition to slavery. Like slavery, freedom is a social process; it is a condition under which individuals live. Unlike slavery, however, freedom is not an institution; it is not well defined, and it is difficult indeed to articulate what it means to be free. In contrast, it is relatively easy to define what it is to be a slave: to be under the condition of slavery is to be an individual constrained by the will of another, a will that is exercised to extract wealth while exerting control over agency. In many ways, freedom is defined in opposition to slavery; to be free is to exist in a state of liberation from such constraints. Yet even in the most progressive societies, the actions of individuals are constrained, either through state institutions, such as the law, or through social conventions, such as polite manners (Goodwin 1999). There are no absolutely free members of any society, and therein lies the problem. Given institutional and conventional constraints on agency, how do people define their freedom? I propose that in the context of any hierarchical social organization, definitions of freedom will differ depending on the place individuals and groups stand in the social order. Under racist social orders, like the one in place in early nineteenth-century Jamaica, members of elite and oppressed races and classes will have very different understandings of what it is to be free. As such, the institutions defining and reproducing the meanings of freedom will be contested. Such was the case with the missionizing Christian churches in early nineteenth-century Jamaica.

In contexts where social relations are mediated by racist understandings of a social order, many ideas—including Christian ideas—can on the surface seem liberating, but when put into practice can be used as just one more tool of subjugation. How ironic that the ideas of a man who, in translation, is attributed as saying, "It is easier for a camel to pass through the eye of a needle than for a rich man to pass through the gates of heaven" were preached, largely uncontextualized, to people who were legally defined as being the property of such rich men. As I assume is often the case in colonial missionizing projects, the meanings intended by the missionizers were far from the meanings interpreted by the missionized. In the end, British slavery in the West Indies ended through means that would have appeared familiar to Moses, Jesus, or Spartacus for that matter. In 1833, some months after a slave rebellion of unprecedented (at least in the British experience) magnitude, organized by converted Christian preachers who themselves were enslaved, a frightened, and reformed, Parliament legislated emancipation for its colonial possessions. While this action may have ended the practice of slavery, the Emancipation Act did not legislate an end to racism in Jamaica. Struggles for liberation and freedom against colonial masters are rarely won outright, and freedom, being difficult to define, is by its nature difficult to attain. Such is true, I believe, because embedded in the idea and struggle for freedom is the necessity to gain equality, which cannot be achieved under any system that is based on strictly defined hierarchies of power and wealth, and thus is a system dependent on the perpetuation of inequality reified, as in this case, by racism. Furthermore, who is empowered in a stratified system to define just what "freedom" means? If freedom is defined by those in positions of authority, who feel empowered to "grant" freedom, can those who are "granted" freedom truly be liberated?

These are questions that have plagued me as I consider the locus of my own archaeological work, which is nineteenth-century Jamaica. Despite a history of fierce and often armed resistance to the system of slavery that brutalized hundreds of thousands of diasporic Africans, emancipation was not won in Jamaica as it had been, for example, in Haiti, but rather was granted by an act of the British Parliament, an institution that had no interest in establishing racial or economic equality in its colonial possessions. Understanding why the British government enacted the abolition of slavery has been a concern of generations of scholars who have struggled to explain emancipation variously as an economic, religious, moral, or political phenomenon (e.g., Anstey 1974; Bolt and Drescher 1980; Drescher 1977; Green 1976; Midgley 1992; Oldfield 1995; Williams 1944). While no consensus is likely to emerge on defining why emancipation was enacted, it is difficult to dispute that despite the final abolition of slavery in 1838, Jamaica did not become a free land. Jamaica developed into an arena of contestation between white and black definitions of what it was to be a free member of society—a land of complex and often violent negotiation between the colonialist understanding that to be an emancipated slave was to become free to work for the planters as a dependent wage earner, and a black understanding that to be fully free was to be empowered with both the right to self-determination and the ability and opportunity to be self-sufficient. Many individuals and institutions debated and attempted to codify the conditions of Jamaican freedom. Among them, and the focus of this chapter, are the Christian missions.

In the pages that follow, I present a brief review of the history of Christian missions in

Jamaica, discuss the roles that missionaries played in constructing the discourse surrounding freedom in the years leading to the abolition of slavery, consider the roles that missions played in the construction of post-emancipation Jamaica, and evaluate how these phenomena can be related to archaeological work on African-Jamaican sites, particularly through the example of the villages of Marshall's Pen, a coffee plantation site currently under excavation. In doing so, I will reveal that missionaries had a complex understanding of race relations which influenced how they contributed to the material and social definitions of just what a free Jamaica would be.

PRE-EMANCIPATION MISSIONS, 1754–1832

In the decades preceding the passage of the Emancipation Act, the Baptist Church was the largest of several missionizing institutions ministering to enslaved and free blacks in Jamaica. Other missionary sects included the Moravians, Wesleyan Methodists, and Scottish Presbyterians. First established in the middle of the eighteenth century in Jamaica, the missionary movement reached its pre-emancipation pinnacle in the late 1820s, when a total of forty-four missionaries from these various denominations ministered to flocks in Jamaica totaling about 27,000 converts (Turner 1998:21). From its establishment to emancipation, the missionary movement was largely restricted to what are known as nonconformist sects—that is, Protestant denominations that did not conform to the strictures of the established Church of England. While a few missionaries associated with the established church were sent to Jamaica by the bishop of London to promote Christian education among the enslaved, they were not very successful, particularly given the ambivalence many Jamaican planters felt about the education and Christianization of the enslaved (Dayfoot 1999:135; Turner 1998:10, 14–15).

The first missionaries to arrive in Jamaica were the Moravians, in 1754 (Dayfoot 1999:121; Gordon 1996:4; King 1850:86). In the first fifty years, Moravian missionaries baptized fewer than a thousand of the several hundred thousand people comprising Jamaica's enslaved population. This was due in large measure to the mission's hierarchical nature. A person could present him or herself as a candidate for baptism, only to remain a candidate for decades until a missionary determined that the candidate had demonstrated a full understanding of the Moravian version of Christianity and had completely abandoned "heathen" African practices. Complicating their relationship with enslaved Africans, the Moravians began by baptizing men only and had to be convinced by their own converted that women played extremely important roles in African-Jamaican society, and thus should be included more actively in the mission (Gordon 1996:22).

Upon their arrival in Jamaica, the Moravians had little if any interest in questioning the existing social hierarchy, including slavery. In many ways dependent on the good graces of planters and overseers, the Moravians limited their early mission work to specific estates to which they were invited by the proprietors. Despite the racist and sexist overtones of their actions, the Moravian message spread through the estates and introduced many enslaved Africans to Christian ideology. The Moravian Church remains an important part of the Christian scene in Jamaica, particularly in the central parishes.

Methodist missionizing began in 1789 with Thomas Coke's arrival in Montego Bay (Gordon 1996:5; King 1850:88–89). Unlike the Moravians, who limited their mission to a few estates in the remote center of the island, the Wesleyan Methodists created a conspicuous presence, focusing their activities in the main urban centers of Montego Bay, Spanish Town, and Kingston, where they acquired property and built chapels (Gordon 1996:5; Turner 1998:12–13). The Methodists were mistrusted by the plantocracy, and in reaction to the Wesleyan presence in Morant Bay, the principal town of the parish of St. Thomas-in-the-East, Sir Simon Taylor, custos (parish magistrate) of that parish, pushed legislation

Figure 11.1. An early nineteenth-century school established by the Baptist Missionary Society. (From Phillippo 1843)

through the island legislature, the Jamaica Assembly, outlawing preaching by anyone not qualified by law. Although such qualifications were not well defined, anyone found guilty of illegal preaching was to be sentenced to one month's hard labor for the first offense, and six months for the second (Turner 1998: 15). In a further attempt to limit Methodist activity, the Jamaica Assembly suspended the license of the Wesleyan chapel in Kingston for seven years following 1807 (Gordon 1996: 5–6). Eventually, the British Parliament had to intervene to limit such local regulations against missionaries, which were found to be in opposition to existing British law (Turner 1998:15–17).

A more limited mission was established by Scottish Presbyterians, who, under the aegis of the Scottish Missionary Society, sent three missionaries to Kingston in 1799 (King 1850:94). Never a large presence, the Presbyterians were thwarted both by demographics (two of the first three missionaries died within weeks of their arrival in Jamaica) and by opposition from the Jamaica Assembly. The local government, apparently uncomfortable with the prospect of a black Presbyterian congregation, barred the surviving catechist, Ebenezer Reid, from ministering in 1802. Not permitted to preach, Reid limited his mission to teaching school. The Presbyterians did little to reinforce their fledgling mission, sending only a handful of missionaries to Jamaica through 1831 (Dayfoot 1999: 135; Gordon 1996:6–7; King 1850:94).

Among the most radical of the missionaries were members of the Baptist Missionary Society, who first arrived in Jamaica in 1814 at the invitation of existing Baptist communities whose black leaders were forbidden to preach by an act passed in the Jamaica Assembly in 1807 (Dayfoot 1999:138; Turner 1998:17). The British Baptists began their mission by opening schools in Falmouth and Kingston (Figure 11.1), where they began to teach free blacks and some enslaved people to read and write (Dayfoot 1999:138; Gordon 1996:6). Like the Presbyterians, the Baptists got off to a relatively slow start. Their first missionary, John Rowe, died two years after his arrival in 1814; his successors also became ill and died, contributing to Jamaica's high mortality rate (Dayfoot 1999:138). The Baptist Missionary Society refocused their efforts in the 1820s, sending the charismatic and influential trio of James Phillippo, Thomas Burchell, and William Knibb to establish what would become significant mission stations in Spanish Town (then the capital of Jamaica), Montego Bay, and Falmouth, respectively (Dayfoot 1999:177).

None of the missionary groups were strong in numbers, and all relied on the local black population to reach the flock in distant areas. In the early years of their mission, the Moravians received little financial support from abroad and depended either on the patronage of specific planters or on raising their own funds, including through employment. Whereas the Moravians were literally visitors living on specific estates in the country, particularly in the rural areas of remote parishes such as St. Elizabeth, the Methodist and Baptist missionaries tended to station themselves in population centers, preaching to the significant population of blacks living in the cities or on nearby plantations, and to those who traveled to the principal towns to conduct business for their owners. Of the various missionary sects, the Baptists were the most active in engaging local people directly in their mission, particularly by creating a system of leadership among the enslaved to spread the word (Gordon 1996:7).

With the probable exception of the Baptists, missionaries in Jamaica were a relatively apolitical group. Being aware that antislavery agitation on the island would provoke hostility among the planters, the societies in the United Kingdom gave strict instructions to all of their missionaries not to engage in local politics, nor to criticize the slave system (Turner 1998:9–10), even though their related London congregations were centers for antislavery agitation (Gordon 1996:7). Despite—and in some cases because of—their political neutrality, the missionaries were greeted with responses ranging from open hostility to accommodation from the planters and other Jamaican whites, as well as the enslaved blacks. Sunday services interfered with the traditional Sunday markets that had long been a focus of social and economic activities for the enslaved (Mintz and Hall 1960). The enslaved also were legally barred from working for the planters on Sundays, and many people used this time to tend their gardens and provision grounds. Many overseers, and undoubtedly many enslaved workers who depended on working the provision grounds for food and on the markets for access to cash, saw missionary work as interfering with the already uncomfortable estate social structure. Overseers and other white estate employees believed that the presence of the missionaries—sometimes condoned by their employers—disrupted the operation of the estates (Gordon 1996:8; Turner 1998:15).

Most members of the Jamaican planter class were nominally members of the established Church of England, which, traditionally considered to be the church of the elite, had a weak presence among the white colonials, never mind the enslaved members of Jamaican society (Harvey and Brewin 1866; Stewart 1992). The presence of nonconformist missionaries actually living out the old racist justification that slavery would bring Christianity to "heathen" Africans prompted members of the Church of England to begin baptizing their slaves. In 1816, the Jamaica Assembly began to earmark funds to employ Church of England curates to visit estates, primarily to baptize the enslaved population. This seems to have been largely what we would today call a public relations move; it has been suggested that these curates did little to instruct people about Christianity, concentrating instead on increasing parish rolls through mass baptisms (Gordon 1996:9; King 1850:80; Turner 1998:14, 21). The Church of England further reacted to the early successes of the nonconformist missionaries by appointing the first bishop of Jamaica, Christopher Lipscomb, in 1825, providing him with a staff of clergy and missionaries to carry out the work of increasing the church's membership rolls. After a century and a half in Jamaica, the Church of England did become a Christianizing force, but only in the decade immediately prior to the final abolition of slavery in 1838. By most accounts, however, the established church did little to spread Christianity among the enslaved people of Jamaica (Dayfoot 1999:165–166; Gordon 1996:9; Turner 1998:14).

RACE AND RACISM AMONG THE MISSIONS

As members of a dominant colonial group, the white missionaries to Jamaica tended to have a paternalistic attitude toward the African peoples they were attempting to Christianize. It was not uncommon for missionaries to be referred to as "Massa" by their enslaved flock, and many missionaries chose to live and socialize with planters, overseers, and other members of the white establishment (Gordon 1996:x). The white clergy's paternalistic attitude is well represented by the comments of David King, a Presbyterian minister who toured Jamaica in the decade following emancipation. King noted that the prosperity of the island was "entrusted to its white inhabitants. Very much depends on the moral example which they set before their servants—on the encouragement which they give to ecclesiastical and educational institutions" (King 1850:29). In discussing why church attendance had fallen off in the years following emancipation, King attempted to dispute the widely held contention that the missionaries themselves were incompetent. In so doing, King revealed a bit of his own racism. Although he previously had argued that black children did as well as white children in mission schools, he goes on to report that "it is a difficult task, indeed, to bring down exposition to the apprehension of such a people" (King 1850:98). The missionaries, King claimed, were doing their utmost to speak down to the blacks. Despite such overt paternalistic racism, many missionaries undoubtedly believed they were acting in the best interest of the enslaved. In fact, they were contributing to the perpetuation of the racist underpinnings of the slave system, if in no other way by acknowledging its right to exist.

A good example of how this played itself out is the early history of the Moravians in Jamaica. As I have previously mentioned, the Moravian mission was the first such enterprise in Jamaica, beginning as early as 1754. Its first missionaries were invited to Jamaica to convert estate slaves to Christianity but had few resources at their disposal. The Moravians thus began their work as guests of the white establishment, living with overseers and planters in their quarters on estates. The Moravians further contributed to the existence of racism by owning slaves themselves, even as they preached to the enslaved (Gordon 1996:4, 16–17).

Perhaps not surprisingly, the Moravian missionaries' message was tailored to the realities of the slave system and in very profound ways contributed to the perpetuation of the idea of racial inequality. Consider, for example, how one of the earliest Moravian missionaries, Brother Caries, explained the Christian concept of heaven to a dubious would-be convert: "You get new bodies made better than they are now—you will be no more Blacks, no more Slaves, and your Souls and bodies will meet together" (quoted in Gordon 1996:21). Within this sentiment lies the idea that to be in heaven one must no longer be black—which was not communicated by telling people that heaven existed beyond corporeal reality, but by telling them that they "get new bodies made better... no more Blacks."

Caries, though reportedly a benevolent man, did little to challenge the idea that slaves were at the bottom of an established social order. As overseers claimed control over the bodies of the slaves, Caries and his brother missionaries claimed control over their souls. It was only at the bidding of one of the missionaries that a person could receive baptism, and because many people were willing to accept this new religion, candidates always outnumbered the baptized at ceremonies (Gordon 1996:21). Caries also seems to have accepted the commonly held opinion that Africans were intellectually inferior to whites

Figure 11.2. African burial practices in Jamaica, disparaged by the missionaries as "heathen." (From Phillippo 1843)

and is reported to have said that the enslaved "have a great deal more in their hearts than they are able to express" (quoted in Gordon 1996:21).

As guests of the planter class, the Moravians apparently catered to the wishes of their sponsors, absentee planters, and the resident plantation staff, who hoped that a Christian slave would be an obedient slave. For example, when asked, a converted African named Lewis said, "Before I was forced to do my work, now I do it faithfully and cheerfully" (quoted in Gordon 1996:22). Whether this represented reality or not is hard to say. It does seem obvious that such obedience to God was part of the missionary message.

After about a decade, attendance at Moravian services began to decline except where it was ordered by overseers (Gordon 1996:26). It would seem that after an initial curiosity about Christianity, many enslaved Africans began to see the Moravians and their mission as part of the system of oppression operating in pre-emancipation Jamaica. Moravian missionaries—house guests of the slaveholding class, some slave holders themselves—denied their own bondsmen food when they neglected to attend Sunday services. Whether the absentees were working to produce food for themselves and their families seemed of little consequence, as anyone who did not hold the Sabbath holy was punished. It seems likely that the missionaries were seen by many as participating in a system that enslaved rather than liberated them (Gordon 1996:26). An anecdote related by Gordon (1996:28–29) is revealing. After denying a convert named Agnes a Christian burial in 1814, the Moravian missionaries witnessed her family and friends organizing a lavish funeral, complete with a coffin covered with gold tinsel (Figure 11.2). The missionary Brother Becker commented, "We were pleased to hear our Christian negroes expressing their contempt of this ridiculous finery, observing that it was quite inconsistent with the situation of a negro" (quoted in Gordon 1996:29).

The Moravians were not alone in accepting the racist mindset in place in pre-emancipation Jamaica. All missionaries, of all stripes, were considered by the planters either as employees or protégés (Turner 1998:23). Dependent on the planters both financially and for the legal right to preach, missionaries adopted many elements of white Jamaican culture, conforming to the expectations of their employers and patrons. Mission families employed domestic servants, who often were slaves hired or borrowed from sympathetic planters, and whipping disobedient servants was not unknown among the missionaries (Turner 1998:26, 70). Wesleyan missionaries ignored the strictures of their home missionary committee by spending three times as much on domestic servants than their counterparts in London. Respectability in white society also demanded that missionaries use horses for transportation rather than walking, the humble custom of missionaries in the United Kingdom. Despite protests from home, some Baptist and Wesleyan missionaries extended this husbandry to keeping a chaise and two horses (Turner 1998:26). Further perpetuating the system of inequality, some missionaries taught the enslaved to willingly accept their subordinate role in society. For example, in a catechism written by the Wesleyan missionary John Shipman, converts were taught to be obedient and submissive servants; lying and stealing from masters was condemned, and converts were taught to labor diligently (Turner 1998:76). A group of Wesleyan missionaries went so far as to draft a resolution in 1824 condemning anti-slavery agitation in England and even defending the institution (Turner 1998:112–115). Finally, missionaries were expected to respect the existing racial hierarchy in Jamaica; free coloreds and blacks were not allowed by the missionaries to preach until 1831, when some measure of civil rights was extended to this growing element of Jamaican society. Similarly, missionaries were prohibited from marrying free women of color (Stewart 1992:76–78). By necessity if not design, the missionaries accepted the racist foundations of pre-emancipation Jamaican society. In doing so, they were viewed suspiciously by some members of the African-Jamaican population as being too closely allied with the enslaving class (Stewart 1992:72).

ANTI-MISSIONARIES? THE NATIVE BAPTIST MOVEMENT

Given the racist worldview accepted, if not espoused, by the white missionaries, it seems quite understandable that some people of African descent who chose to follow Christianity preferred hearing the word of God spoken by other black men and women to being preached to by slaveholders and their friends. This phenomenon was manifest in at least two ways: by the white missionaries' use of black "class leaders," and the growth and development of the Native Baptist movement.

Class leaders were able to communicate with the enslaved in ways that European missionaries could not, particularly in the use of the creole patois language commonly spoken by African-Jamaicans. Given the class leaders' ability to reach the flock, missionaries trusted them to explain the nuances of Christian thought to African-Jamaican converts. Class leaders also were taught to read and write, and often taught those in their classes. Although forbidden from preaching, the leaders were in charge of prayer groups and, in fact, exerted great influence among the flock (Turner 1998:90–91).

The white missionaries also found themselves in competition with another growing Christian movement, a group known as the Native Baptists, led by self-appointed spiritual leaders of African descent who followed a syncretic and unorthodox version of Christianity. The Native Baptist movement was established in Jamaica by servants and slaves of American southern loyalists who settled in Jamaica during the Revolutionary War (Gordon 1996:4). Led by a former slave, George Leile, the movement was originally centered in Kingston but soon spread into the western parish of St. James, primarily through the preachings of Leile's student Moses Baker.

Leile accompanied the four hundred or so white American loyalist families who settled in Jamaica after the War for Independence. Two years after arriving, Leile was freed, and he purchased a small parcel of land and a cart (and presumably a donkey or mule). He then embarked on a career as an itinerant trader and preacher (Gordon 1996:41; Turner 1998: 11). His student Moses Baker, a barber from New York, was a free "colored" man (in Jamaican understanding, this would be a person of mixed African and European descent). After his conversion to Christianity by Leile, he was hired by a man named Wynn to preach to the slaves on his St. James estate. Baker established local leaders (called "daddies" and "mammies"), who maintained the congregation in his absence, and organized a system of internal justice adjudicated by "judges" within each group (Gordon 1996:42). Other notable members of the early Native Baptist movement included George Gibb, who preached in the northern parishes of St. Mary and St. Thomas-in-the-Vale, and George Lewis, an enslaved peddler who traveled the countryside selling wares for his mistress, preaching as he traveled through the southern parishes of Vere, Manchester, and St. Elizabeth. Lewis had connections with the Moravians, as missionaries and converted slaves had contributed to the purchase of his freedom (Gordon 1996:4, 42). (Lewis is of particular interest because he preached in Manchester, the parish in which the focus of my field study, Marshall's Pen, is located.)

The influence of the Native Baptist movement was so great that the Jamaica Assembly eventually prohibited the group's ministers from preaching. Nevertheless, the Native Baptists remained influential, and some class leaders, educated in the scriptures by the missionaries, began to question the relationship between Christianity and the slave system defended by many of the missionaries. Newly literate, these leaders began to read the Bible for themselves, and began to understand Christianity's potential as an ideology of liberation. Some of them, no doubt inspired by the stories of the Babylonian captivity and the liberation of the Israelite slaves by Moses, began to preach their own interpretations of Christianity in the Native Baptist tradition. Because they were either associated directly to a mission station or protected by the aegis of the British Baptist Missionary Society, class leaders and Native Baptists found a way to legally spread their own interpretation of the word—an interpretation that called not for submission, but for liberation.

THE BAPTIST WAR

As one might imagine, empowering enslaved workers through the word of God was resisted by some planters, particularly after the Baptist and Wesleyan Methodist Churches placed their full support behind an 1823 initiative to abolish slavery in the British Empire (Turner 1998:102). The most aggressive and visible of the missionary groups, the Baptists, and the Native Baptist preachers were already seen as a threat by some planters. The Native Baptists encouraged the development of community across plantations, preaching a version of Christianity created and understood by members of the African diaspora, and based on an ideology of liberation. The white missionaries taught slaves to read and empowered them by involving them directly in church leadership and granting them power as class leaders, albeit in subordinate positions to the missionaries themselves. By 1836, two years prior to the declaration of full emancipation in the British West Indies, 15 Baptist missionaries supervised 52 stations, ministering to approximately 14,000 communicants; one missionary, James Phillippo, alone supervised more than 40 "class leaders."

The planters' fears that the Baptists were instilling both a sense of entitlement and the ability to organize resistance among the enslaved was realized in December of 1831 with the outbreak of the largest slave rebellion in Jamaica's history, an uprising known historically as the Baptist War or the Christmas Rebellion. According to Phillippo's account of the events leading up to the rebellion, a number of enslaved people in the western parishes of Trelawney and St. James became convinced that the king had ordered Jamaica's slaves to be freed, only to have the planters withhold their manumission papers. In protest, a labor strike against the condition of slavery was planned for the week after

Christmas 1831; the strikers would refuse to work unless paid a wage. Things became violent when martial law was declared, and the militia and British regulars engaged the strikers in several skirmishes. The strikers, now numbering in the tens of thousands, began to burn estates. When the dust from this well-organized uprising had settled, some 250 sugar estates had suffered more than £1 million in damages, 16 whites had been killed, 200 slaves had died in combat, and another 340 were executed for taking part in the uprising (Phillippo 1843:164–165; see also Turner 1998:148–178).

The Christmas Rebellion was also called the Baptist War because all of the presumed leaders were either class leaders or deacons in the Baptist Church. Sam Sharpe, who has come to be known as the mastermind of the insurrection, was a class leader who, even though enslaved, moved freely from plantation to plantation. He was one of those executed in the wake of the uprising and is now recognized as one of Jamaica's seven national heroes.

In the weeks following suppression of the rebellion, white Baptist missionaries attempted to distance themselves from the uprising, which, in fact, they had had no part in planning (Gordon 1996:12) Nevertheless, the nonconformist missionaries, many of whom were thought by the planters to be active abolitionists, were arrested by the parish governments and tried for treason (though none were convicted). They were subsequently targeted for violent retribution by the planters, who had organized their own group, the Colonial Church Union (CCU), which in many cases acted as a lynch mob to terrorize both black converts and white missionaries while destroying their property and churches (Gordon 1996:12). Some Baptists were physically attacked, and most of their chapels destroyed. Many missionary leaders were forced to flee Jamaica for England. Despite the fact that the CCU was outlawed by the Jamaica Assembly, and that free colored followers of the missionaries served as guards at many chapels and mission stations (Gordon 1996:12), the missionary James Phillippo reported that fourteen chapels belonging to the Baptist Missionary Society were destroyed, as were the houses and other property of the Baptist missionaries; the property damage inflicted by the planters on the Baptists reportedly exceeded £23,000. In their wrath the planters also attacked the Wesleyans. Although there was no evidence that they had participated in the uprising, the planters destroyed six Wesleyan chapels valued at about £6,000. According to Phillippo, only the Evangelical and Presbyterian clergy were spared (Phillippo 1843:166–167).

In the wake of this pogrom, many newly exiled missionaries lobbied for emancipation back in England, which some have argued was successful, as Parliament enacted the Emancipation Act less than two years after the outbreak of the Baptist War.

POST-EMANCIPATION MISSIONS

The missionizing work of the Baptists and other nonconformist sects continued for several decades after emancipation, and, in fact, whereas few African-Jamaicans would have identified themselves as Christians at the end of the eighteenth century, most would identify themselves as such by the end of the nineteenth. How, though, did the missionaries contribute to the construction of post-slavery Jamaica, and how can this be understood archaeologically?

Empowered by Parliament's decision to end slavery in the West Indies, missionary activity soon resumed as many of the clergymen exiled in the wake of the Baptist War returned to Jamaica. According to King, by the late 1840s the Moravians had thirteen active stations in Jamaica; the Wesleyan Methodists counted twenty-four British and four colored Jamaican missionaries on the island; the Baptist mission included twenty-eight European and "five or six native" pastors; and the Presbyterians were represented by "about twenty European missionaries" (King 1850:86–93). Among those resuscitating the missionary movement were members of the London Missionary Society (LMS), an interdenominational mission charged with bringing religious instruction to the former slaves. Six missionaries affiliated with the LMS arrived in Jamaica in December 1834; by 1849, eleven stations had been established.

The stated goal of the London Missionary Society was to assist the emancipated workers in their transition to becoming orderly and disciplined wage laborers. The LMS apparently hoped not to "preach to the converted," as it instructed its agents to concentrate efforts in regions not previously missionized (Gordon 1996:14). In the years following the end of slavery, LMS missionaries found the task of converting emancipated slaves to Christianity daunting, especially given the strength of the Native Baptist movement. For example, at Porus, which is just a few miles from Marshall's Pen, one LMS missionary, Brother Slayter, reported that he found himself surrounded by five black Baptist groups, which he regarded as "a barrier to the spread of true religion" (quoted in Gordon 1996:14), again revealing the prejudice against black understandings of Christianity. King reports that frustration with their lack of success in attracting converts led several missionaries to return to the United Kingdom (King 1850:93).

In the years spanning the passage of the Emancipation Act (1833) and the actual abolition of slavery (1838), Baptist missionaries actively incorporated into their mission a paternalistic attempt to help emancipated slaves make the transition to freedom. At the heart of this attempt was the creation of what were called "free townships," carved out of land purchased by missionary groups or donated by planters, and either sold at a discount or given outright to converted African-Jamaicans who agreed to live in these newly created villages. Usually these townships were established on the edges of existing estates.

Interestingly, the planters and the missionaries seem to have found common ground following emancipation, as both the missionaries and the planters wanted the population to remain near white settlements rather than moving into the vast unsettled interior. When missions bought land, which was widely available after emancipation, they would sell it cheaply in small lots to the missionized, usually with the understanding that members of the flock would become wage laborers on the nearby estate. The stated goal of the missionaries was to create a new Jamaican society, one in which the emancipated slaves would become God-fearing holders of private property engaged in the cash economy developing under nineteenth-century capitalism (Austin-Broos 1997:39–42; Hinton 1847:117). This, of course, suited the planters' interests, given the realities of a post-slavery world; to make their estates profitable, they required access to a pliant, disciplined, and obedient workforce. What could be better than mild Christians living close by and under the watchful eye of a missionary?

MISSIONARIES AND THE DESIGN OF FREE TOWNSHIPS

The understanding of spatial behavior and landscape design is central to archaeological practice. Like other types of documentary archaeology, such analysis requires the consideration not only of artifacts recovered from the ground, but of documentary and cartographic data as well (Beaudry 1988; Little 1992). Such analysis can demonstrate the ways in which the missionaries' worldviews were written into the landscapes of the free townships, and thus help us to consider how preconceived sociospatial relations contributed to the definition of racial hierarchies in post-emancipation Jamaica. Take, for example, a contemporary rendition of one of the first of these townships, known as Sligoville, which was founded by James Phillippo in 1835 and named after the governor of Jamaica, the Marquis of Sligo (Figure 11.3). The design of the township was an amalgam of Jamaican plantation and British parochial village. In the context of post-emancipation Jamaica, rather than building the village in the shadow of the overseer's or planter's house (which were often elevated to maximize surveillance over the villages of the enslaved), the missionaries built the free townships around the church, school, and mission house or rectory, which served as the locus of surveillance. As the planters had done before them, the missionaries created a landscape of

Figure 11.3. Sligoville, a free township founded by James Phillippo in 1835. (From Phillippo 1843)

domination with themselves in the elevated position. Also key to township design was the subdivision of the land into small plots, with individual ownership of land and cottages. By ensuring that people lived on plots too small to produce any significant surplus, the missionaries and their new-found allies, the planters, planned to create spiritual dependence on the missionary and economic dependence on plantation work, and thus the plantation owner.

A similar layout can be seen in the subdivision plat of a township known as Priory (Figure 11.4) created out of the Seville estate near St. Ann's Bay. As was the case with Sligoville, the parcel of land that became the Priory township was divided into small lots, each conveyed to separate, formerly enslaved individuals. The layout of the village was such that the rectory—the missionary's house—was at the end of an avenue, uphill from the small lots of the parishioners. The church was at the opposite end of the avenue, downhill from the rectory and the lots. This layout was designed to accomplish two things. First, by creating a class of landowners whose lots might be large enough to support a kitchen garden, but little else, the missionaries and planters who actualized the design hoped to reinforce an emerging class system in which formerly enslaved blacks would simultaneously be endowed with the ethics of a landholder with title to private property. Because the lots were too small to produce any significant surplus to sell in the St. Ann's Bay market, this new class of small landholders would thus be dependent on wage labor to supplement their income. In order to buy imported goods, such as cloth, metal cooking pots, imported ceramics, and food staples, including rice and salted meat, the emerging class of black workers—particularly those who had no marketable artisanal skills—would have little choice but to continue working on neighboring estates for a wage. In both Sligoville and Priory, labor discipline would be reinforced by the constant gaze of a white Christian missionary.

As revealed in the layout of mission townships, surveillance was a key element of the overall design. This was a concept upon which the planters and missionaries could

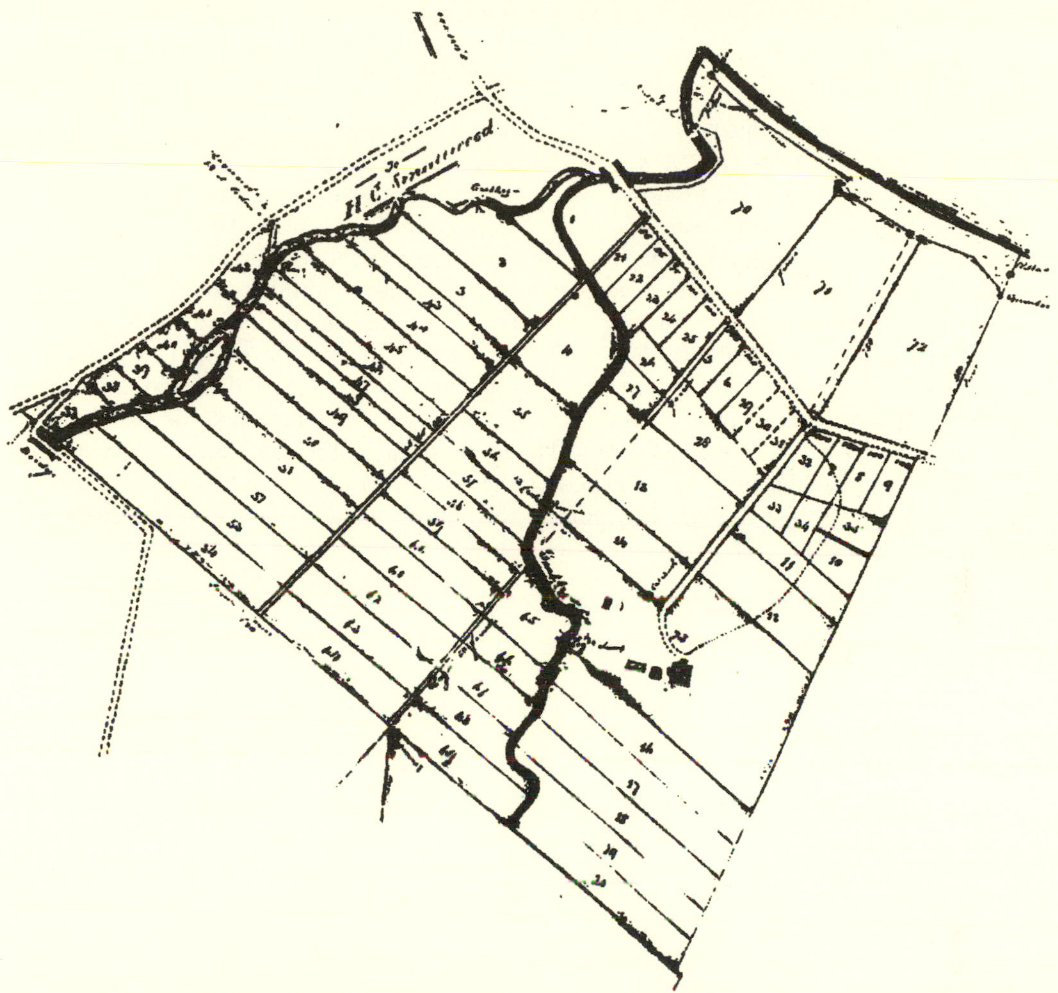

Figure 11.4. Plan of the subdivision of part of the Seville estate into Privy Township, bordered on the north by the sea, to the east by the estate, and to the south by the mission compound. North is to the top. Redrawn from an original in the National Library of Jamaica. (Courtesy of the National Library of Jamaica)

agree: the emancipated labor force needed to be watched. From the earliest days of the Christianizing movement, the missionaries made it their business to change certain behaviors they found reprehensible, including such customs as polygamy, serial monogamy, the use of sorcery (in Jamaica known as "obeah"), and premarital sex ("fornication" in the language of the missionaries) (see Stewart 1808:276–277 for a discussion of polygamy from a planter's perspective). Missionaries of each of the various nonconformist sects found it necessary to expel individuals from the church for failing to abandon such "sinful" practices. Of course, in order for such expulsions to occur, the sinners had to be exposed, which required surveillance over private behavior, a key part of the mission. Missionaries occasionally put their class leaders in uncomfortable positions by requiring them to report on the activities of their class members (Turner 1998:90–91). Surveillance had long been part of the labor-control strategy of pre-emancipation Jamaica (Delle 1998; Delle et al. 1999); given this logic, the importance of surveillance in the township design as a mechanism to control unwanted behaviors is quite understandable.

DIALECTICAL SPATIAL UNDERSTANDINGS AT MARSHALL'S PEN

Given the intentions of the missionary-inspired township designs, how were these intended spaces actualized, and how well were the intended race-reified social structures imagined by the missionaries and planters actually formed in post-emancipation Jamaica? A parallel question concerns how such social engineering and processes can be studied archaeologically. To probe these questions, I now turn to a discussion of recent archaeological work at Marshall's Pen, an early nineteenth-century coffee plantation in central Jamaica, located in that part of the modern parish of Manchester that in the early nineteenth century was part of the parish of Clarendon.

Marshall's Pen is the southernmost of a series of estates owned and operated by Alexander Lindsay, the sixth earl of Balcarres, and passed upon his death in 1825 to his son, James Lindsay, the twenty-fourth earl of Crawford. Balcarres is a relatively important character in Jamaican history. A Scottish nobleman who served in the British army as a lieutenant colonel in the American Revolution, the twenty-five-year-old earl commanded a regiment that surrendered to the Continental Army with General Burgoyne at Saratoga in 1777. In 1793 he served as the commander of His Majesty's forces in Jersey, and in 1794 was appointed lieutenant governor of Jamaica—the de facto viceroy of what was then Britain's most valuable colonial possession, a position he maintained until 1801. During the first year of his term as lieutenant governor, Balcarres personally directed military operations during the Maroon War of 1795. Apparently a ruthless military man, Balcarres imported trained mastiffs from Cuba and used these fierce dogs as part of a strategy to dishearten and defeat the maroon guerillas. Upon the maroons' capitulation in 1796, Balcarres deported six hundred of them to Nova Scotia (Campbell 1988; Matheson and Taylor 1976; S. Walker 1988).

During his regime, Balcarres invested in several lucrative ventures, among them a scheme to rent enslaved men to the armed forces as laborers. To our point here, from 1799 on, Balcarres invested in a series of coffee estates in the northwestern parish of St. George and in central Jamaica, in what is now the parish of Manchester. During this time, Balcarres purchased three estates in central Jamaica, including Martin's Hill, Shooter's Hill, and Marshall's Pen. After leaving Jamaica in 1801, Balcarres managed his estates as an absentee proprietor. Upon his death in 1825, his son continued to manage the estate through emancipation but sold off the Jamaican properties by the early 1840s (S. Walker 1988:359).

Archaeologically, Marshall's Pen is the most interesting of the three Manchester estates. Martin's Hill and Shooter's Hill were purchased by Alcan, which mined the former coffee estates for bauxite, a raw material the company uses to produce aluminum. The mining operations have severely disturbed the archaeological integrity of these two plantations. In contrast, Marshall's Pen has not yet been mined for bauxite. Since 1939 the estate has been owned by the Sutton family, who have operated the estate as both a dairy and beef cattle farm.

Marshall's Pen is an ideal location to examine spatial dialectics during the peak of missionary activity in Jamaica. Documentary evidence suggests that the estate was first surveyed and improved in 1785; it was acquired by Balcarres in 1799. By 1802 at the latest, a slave settlement at Marshall's Pen had been established on what is known both historically and contemporarily as "Negro House Hill." The documentary evidence suggests that this village may have been designed and constructed by the enslaved Africans working the estate. The site was mapped as part of the Marshall's Pen African-Jamaican Archaeological Project in the summer of 1999 (Figure 11.5). Surface remains of houses, fences, retaining walls, and animal pens indicate that the village was organized into ten compounds, each bounded by retaining walls and fences. Eight of the ten contained more than

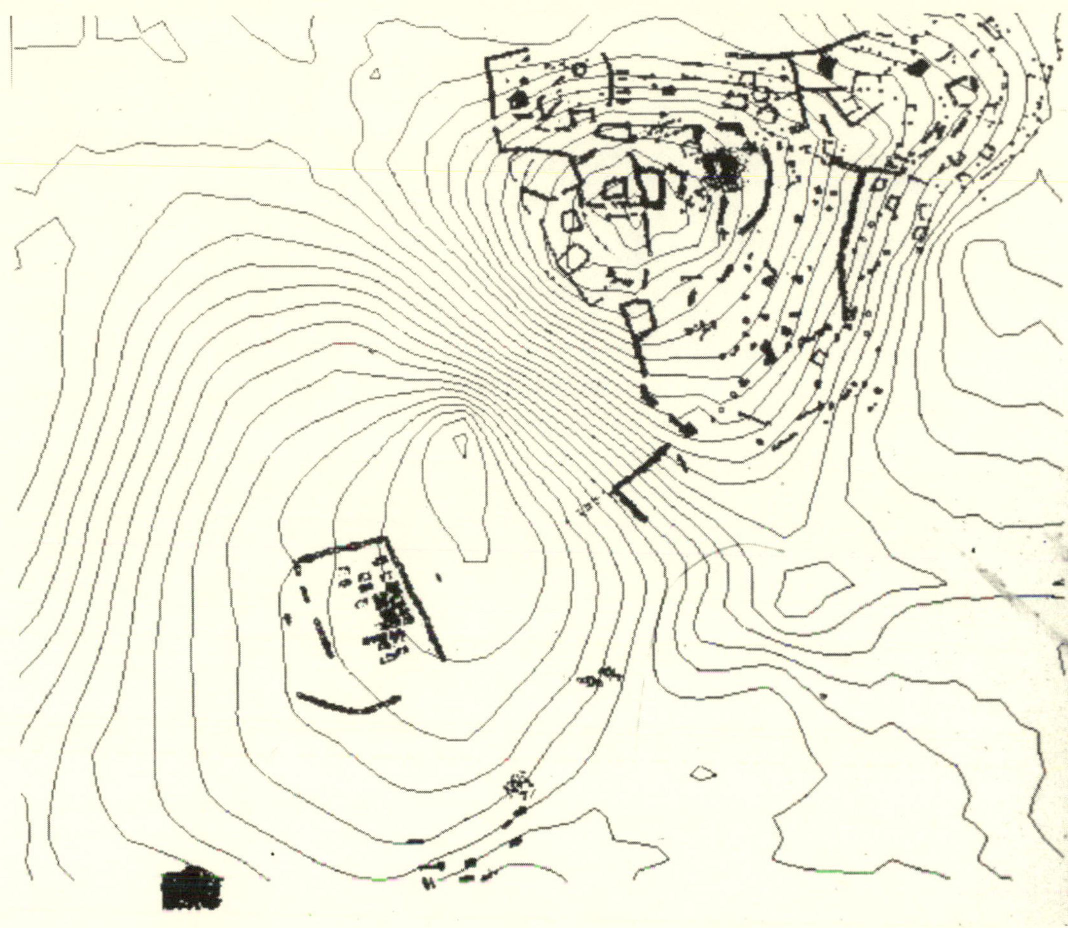

Figure 11.5. The village at Marshall's Pen. Clusters of house compounds can be seen bounded by stone walls to the upper right. Center left, also bounded by a stone wall, is the cemetery. The large structure at the bottom left is likely the slave hospital. (Drawn by William Burdick)

one house foundation visible on the surface (Figure 11.6). Several compounds featured a shared animal pen. Given the clustered settlement pattern of house compounds with shared animal pens, it seems likely that the village was organized into communal groups. The compounds probably were inhabited by kin groups, as was the case in other Jamaican villages with a similar settlement pattern (Higman 1998).

When it was quite clear that Parliament was going to legislate the end of slavery, a free township was carved out of Marshall's Pen. Balcarres Township was established on the northeastern periphery of the estate in 1838 by James Lindsay, the twenty-fourth earl of Crawford, who removed the entire enslaved population of more than two hundred people to Balcarres Township at this time. Just how many people actually settled there is uncertain, but it seems clear that the descendant community still resides in Balcarres Township. Unlike the clustered settlement pattern of Negro House Hill, the New Village at Balcarres Township was constructed on a linear pattern with individual houses sitting on small lots, similar to the layout of townships designed and implemented on other estates by missionaries. It is unclear at this time whether any missionaries were directly involved in the design of Balcarres Township, but there is clear evidence that the missionary movement impacted the enslaved population on the Balcarres estates. The estate records,

Figure 11.6. The foundation of House 5, in House Area 6, prior to excavation. (Photo by James A. Delle)

housed at the National Library of Scotland, indicate that in the mid-1820s many enslaved people owned by Balcarres were baptized, and that they abandoned their assigned or African names in favor of English, Christian names.

Archaeological remote sensing has suggested another line of evidence that may corroborate the influence of Christianity on the enslaved population of Marshall's Pen. One of the remarkable features of the site is a graveyard associated with the village on Negro House Hill in which there are twenty-six visible aboveground grave markers (Figure 11.7). While local oral histories suggest that these graves once had inscribed headstones, these were reportedly robbed in the late nineteenth century (Robert Sutton, pers. comm.). During the 1999 field season, the graveyard was mapped, and geophysical remote sensing was conducted in the pasture surrounding the visible graves. The magnetometer survey revealed several linear series of subsurface anomalies, signatures that may in fact reveal the location of grave shafts. Should these anomalies indeed be caused by grave shafts, it may be hypothesized that sometime during the graveyard's use-life, burial practices changed. It is possible that the aboveground markers, similar to burial markers in West Africa (Agorsah 1999), may have been associated with "heathen" African practices and abandoned after the Marshall's Pen population was baptized into Christianity.

Shared spaces like the compounds at Marshall's Pen suggest a communal mode of social organization, much different from the segmented, individualized settlement systems pushed by the missionaries through their township schemes. While it was in the best interest of the planters to fragment African-Jamaican society into the lowest common denominator, the individual, it was in the best interest of those individuals to create social bonds and to consider themselves part of a social whole, distinct from the society of the whites. Therein lies the key to understanding the dialectic between the individual and the whole: societies created out of individual components are disempowered both in whole and in part, as those individuals will nearly inevitably be caught up in competition great

Figure 11.7. One of the grave markers still visible in the cemetery at Marshall's Pen. (Photo by James A. Delle)

and small, not only for resources (including, of course, wages) but for their very survival. Social groups held together through a communal organization such as that evident in the layout of the village at Marshall's Pen can rely on shared resources and spaces. By placing emphasis on the community, family, or group, communal agency is exerted to benefit not isolated individuals, but society as a whole. Consciously or not, it was this very solidarity that the planters and missionaries sought to undermine by creating villages of individuals dependent on wages. Nevertheless, this solidarity led even privileged members of the enslaved class to risk their lives to bring an end to the institution that enslaved them. The leaders of the 1831 Baptist War, men like Sam Sharpe, were the slave owners' most trusted and valuable workers—the very men and women who were best able to use communal bonds to organize collective action. This fact was not lost on Lord Balcarres. Presaging the Baptist War of 1831–1832 was a mutiny plan hatched by a number of enslaved people during the Christmas holidays of 1823. Unlike the Christmas Rebellion of 1831, the 1823 insurrection was detected by the planters before it was executed. Seven men enslaved by Balcarres on his St. George estate were convicted as being ringleaders. Balcarres's head driver, second driver, and head mason—all privileged and trusted members of the enslaved population—were hanged; the other four men were transported from the island. Balcarres and his heir were well aware of the necessity of breaking down communal solidarity among the African-Jamaican population, a message inherent in the township plans preached by the post-emancipation missionaries and executed in the design of Balcarres Township.

CONCLUSION

By the early 1850s, the tide of European missionary work in Jamaica had turned. The island's economy, at least in terms of export products, was in a serious decline brought on by a series of labor and production crises (Delle 1998). It had been the expressed hope of the missionaries in Jamaica, encouraged by their initial success in converting enslaved Jamaicans to their various denominations, that soon after slavery had ended, the congregations would be self-supporting. The opposite was the case. In another example of a dialectical conflict over the importance of established religion to the colonizers and the colonized, many African-Jamaicans began to abandon their missionary instructors as the empty promises of emancipation were exposed. Good Christians were expected to tithe to their church, and students in most missionary schools were expected to pay tuition. As King reported, "Many members of congregations would be pleased to have their names quietly dropped from the roll... if they were to be exempted in consequence from all demands on their pocket.... They are willing or desirous to be let alone"(King 1850:96). Concerning the drop in attendance at mission schools, King suggested that "the attendance of pupils in the schools is, in many places, falling off, and parents grudge or positively refuse to pay the smallest fee for the instruction of their offspring" (King 1850:97). It seems quite obvious that many were not willing to pay the whites for the privilege of participating in their religion.

In the years prior to abolition, many African-Jamaicans believed that Christianity could be a liberating movement; witness the role that Baptist ministers played in the Christmas Rebellion of 1831–1832. Once emancipation was attained, and people began to understand that freedom would not be equated with social equality, interest in the new religions began to wane. As King related in 1850, the "present negroes were not slaves, or they have been so long free that they have grown familiar with emancipation, and are not easily stirred by the consideration of it to any special thankfulness or activity" (King 1850:102). As wages fell, many African-Jamaicans abandoned their townships and their connection to the export economy, choosing instead to create an independent subsistence on farms deep in the interior. King reports that a meeting of the Wesleyan Methodists in Kingston ended with a resolution that, in part, acknowledged this fact: the "prostrate condition of [Jamaica's] agriculture and commerce... induces numbers of negro labourers to retire from estates... to seek the means of subsistence in the mountains, where they are removed in general from moral training and superintendence" (King 1850:111).

In conclusion, it is my belief that the creation of townships on peripheries of estates was part of a larger strategy of limiting the freedom of emancipated slaves. It is little wonder that many chose to abandon this system and attempted to create an independent existence "removed... from moral training and superintendence." Missionaries and planters had worked together to remove laborers from the property owned by estates, but to keep them close by with the intention of building unequal social relations under a wage system. It was the hope of planters and missionaries alike that the African-Jamaican population would remain dependent on white landowners and church leaders, and that communal relations developed under the harsh realities of slavery, and visible in the layout of the village at Marshall's Pen, would break down. In selling, renting, or giving small houses on tiny plots to isolated individuals living in monogamous nuclear families, planters and missionaries hoped to create a population of disciplined, obedient wage slaves who respected the existing power structure and its material manifestations, especially the lives and property of the white elites. Living as wage-dependent Christians, the newly converted had to accept the racist social order created and perpetuated by the whites, even after slavery had been abolished. Living apart from this social order would be the only way to attain some measure of autonomy and a true emancipation.

In the case of Marshall's Pen, it is possible that even though Balcarres Township was not created by missionaries, the design and creation of places like Priory and Sligoville influenced its creation. Even the use of the term "township" suggests the missionaries' influence on the younger earl's designs for moving the emancipated workers into this newly created village. Despite these well-laid plans, however, the African-Jamaican population did not miraculously transform into an obedient, acquiescent labor force. It would take more than new township designs to transform the social realities of African-Jamaicans.

The forms of limited freedom envisioned by the missionaries and planters who designed places like Balcarres Township conflicted dialectically with the goal of many of the emancipated African-Jamaicans, which was to attain economic self-sufficiency. The white goal of restricting self-sufficiency resulted in collusion between formerly conflicting groups (planters and missionaries) and, I think, resistance on the part of the newly freed African-Jamaicans. Such acts of resistance can be seen, for example, in two 1850 riots of his own parishioners against the Baptist missionary James Phillippo, the man most responsible for pushing the township scheme in post-emancipation Jamaica. As it turned out, Phillippo's authority as a church leader was challenged by his flock, who apparently had tired of the missionary's paternalistic ways. In 1850 Phillippo's communicants occupied his chapel, hoping to replace the white missionary with a black leader from their own ranks. In response, Phillippo secured a court order maintaining English Baptist claims to the church property in Spanish Town, and he had the people forcibly removed from the church. The militant response to these strong-arm tactics was rioting. The first riot involved only twenty people, including sixteen women; the second involved about five hundred people who nearly destroyed Phillippo's house. This latter group had to be disbursed by the military (Holt 1992). Clearly, the missionary vision of what a free Jamaica should look like, espoused by the likes of Phillippo, had little to do with liberation.

Note

Thanks to Ann and Robert Sutton, Rosemary Whitaker, Dorrick Gray, Roderick Ebanks, Chuck Orser, James Skibo, my fellow participants in the 1999 symposium on race and archaeology, and, of course, the students and staff of the Franklin and Marshall College Summer Field School in Historical Archaeology, especially Patrick Heaton, Will Burdick, and Lizzie Martin.

12

Class, Race, and Identity among Free Blacks in the Antebellum South

Theresa A. Singleton

Communities of free blacks or free persons of color arose in every slave society throughout the Americas. The terms "free persons of color," "free blacks," or "free African Americans" refer to people of African descent who obtained their freedom from slavery legally either through self-purchase or some form of gratis manumission.[1] Though legally free, free African Americans had to struggle for their civil rights due to legal restrictions that in many cases reduced them to a near-slave status. Even the titles of many classic historiographies on free African Americans, such as Ira Berlin's *Slaves Without Masters* (1974), David Cohen and Jack Green's *Neither Slave Nor Free* (1972), and Jerome Handler's *The Unappropriated People* (1974), speak to the ambivalent status of free people of color wherever they resided in the Americas.

In the southern United States, both white slaveholders and white non-slaveholders viewed free African Americans with contempt and were vested in keeping them subordinate. Slaveholders regarded free blacks as a threat to slavery. They feared free African Americans would assist enslaved men and women in running away or inciting rebellions. When such fears were realized, as in the Denmark Vesey conspiracy, slaveholders redoubled their efforts through the passage of legislation aimed to discourage fraternization between free and enslaved segments of the black community. Denmark Vesey was an enslaved blacksmith who purchased his freedom in 1800. He and several enslaved persons plotted a slave revolt in Charleston, South Carolina, but it was revealed to a slaveholder who, in turn, contacted the authorities. In the end, thirty-five people, including Vesey, were executed for planning the alleged plot in 1822. Thus, the Vesey conspiracy became a symbol throughout the South of the potential dangers of free black/slave associations (Goldfield 1991:140).[2]

White non-slaveholders, particularly skilled laborers, saw free blacks as competitors because blacks would work for less money. Throughout the Old South, white laborers sought legislation to prohibit blacks, enslaved and free, from entering many skilled occupations (Singleton 1984).[3] Consequently, few blacks were apprenticed in prestigious crafts such as silversmithing or cabinetmaking, or many mechanical trades requiring a high level of technical expertise, such as that of millwright.[4] Whites considered many of the jobs free blacks performed to be beneath them and pejoratively labeled them "nigger work" (Goldfield 1991:133). The occupations most often relegated to black laborers included barbering, carting, stable work, or carpentry for men, and cooking, laundering, housekeeping, sewing, and peddling of handicrafts and produce for women. Both free black men and women were engaged in catering, an activity free blacks monopolized in several southern cities (Goldfield 1991:133–134). The following examples illustrate how free blacks took advantage of opportunities to work jobs that whites found demeaning and, in the process, sometimes became quite prosperous.

How free blacks responded to the racial subordination imposed on them by whites is the subject of this chapter. Using archaeological and written sources, this chapter explores the strategies used by free African Americans to contest white efforts to reduce them to a form of bondage just slightly above that of slavery. Undoubtedly, these strategies varied widely and changed according to particular circumstances. Additionally, an examination of such strategies provides insights into their agency, defined here as direct or indirect individual or collective action (for various definitions and approaches to agency, see Dobres and Robb 2000:9). The study of free blacks lends itself to the study of individual action because most of the historiography of free blacks has been derived from constructing the histories of individuals through exhaustive research of manumission, military, and governmental records; property deeds; and parish registers. These histories are then "patched together to form whole patterns" (Landers 1996:viii) of the larger free black community.

In a vein similar to that of historians, I focus on individual free blacks to better understand them as a segment of southern antebellum society. Because of their multiple yet contradictory identities as former slaves, slaveholders, and often emancipators, free blacks offer the opportunity to examine the negotiation of their racial identity. Michael Johnson and James Roark (1984a:50) observe that southern free blacks either sympathized with the plight of enslaved people and accepted a shared identity, or distanced themselves because they saw their fate as separate and distinct from the enslaved. Although these two tendencies are diametrically opposed, free blacks used both strategies in varying degrees depending on the situation. This fluidity allows us to move beyond essentialist notions of identity and begin analyses of the complexities associated with identity formation.

Identity is closely tied to agency. Actors' sense about who they are and how they should act influences their action, but there is no guarantee that they will act predictably, even when confronted with identical circumstances, because of their individual subjectivities (Brumfiel 2000:252). The following examples show the different ways that free blacks responded to the racist structures of the antebellum South.

SOUTHERN FREE BLACKS IN COMPARATIVE PERSPECTIVE

Free blacks arose in every slave society in the Americas, but their place within any given regime depended on a wide range of economic, cultural, political, and religious circumstances. Moreover, the laws and practices governing manumission reflected changing attitudes that varied through time and in different places. Yet despite the idiosyncrasy that characterized the lives of free blacks, some general tendencies are observable: they often entered the lowest stratum of free society; they faced hostility from white neighbors and former masters; and freedom never meant total acceptance because racism existed in all American slave societies (Klein 1986:217–218). The degree of acceptance and/or hostility often depended on whether or not free blacks filled an unoccupied niche within the particular society that served as a buffer between slaveholders and enslaved black laborers.

In the southern United States, manumissions were initially more widespread in the Upper South than in the Lower South. The creation of a free black class through manumissions had been an important feature of slavery in seventeenth-century Virginia. As the slave population grew in the eighteenth century, however, manumissions were fewer, and efforts toward restricting the privileges of free blacks increased (Deal 1988:277–280). Manumissions occurred with greater frequency later in the eighteenth century when the agricultural economy of the Chesapeake shifted from tobacco to wheat. Planters' dependency on slave labor diminished, and many enslaved laborers were freed. During the first two decades following the American Revolution, many slaveholders granted manumissions; consequently the free black population of the Upper South tripled (Johnson and Roark 1984a:31).

The history of free blacks in the English colonies of the Lower South has been obscured because most studies of free blacks in that region begin with the 1790 census. Additionally, South Carolina's act "For the Better Ordering, and Governing of Negroes and Other Slaves," popularly known as the Negro Act of 1740, conflated free blacks with enslaved people (Olwell 1996:2). This legislation implied that the free black population was insignificant, and that their situation was not much better than that of enslaved people. Although free blacks in eighteenth-century South Carolina failed to develop a rural land base, an urban, artisanal, free black community did emerge, just as in many of the black communities of Chesapeake. These free blacks were the forebears of the free black households identified in the 1790 census (Olwell 1996). Beginning in the 1790s, hundreds of mulatto refugees fleeing St. Domingue during the Haitian revolution sought refuge in southern cities, namely Charleston, Mobile, and New Orleans, which greatly added to the free black population in those cities.

After 1820, when the spread of cotton culture revived the need for enslaved labor, manumissions dropped considerably throughout the South. The free black population increased primarily by natural means. Manumissions became so restrictive in some states that only state legislatures had the authority to free a person who was born enslaved. In the 1850s, free blacks faced two new challenges: first, competition from waves of new European immigrants who were willing to do work that only free blacks had previously done (Goldfield 1991); second, growing hostility from white slaveholders, who had become paranoid of having a black community that represented a contradiction to their efforts to defend slavery (Johnson and Roark 1984b). These circumstances forced many free blacks to accept the imposed racial identity they shared with enslaved blacks, and many emerged as the leaders of a united black community during the Civil War and Reconstruction (Boles 1984:138).

THE ARCHAEOLOGY OF FREE BLACKS

Archaeological studies of free black communities have been undertaken in both the Upper and Lower South, and have primarily focused on urban communities where at least a third of the free black population of the South resided. These studies were undertaken primarily for the purpose of cultural resource management and other historic preservation projects such as architectural restoration, and therefore have not directly addressed the questions concerning free blacks' responses to racism or their identity formation. Also, most of these studies have been published as "gray literature" site reports that are often difficult to locate. Despite these limitations of the archaeological literature on free blacks, it is possible to begin analyses of their agency as seen in material culture. My goal here is to offer alternative ways of interpreting material culture associated with free blacks as symbolic of strategies they used to resist racial subordination.

This discussion examines the lives of three African Americans living during the antebellum period. William Johnson, a well-documented barber of Natchez, Mississippi, amassed a small fortune in substantial holdings in rental property, large acreage of farm and timber land, several businesses, and fifteen enslaved laborers (Davis and Hogan 1973:8–9; Hogan and Davis 1993:34); William Cuff of Chestertown, Maryland, identified simply as a "laborer" in census records, owned property and several enslaved persons, some of whom were apparently family members (Catts and McCall 1991); Hannah Jackson, a laundress in Alexandria, Virginia, was one the earliest-known African Americans to own property in Alexandria (Revis 1991). As did William Cuff, she purchased several enslaved persons, all of them apparently relatives.

I selected these examples primarily because they represent different social positions within free black society. It is difficult to discuss free blacks without discussing class because clearly a class structure existed among them (see discussion in Hogan and Davis 1993:11–12). At the same time, however, this class structure did not necessarily mirror the corresponding white society. Moreover, archaeological approaches to class are problematic because class is often treated as consisting of objective attributes rather than operating in particular sociohistorical contexts and at different scales of social relations (Wurst 1999:9–10). What distinguishes the three individuals in this study, at least on a superficial level, are not different occupational or skill levels but the different amounts of real property they owned. William Johnson was considerably more affluent than the other two. His estate was appraised at $8,770 at the time of his death (Building Conservation Technology 1979:121–124), whereas the estates of other two together were valued at less than $100. Despite his relative wealth, Johnson was not a member of the free black elite, as was William Ellison of South Carolina, a master craftsman and slaveholder who owned more than sixty enslaved people (Johnson and Roark 1984a).

William Cuff is more of an enigma. He was identified simply as a laborer in the census, but he acquired a fair amount of property. Some he resold to other free blacks, and he appears to have donated some property to a black congregation for the construction of a church. Cuff's material world, as indicated in a probate inventory and archaeological investigations, was modest compared to Johnson's but may well have been characteristic of small landholders of the time.

Unlike Johnson and Cuff, who owned properties other than their residence, Jackson's real property was confined to the front and rear houses on the lot she purchased in Alexandria. Although the residence directly associated with Hannah Jackson has not been excavated, several other free black sites along the same block have been. Jackson's residence and those excavated were part of a free black neighborhood known as "Hayti." The artifacts from Hayti exhibit considerable wear and were quite old when discarded. This pattern of artifact use sharply contrasts with those of William Johnson and Thomas Cuff. Upon her death, however, Harriet Jackson's net cash worth was considerably higher than the appraised value of Cuff's estate. This factor complicates class distinctions between Jackson and Cuff, and supports the notion that class is a dynamic social formation, not fixed rungs on a social ladder (Wurst 1999:8).

A second reason for selecting these individuals was that their life histories correspond with the first half of the nineteenth century and sites that are roughly contemporaneous. Each has discrete archaeological components dating to the antebellum period. William Johnson occupied the site from 1841 until his death in 1851, and family members occupied it well into the twentieth century. The ceramic assemblage at the Thomas Cuff site dates to between 1830 and 1860 (Catts and McCall 1991:175). Hannah Jackson bought her residence in the Hayti neighborhood in 1820, and 1830 is the beginning date for the free black assemblages there.

WILLIAM JOHNSON, THE BARBER OF NATCHEZ

William Johnson, a mulatto, was born into slavery. He was presumably the son of William Johnson, a slaveholder, and Amy, an enslaved woman. Johnson, Amy's owner, reputedly manumitted her from slavery by crossing the Mississippi River from Natchez, Mississippi, to Videlia, Louisiana. Louisiana civil law, based on French and Spanish precedents, was more lenient toward slave manumission than Mississippi. Johnson appeared before a judge and declared Amy free in 1814. Six years later, Johnson petitioned the Mississippi legislature to emancipate Amy's son William, who was eleven at the time (Davis and Hogan 1973:17–18).

The young Johnson learned the barber business from his brother-in-law and opened his first barbershop at the age of nineteen in Port Gibson, Mississippi, about fifty miles south of Natchez. Two years later, he returned to Natchez and purchased his brother-in-law's shop. He began to augment the business with other ventures such as money lending, rental property, and a dairy farm. He also opened two more barber shops, which were operated by enslaved workers as well as free blacks he had employed.

Johnson is best known to students of southern history for the diary he kept in which he recorded his business and personal dealings (Hogan and Davis 1951, 1993). It is also an important document of life in antebellum Natchez, southern life in general, and black/white relations. Moreover, for the purposes of this chapter, his diary provides a rare glimpse into the thoughts and motivations of a free African American. Johnson's diary therefore facilitates interpretations of his agency.

It is very clear from Johnson's diary that he saw the experience of free blacks as separate and distinct from that of enslaved people. Johnson worked very hard to emulate what he perceived as the high moral standards of white gentlemen. He accepted slavery and was a slaveholder. He maintained his distance from enslaved people and expected his family and free black apprentices to do the same. Nevertheless, all but one of his apprentices routinely went to social events with enslaved people, which greatly annoyed Johnson. He wanted his apprentices to follow the standards of conduct he and other free blacks at the top of their social strata had established (Davis and Hogan 1973:92).

Yet Johnson was not unsympathetic to the plight of enslaved people. He became the mentor and advocate for an enslaved young man named William Winston, whom he hired from his white slave owner, training him in barbering and teaching him to read and write (Hogan and Davis 1993:527). Winston was eventually manumitted in the will of his slaveholder and later moved to the North (Hogan and Davis 1993:576, 723). On another occasion, Johnson was deeply upset at the prospect of having to sell an enslaved laborer named Steven on the eve of 1844: "Today has been to me a very Sad Day; many tears was in my Eyes today On acct. of my Selling poor Steven.... I gave Steven a pair [of] suspenders and a pr. of Socks and 2 Cigars, Shook hands with him and see [him] go On Board for the Last Time I felt hurt but Liquor is the cause of his troubles" (Hogan and Davis 1993:470). Three years later, Johnson was saddened to hear of the recent sale of two little girls and an older woman of a local slaveholder: "Poor creatures I am Sorry for them" (Hogan and Davis 1993:572). Although Johnson was a slaveholder, these examples hint at his internal struggle regarding slavery. He never discussed the morality of slavery in his diary, but as a former slave himself, perhaps there were times when he could identify with their situation.

White citizens respected Johnson and recognized that he was at top of the free black social ladder in Natchez. They thought he was a fair and earnest businessman who was community-minded. Several of his white clients befriended him, but they never accepted him socially. The color-line also prohibited Johnson from sitting with white men in public gatherings, riding in a public or private vehicle with them, voting, participating in civic meetings, belonging to the local militia, and becoming a member of the local civic board. In his later years, Johnson recognized that he had failed in his quest for white social acceptance. Perhaps, realizing that white acceptance was a lost cause, Johnson directed his attention to maintaining his social standing among free blacks.

In 1851, Johnson was murdered by Baylor Winn, who had been engaged in a land dispute over Johnson's timberlands for several years. Johnson had traveled to his timberlands accompanied by a free black apprentice and two enslaved men. On his return trip to Natchez, Winn murdered him. After several failed attempts to convict Winn for the murder, he was set free. The prosecution was unable to convict him because the only witnesses to the murder were black, and according to Mississippi laws of the time, blacks could not testify against whites. The

Figure 12.1. William Johnson House, Natchez, Mississippi (front facing view), 1982. (Photo courtesy of the Mississippi Department of Archives and History)

Figure 12.2. William Johnson House (view of backyard, the site of excavations), 1989. (Photo by Theresa Singleton)

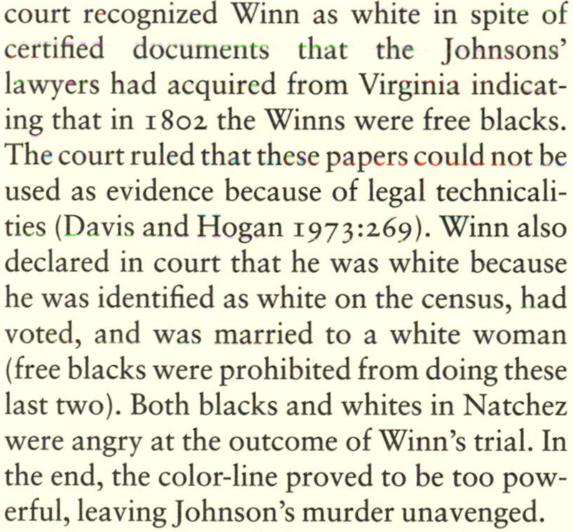

court recognized Winn as white in spite of certified documents that the Johnsons' lawyers had acquired from Virginia indicating that in 1802 the Winns were free blacks. The court ruled that these papers could not be used as evidence because of legal technicalities (Davis and Hogan 1973:269). Winn also declared in court that he was white because he was identified as white on the census, had voted, and was married to a white woman (free blacks were prohibited from doing these last two). Both blacks and whites in Natchez were angry at the outcome of Winn's trial. In the end, the color-line proved to be too powerful, leaving Johnson's murder unavenged.

Johnson acquired the property where the present William Johnson House now stands when he married Ann Battles, a free black woman, in 1835 (Figure 12.1). The first house was framed and was destroyed in a fire that took the entire block. A new three-story brick house was built at the site under Johnson's direction using both hired white and slave labor between August 1840 and November 1841 (Hogan and Davis 1993:33). Behind the house was a two-story brick kitchen with servant quarters upstairs, a bricked patio, a cistern, a stable, and small frame buildings for animals (Figure 12.2).

Archaeological investigations were undertaken at William Johnson's house in Natchez in 1978 for the purpose of architectural restoration. In 1976, the Garden Club of Natchez purchased the Johnson House and deeded it to the Preservation Society of Ellicott Hill so that it could be restored and preserved. The excavations were directed in the backyard for the purpose of obtaining information on outbuildings, determining if the structure in the rear of lot was original, and locating the cistern, patio, and privies. Artifacts were recovered primarily from sheet deposits, with the highest concentration found around privy holes. Most of the artifacts date to the first half of the nineteenth century. Ceramics comprise about half of the assemblage and include a variety of pearlwares, whitewares, coarse earthenwares, and stonewares.

No makers' marks were identified, and the only decorative motif noted was the "blue willow" pattern on transfer-printed ceramics (Padgett 1978:12). Glass was the second most important category of artifacts, and many different kinds of bottles, jars, and drinking vessels were recovered.

The aspect of William Johnson's material culture that speaks the loudest to his agency is the house itself. Located in a prominent area of Natchez that served as a hub of social and business activity, it was only a block from Main Street and two blocks from the river bluff where Natchez folk took evening walks (Davis and Hogan 1973:78). Johnson apparently worked hard to make the house a showplace. He directed most of the construction himself (Hogan and Davis 1993:313, 316, 317, 319–320) and detailed the costs in his diary (Hogan and Davis 1993:324–326). The house was furnished with items of very good quality, many of them purchased at auctions (Hogan and Davis 1993:296, 354). He also provided his family with many cultural amenities. He had a well-stocked library of books and magazines, and his musical instruments included a piano, a music box, and violins. Johnson apparently played the violin and occasionally performed for his family and guests.

Recovered glass fragments also hint at Johnson's desire to emulate the taste of white gentry. Although only five complete bottles were recovered, at least forty-five bottles and jars are represented in the assemblage (Padgett 1978:14). These include wine and other alcoholic beverage bottles, medicine bottles and jars, an ink bottle, decanter stoppers, and the base of a wine glass. The records of the Johnson family's purchases indicate that from time to time quantities of what were considered luxury items were purchased: "eighteen bottles of lime juice, nine bottles of London mustard, a barrel of oysters, two boxes of tea, two gallons peach brandy, keg of Gocian butter, and a barrell of cranburys" (Davis and Hogan 1973:80). Analysis of food remains could have been used to support the statement "Johnson table was both plentiful and varied" (Davis and Hogan 1973:80). Although faunal remains were recovered from the site, they were neither listed nor analyzed in the archaeological report.

The archaeological evidence and written descriptions of William Johnson's material world reflect Johnson's conscious efforts to present himself and his family as different from enslaved blacks. He clearly wanted acceptance from the white slaveholding elite and fashioned everything in his life—from the way he carried himself, dressed, and designed and decorated his house—to show that he could fit into their world. He may have even thought that if he presented a convincing case, showing he was just like them, some of the prohibitions of the color-line would be lifted for him and other free blacks. This never happened. Ironically, the white acceptance that eluded Johnson was achieved by his murderer, Baylor Winn, who was able to convince the court that he was *legally white*.

THOMAS CUFF, A FREE BLACK LABORER

It is unknown whether Thomas Cuff was born enslaved or free, but he evidently was born in the 1790s, because when he died in 1858, his age was estimated to be sixty-eight years (Catts and McCall 1991:165). Cuff was the son of a woman named Dinah, who was a cook, presumably enslaved, for Peregrine Wroth's mother. Peregrine Wroth, an abolitionist and advocate of black colonization of Liberia, was a longtime white friend of Cuff. Wroth was also possibly Cuff's white sponsor. Most of the slave states required that free blacks have a white sponsor who would make certain that they obeyed the laws regulating their activities.

In 1819 Cuff purchased property in a neighborhood in Chestertown, Maryland, that became known as Scott's Point. He bought the house and lot at 108 Cannon Street, the site of excavations, in 1830 from his friend Wroth. Over the next several years Cuff purchased the remaining houses in Scott's Point and later sold them to other free blacks. An advocate and benefactor for the black community in several ways, Cuff purchased property for the site of the Bethel African Methodist Episcopal meeting house in Chestertown; he was a founder and trustee the church; he sold property to free blacks; and he purchased several enslaved persons, many of whom he emancipated. How Cuff amassed enough money to buy property and enslaved people is still unclear, but he became one of wealthiest members of the black community (Catts and McCall 1991:164–165).

Archaeological investigations were undertaken at the Cuff residence to salvage materials from the crawl space underneath the house during renovations of the property. Various artifacts were uncovered, but the analysis centered on the ceramic assemblage that corresponds with the Thomas Cuff occupation. In analyzing the ceramics, Catts and McCall used the Miller Ceramic Index (Miller 1980) for determining their economic value and then compared values for the Cuff assemblage to those for assemblages from eleven other sites, five of which were occupied by African Americans. Faunal remains recovered from the site were also used to infer Cuff's socioeconomic position, although the materials came from a mixed context. (For a critique of the faunal assemblage, see Warner 1998:180–182.) The diet included some cuts of meat that archaeologists often associate with people of limited means, such as ham hocks, hog jowls, and ribs, as well as beef and loins, which may have been considered better cuts of meat. The authors also suggest that "Cuff's meat varieties were due to his relationships with these [free black] butchers" (Catts and McCall 1991:177). From this analysis, they conclude that Cuff's material world, while better than that of many of his black contemporaries, was more reflective of a laborer than of a landowner.

According to written records, Cuff directed his agency toward purchasing property and enslaved people. He was a supporter of the black community and an emancipator of enslaved people. Cuff manumitted most of the enslaved people he purchased, and they became part of his household. Acquiring enough money for self-purchase or the manumission of others was always a long, arduous process that could take many years (Landers 1996). The ability to save enough money to purchase one's freedom was by far the most important item enslaved people routinely mentioned in the antebellum African American autobiographies.[5] If saving money for manumission was a top priority, it should not be surprising that acquiring household objects became a secondary concern.

Cuff's probate inventory is more telling of his material world than is the archaeological record of his lot, but Catts and McCall (1991: 165) not only dismiss it in their interpretation, but also underestimate its potential value in the mid-nineteenth century: "The inventory of his estate suggested that he owned few material items. Total value of his estate was only $27.52, and this included a brass clock valued at $3.00, a cupboard, bureau, desk, feather bed and bedstead, nine chairs, an easy chair, rocking chair, stove, carpeting, and dishes, candlesticks, andirons, and other sundry items." Without comparable probate records for the time and place, it is difficult to evaluate Cuff's material world. While certainly spartan from the perspective of a wealthy antebellum landowner or by present-day standards, Cuff's household objects may have been typical of small propertyholders and sufficient for furnishing his house, particularly in his declining years.[6]

HANNAH JACKSON, A FREE BLACK LAUNDRESS

Considerably less is known about Hannah Jackson than the other two individuals. She first appears in the written records of Alexandria, Virginia, in 1816, when she submitted to the U.S. Circuit Court five actions on her behalf. Three of these actions involved purchasing enslaved persons: "a man named Solomon" (her son) for $135; Anne Weaver (her granddaughter) for $65 and a deed of sale for five slaves: Ester (her sister, also a laundress) and Ester's four children (Revis 1991:1) for $1,000. The other two actions were for manumissions for Ester and her children, and for John Weaver, Jackson's son-in-law. As did Thomas Cuff, Jackson was purchasing enslaved people for the purpose of manumitting them, and these individuals were all family members.

In 1820 Jackson purchased a house at what became 406–408 South Royal Street for five shillings. Jackson is one of the earliest-known African Americans to own property in this area of Alexandria. The 400 block of South Royal Street was the first free block of the neighborhood that became known as "Hayti," a name obviously derived from that of the island of Haiti, the name given to St. Domingue after the enslaved people there won their freedom from the French in 1803.

Excavations were undertaken at several sites along the 400 block of South Royal, including Lots 404, 418, 420, and 422. The ceramics and glassware were inexpensive and unmatched, like the artifacts recovered from the Bottoms, another free black neighborhood in Alexandria (Shephard 1987). They also exhibited heavy signs of wear on their bases, indicating many years of use. In general, the ceramics were quite old when they were discarded. Numerous shirt and underwear buttons along with small cylinders of decomposed wood from the poles used for laundry lines indicate that several women living on South Royal Street were laundresses, as were Jackson and her sister Ester (Alexandria Archaeology 1993; Cressey 1985).

When compared with Thomas Cuff's material world, the archaeological materials recovered from the Hayti sites suggest a more spartan way of life. Even a collection of artifacts recovered from an urban slave quarter occupied by Harriet Williams from 1849 to 1855 had more expensive items than those recovered from the free black sites of Hayti. The items recovered from Harriet Williams's home included a lead crystal wine glass, a French wine bottle seal, nine porcelain teacups, and a Canton fruit basket (Alexandria Archaeology 1993).

Are the nicer objects at the slave quarter of Harriet Williams necessarily an indicator that her material life was better than that of Hannah Jackson and Hayti's other residents? Like Cuff, Jackson focused her energy on purchasing her relatives from slaveholders and manumitting them. Evidently, it had taken her a long time to accumulate enough money to do this. Jackson's age at the time of these purchases in 1816 is not given, but her children appear to have been adults. Her daughter was married and had a child. The age of Ester, Jackson's sister, is given at about forty-five years, and she appears to have been younger than Hannah given that her children were considerably younger than Hannah's (one to eleven years old). A further suggestion that Jackson acquired the money to purchase her family later in life is seen in the fact that her will was probated in 1827, only eleven years after she submitted the actions to purchase and manumit her family. In the will, Jackson left the "front house" on Royal Street to her daughter and son-in-law, John Weaver, and the "back house" to her son Solomon and his family (Revis 1991:4). She also left twenty-five dollars to each of Solomon's two children, a considerable sum of money at the time. The cash portion alone of her estate was worth almost twice the value of Cuff's entire estate ($27.52). Rather than spending money on household objects, Jackson may have preferred saving cash. Apparently it took her a lifetime of saving to purchase and manumit her family members.

CLOSING COMMENTS

I initiated this project to begin an analysis of the archaeology of free blacks in the antebellum South. Although several archaeological projects have been undertaken, very little has been published or compared with other related free black assemblages. While the sites included in this chapter may not have the best contexts, I became intrigued with these individuals and what they were able to accomplish during one of the most overtly racist periods in U.S. history. It is so clear to me that materialist approaches focusing on the quality or quantity of goods consumed do not permit us to see how people lived their lives, the decisions they made, or the strategies they used to divert racist structures.

I was motivated to write this chapter for

several academic and personal reasons. Although I have devoted a great deal of attention to the study of slavery, I do not believe it is possible to fully comprehend a slave society until one understands the roles of all the other players: white slaveholders, white non-slaveholders, free blacks, maroons, and so on. This does not mean one has to conduct primary research on each of these groups, but rather that one should at least know the literature, the major arguments, debates, and so forth for each of these groups. One of my goals for writing this chapter was to expand my understanding of free blacks in southern antebellum society.

I also entered this project with a definite mission. I wanted to explore the question, In what ways were the lives of free blacks different from those of enslaved people? Several years ago I had a discussion with an advanced graduate student of southern history (he has since received a Ph.D.) who insisted that Berlin's *Slaves Without Masters* was inappropriately titled. He felt that many free blacks of the Old South, such as William Johnson, had money, property, and prestige, and therefore their lives could not be considered comparable to those of slaves. I did not argue with him, but I did not agree with him. I had read Berlin's work, and agreed with Berlin that the *vast majority* of free blacks were probably just a rung above enslaved people socially, materially, and politically. Free blacks, unlike enslaved people, did have some control over their labor. Because of the racializing of labor (see discussion in Mullins 1999a:129–140), free blacks were able to fill a niche in the workplace that often permitted them to acquire the financial resources to purchase enslaved people and real estate.[7]

When the prohibitions of the color-line are considered, however, the social position of free blacks takes on a different meaning. Despite all his material accomplishments, William Johnson could not sit with white men or attend a public meeting. When a noted white religious speaker came to Natchez, for example, Johnson recorded: "I went to the Methodist Church and Listened on the Out Side of it at Mr. Maffitt preaching—He is a splendid speaker, The best I Ever herd in all my life" (Hogan and Davis 1993:231). Johnson's money and prestige were insufficient to cushion him from the racist social structure.

Even today, wealthy and accomplished African Americans recount incidents of being discriminated against, demeaned, and treated like stereotypes during the post-Civil Rights Act era. I encounter many people, black and white, who seem to think education, money, or respect can insulate people from racism and other forms of discrimination, but it can't. The unfortunate consequence of people who follow Johnson's strategy of emulating whites in order to achieve white acceptance and equality is hatred of the criteria used by others, and perhaps themselves, to define their racial identity. Johnson is a complex, tragic figure who should not be simply dismissed as an *Uncle Tom.* We must strive to understand his agency on its own terms.

A personal reason for writing this chapter is that I have been curious about free blacks for a long time. As a child, my maternal grandmother spoke proudly of her free black heritage. Her maternal grandfather (my great-great-grandfather), John Whiteman (also spelled "Whitman" and "Wightman") lived during the time of slavery and presumably was a free black living in Charleston, South Carolina. I do not know the particulars of his manumission, but he is identified as a stonecutter, always with a small *c* for "colored" directly after his name in Charleston directories. Family tradition has it that he worked on the U.S. Custom House, a granite and marble building with Greek and Roman elements still standing in downtown Charleston (Figure 12.3). Construction on the building began in 1854, and it was finally completed in 1879 (Severens 1988:175–176). My childhood image of John Whiteman was that of an enormous man with large, muscular hands who single-handedly worked and shaped each stone of the massive structure.

Although my grandmother did not know how or why John Whiteman was free, she remembered seeing papers that indicated he was free, but these were lost. Free blacks had

Figure 12.3. U.S. Custom House, Charleston, South Carolina, 2000. (Photo by Theresa Singleton)

to produce such papers when asked to show their identification to white authorities. A free black without papers could legally be reenslaved, a situation that became a real threat to free blacks in South Carolina on the eve of the Civil War (see Johnson and Roark 1984b).

Although a skilled craftsman, Whiteman does not appear to have been as materially successful as Johnson, Cuff, or even Jackson because he did not own any real estate. Whiteman's children and grandchildren followed his lead by pursuing and excelling in a variety of skilled and semiskilled occupations. My grandmother was a seamstress, but her skill was comparable to that of the small, independent fashion designers of today. She often made original garments without a pattern, including coats and jackets. In antebellum Charleston, she would have been referred to as a "mantu-maker," a seamstress who makes cloaks and other fine clothes and accessories.[8]

I do not know whether John Whiteman associated with enslaved people or identified with them. His name is absent from the directories of affluent free black organizations such as the Brown Fellowship Society, Charleston's most exclusive free mulatto benevolent society (Johnson and Roark 1984a:107). He and his children and grandchildren, however, were members of Centenary Methodist Church. It was one of the favorite churches of the black upper class, and a large number of its leaders and members had been free persons of color before emancipation (Powers 1994:215).

As for my grandmother, I am still puzzled about why her free black heritage meant so much to her. My grandmother, Serena Mitchell, was born in 1888 and died in 1963. She lived her entire life in the racially segregated South. She was among the last of the first generation of African Americans born after emancipation. Historian Leon Litwack (1989) characterized that generation of African Americans as having been subjected to the worst racist atrocities in U.S. history. Serena was just six years old when the Supreme Court legalized segregation with its *Plessy v. Ferguson* decision in 1896. She was a young adult when the film *Birth of a Nation,* which celebrated the rise of the Ku Klux Klan, was released. She was a young wife and mother when southern blacks began their Great Migration to northern cities to escape peonage and lynching.

After World War I, three of Serena's siblings migrated north. Two of her brothers she would never hear from again. Family tradition has it that because of their pale-colored skin, wavy hair, and "keen" facial features, they fled the South so they could "pass" for white, as Baylor Winn allegedly did. Identity, including racial identity, is not only fluid and situational, but can also be highly variable even among members of the same nuclear family.

Serena and her husband, Joseph, had a different vision. They remained in Charleston and raised five children, making sure that they all received a post-secondary education. Eventually all five earned bachelor's degrees, and one a master's degree. A strong advocate of higher education, Joseph had attended Tuskegee Institute in Alabama and had received a degree in building arts and construction in what later became the school of architecture. In Charleston, Joseph struggled to make a living restoring old houses and building new ones. The last house he designed was built for my grandmother. My mother lives there now.

I think my grandmother embraced her free black heritage to encourage her children and her grandchildren to be like John Whiteman, who worked hard in the midst of racial adversity to garner whatever he could from his free status. I suspect it may have been comforting at times for her to reflect on Whiteman's history as a way to get through the period when race relations took the insidious turn it did in the first decades of the twentieth century. Her knowledge of free black society may have helped her accept her brothers' decision to deny who they were and cross over the colorline, but I think her free black heritage probably symbolized many things to her that I could not know, appreciate, or experience.

The final reason I wrote this chapter is that I have been unable to write John Whiteman's story. As for the vast majority of free blacks of the antebellum South, there are too few written references to him in public records. But through William Johnson, Thomas Cuff, and Hannah Jackson, I have gained a better understanding of what his life, and that of many other free blacks, may have been like. This chapter commemorates John Whiteman, for I am very grateful for the legacy he has bestowed upon me.

Notes

1. I use these terms interchangeably in this chapter, but for the sake of brevity I use "free blacks" most often.
2. In the 1830s, the Nat Turner Rebellion generated a similar concern among slaveholders regarding association between free blacks and slaves.
3. White laborers sought similar legislation in the antebellum North to prohibit blacks from entering trades and to restrict their activities (see, for example, Nash 1988).
4. There are notable exceptions to this general rule, particularly in Louisiana. New Orleans was a center for skilled artisans of color (see, for example, Patton 1995). Exceptions also existed elsewhere in the South. For example, Thomas Day was a well-known furniture maker in North Carolina (see S. Jones 1985). Charleston, South Carolina, also had better opportunities for free blacks to enter trades than some other southern cities (see Goldfield 1991 and Powers 1994).
5. This insight comes from a survey I conducted of antebellum African American autobiographies, presented in a paper coauthored with Brian Crane (Singleton and Crane 1995).
6. My research of probate inventories in South Carolina during the eighteenth and nineteenth centuries suggests that Cuff's inventory was worth far more than that of the average yeoman farmer or unskilled or semiskilled workers. I discuss these inventories in terms of textile equipment and textile ownership (see Singleton 1985a).
7. Although there is a growing literature on the propertyholding of enslaved people, this property did not include the land or structures (real estate), at least not in the United States. The one thing that free blacks could purchase that slaves could not is real estate.
8. The skill levels of seamstresses in Charleston are discussed in Rosengarten et al. (1987).

References

Abelson, E. S.
1989 *When Ladies Go A-Thieving: Middle-Class Shoplifters in the Victorian Department Store.* Oxford University Press, New York.

Abrahams, R. D.
1992 *Singing the Master: The Emergence of African American Culture in the Plantation South.* Pantheon, New York.

Adams, D. L.
1989 *Lead Seals from Fort Michilimackinac, 1715–1781.* Archaeological Completion Report Series, no. 14. Mackinac State Historic Parks, Mackinac Island, Michigan.

Adams, W. H.
1980 *Waverly Plantation: Ethnoarchaeology of a Tenant Farming Community.* National Technical Information Service, Washington, D.C.

Adams, W. H., and S. D. Smith
1985 Historical Perspectives on Black Tenant Farmer Material Culture: The Henry C. Long General Store Ledger at Waverly Plantation, Mississippi. In *The Archaeology of Slavery and Plantation Life,* edited by T. A. Singleton, pp. 309–334. Academic Press, Orlando.

Agee, J., and W. Evans
1941 *Let Us Now Praise Famous Men.* Houghton Mifflin, Boston.

Agnew, J.-C.
1993 Coming Up for Air: Consumer Culture in Historical Perspective. In *Consumption and the World of Goods,* edited by J. Brewer and R. Porter, pp. 19–39. Routledge, London.

Agorsah, K.
1999 Archaeological Implications of African Burial Systems for Reconstructing the Heritage of the African Diaspora. Paper presented at the fourth World Archaeological Congress, Cape Town, South Africa.

Aiello, E., and J. L. Seidel
1994 *Three Hundred Years in Annapolis: Phase III Archaeological Investigations of the Anne Arundel County Courthouse Site (18AP63), Annapolis, Maryland.* 2 vols. Prepared by Archaeology in Annapolis, submitted to Spillis Candela/Warnecke. Historic Annapolis Foundation, Annapolis.

Alexandria Archaeology
1993 *To Witness the Past: African American Archaeology in Alexandria, Virginia.* Alexandria Archaeology Museum, Alexandria, Virginia.

Allain, M.
1988 *Not Worth a Straw: French Colonial Policy and the Early Years of Louisiana.* Center for Louisiana Studies, University of Southwestern Louisiana, Lafayette.

Allen, T. W.
1994 *The Invention of the White Race.* Vol. 1, *Racial Oppression and Social Control.* Verso, London.
1997 *The Invention of the White Race.* Vol. 2, *The Origin of Racial Oppression in Anglo-America.* Verso, London.

Ameri, A. H.
1997 Housing Ideologies in the New England and Chesapeake Bay Colonies, c. 1650–1700. *Journal of the Society of Architectural Historians* 56:6–15.

Andrews, S. T., S. Atkins, J. Bowen, and J. Dandoy
1997 The Zooarchaeological Remains from a Rich Neck Plantation Site. Paper presented at the annual

meeting of the Society for Historical Archaeology, Corpus Christi, Texas.

Anesko, M.

1985 So Discreet a Zeal: Slavery and the Anglican Church in Virginia, 1680–1730. *Virginia Magazine of History and Biography* 93:247–278.

Angelou, M.

1969 *I Know Why the Caged Bird Sings.* Bantam, New York.

Anonymous

1837 A Visit. *Gazette and Mercury.* Greenfield, Massachusetts.

1838 Obituary of Ebeneezer Hinsdale Williams (1761–1838) of Deefield. *Gazette and Mercury.* Greenfield, Massachusetts.

Anstey, R.

1974 *The Atlantic Slave Trade and British Abolition, 1760–1810.* Macmillan, London.

Anthony, E. H.

1939 A Sightseeing Tour Along Seventh Street in the Late Eighties or Early Nineties. *West of Market Boys' Journal* (November 6–10).

Anzilotti, C.

1997 Autonomy and the Female Planter in Colonial South Carolina. *Journal of Southern History* 63:239–268.

Appiah, K. A.

1990 Racisms. In *Anatomy of Racism,* edited by D. T. Goldberg, pp. 3–17. University of Minnesota Press, Minneapolis.

Armour, D. A., and K. R. Widder

1978 *At the Crossroads: Michilimackinac During the American Revolution.* Mackinac Island State Park Commission, Mackinac Island, Michigan.

Asad, T., J. W. Fernandez, M. Herzfeld, A. Lass, S. C. Rogers, J. Schneider, and K. Verdery

1997 Provocations of European Ethnology. *American Anthropologist* 99(4):713–730.

Ascher, R., and C. H. Fairbanks

1971 Excavation of a Slave Cabin: Georgia, U.S.A. *Historical Archaeology* 5:3–17.

Askin, J.

1766 Memorandum Book of John Askin. Original in the John Askin Papers, Ontario Archives, Toronto, Canada. Microfilmed by the Toronto Public Library, July 1942. Microfilm copy in the collections of the Mackinac Island State Park Commission, Lansing, Michigan.

1776–1779 Estate Inventories. Originals in the Askin Papers, National Archives of Canada, Ottawa, MG 19, A3. Photocopies in the collections of the Mackinac Island State Park Commission, Lansing, Michigan.

Askins, W.

1988 Sandy Ground: Historical Archeology of Class and Ethnicity in a Nineteenth-Century Community on Staten Island. Doctoral dissertation, City University of New York, New York.

Atkins, S. C.

1994 An Archaeological Perspective on the African-American Slave Diet at Mount Vernon's House for Families. Master's thesis, College of William and Mary, Williamsburg, Virginia.

Austin-Broos, D. J.

1997 *Jamaica Genesis: Religion and the Politics of Moral Order.* University of Chicago Press, Chicago.

Avery, G.

1995 More Friend Than Foe: Eighteenth-Century Spanish, French, and Caddoan Interaction at Los Adaes, a Capital of Texas Located in Northwestern Louisiana. *Louisiana Archaeology* 22:163–193.

Axtell, J.

1981 The Invasion Within: The Contest of Cultures in Colonial North America. In *The Frontier in History: North America and Southern Africa Compared,* edited by H. Lamar and L. Thompson, pp. 237–269. Yale University Press, New Haven.

Ayer Collection

c. 1717 Anonymous map of Michilimackinac in the Ayer Collection, Newberry Library, Chicago. Photocopy in the collections of the Mackinac Island State Park Commission, Lansing, Michigan.

Babson, D. W.

1990 The Archaeology of Racism and Ethnicity on Southern Plantations. *Historical Archaeology* 24(4):20–28.

Baker, L. D., and T. C. Patterson

1994a Race, Racism, and the History of

U.S. Anthropology. *Transforming Anthropology* 5(1–2):1–7.

———, editors

1994b Race, Racism, and the History of U.S. Anthropology. *Transforming Anthropology* 5(1–2):1–41.

Baker, N.

1986 Annapolis, Maryland 1695–1730. *Maryland Historical Magazine* 81:191–209.

Baker, V. G.

1978 *Historical Archaeology at Black Lucy's Garden, Andover, Massachusetts: Ceramics from the Site of a Nineteenth Century Afro-American.* Phillips Academy, Andover, Massachusetts.

1980 Archaeological Visibility of Afro-American Culture: An Example from Black Lucy's Garden, Andover, Massachusetts. In *Archaeological Perspectives on Ethnicity in America: Afro-American and Asian American Culture History,* edited by R. L. Schuyler, pp. 29–37. Baywood, Farmingdale, New York.

Barnard, Sumner, and Putnam Company

1903 *The Artistic Home.* Barnard, Sumner and Putnam Company, Worcester, Massachusetts.

Baron, D. K., J. E. Hood, and H. V. Izard

1996 They Were Here All Along: The Native American Presence in Lower-Central New England in the Eighteenth and Nineteenth Centuries. *William and Mary Quarterly* 53:561–586.

Baudrillard, J.

1988 *Selected Writings.* Stanford University Press, Stanford, California.

Bear, J. A., Jr., and L. C. Stanton, editors

1997 *Jefferson's Memorandum Books, Accounts, with Legal Records and Miscellany, 1767–1826.* Vol. 1. Princeton University Press, Princeton, New Jersey.

Beaudry, M., editor

1988 *Documentary Archaeology in the New World.* Cambridge University Press, Cambridge.

Beaudry, M. C., L. J. Cook, and S. A. Mrozowski

1991 Artifacts and Active Voices: Material Culture as Social Discourse. In *The Archaeology of Inequality,* edited by R. H. McGuire and R. Paynter, pp. 150–191. Blackwell, Oxford.

Beecher, C. E., and H. B. Stowe

1869 *The American Woman's Home: or, Principles of Domestic Science.* J. B. Ford, New York.

1873 *The New Housekeeper's Manual: Embracing a New Revised Edition of* The American Woman's Home: or, Principles of Domestic Science. J. B. Ford, New York.

Beeghley, L.

1989 *The Structure of Social Stratification in the United States.* Allyn and Bacon, Boston.

Bell, C. C.

1997 *Revolution, Romanticism, and the Afro-Creole Protest Tradition in Louisiana, 1718–1868.* Louisiana State University Press, Baton Rouge.

Bell, W. J., Jr.

1957 Medical Practices in Colonial America. *Symposium on Colonial Medicine.* The Jamestown-Williamsburg-Yorktown Celebration Commission and the Virginia 350th Anniversary Commission, pp. 52–63. Williamsburg, Virginia.

Benson, A. B., editor

1987 *Peter Kalm's Travels in North America: The English Version of 1770.* Dover, New York.

Beoku-Betts, J. A.

1994 "She Make Funny Flat Cake She Call Saraka": Gullah Women and Food Practices under Slavery. In *Working Toward Freedom: Slave Society and Domestic Economy in the American South,* edited by L. E. Hudson Jr., pp. 211–231. University of Rochester Press, Rochester, New York.

Berlin, I.

1974 *Slaves Without Masters: The Free Negro in the Antebellum South.* Oxford University Press, New York.

1998 *Many Thousands Gone: The First Two Centuries of Slavery in North America.* Belknap Press of Harvard University Press, Cambridge.

Beverly, R.

1971 *The History and Present State of Virginia: A Selection.* 1705. Reprint, Bobbs-Merrill, Indianapolis.

Biben, D.
1993 Interview at Riverlake Plantation, Oscar, Louisiana.

Bieder, R. E.
1986 *Science Encounters the Indian, 1820–1880: The Early Years of American Anthropology.* University of Oklahoma Press, Norman.

Billings, W. M, editor
1975 *The Old Dominion in the Seventeenth Century: A Documentary History of Virginia, 1606–1689.* University of North Carolina Press, Chapel Hill.

Binford, L. R.
1983 *Working at Archaeology.* Academic Press, New York.
1987 Researching Ambiguity: Frames of Reference and Site Structure. In *Method and Theory for Activity Area Research: An Ethnoarchaeological Approach,* edited by S. Kent, pp. 449–512, Columbia University Press, New York.

Blakey, M. L.
1988 Racism through the Looking Glass: An Afro-American Perspective. *World Archaeological Bulletin* 2:46–50.
1995 Race, Nationalism, and the Afrocentric Past. In *Making Alternative Histories: The Practice of Archaeology and History in Non-Western Settings,* edited by P. R. Schmidt and T. C. Patterson, pp. 213–228. School of American Research Press, Santa Fe, New Mexico.
1998 The New York African Burial Ground Project: An Examination of Enslaved Lives, A Construction of Ancestral Ties. *Transforming Anthropology* 7(1):53–58.

Blanton, W. B.
1931 *Medicine in Virginia in the Eighteenth Century.* Garrett and Massie, Richmond, Virginia.

Blassingame, J. W.
1972 *The Slave Community: Plantation Life in the Ante-Bellum South.* Oxford University Press, New York.

Bogger, T. L., and the Black Church Cultural Affairs Committee
1994 *A History of African-Americans in Middlesex County, 1646–1992.* Privately published.

Bograd, M. D.
1989 Whose Life Is It Anyway? Ceramics, Context, and the Study of Status. Master's thesis, University of Massachusetts, Amherst.

Boles, John B.
1984 *Black Southerners, 1619–1869.* New Perspectives on the South Series. University Press of Kentucky, Lexington.

Bolt, C., and S. Drescher, editors
1980 *Anti-Slavery, Religion, and Reform.* Archon, Hamden, Connecticut.

Bond, E. L.
1996 Anglican Theology and Devotion in James Blair's Virginia, 1685–1743: Private Piety in the Public Church. *Virginia Magazine of History and Biography* 104:313–340.

Bourdieu, P.
1977 *Outline of a Theory of Practice.* Cambridge University Press, Cambridge.
1984 *Distinction: A Social Critique of the Judgment of Taste.* Translated by R. Nice. Harvard University Press, Cambridge.

Bowen, J.
1993 *Faunal Remains from the House for Families Cellar.* Manuscript on file at the DAR, Colonial Williamsburg Foundation, Williamsburg, Virginia.
1995 Slavery at Mount Vernon: A Dietary Analysis. Paper presented at the annual meeting of the Society for Historical Archaeology, Washington, D.C.
1996 Foodways in the Eighteenth-Century Chesapeake. In *The Archaeology of Eighteenth-Century Virginia,* edited by T. R. Reinhart, pp. 87–130. Spectrum Press, Richmond, Virginia.

Bower, B. A.
1991 Material Culture in Boston: The Black Experience. In *The Archaeology of Inequality,* edited by R. H. McGuire and R. Paynter, pp. 55–63. Blackwell, Oxford.
n.d. *The African Meeting House, Boston, Massachusetts, Summary Report of Archaeological Excavations,*

1975–1986. The Museum of Afro American History, Boston, Massachusetts.

Bower, B. A., and B. Rushing
1980 The African Meeting House: The Center for Nineteenth Century Afro-American Community in Boston. In *Archaeological Perspectives on Ethnicity in America: Afro-American and Asian American Culture History,* edited by R. L. Schuyler, pp. 69–75. Baywood Publishing, New York.

Braman, D.
1999 Of Race and Immutability. *UCLA Law Review* 46:1375–1464.

Braxton, J. M.
1989 *Black Women Writing Autiobiography: A Tradition Within a Tradition.* Temple University Press, Philadelphia.

Breeden, J. O., editor
1980 *Advice Among Masters: The Ideals in Slave Management in the Old South.* Greenwood, Westport, Connecticut.

Breen, T. H.
1988 "Baubles of Britain": The American and Consumer Revolutions of the Eighteenth Century. *Past and Present* 119:73–104.

Breen, T. H., and S. Innes
1980 *"Myne Owne Ground": Race and Freedom on Virginia's Eastern Shore, 1640–1676.* Oxford University Press, New York.

Briggs, A.
1988 *Victorian Things.* University of Chicago Press, Chicago.

Briggs, W.
1990 Le Pays des Illinois. *William and Mary Quarterly* 47(1): 30–56.

Brodeur, P.
1985 *Restitution: The Land Claims of the Mashpee, Passamaquoddy, and Penobscot Indians of New England.* Northeastern University Press, Boston.

Brodkin, K.
1998a *How Jews Became White Folks and What That Says About Race in America.* Rutgers University Press, New Brunswick, New Jersey.
1998b Race, Class, and Gender: The Metaorganization of American Capitalism. *Transforming Anthropology* 7(2):46–57.

Brooks, B. C.
1994 Clarity, Contrast, and Simplicity: Changes in American Interiors, 1880–1930. In *The Arts and the American Home, 1890–1930,* edited by J. H. Foy and K. A. Marling, pp. 14–43. University of Tennessee Press, Knoxville.

Brown, J. A.
n.d. Final Report of the Excavations at Fort Michilimackinac, Emmet County, Michigan, Conducted by the Department of Anthropology and Museum, Michigan State University: 1967, 1968, 1969. Manuscript on file at the Mackinac Island State Park Commission, Lansing, Michigan.

Brown, J. S. H.
1980 *Strangers in Blood: Fur Trade Company Families in Indian Country.* University of British Columbia Press, Vancouver.

Brown, K. L., and D. C. Cooper
1990 Structural Continuity in an African American Slave and Tenant Community. *Historical Archaeology* 24(4):7–19.

Brown, L. K., and K. Mussell, editors
1984a *Ethnic and Regional Foodways in the United States: The Performance of Group Identity.* University of Tennessee Press, Knoxville.
1984b Introduction to *Ethnic and Regional Foodways in the United States: The Performance of Group Identity,* edited by L. K. Brown and K. Mussell, pp. 3–15. University of Tennessee Press, Knoxville.

Brown, M. R., and P. Samford
1991 Recent Evidence of Eighteenth-Century Gardening in Williamsburg, Virginia. In *Earth Patterns: Essays in Landscape Archaeology,* edited by W. M. Kelso and R. Most, pp. 103–121. University Press of Virginia, Charlottesville.

Brugger, R. J.
1988 *Maryland: A Middle Temperament,*

1634–1980. Johns Hopkins University Press, Baltimore.

Brumfiel, E. M.
2000 On the Archaeology of Choice: Agency Studies as Research Strategem. In *Agency and Archaeology,* edited by M-A. Dobres and J. Robb, pp. 246–255. Routledge, London.

Bugg, L. H.
1891 *The Correct Thing for Catholics.* Benzinger Brothers, New York.

Building Conservation Technology
1979 Historic Structures Report of William Johnson House, Natchez, Mississippi. Preservation Society of Elliott Hill, Natchez, Mississippi. Typescript.

Bullen, A. K., and R. P. Bullen
1945 Black Lucy's Garden. *Bulletin of the Massachusetts Archaeological Society* 6(2):17–28.

Bumsted, J. M.
1982 *The People's Clearance: Highland Emigration to British North America, 1770–1815.* Edinburgh University Press, Edinburgh.

Bushman, R. L.
1993 *The Refinement of America: Persons, Houses, Cities.* Vintage, New York.

Butler, R. L., translator and editor
1934 *Journal of Paul Du Ru.* Caxton Club, Chicago.

Butler, J.
1990 *Gender Trouble: Feminism and the Subversion of Identity.* Routledge, London.

Calloway, C. G., editor
1997 *After King Philip's War: Presence and Persistence in Indian New England.* University Press of New England, Hanover, New Hampshire.

Campbell, C.
1987 *The Romantic Ethic and the Spirit of Modern Consumerism.* Basil Blackwell, Oxford.

Campbell, J.
1994 "My Constant Companion": Slaves and Their Dogs in the Antebellum South. In *Working toward Freedom: Slave Society and Domestic Economy in the American South,* edited by L. E. Hudson Jr., pp. 53–76. University of Rochester Press, Rochester, New York.

Campbell, M.
1988 *The Maroons of Jamaica, 1655–1796: A History of Resistance, Collaboration, and Betrayal.* Bergin and Garvey, Granby, Massachusetts.

Campisi, J.
1991 *The Mashpee Indians: Tribe on Trial.* Syracuse University Press, Syracuse, New York.

Canny, N. P.
1976 *The Elizabethan Conquest of Ireland: A Pattern Established.* Barnes and Noble, New York.

Carby, H.
1987 *Reconstructing Womanhood: The Emergence of the Afro-American Woman Novelist.* Oxford University Press, New York.

Carlson, C.
1998 *Native American Presences in Deerfield, Massachusetts: An Essay and Resource Guide.* Historic Deerfield, Deerfield, Massachusetts.

Carr, L. G., and R. R. Menard
1979 Immigration and Opportunity: The Freedman in Early Colonial Maryland. In *The Chesapeake in the Seventeenth Century: Essays on Anglo-American Society and Politics,* edited by T. W. Tate and D. L. Ammerman, pp. 206–242. University of North Carolina Press, Chapel Hill.

Carson, C., N. Barka, W. Kelso, G. W. Stone, and D. Upton
1981 Impermanent Architecture in the Southern American Colonies. *Winterthur Portfolio* 16:135–196.

Carson, J.
1985 *Colonial Virginia Cookery: Procedures, Equipment, and Ingredients in Colonial Cooking.* Colonial Williamsburg Foundation, Williamsburg, Virginia.

Cartmill, M.
1998 The Status of the Race Concept in Physical Anthropology. *American Anthropologist* 100:651–660.

Castelvecchi, L.
1885 *Catalogue and Price List of Antique, Grecian, Roman, Medaeval and Plaster of Paris Statues, Statuettes,*

Busts, Etc. L. Castelvecchi, New York.

Catts, W., and D. McCall

1991 A Report of the Archaeological Investigations at the House of Thomas Cuff, a Free Black Laborer, 108 Cannon Street, Chestertown, Kent County, Maryland. *North American Archaeologist* 12(2):155–181.

Chappell, E.

1982 Slave Housing. *Fresh Advices,* pp. i–ii, iv. Colonial Williamsburg Foundation, Williamsburg.

Chinard, G.

1934 *A Huguenot Exile in Virginia: or Voyages of a Frenchman exiled for his religion with a description of Virginia and Maryland.* 1687. Reprint, Press of the Pioneers, New York.

Clark, B.

1996 Amache Ochinee Prowers: The Archaeobiography of a Cheyenne Woman. Master's thesis, University of Denver, Colorado.

Clark, J. G.

1970 *New Orleans, 1718–1812: An Economic History.* Louisiana State University Press, Baton Rouge.

Clayton, R. W., editor

1990 *Mother Wit: The Ex-Slave Narratives of the Louisiana Writers' Project.* Peter Lang, New York.

Clements, W. L., editor

1918 Roger's Michilimackinac Journal. *American Antiquarian Society Proceedings* 28(2):224–273.

Clifford, J.

1994 Diasporas. *Cultural Anthropology* 9(3):302–338.

Cochran, M., and J. Neuwirth

2000 In My Father's Kingdom There Are Many Houses: Interior Space and Contested Meanings in Nineteenth-Century African American Annapolis. Paper delivered at the annual meeting of the Society for Historical Archaeology, Quebec.

Cohen, D. W., and J. P. Green, editors

1972 *Neither Slave Nor Free: The Freedmen of African Descent in Slave Societies of the New World.* Johns Hopkins University Press, Baltimore.

Cohn, B. S.

1996 *Colonialism and Its Form of Knowledge: The British in India.* Princeton University Press, Princeton, New Jersey.

Collins, P. H.

1991 *Black Feminist Thought: Knowledge, Consciousness, and the Politics of Empowerment.* Routledge, New York.

2000 *Black Feminist Thought: Knowledge, Consciousness, and the Politics of Empowerment.* 2nd ed. Routledge, New York.

Combahee River Collective

1982 A Black Feminist Statement. In *All the Women Are White, All the Blacks Are Men, but Some of Us Are Brave,* edited by G. T. Hull, P. B. Scott, and B. Smith, pp. 13–22. Feminist Press, New York.

Conrad, D. E.

1965 *The Forgotten Farmers: The Story of Sharecroppers in the New Deal.* University of Illinois Press, Urbana.

Cook, C.

1878 *The House Beautiful: Essays on Beds and Tables, Stools and Candlesticks.* Scribner and Armstrong, New York. Reprint, North River Press, New York, 1980.

Coronil, F.

1996 Beyond Occidentalism: Toward Nonimperial Geohistorical Categories. *Cultural Anthropology* 11:51–87.

Costello, J. G.

1992 Purchasing Patterns of the California Missions in ca. 1805. *Historical Archaeology* 26(1):59–66.

Costello, J. G., A. Praetzellis, M. Praetzellis, J. Marvin, M. D. Meyer, E. S. Gibson, and G. H. Ziesing

1998 *Historical Archaeology at the Headquarters Facility Project Site, the Metropolitan Water District of Southern California.* Anthropological Studies Center, Sonoma State University, Rohnert Park, California.

Costlin, C. L.

1999 Formal and Technological Variability and the Social Relations of Production: *Crisoles* from San José de Moro, Peru. In *Material Meanings: Critical Approaches to*

Interpretation of Material Culture, edited by E. S. Chilton, pp. 85–102. University of Utah Press, Salt Lake City.

Cottrol, R. J.
1982 *The Afro-Yankees: Providence's Black Community in the Antebellum Era.* Greenwood Press, Westport, Connecticut.

Cox, O. C.
1942 The Modern Caste School of Race Relations. *Social Forces* 21:218–226.
1945 Race and Caste: A Distinction. *American Journal of Sociology* 50:360–368.
1948 *Caste, Class, and Race: A Study in Social Dynamics.* Doubleday, Garden City, New York.

Crader, D. C.
1990 Slave Diet at Monticello. *American Antiquity* 55:690–717.

Crawford, F. M.
1882 False Taste in Art. *North American Review* 308:89–98.

Crenshaw, K., N. Gotanda, G. Peller, and K. Thomas
1995 Introduction to *Critical Race Theory: The Key Writings That Formed the Movement,* edited by K. Crenshaw, N. Gotanda, G. Peller, and K. Thomas, pp. xiii–xxxii, New Press, New York.

Cressey, P. J.
1985 The Archaeology of Free Blacks in Alexandria, Virginia. *Alexandria Archaeology Publications* 19. City of Alexandria, Virginia.

Cromwell, A. M.
1994 *The Other Brahmins: Boston's Black Upper Class, 1750–1950.* University of Arkansas Press, Fayetteville.

Cruzat, H. H.
1929 Louisiana in 1724: Banet's Report to the Company of the Indies, Dated Paris, December 20, 1724. *Louisiana Historical Quarterly* 12:121–133.

Culp, J. McC., Jr.
1999 To the Bone: Race and White Privilege. *Minnesota Law Review* 83:1637–1679.

Curry, L. P.
1981 *The Free Black in Urban America, 1800–1850.* University of Chicago Press, Chicago.

Curtis, S.
1991 *A Consuming Faith: The Social Gospel and Modern American Culture.* Johns Hopkins University Press, Baltimore.

Dalton, G.
1969 Theoretical Issues in Economic Anthropology. *Current Anthropology* 10:63–102.
1982 Aboriginal Economies in Stateless Societies. In *Contexts for Prehistoric Exchange,* edited by T. K. Earle and J. E. Ericson, pp. 119–212. Academic Press, New York.

Databank 2000
2000 African-American Spirit Management Databank. On file, Department of Anthropology, University of Maryland, College Park.

Davis, E. A., and W. R. Hogan
1973 *The Barber of Natchez.* Louisiana State University Press, Baton Rouge.

Davis, E. A., and W. R. Hogan, editors
1951 *William Johnson's Natchez: The Ante-Bellum Diary of a Free Negro.* Louisiana State University Press, Baton Rouge.

Davis, R. B., editor
1963 *William Fitzhugh and His Chesapeake World, 1676–1701: The Fitzhugh Letters and Other Documents.* University of North Carolina Press, Chapel Hill.

Dawdy, S. L.
1998 *Madame John's Legacy Revisited: A Closer Look at the Archaeology of Colonial New Orleans.* Prepared by the Greater New Orleans Archaeology Program for the Friends of the Cabildo, New Orleans.

Dayfoot, A. C.
1999 *The Shaping of the West Indian Church.* University Press of Florida, Gainesville.

Deagan, K.
1991 Historical Archaeology's Contribution to Our Understanding of Early America. In *Historical Archaeology in Global Perspective,* edited by L. Falk, pp. 97–112. Smithsonian Institution Press, Washington, D.C.
1995 After Columbus: The Sixteenth-

Century Spanish-Caribbean Frontier. In *Puerto Real: The Archaeology of a Sixteenth-Century Spanish Town in Hispaniola,* edited by K. Deagan, pp. 419–456. University Press of Florida, Gainesville.

———, editor
1983 *Spanish St. Augustine: The Archaeology of a Colonial Creole Community.* Academic Press, New York.

Deal, D.
1988 A Constricted World, Free Blacks on Virginia's Eastern Shore, 1680–1750. In *Colonial Chesapeake Society,* edited by L. G. Carr, P. Morgan, and J. B. Russo, pp. 275–305. University of North Carolina Press, Chapel Hill.

DeBusk, J. M., C. L. Price, L. E. Gray, and D. M. Price, compilers
1982 *Family Histories of Middlesex County, Virginia.* Ralph Wormeley Branch, Association for the Preservation of Virginia Antiquities, Urbanna.

de Certeau, M.
1984 *The Practice of Everyday Life.* University of California Press, Berkeley.

De Cunzo, L. A.
1998 A Future After Freedom. *Historical Archaeology* 32(1):42–54.

Deetz, J.
1977 *In Small Things Forgotten: The Archaeology of Early America.* Anchor Press, New York.
1993 *Flowerdew Hundred: The Archaeology of a Virginia Plantation, 1619–1864.* University Press of Virginia, Charlottesville.

Delle, J. A.
1998 *An Archaeology of Social Space: Analyzing Coffee Plantations in Jamaica's Blue Mountains.* Plenum, New York.

Delle, J. A., M. P. Leone, and P. R. Mullins
1999 Archaeology of the Modern State: European Colonialism. In *Companion Encyclopedia of Archaeology,* edited by G. Barker, pp. 1107–1159. Routledge, London.

Demos, J.
1994 *The Unredeemed Captive: A Family Story from Early America.* Alfred A. Knopf, New York.

DePeyster, A. S.
1813 *Miscellanies by an Officer.* Dumfries.

Dietler, M.
1994 "Our Ancestors the Gauls": Archaeology, Ethnic Nationalism, and the Manipulation of Celtic Identity in Modern Europe. *American Anthropologist* 96:584–605.

di Leonardo, M.
1998 *Exotics at Home: Anthropologies, Others, American Modernity.* University of Chicago Press, Chicago.

Dobres, M-A., and J. Robb
2000 Agency in Archaeology: Paradigm or Platitude? In *Agency in Archaeology,* edited by M-A. Dobres and J. Robb, pp. 3–17. Routledge, London.

Donnelly, J. P.
1971 *Pierre Gibault, Missionary 1737–1802.* Loyola University Press, Chicago.

Doughton, T. L.
1997 Unseen Neighbors: Native Americans of Central Massachusetts, A People Who Had "Vanished." In *After King Philip's War: Presence and Persistence in Indian New England,* edited by C. Calloway, pp. 207–230. University Press of New England, Hanover, New Hampshire.

Douglass, F.
1994 *Life and Times of Frederick Douglass, Written by Himself.* 1893. Reprint, Literary Classics, New York.

Drake, S. C.
1987 *Black Folk Here and There: An Essay in History and Anthropology.* Vol. 1. Center for Afro-American Studies, University of California, Los Angeles.
1990 *Black Folk Here and There: An Essay in History and Anthropology.* Vol. 2. Center for Afro-American Studies, University of California, Los Angeles.

Dreiser, T.
1900 *Sister Carrie.* Reprint, W. W. Norton, New York, 1970.

Drescher, S.
1977 *Econocide: British Slavery in the Era of Abolition.* University of Pittsburgh Press, Pittsburgh.

Drinnon, R.
1980 *Facing West: The Metaphysics of Indian-Hating and Empire-Building.* New American Library, New York.

Drummond, L.
1980 The Cultural Continuum: A Theory of Intersystems. *Man* 15:352–374.

Dublin, L. S.
1987 *The History of Beads: From 30,000 B.C. to the Present.* Harry N. Abrams, New York.
1998 *The History of Beads: From 30,000 B.C. to the Present.* Harry N. Abrams, New York.

Du Bois, W. E. B.
1920 *Darkwater: Voices from Within the Veil.* Harcourt Brace, New York.
1939 *Black Folk, Then and Now: An Essay in the History and Sociology of the Negro Race.* Henry Holt, New York.
1968 *The Autobiography of W. E. B. Du Bois: A Soliloquy on Viewing My Life from the Last Decade of Its First Century.* International, New York.
1984 *Dusk of Dawn: An Essay Toward an Autobiography of a Race Concept.* Transaction, New Brunswick, New Jersey.

Duke, M.
1995 *Don't Carry Me Back: Narratives by Former Virginia Slaves.* Dietz, Richmond, Virginia.

Dunnigan, B. L.
1973 *King's Men at Mackinac: The British Garrisons, 1780–1796.* Reports in Mackinac History and Archaeology, 3. Mackinac Island State Park Commission, Mackinac Island, Michigan.

Dyer, R.
1997 *White.* Routledge, New York.

Edsforth, R.
1987 *Class Conflict and Cultural Consensus: The Making of a Mass Consumer Society in Flint, Michigan.* Rutgers University Press, New Brunswick, New Jersey.

Edwards, Y. D.
1998 "Trash" Revisited: A Comparative Approach to Historical Descriptions and Archaeological Analysis of Slave Houses and Yards. In *Keep Your Head to the Sky: Interpreting African American Home Ground,* edited by G. Gundaker, pp. 245–271, 325–329. University Press of Virginia, Charlottesville.

Edwards-Ingram, Y. D.
1997 An Inter-Disciplinary Approach to African-American Medicinal and Health Practices in Colonial America. *The Watermark: Newsletter of the Archivists and Librarians in the History of the Health Sciences* 20(3):67–73.
1999 The Recent Archaeology of Enslaved Africans and African Americans. In *Old and New Worlds,* edited by G. Egan and R. L. Michael, pp. 155–164. Oxbow, Oxford.

Edwards-Ingram, Y. D., and M. R. Brown III
1998 Worlds Made Together? Critical Reflections on the Use of the Creolization Model in Historical Archaeology. Paper presented in the symposium "Creolization": Emerging Paradigms or Passing Fad at the annual meeting of the Society for Historical Archaeology, Atlanta, Georgia.

Egerton, J.
1993 *Southern Food: At Home, on the Road, in History.* University of North Carolina Press, Chapel Hill.

Ekberg, C. J.
1998 *French Roots in the Illinois Country: The Mississippi Frontier in Colonial Times.* University of Illinois Press, Urbana.

Emerson, M. C.
1994 Decorated Clay Tobacco Pipes from the Chesapeake: An African Connection. In *Historical Archaeology of the Chesapeake,* edited by P. A. Shackel and B. J. Little, pp. 35–49. Smithsonian Institution Press, Washington, D.C.
1999 African Inspirations in a New World Art and Artifact: Decorated Pipes from the Chesapeake. In *"I, Too, Am America": Archaeological Studies of African-American Life,* edited by T. A. Singleton, pp. 47–82. University Press of Virginia, Charlottesville.

Epperson, T. W.
1990a Race and the Disciplines of the Plan-

tation. *Historical Archaeology* 24(4):29–36.

1990b "To Fix a Perpetual Brand": The Social Construction of Race in Virginia, 1675–1750. Doctoral dissertation, Temple University, Philadelphia.

1994 The Politics of Empiricism and the Construction of Race as an Analytical Category. *Transforming Anthropology* 5(1–2):15–19.

1996 The Politics of "Race" and Cultural Identity at the African Burial Ground Excavations, New York City. *World Archaeological Bulletin* 7:108–117.

1997 Whiteness in Early Virginia. *Race Traitor* 7:9–20.

1998 Critical Race Theory and the Archaeology of the African Diaspora. Paper presented at the annual meeting of the Society for Historical Archaeology, Atlanta, Georgia.

1999a Constructing Difference: The Social and Spatial Order of the Chesapeake Plantation. In *"I, Too, Am America": Archaeological Studies of African-American Life,* edited by T. A. Singleton, pp. 159–172. University Press of Virginia, Charlottesville.

1999b The Contested Commons: Archaeologies of Race, Repression, and Resistance in New York City. In *Historical Archaeologies of Capitalism,* edited by M. P. Leone and P. B. Potter, Jr., pp. 81–110. Kluwer Academic/Plenum, New York.

Erichsen-Brown, C.

1989 *Medicinal and Other Uses of North American Plants: A Historical Survey with Special Reference to the Eastern Indian Tribes.* Dover, New York. First published in 1979 under the title *Use of Plants for the Past Five Hundred Years,* Breezy Creek Press, Canada.

Eriksen, T. H.

1993 *Ethnicity and Nationalism: Anthropological Perspectives.* Pluto Press, London.

Escott, P. D.

1979 *Slavery Remembered: A Record of Twentieth-Century Slave Narratives.* University of North Carolina Press, Chapel Hill.

Ewen, S.

1988 *All Consuming Images: The Politics of Style in Contemporary Culture.* Basic, New York.

Fabian, J.

1983 *Time and the Other: How Anthropology Makes Its Object.* Columbia University Press, New York.

Fabre, G., and R. O'Meally, ed.

1994 *History and Memory in African-American Culture.* Oxford University Press, New York.

Fairbanks, C. H.

1974 The Kingsley Slave Cabins in Duval County, Florida, 1968. *Conference on Historic Site Archaeology Papers* 7:62–93.

1983 Historical Archaeological Implications of Recent Investigations. *Geoscience and Man* 23:17–26.

1984 The Plantation Archaeology of the Southeastern Coast. *Historical Archaeology* 18(1):1–14.

Farish, H. D., editor

1957 *Journal and Letters of Philip Vickers Fithian 1773–1774: A Plantation Tutor of the Old Dominion.* Colonial Williamsburg, Williamsburg, Virginia.

Feder, K. L.

1994 *A Village of Outcasts: Historical Archaeology and Documentary Research at the Lighthouse Site.* Mayfield, Mountain View, California.

Federal Writers Project

1938a Interview, Henry W. Black, November, 7, 1938. http://lcweb2.loc.gov/wpaintro/wpahome.html

1938b Interview, Mrs. John Albert Williams, November 27, 1938. http://lcweb2.loc.gov/wpaintro/wpahome.html

1938c Interview, Rudolph Dunbar, November 28, 1938. http://lcweb2.loc.gov/wpaintro/wpahome.html

1938d Interview, Josiah Waddle, December 1, 1938. http://lcweb2.loc.gov/wpaintro/wpahome.html

Ferguson, L.
1991 Struggling with Pots in South Carolina. In *The Archaeology of Inequality,* edited by R. H. McGuire and R. Paynter, pp. 28–39. Blackwell, Oxford.
1992 *Uncommon Ground: Archaeology and Early African America, 1650–1800.* Smithsonian Institution Press, Washington, D.C.

Fesler, G. R.
1996 Interim Report of Excavations at Utopia Quarter (44JC32): An Eighteenth-Century Slave Complex at Kingsmill on the James in James City County, Virginia. Unpublished manuscript in possession of the author.
1998a Relations between Enslaved Women and Men at an Early Eighteenth-Century Virginia Quartering Site. Paper presented at the annual meeting of the Society for Historical Archaeology, Atlanta Georgia.
1998b The Utopia Quarter: Patterns of Submission and Perseverance at an Eighteenth-Century Chesapeake Archaeological Site Occupied by Enslaved Africans and Their Descendants, ca. 1670 to 1780. Dissertation proposal, Department of Anthropology, University of Virginia, Charlottesville.

Fessenden, J.
1837 *Sermon Preached to the First Congregational Society in Deerfield, Mass., and in the Hearing of Several Indians of Both Sexes Supposed to be Descendants of Eunice Williams, Daughter of Rev. John Williams, First Minister of Deerfield.* Phelps and Ingersoll, Greenfield, Massachusetts.

Fields, B. J.
1982 Ideology and Race in American History. In *Region, Race, and Reconstruction: Essays in Honor of C. Vann Woodward,* edited by J. M. Kousser and J. M. McPherson, pp. 143–177. Oxford University Press, New York.
1983 The Nineteenth-Century American South: History and Theory. *Plantation Society in the Americas* 2:7–27.
1985 *Slavery and Freedom on the Middle Ground: Maryland During the Nineteenth Century.* Yale University Press, New Haven.
1990 Slavery, Race, and Ideology in the United States of America. *New Left Review* 181:95–118.

Fike, R. E.
1987 *The Bottle Book: A Comprehensive Guide to Historic, Embossed Bottles.* Peregrine Smith Books, Salt Lake City, Utah.

Fine, M., L. Weis, L. C. Powell, and L. M. Wong, editors
1997 *Off White: Readings on Race, Power, and Society.* Routledge, New York.

Fischer, D. H.
1989 *Albion's Seed: Four British Folkways in America.* Oxford University Press, New York.

Fitts, R. K.
1996 The Landscapes of Northern Bondage. *Historical Archaeology* 30(2):54–73.

Force, P., compiler
1836 A Voyage to Virginia, by Colonel Norwood. In *Tracts and Other Papers, Relating Principally to the Origin, Settlement, and Progress of the Colonies in North America from the Discovery of the Country to the Year 1776,* vol. 3, tract 10. P. Force, Washington, D.C.

Foster, M. K., and W. Cowan, editors
1998 *In Search of New England's Native Past: Selected Essays by Gordon M. Day.* University of Massachusetts Press, Amherst.

Foucault, M.
1979 *Discipline and Punish.* Vintage, New York.

Fox-Genovese, E.
1988 *Within the Plantation Household: Black and White Women of the Old South.* University of North Carolina Press, Chapel Hill.

Frankenberg, R.
1993 *The Social Construction of Whiteness: White Women, Race Matters.* University of Minnesota Press, Minneapolis.
1995 Whiteness and Americanness: Examining Constructions of Race, Culture, and Nation in White Women's

Life Narratives. In *Race,* edited by S. Gregory and R. Sanjek, pp. 62–77. Rutgers University Press, New Brunswick, New Jersey.

———, editor

1997 *Displacing Whiteness: Essays in Social and Cultural Criticism.* Duke University Press, Durham, North Carolina.

Franklin, M.

1997a Out of Site, Out of Mind: The Archaeology of an Enslaved Virginian Household, c. 1740–1778. Doctoral dissertation, University of California, Berkeley. University Microfilms, Ann Arbor.

1997b "Power to the People": Sociopolitics and the Archaeology of Black Americans. *Historical Archaeology* 31(3):36–50.

1998 The Racial Divide and Its Influence on Creole Cultures in the Chesapeake. Paper presented at the annual meeting of the Society for Historical Archaeology, Atlanta, Georgia.

Frazier, E. F.

1957 *Black Bourgeoisie.* Free Press, New York.

1964 *The Negro Church in America.* Schocken, New York.

Friedman, J.

1992 General Historical and Culturally Specific Properties of Global Systems. *Review* 15:335–372.

Gailey, C. W.

1994 Politics, Colonialism, and the Mutable Color of Southern Pacific Peoples. *Transforming Anthropology* 5(1–2):34–40.

Gaines. E. J.

1971 *The Autobiography of Miss Jane Pittman.* Bantam, New York.

1976 *Bloodline.* W. W. Norton, New York.

1983 *A Gathering of Old Men.* Vintage, New York.

Galenson, D. W.

1986 *Traders, Planters, and Slaves: Market Behavior in Early English America.* Cambridge University Press, Cambridge.

Garman, J. C.

1992 "Faithful and Loyal Servants": The Masking and Marking of Ethnicity in the Material Culture of Death. Master's thesis, University of Massachusetts, Amherst.

1998 Rethinking "Resistant Accommodation": Toward an Archaeology of African-American Lives in Southern New England, 1638–1800. *International Journal of Historical Archaeology* 2:133–160.

Garrison, J. R.

1991 *Landscape and Material Life in Franklin County, Massachusetts, 1770–1860.* University of Tennessee Press, Knoxville.

1996 Introduction to *Family and Landscape: Deerfield Homelots from 1671,* edited by S. McGowan and A. F. Miller, pp. xvii–xxxi. Pocumtuck Valley Memorial Association, Deerfield, Massachusetts.

Gaspar, D. B., and D.C. Hine, editors

1996 *More Than Chattel: Black Women Slavery in the Americas.* Indiana University Press, Bloomington.

Gatewood, W. B.

1990 *Aristocrats of Color: The Black Elite, 1880–1920.* Indiana University Press, Bloomington.

Geismar, J. H.

1982 *The Archaeology of Social Disintegration in Skunk Hollow: A Nineteenth-Century Rural Black Community.* Academic Press, New York.

Genovese, E. D.

1972 *Roll, Jordan, Roll: The World the Slaves Made.* Pantheon, New York.

Gérin-Lajoie, M.

1976 *Fort Michilimackinac in 1749, Lotbiniere's Plan and Description.* Mackinac History, Vol. 2, leaflet 5. Mackinac Island State Park Commission, Mackinac Island, Michigan.

Gibbs, P. A.

1999 "Little Spots Allow'd Them": Slave Garden Plots and Poultry Yards. *The Colonial Williamsburg Interpreter* 20(4):9–13.

Giddens, A.

1984 *The Constitution of Society.* University of California Press, Berkeley.

Gill, H. B., Jr.

1972 *The Apothecary in Colonial Virginia.*

University Press of Virginia, Charlottesville.

Gill, J.
1997 *The Lords of Misrule: Mardi Gras and the Politics of Race in New Orleans.* University of Mississippi Press, Oxford.

Gilroy, P.
1993 *The Black Atlantic: Modernity and Double Consciousness.* Harvard University Press, Cambridge, Massachusetts.

Giraud, M.
1987 *A History of French Louisiana.* Vol. 5, *The Company of the Indies, 1718–1731.* Translated by B. Pearce. Louisiana State University Press, Baton Rouge.

Godwyn, M.
1680 *The Negro's & Indians Advocate, Suing for their Admission into the Church: or A Persuasive to the Instructing and Baptizing of the Negro's and Indians in our Plantations.... To Which is added, A brief Account of Religion in Virginia.* London.

Goldberg, D. T.
1993 *Racist Culture: Philosophy and the Politics of Meaning.* Blackwell, Oxford.

Goldfield, D.
1991 Black Life in Old Southern Cities. In *Before Freedom Came: African-American Life in the Antebellum South,* edited by E. D. C. Campbell Jr. and K. Rice, pp. 123–153. University Press of Virginia, Charlottesville.

Golf Magazine Online
1997 http://www.salon.com/news/featu

Gomez, M. A.
1998 *Exchanging Our Country Marks: The Transformation of African Identities in the Colonial and Antebellum South.* University of North Carolina Press, Chapel Hill.

Goodwin, L. B. R.
1999 *An Archaeology of Manners: The Polite World of the Merchant Elite of Colonial Massachusetts.* Kluwer Academic/Plenum Press, New York.

Goodwin, R. C.
1993 *Phase II/III Archaeological Investigations of the Gott's Court Parking Facility, Annapolis, Maryland.* R. Christopher Goodwin and Associates, Inc., Frederick, Maryland.

Gordon, E. T.
1998 *Disparate Diasporas: Identity Politics in an Afro-Nicaraguan Community.* University of Texas Press, Austin.

Gordon, E. T., and M. Anderson
1999 The African Diaspora: Toward an Ethnography of Diasporic Identification. *Journal of American Folklore* 112:282–296.

Gordon, S. C.
1996 *God Almighty Make Me Free: Christianity in Preemancipation Jamaica.* Indiana University Press, Bloomington.

Gramsci, A.
1971 *Selections from the Prison Notebooks.* Edited and translated by Q. Hoare and G. N. Smith. International, New York.

Gran, P.
1994 Race and Racism in the Modern World: How It Works in Different Hegemonies. *Transforming Anthropology* 5(1–2):8–14.

Graves-Brown, P., S. Jones, and C. Gamble, editors
1996 *Cultural Identity and Archaeology: The Construction of European Communities.* Routledge, New York.

Gray, L. E., E. Q. Ryland, and B. J. Simmons
1978 *Historic Buildings in Middlesex County, Virginia, 1650–1875.* Delmar Printing, Charlotte, North Carolina.

Green, W. A.
1976 *British Slave Emancipation: The Sugar Colonies and the Great Experiment, 1830–1865.* Clarendon Press, Oxford.

Greene, J. P., editor
1965 *The Diary of Colonel Landon Carter of Sabine Hall, 1752–1778.* Vol. 1. University Press of Virginia, Charlottesville.

Greene, L. J.
1942 *The Negro in Colonial New England, 1620–1776.* Columbia University Press, New York.

Greenwood, R. S.
1996 *Down by the Station: Los Angeles Chinatown, 1880–1933*. Institute of Archaeology, University of California, Los Angeles.

Gregory, S., and R. Sanjek, editors
1994 *Race*. Rutgers University Press, New Brunswick, New Jersey.

Grier, K. C.
1988 *Culture and Comfort: Parlor Making and Middle-Class Identity, 1850–1930*. Smithsonian Institution Press, Washington, D.C.

Grimé, W. E.
1979 *Ethno-Botany of the Black Americans*. Reference Publications, Algonac, Michigan.

Groover, M. D., and T. E. Baumann
1996 "They Worked Their Own Remedy": African-American Herbal Medicine and the Archaeological Record. *South Carolina Antiquities* 28(1–2):21–32.

Gross, A. J.
1998 Litigating Whiteness: Trials of Racial Determination in the Nineteenth-Century South. *The Yale Law Journal* 108:109–188.

Grossinger, R.
1990 *Planet Medicine: From Stone Age Shamanism to Post-Industrial Healing*. 5th ed. North Atlantic Books, Berkeley, California.

Groth, P., and M. Gutman
1997 Workers' Houses in West Oakland. In *Sights and Sounds: Essays in Celebration of West Oakland*, edited by S. Stewart and M. Praetzellis, pp. 31–84. Anthropological Studies Center, Sonoma State University, Rohnert Park, California.

Gruber, A.
1990 The Archaeology of Mr. Jefferson's Slaves. Master's thesis. University of Delaware, Newark.

Grumet, R. S., editor
1996 *Northeastern Indian Lives, 1632–1816*. University of Massachusetts Press, Amherst.

Gums, B. L.
1998 *The Archaeology of an African-American Neighborhood in Mobile, Alabama*. Center for Archaeological Studies, University of South Alabama, Mobile.

Gundaker, G.
1993 Tradition and Innovation in African-American Yards. *African Arts* 26(2):58–71, 94–96.
1998a *Signs of Diaspora/Diaspora of Signs: Literacies, Creolization, and Vernacular Practice in African America*. Oxford University Press, New York.

———, editor
1998b *Keep Your Head to the Sky: Interpreting African American Home Ground*. University Press of Virginia, Charlottesville.

Gutierrez, C. P.
1984 The Social and Symbolic Uses of Ethnic/Regional Foodways: Cajuns and Crawfish in South Louisiana. In *Ethnic and Regional Foodways in the United States: The Performance of Group Identity*, edited by L. K. Brown and K. Mussell, pp. 169–182. University of Tennessee Press, Knoxville.

Gutman, H. G.
1976a *The Black Family in Slavery and Freedom, 1750–1925*. Vintage, New York.
1976b *Work, Culture, and Society in Industrializing America*. Vintage, New York.

Habermas, J.
1984 *The Theory of Communicative Action*. Vol. 1, *Reason and the Rationalization of Society*. Beacon Press, Boston.
1987 *The Theory of Communicative Action*. Vol. 2, *Lifeworld and System: A Critique of Functionalist Reason*. Beacon Press, Boston.

Hacking, I.
1997 An Aristotelian Glance at Race and the Mind. *Ethos* 25:107–112.
1999 *The Social Construction of What?* Harvard University Press, Cambridge.

Haefeli, E., and K. Sweeney
1995 Revisiting *The Redeemed Captive*: New Perspectives on the 1704 Attack on Deerfield. *The William and Mary Quarterly*, 52:3–46.

Halchin, J. Y.
1985 *Excavations at Fort Michilimack-*

inac, 1983–1985: House C of the Southeast Row House. Archaeological Completion Report Series, 11. Mackinac Island State Park Commission, Mackinac Island, Michigan.

Hale, G. E.
1998 *Making Whiteness: The Culture of Segregation in the South, 1890–1940.* Vintage, New York.

Hall, G. M.
1992 *Africans in Colonial Louisiana: The Development of Afro-Creole Culture in the Eighteenth Century.* Louisiana State University Press, Baton Rouge.

Hall, M.
1992 Small Things and the Mobile, Conflictual Fusion of Power, Fear, and Desire. In *The Art and Mystery of Historical Archaeology,* edited by A. E. Yentsch and M. C. Beaudry, pp. 373–399. CRC Press, Boca Raton, Florida.

Hall, R. L.
1984 "Do Lord, Remember Me": Religion and Cultural Change among Blacks in Florida, 1565–1906. Doctoral dissertation, Florida State University.
1989 Religious Symbolism of the Iron Pot: The Plausibility of a Congo-Angola Origin. *The Western Journal of Black Studies* 13:125–129.
1991 Savoring Africa in the New World. In *Seeds of Change: Five Hundred Years Since Columbus,* edited by H. J. Viola and C. Margolis, pp. 161–171. Smithsonian Institution Press, Washington D.C.

Hall, W. H.
1966 The History of Public Education in West Feliciana Parish, 1893–1964. Master's thesis, Louisiana State University, Baton Rouge.

Handler, J. S.
1974 *The Unappropriated People: Freedmen in the Slave Society of Barbados.* Johns Hopkins University Press, Baltimore.

Handsman, R. G., and M. P. Leone
1989 Living History and Critical Archaeology in the Reconstruction of the Past. In *Critical Traditions in Contemporary Archaeology: Essays in the Philosophy, History, and Socio-Politics of Archaeology,* edited by V. Pinsky and A. Wylie, pp. 117–135. Cambridge University Press, Cambridge.

Hanger, K. S.
1997 *Bounded Lives, Bounded Places: Free Black Society in Colonial New Orleans, 1769–1803.* Duke University Press, Durham.

Harris, J. B.
1989 *Iron Pots and Wooden Spoons: Africa's Gifts to New World Cooking.* Atheneum, New York.
2001 Black and Unknown Hands. *American Legacy* 7:14–16.

Harrison, F. V.
1991 Ethnography as Politics. In *Decolonizing Anthropology: Moving Further toward an Anthropology for Liberation,* edited by F. V. Harrison, pp. 88–109. American Anthropological Association, Washington, D.C.
1995 The Persistent Power of "Race" in the Cultural and Political Economy of Racism. *Annual Reviews of Anthropology* 24:47–74.
1998 Introduction: Expanding the Discourse on "Race." *American Anthropologist* 100:609–631.

Harrison, W. S., and E. Massengill
1939 I Has a Garden. In *The Federal Writers' Project: These Are Our Lives,* pp. 45–54. University of North Carolina Press, Chapel Hill. Reprint, W. W. Norton, New York, 1967.

Hartigan, J., Jr.
1997a Establishing the Fact of Whiteness. *American Anthropologist* 99:495–505.
1997b When White Americans Are a Minority. In *Cultural Diversity in the United States,* edited by L. L. Naylor, pp. 103–115. Bergin and Garvey, Westport, Connecticut.

Hartley, F.
1860 *The Ladies' Book of Etiquette and Manual of Politeness.* G. W. Cottrell, Boston.

Harvey, D.
2000 *Spaces of Hope.* University of California Press, Berkeley.

Harvey, T., and W. Brewin
1866 *Jamaica in 1866.* A. W. Bennett, London.

Hattersley-Drayton, K.

1997 Melting Pot or Not? Ethnicity and Community in Pre-World War II West Oakland. In *Sights and Sounds: Essays in Celebration of West Oakland,* edited by S. Stewart and M. Praetzellis, pp. 183–210. Anthropological Studies Center, Sonoma State University, Rohnert Park, California.

Hauptman, L. M., and J. Wherry, editors

1990 *The Pequots in Southern New England: The Fall and Rise of an American Indian Nation.* University of Oklahoma Press, Norman.

Heath, B. J., and A. Bennett

2000 "The Little Spots Allow'd Them": The Archaeological Study of African-American Yards. *Historical Archaeology* 34(2):38–55.

Hebdige, D.

1979 *Subculture: The Meaning of Style.* Routledge, London.

Heldman, D. P.

1977 *Excavations at Fort Michilimackinac, 1976: The Southeast and South Southeast Row Houses.* Archaeological Completion Report Series 1. Mackinac Island State Park Commission, Mackinac Island, Michigan.

1978 *Excavations at Fort Michilimackinac, 1977: House One of the South Southeast Row House.* Archaeological Completion Report Series 2. Mackinac Island State Park Commission, Mackinac Island, Michigan.

1980 Coins at Michlimackinac. *Historical Archaeology* 14:82–107.

1984 East Side, West Side, All Around the Town: Stratigraphic Alignment and Resulting Settlement Patterns at Fort Michilimackinac, 1715–1781. Paper presented at the annual meeting of the Society for Historical Archaeology, Williamsburg, Virginia.

1986 Michigan's First Jewish Settlers: A View From the Solomon-Levy Trading House at Fort Michilimackinac, 1765–1781. *Journal of New World Archaeology* 6(4):21–34.

1999 Euro-American Archaeology in Michigan: The French Period. In *Retrieving Michigan's Buried Past: The Archaeology of the Great Lakes State,* edited by John R. Halsey, pp. 292–311. Bulletin 64, Cranbrook Institute of Science, Bloomfield Hills, Michigan.

Heldman, D. P., and R. T. Grange, Jr.

1981 *Excavations at Fort Michilimackinac, 1978–1979: The Rue de la Babillardee.* Archaeological Completion Report Series 3. Mackinac Island State Park Commission, Mackinac Island, Michigan.

Henderson, C. R.

1897 *The Social Spirit in America.* Chautaqua-Century Press, New York.

Hening, W. W.

1809 *The Statutes at Large; Being a Collection of All the Laws of Virginia from the First Session of the Legislature in the Year 1619.* Vol. 3. Thomas Desilver, Philadelphia.

1819 *The Statutes at Large; Being a Collection of all the Laws of Virginia.* Vol. 6. Franklin Press, Richmond, Virginia.

Herron, L., and A. M. Bacon

1985 Conjuring and Conjure-Doctors. *Southern Workman* 24:117–118, 193–194, 209–211.

Herskovits, M. J.

1958 *The Myth of the Negro Past.* Beacon, Boston.

Hess, K.

1992 *The Carolina Rice Kitchen: The African Connection.* University of South Carolina, Columbia.

Higgins, T. F., B. Ford, C. Downing, V. L. Deitrick, S. C. Pullins, and D. B. Blanton

2000 *Wilton Speaks: Archaeology at an Eighteenth-Nineteenth-Century Plantation. Data Recovery at Site 44HE493, Associated with the Proposed Route 895 Project, Henrico County, Virginia.* The College of William and Mary Center for Archaeological Research, Williamsburg, Virginia.

Higman, B.

1998 *Montpelier.* University Press of the West Indies, Kingston.

Hill, J. H.

1998 Language, Race, and White Space.

American Anthropologist 100:680–689.

Hilliard, S. B.

1972 *Hog Meat and Hoecake: Food Supply in the Old South 1840–1860.* Southern Illinois University Press, Carbondale.

1988 Hog Meat and Cornpone: Foodways in the Antebellum South. In *Material Life in America, 1600–1860,* edited by R. B. St. George, pp. 311–332. Northeastern University Press, Boston.

Hinsley, C. M.

1989 Revising and Revisioning the History of Archaeology: Reflections on Region and Context. In *Tracing Archaeology's Past: The Historiography of Archaeology,* edited by A. L. Christenson, pp. 79–96. Southern Illinois University Press, Carbondale.

Hinton, J.

1847 *Memoir of William Knibb, Missionary in Jamaica.* Houlston and Stoneman, London.

Hodder, I.

1982 Toward a Contextual Approach to Prehistoric Exchange. In *Contexts for Prehistoric Exchange,* edited by T. K. Earle and J. E. Ericson, pp. 199–212. Academic Press, New York.

1997 "Always Momentary, Fluid, and Flexible": Towards a Reflexive Excavation Methodology. *Antiquity* 71:691–700.

Hodgen, M. T.

1971 *Early Anthropology in the Sixteenth and Seventeenth Centuries.* University of Pennsylvania Press, Philadelphia.

Hoffman, K.

1997 Cultural Development in La Florida. *Historical Archaeology* 31(1):24–35.

Hogan, W. R., and E. A. Davis, editors

1951 *William Johnson's Natchez: The Ante-Bellum Diary of a Free Negro.* Louisiana State University Press, Baton Rouge.

1993 *William Johnson's Natchez: The Ante-Bellum Diary of a Free Negro.* With a new introduction by W. L. Andrews. Louisiana State University Press, Baton Rouge.

Holt, T.

1992 *The Problem of Freedom: Race, Labor, and Politics in Jamaica and Britain, 1832–1938.* Johns Hopkins University Press, Baltimore.

Hood, J. E.

1996 Social Relations and the Cultural Landscape. In *Landscape Archaeology: Reading and Interpreting the American Historical Landscape,* edited by R. Yamin and K. B. Metheny, pp. 121–146. University of Tennessee Press, Knoxville.

hooks, b.

1981 *Ain't I a Woman: Black Women and Feminism.* South End Press, Boston.

1992 *Black Looks: Race and Representation.* South End Press, Boston.

1994 *Outlaw Culture: Resisting Representations.* Routledge, London.

Horowitz, D.

1985 *The Morality of Spending: Attitudes toward the Consumer Culture in America, 1875–1940.* Johns Hopkins University Press, Baltimore.

Horsman, R.

1981 *Race and Manifest Destiny: The Origins of American Racial Anglo-Saxonism.* Harvard University Press, Cambridge.

Horton, J. O.

1993 *Free People of Color: Inside the African American Community.* Smithsonian Institution Press, Washington, D.C.

Horton, J. O., and L. E. Horton

1979 *Black Bostonians: Family Life and Community Struggle in the Antebellum North.* Holmes and Meier, New York.

The House Beautiful

1898 Notes, Household Decoration. 32(2):61–62.

The Household: A Monthly Journal Devoted to the Interests of the American Housewife

1887 False Economy. 20(1):23.

Howson, J.

1990 Social Relations and Material Culture: A Critique of the Archaeology of Plantation Slavery. *Historical Archaeology* 24(4):78–91.

Hu-DeHart, E.
1995 P.C., and the Politics of Multiculturalism in Higher Education. In *Race,* edited by S. Gregory and R. Sanjek, pp. 243–256. Rutgers University Press, New Brunswick, New Jersey.

Hudgins, C. L.
1990 Robert "King" Carter and the Landscape of Tidewater Virginia in the Eighteenth Century. In *Earth Patterns: Essays in Landscape Archaeology,* edited by W. M. Kelso and R. Most, pp. 59–70. University Press of Virginia, Charlottesville.

Hull, G. T., P. B. Scott, and B. Smith, editors
1982 *All the Women Are White, All the Blacks Are Men, But Some of Us Are Brave.* Feminist Press, New York.

Hurston, Z. N.
1931 Hoodoo in America. *Journal of American Folk-Lore* 44:317–417.

Hyatt, H. M.
1965 *Folk-Lore from Adams County, Illinois.* 2nd ed. Western Printing, Hannibal, Missouri.
1970–1978 *Hoodoo-Conjuration-Witchcraft-Rootwork: Beliefs Accepted by Many Negroes and White Persons, These Being Orally Recorded Among Blacks and Whites.* Western Publishing, Hannibal, Missouri.

Hyde, L.
1979 *The Gift: Imagination and the Erotic Life of Property.* Random House, New York.

Igartua, J. E.
1974 The Merchants and Negociants of Montreal, 1750–1775: A Study in Socio-Economic History. Doctoral dissertation, Michigan State University, East Lansing.

Ignatiev, N.
1995 *How the Irish Became White.* Routledge, New York.

Ingersoll, T. N.
1990 Old New Orleans: Race, Class, Sex, and Order in the Early Deep South, 1718–1819. Doctoral dissertation, University of California, Los Angeles.

Isaac, R.
1982 *The Transformation of Virginia, 1740–1790.* University of North Carolina Press, Chapel Hill.

James, E. T., J. W. James, and P. S. Boyer, editors
1971 *Notable American Women, 1607–1950.* Harvard University Press, Cambridge.

Jenkins, C.
1999 Slave Subsistence at Saragossa Plantation. Paper presented at the Southeastern Archaeological Conference, Pensacola, Florida.

John, B.
1999 The Construction of Racial Meaning by Blacks and Whites in Plantation Society. In *Plantation Society and Race Relations: The Origins of Inequality,* edited by T. J. Durant Jr., and J. D. Knottnerus, pp. 41–50. Praeger, Westport, Connecticut.

Johnson, M.
1996 *An Archaeology of Capitalism.* Blackwell, Oxford.

Johnson, M., and J. Roark
1984a *Black Masters: A Free Family of Color in the Old South.* W. W. Norton, New York.

———, editors
1984b *No Chariot Let Down: Charleston's Free People of Color on the Eve of the Civil War.* University of North Carolina Press, Chapel Hill.

Johnson, W.
1921–1965 *The Papers of Sir William Johnson.* Vols. 4, 5, 7, and 8. Edited by M. W. Hamilton. University of the State of New York Press, Albany.

Jones, J.
1985 *Labor of Love, Labor of Sorrow.* Basic, New York.

Jones, L. D.
1995 The Material Culture of Slavery from an Annapolis Household. Paper presented at the annual meeting of the Society for Historical Archeology, Annapolis.
2000 *Archaeological Investigations at Slayton House, 18AP74, Annapolis, Maryland.* Historic Annapolis Foundation, Annapolis, Maryland.

Jones, S. L.
1985 Afro-American Vernacular Architecture. In *The Archaeology of Slavery and Plantation Life,* edited by T. A. Singleton, pp. 195–121. Academic Press, Orlando.

Jones, S.
1997 *The Archaeology of Ethnicity: Constructing Identities in the Past and Present.* Routledge, London.
1999 Historical Categories and the Praxis of Identity: The Interpretation of Ethnicity in Historical Archaeology. In *Historical Archaeology: Back From the Edge,* edited by P. P. A. Funari, M. Hall, and S. Jones, pp. 119–232. Routledge, London.

Jordan, D. W.
1979 Political Stability and the Emergence of a Native Elite in Maryland. In *The Chesapeake in the Seventeenth Century: Essays in Anglo-American Society,* edited by T. W. Tate and D. L. Ammerman, pp. 243–273. University of North Carolina Press, Chapel Hill.

Jordan, P. B.
1986 *Herbal Remedies and Home Remedies: A Potpourri in Bahamian Culture.* Nassau Guardian Press, Nassau, Bahamas.

Jordan, W. D.
1968 *White Over Black: American Attitudes Toward the Negro, 1550–1812.* University of North Carolina Press, Chapel Hill.

Joyner, C.
1985 *Down by the Riverside: A South Carolina Slave Community.* University of Illinois Press, Urbana.

———, editor
1986 *Drums and Shadows: Survival Studies among the Georgia Coastal Negroes.* University of Georgia Press, Athens.

Kalcik, S.
1984 Ethnic Foodways in America: Symbol and the Performance of Identity. In *Ethnic and Regional Foodways in the United States: The Performance of Group Identity,* edited by L. K. Brown and K. Mussell, pp. 37–65. University of Tennessee Press, Knoxville.

Karnegis, T.
1996 Former West Oakland resident. Taped interview, September 4, 1996, for the Oakland Neighborhood History Project, Oakland. Verbatim transcription on file at the Anthropological Studies Center, Sonoma State University, Rohnert Park, California.

Kelly, M. C. S., and R. E. Kelly
1980 Approaches to Ethnic Identification in Historical Archaeology. In *Archaeological Perspectives on Ethnicity in America: Afro-American and Asian American Culture History,* edited by R. L. Schuyler, pp. 133–143. Baywood, Farmingdale, New York.

Kelso, W. M.
1984 *Kingsmill Plantations, 1619–1800: Archaeology of Country Life in Colonial Virginia.* Academic Press, New York.

Kern, S.
1999 Where Did the Indians Sleep? An Archaeological and Ethnohistorical Study of Mid-Eighteenth-Century Piedmont Virginia. In *Historical Archaeology, Identity Formation, and the Interpretation of Ethnicity,* edited by M. Franklin and G. Fesler, pp. 33–48. The Colonial Williamsburg Foundation, Williamsburg, Virginia.

Killion, R., and C. Waller, editors
1973 *Slavery Time When I Was Chillun Down on Marster's Plantation.* Beehive Press, Savannah.

King, D.
1850 *The State and Prospects of Jamaica.* Johnstone and Hunter, London.

King, J.
1984 Ceramic Variability in Seventeenth-Century St. Augustine, Florida. *Historical Archaeology* 18(2):75–82.

Klein, H.
1986 *African Slavery in Latin America and the Caribbean.* Oxford University, New York.

Klingelhofer, E.
1987 Aspects of Early Afro-American Material Culture: Artifacts from the Slave Quarters at Garrison Plantation, Maryland. *Historical Archaeology* 21:112–119.

Kohl, P. L.
1998 Nationalism and Archaeology: On the Constructions of Nations and the Reconstructions of the Remote Past. *Annual Review of Anthropology* 27:223–246.

Krass, D. S., and B. O'Connell, editors
1992 *Native Peoples and Museums in the Connecticut Valley: A Guide for Learning*. Historic Northampton, Northampton, Massachusetts.

Krause, E. L.
1998 "The Bead of Raw Sweat in a Field of Dainty Perspirers": Nationalism, Whiteness, and the Olympic-Class Ordeal of Tonya Harding. *Transforming Anthropology* 7(1): 33–52.

Kulikoff, A.
1986 *Tobacco and Slaves: The Development of Southern Cultures in the Chesapeake, 1680–1800*. University of North Carolina Press, Chapel Hill.

Laguerre, M.
1987 *Afro-Caribbean Folk Medicine*. Bergin and Garvey, South Hadley, Massachusetts.

Landers, J. G., editor
1996 *Against the Odds: Free Blacks in Slave Societies of the Americas*. Frank Cass, London.

La Roche, C. J.
1994 Beads from the African Burial Ground, New York City: A Preliminary Assessment. *Beads: Journal of the Society of Bead Researchers* 6:3–20.

La Roche, C. J., and M. L. Blakey
1997 Seizing Intellectual Power: The Dialogue at the New York African Burial Ground. *Historical Archaeology* 31(3):84–106.

Larson, P. M.
1999 Reconsidering Trauma, Identity, and the African Diaspora: Enslavement and Historical Memory in Nineteenth-Century Highland Madagascar. *William and Mary Quarterly*, 3rd series, 56:335–362.

Lears, T. J. J.
1983 From Salvation to Self-Realization: Advertising and the Therapeutic Roots of the Consumer Culture, 1880–1930. In *The Culture of Consumption: Critical Essays in American History, 1880–1980*, edited by R. W. Fox and T. J. J. Lears, pp. 1–38. Pantheon, New York.

Lebsock, S.
1987 *Virginia Women, 1600–1945: A Share of Honour*. Virginia State Library, Richmond.

Lee Family Papers
1638–1867 Ludwell III Appraisal. Mss. 1L51f. Microfilm reels C227, frames 65–68. On file at the Virginia Historical Society, Richmond.

Lemann, N.
1991 *Promised Land*. Alfred A. Knopf, New York.

Lemelle, S. J., and R. D. G. Kelley, editors
1994 *Imaging Home: Class, Culture, and Nationalism in the African Diaspora*. Verso, London.

Lemon, J. T.
1984 Spatial Order: Households in Local Communities and Regions. In *Colonial British America: Essays in the New History of the Early Modern Era*, edited by J. P. Greene and J. R. Pole, pp. 86–122. Johns Hopkins University Press, Baltimore.

Leone, M. P.
1981 Archaeology's Relationship to the Present and the Past. In *Modern Material Culture: The Archaeology of Us*, edited by R. Gould and M. Schiffer, pp. 5–13. Academic Press, New York.

1984 Interpreting Ideology in Historical Archaeology: The William Paca Garden in Annapolis, Maryland. In *Ideology, Power, and Prehistory*, edited by D. Miller and C. Tilley, pp. 25–35. Cambridge University Press, Cambridge.

1988 The Georgian Order as the Order of Merchant Capitalism in Annapolis, Maryland. In *The Recovery of Meaning: Historical Archaeology in the Eastern United States*, edited by M. P. Leone and P. B. Potter, Jr., pp. 235–261. Smithsonian Institution Press, Washington, D.C.

1995 A Historical Archaeology of Capitalism. *American Anthropologist* 97(2): 251–268.

1999 Ceramics from Annapolis, Maryland: A Measure of Time Routines and Work Discipline. In *Historical Archaeologies of Capitalism*, edited by M. P. Leone and P. B. Potter Jr., pp. 195–216. Kluwer Academic/Plenum, New York.

Leone, M. P., and G-M. Fry
1999 Conjuring in the Big House Kitchen: An Interpretation of African American Belief Systems Based on the Uses of Archaeology and Folklore Sources. *Journal of American Folklore* 112:372–403.

Leone, M. P., E. Kryder-Reid, and J. Bailey-Goldschmidt
1992 The Rationalization of Sound in Mid-Eighteenth-Century Annapolis, Maryland. In *The Art and Mystery of Historical Archaeology,* edited by A. E. Yentsch and M. C. Beaudry, pp. 229–245. CRC Press, Boca Raton, Florida.

Leone, M. P., and P. B. Potter, Jr., editors
1999 *Historical Archaeologies of Capitalism.* Kluwer Academic/Plenum, New York.

Leone, M. P., P. B. Potter Jr., and P. A. Shackel
1987 Toward a Critical Archaeology. *Current Anthropology* 28:283–302.

Leone, M. P., and N. A. Silberman, editors
1995 *Invisible America: Unearthing Our Hidden History.* Henry Holt, New York.

Levine, L. W.
1977 *Black Culture and Black Consciousness: Afro-American Folk Thought from Slavery to Freedom.* Oxford University Press, New York.

Lewis, D. L.
1993 *W. E. B. Du Bois: Biography of a Race, 1868–1919.* Henry Holt, New York.

Lewis, M. G.
1834 *Journal of a West India Proprietor, Jamaica, Kept During a Residence in the Island of Jamaica.* John Murray, London.

Lincoln, C. E., and L. H. Mamiya
1990 *The Black Church in the African American Experience.* Duke University Press, Durham, North Carolina.

Linebaugh, D. W.
1994 "All the Annoyances and Inconveniences of the Country": Environmental Factors in the Development of Outbuildings in the Colonial Chesapeake. *Winterthur Portfolio* 29:1–18.

Little, B. J., editor
1992 *Text-Aided Archaeology.* CRC Press, Boca Raton, Florida.

Litwack, L. F.
1961 *North of Slavery: The Negro in the Free States, 1790–1860.* University of Chicago Press, Chicago.
1989 Hellbound on My Trail: Race Relations in the South from Reconstruction to the Civil Rights Movement. Paper delivered at the University of Mississippi, Oxford.
1998 *Trouble in Mind: Black Southerners in the Age of Jim Crow.* Vintage, New York.

Logan, G. C., T. W. Bodor, L. D. Jones, and M. C. Creveling
1992 *1991 Archaeological Excavations at the Charles Carroll House in Annapolis, Maryland, 18AP45.* Historic Annapolis Foundation, Annapolis.

Lotbinière, M. C. de
1764 Memoir by Chartier de Lotbinière (Michel) to Amherst, dated August 4, 1764, concerning "The Western part of Canada from Michilimackinac to the Mississippi River" (in French). Original in the National Archives of Canada, Ottawa, MG 18, L4, packet 18. Photocopy and English translation in the collections of the Mackinac Island State Park Commission, Lansing, Michigan.

Lucentini, J.
2000 Shards of Our Past. *Newsday: Health and Discovery.* November 28, C3, C10.

Lüdtke, A.
1995 Introduction: What Is the History of Everyday Life and Who Are Its Practitioners? In *The History of Everyday Life: Reconstructing Historical Experiences and Ways of Life,* edited by A. Lüdtke, pp. 3–40. Princeton University Press, Princeton, New Jersey.

Luedtke, B. E.
1995 Creating and Interpreting Cultural Identity. *Conference on New England Archaeology Newsletter* 15:1–6.

Lunt, P. K., and S. M. Livingstone
1992 *Mass Consumption and Personal Identity.* Open University Press, Buckingham.

Lyman, R. L., M. J. O'Brien, and R. C. Dunnell
1997 *The Rise and Fall of Culture History.* Plenum, New York.

Lynd, R. S., and H. M. Lynd
1929 *Middletown: A Study in Contemporary American Culture*. Harcourt, Brace, New York.

McBride, K.
1993 "Ancient and Crazie": Pequot Lifeways During the Historic Period. In *Algonkians of New England: Past and Present,* edited by P. Benes, pp. 63–75. Boston University Press, Boston.

McCarthy, J. P.
1993 Burial Practices at the Cemeteries of the First African Baptist Church, Philadelphia: Social Identity in the African-American Community in the Early Nineteenth Century. Paper presented at the annual meeting of the National Council on Public History, Valley Forge, Pennsylvania.

McDannell, C.
1992 Parlor Piety: The Home as Sacred Space in Protestant America. In *American Home Life, 1880–1930: A Social History of Spaces and Services,* edited by J. H. Foy and T. J. Schlereth, pp. 162–189. University of Tennessee Press, Knoxville.

McDavid, C., and D. Babson, editors
1997 In the Realm of Politics: Prospects for Public Participation in African-American and Plantation Archaeology. *Historical Archaeology* 31(3):1–152.

McDermott, J. F.
1941 *A Glossary of Mississippi Valley French, 1673–1850*. Washington University Studies, Language and Literature 12. St. Louis, Missouri.

McDowell, B., and R. W. Madden
1969 Deerfield Keeps a Truce with Time. *National Geographic* 135(6):780–809.

McDowell, J. E.
1978 Therese Schindler of Mackinac: Upward Mobility in the Great Lakes Fur Trade. *Wisconsin Magazine of History* 61(2):125–143.

McEwan, B. G.
1986 Domestic Adaptation at Puerto Real, Haiti. *Historical Archaeology* 20(1):44–49.

McFaden, L., P. Levy, D. Muraca, and J. Jones
1994 *Interim Report: The Archaeology of Rich Neck Plantation, VDHR File Number 97-1411F.* The Colonial Williamsburg Foundation, Williamsburg, Virginia.

McGhan, J.
1993 *Virginia Will Records.* Genealogical Publishing, Baltimore.

McGowan, J. T.
1976 Creation of a Slave Society: Louisiana Plantation in the Eighteenth Century. Doctoral dissertation, University of Rochester, Rochester, New York.

McGowen, S., and A. F. Miller
1996 *Family and Landscape: Deerfield Homelots from 1671.* Pocumtuck Valley Memorial Association, Deerfield, Massachusetts.

McGuire, R. H.
1982 The Study of Ethnicity in Historical Archaeology. *Journal of Anthropological Archaeology* 1:159–178.

McIlwaine, H. R., editor
1925 *Executive Journals of the Council of Colonial Virginia.* Vol. 1, June 11, 1680–June 22, 1699. Virginia State Library, Richmond.

McIntosh, P.
1993 White Privilege: Unpacking the Invisible Knapsack. In *Experiencing Race, Class, and Gender in the United States,* edited by V. Cyrus, pp. 209–213. Mayfield, Mountain View, California.

McKee, L.
1987 Delineating Ethnicity from the Garbage of Early Virginians: Faunal Remains from the Kingsmill Plantation Slave Quarter. *American Archaeology* 6(1):31–39.
1988 Plantation Food Supply in Nineteenth-Century Tidewater Virginia. Doctoral dissertation, University of California, Berkeley.
1992 The Ideals and Realities Behind the Design and Use of Nineteenth-Century Virginia Slave Cabins. In *The Art and Mystery of Historical Archaeology: Essays in Honor of James Deetz,* edited by A. E. Yentsch and M. C. Beaudry, pp. 195–213. CRC Press, Boca Raton, Florida.
1995 Is It Futile to Try and Be Useful? Historical Archaeology and the African-

American Experience. *Northeast Historical Archaeology* 23:1–7.

1999 Food Supply and Plantation Social Order. In *"I, Too, Am America": Archaeological Studies of African-American Life,* edited by T. A. Singleton, pp. 218–239. University Press of Virginia, Charlottesville.

McKern, W. C.

1939 The Midwestern Taxonomic Method as an Aid to Archaeological Culture Study. *American Antiquity* 4:301–313.

McMillen, S.

1985 Mother's Sacred Duty: Breast-Feeding Patterns among Middle- and Upper-Class Women in the Antebellum South. *Journal of Southern History* 51:333–356.

McMullen, A., and R. G. Handsman, editors

1987 *A Key into the Language of Woodsplint Baskets.* American Indian Archaeological Institute, Washington, Connecticut.

McWilliams, R. G., translator and editor

1953 *Fleur de Lys and Calumet: Being the Pénicaut Narrative of the French Adventure in Louisiana.* Louisiana State University Press, Baton Rouge.

Maduell, C. R., compiler and translator

1972 *The Census Tables for the French Colony of Louisiana from 1699 through 1732.* Polyanthos, New Orleans.

Maguire, J.

1975 *On Shares: Ed Brown's Story.* W. W. Norton, New York.

Main, G.

1982 *Tobacco Colony: Life in Early Maryland, 1650–1720.* Princeton University Press, Princeton, New Jersey.

Mair, L. M.

1986 *Women Field Workers in Jamaica During Slavery.* University of the West Indies Press, Mona.

Malone, D., editor

1932 *Dictionary of American Biography.* Vols. 8–9. Charles Scribner's Sons, New York.

Mandle, J. R.

1983 Sharecropping and the Plantation Economy in the United States South. In *Sharecropping and Sharecroppers,* edited by T. J. Byres, pp. 120–129. Frank Cass, Totowa, New Jersey.

Manning-Sterling, E. H.

1994 Great Blue Herons and River Otters: The Changing Perceptions of All Things Wild in the Seventeenth- and Eighteenth-Century Chesapeake. Master's thesis, College of William and Mary, Williamsburg, Virginia.

Marchand, R.

1985 *Advertising the American Dream: Making Way for Modernity, 1920–1940.* University of California Press, Berkeley.

Marcus, J. R.

1951 *Early American Jewry: The Jews of New York, New England, and Canada, 1649–1794.* Jewish Publication Society of America, Philadelphia.

1953 *Early American Jewry: The Jews of Pennsylvania and the South, 1655–1790.* Jewish Publication Society of America, Philadelphia.

1959 *American Jewry—Documents—Eighteenth-Century: Primarily Hitherto Unpublished Manuscripts.* Hebrew Union College Press, Cincinnati.

1970 *The Colonial American Jew, 1492–1776.* Vols. 1–3. Wayne State University Press, Detroit.

Marx, K.

1967 *Capital.* Vol. 1. 1867. Reprint, Random House/Vintage, New York.

1970 Preface to *A Contribution to the Critique of Political Economy,* by K. Marx, pp. 19–23. 1859. Reprint, International, New York.

Massachusetts Department of Education

1997 *History and Social Science Curriculum Framework.* Massachusetts Department of Education, Boston.

Matheson, G. A., and F. Taylor

1976 Hand-List of Personal Papers from the Muniments of the Earl of Crawford and Balcarres. Deposited in the John Rylands University Library of Manchester, England.

Matsuda, M. J.

1989 Public Response to Racist Speech: Considering the Victim's Story. *Michigan Law Review* 87:2320.

Matthews, C. N.
1996 "It is quietly chaotic. It confuses time": Final Report of Excavations at the Bordley-Randall Site in Annapolis, Maryland, 1993–1995. Report on file. Archaeology in Annapolis, Annapolis.
1998 Annapolis and the Making of the Modern Landscape: An Archaeology of History and Tradition. Doctoral dissertation, Columbia University.
1999 *Management Report of Excavations at the St. Augustine Site (16OR148), 1999.* Submitted to the Louisiana Division of Archaeology. On file, the Greater New Orleans Archaeology Program, New Orleans.
n.d. *An Archaeology of History and Tradition: Moments of Danger in the Annapolis Landscape.* Kluwer Academic/Plenum, New York.

Maxwell, M. S., and L. R. Binford
1961 *Excavations at Fort Michilimackinac, Mackinaw City, Michigan, 1959 Season.* Museum Cultural Series, vol. 1, no. 1, Michigan State University, East Lansing.

May, G. S., editor
1960 *The Doctor's Secret Journal,* by Daniel Morison. Mackinac Island State Park Commission, Mackinac Island, Michigan.

Medearis, A. S.
1997 *The African-American Kitchen: Cooking from Our Heritage.* Plume, New York.

Medick, H.
1995 "Missionaries in the Rowboat"? Ethnological Ways of Knowing as a Challenge to Social History. In *The History of Everyday Life: Reconstructing Historical Experiences and Ways of Life,* edited by A. Lüdtke, pp. 41–71. Princeton University Press, Princeton, New Jersey.

Melish, J. P.
1998 *Disowning Slavery: Gradual Emancipation and "Race" in New England, 1780–1860.* Cornell University Press, Ithaca, New York.

Melvoin, R.
1989 *New England Outpost: War and Society in Colonial Deerfield,* W. W. Norton, New York.

Menard, R. R.
1977 From Servants to Slaves: The Transformation of the Chesapeake Labor System. *Southern Studies* 16:355–390.

Metress, S.
1997 The Irish-Americans: From the Frontier to the White House. In *Cultural Diversity in the United States,* edited by L. L. Naylor, pp. 131–144. Bergin and Garvey, Westport, Connecticut.

Middlesex County
1680–1694 Middlesex County, Virginia, Order Books. Microfilm, Library of Virginia, Richmond.

Middleton, A. P.
1953 *Tobacco Coast: A Maritime History of the Chesapeake Bay in the Colonial Era.* Mariners' Museum, Newport News, Virginia.

Midgley, C.
1992 *Women Against Slavery: The British Campaigns, 1780–1870.* Routledge, London.

Miller, A. F.
n.d. *The Bittersweet Life of E. H. Williams, 1761–1838.* On file, Historic Deerfield, Deerfield, Massachusetts.

Miller, G. L.
1980 Classification and Economic Scaling of Nineteenth Century Ceramics. *Historical Archaeology* 14:1–40.

Miller, H. M.
1984 Colonization and Subsistence Change on the Seventeenth-Century Chesapeake Frontier. Doctoral dissertation, Michigan State University, East Lansing.
1988 An Archaeological Perspective on the Evolution of Diet in the Colonial Chesapeake, 1620–1745. In *Colonial Chesapeake Society,* edited by L. G. Carr, P. D. Morgan, and J. B. Russo, pp. 176–199. University of North Carolina Press, Chapel Hill.
1996 Archaeology of the Seventeenth-Century British Immigrant Experience in the Middle Atlantic Region. *Historical Archaeology Guides* 4:25–46.

Mills, E., and A. Mann
1996 *Son of Mashpee: Reflections of Chief*

Flying Eagle, a Wampanoag. Word Studio, North Falmouth, Massachusetts.

Milner, C. A., II
1981 Indulgent Friends and Important Allies: Political Process on the Mississippi Frontier and Its Aftermath. In *The Frontier in History: North America and Southern Africa Compared,* edited by H. Lamar and L. Thompson, pp. 123–148. Yale University Press, New Haven.

Minchinton, W., C. King, and P. Waite
1984 *Virginia Slave-Trade Statistics, 1698–1775.* Virginia State Library, Richmond.

Mintz, S.
1999 *African-American Voices: The Life Cycle of Slavery.* 2nd ed. Brandywine Press, St. James, New York.

Mintz, S. W.
1996 *Tasting Food, Tasting Freedom: Excursions into Eating, Culture, and the Past.* Beacon, Boston.

Mintz, S. W., and D. Hall
1960 *The Origins of the Jamaican Internal Marketing System.* Yale University Publications in Anthropology, New Haven.

Miquelon, D. B.
1966 The Baby Family in the Trade of Canada, 1750–1820. Master's thesis, Carleton University. University Microfilms, Ann Arbor, Michigan.

Mitchell, F.
1978 *Hoodoo Medicine: Sea Islands Herbal Remedies.* Reed, Cannon and Johnson, Berkeley, California.

Mitchell, P. B.
1993 *Soul on Rice: African Influences on American Cooking.* Patricia B. Mitchell, Chatham, Virginia.

Monks, G. G.
1999 On Rejecting the Concept of Socio-Economic Status in Historical Archaeology. In *Historical Archaeology: Back from the Edge,* edited by P. P. A. Funari, M. Hall, and S. Jones, pp. 204–216. Routledge, London.

Montagu, A.
1964 *The Concept of Race.* Free Press, New York.
1974 *Man's Most Dangerous Myth: The Fallacy of Race.* Oxford University Press, New York.

Moody, A.
1968 *Coming of Age in Mississippi.* Laurel Books, New York.

Moore, L. E.
1995 Letter to the Editor. *Bulletin of the Society for American Archaeology* 13(1):3.

Moore, S. G.
1989 Established and Well Cultivated: Afro-American Foodways in Early Virginia. *Virginia Cavalcade* 39: 70–83.

Moore, W. B.
1984 Metaphor and Changing Reality: The Foodways and Beliefs of the Russian Molokans in the United States. In *Ethnic and Regional Foodways in the United States: The Performance of Group Identity,* edited by L. K. Brown and K. Mussell, pp. 91–112. University of Tennessee Press, Knoxville.

Morgan, E. S.
1975 *American Slavery, American Freedom: The Ordeal of Colonial Virginia.* W. W. Norton, New York.

Morgan, P. D.
1998 *Slave Counterpoint: Black Culture in the Eighteenth-Century Chesapeake and Lowcountry.* University of North Carolina Press, Chapel Hill.

Morton, J. C.
1969 Stephen Bordley of Colonial Annapolis. *Winterthur Portfolio* 5:1–14.

Mouer, L. D., M. E. N. Hodges, S. R. Potter, S. L. Henry Renaud, I. Noël Hume, D. J. Pogue, M. W. McCartney, and T. E. Davidson
1999 Colonoware Pottery, Chesapeake Pipes, and "Uncritical Assumptions." In *"I, Too, Am America": Archaeological Studies of African-American Life,* edited by T. A. Singleton, pp. 75–115. University Press of Virginia, Charlottesville.

Mousalimas, A.
1980 Former West Oakland resident. Taped interview, August 30, 1980, for the Oakland Neighborhood His-

tory Project, Oakland. Verbatim transcription on file at the Anthropological Studies Center, Sonoma State University, Rohnert Park, California.

MPHC (Michigan Pioneer and Historical Collection)

1874–1929 *Collections of the Pioneer and Historical Society of Michigan.* Vols. 8–12, 15, 27. Pioneer and Historical Society of Michigan, Lansing.

Mrozowski, S. A.

1999 Colonization and the Commodification of Nature. *International Journal of Historical Archaeology* 3:153–166.

Mrozowski, S. A., and L. Driscoll

1997 Seeds of Learning: An Archaeobotanical Analysis of the Rich Neck Plantation Slave Quarter, Williamsburg, Virginia. Manuscript on file, Department of Archaeological Research, Colonial Williamsburg Foundation, Williamsburg.

Mukhopadhyay, C. C., and Y. T. Moses

1997 Reestablishing "Race" in Anthropological Discourse. *American Anthropologist* 99:517–533.

Mullin, G. W.

1972 *Flight and Rebellion: Slave Resistance in Eighteenth-Century Virginia.* Oxford University Press, New York.

Mullings, L.

1997 *On Our Own Terms: Race, Class, and Gender in the Lives of African American Women.* Routledge, New York.

Mullins, P. R.

1999a *Race and Affluence: An Archaeology of African America and Consumer Culture.* Kluwer Academic/Plenum, New York.

1999b Race and the Genteel Consumer: Class and African-American Consumption, 1850–1930. *Historical Archaeology* 33(1):22–38.

Mullins, P. R., and M. S. Warner

1993 *Final Archaeological Investigations at the Maynard-Burgess House (18AP64), an 1847–1980 African American Household in Annapolis, Maryland.* Historic Annapolis Foundation, Annapolis.

Muraca, D.

1997 *Rich Neck Plantation Open House.* Photocopied brochure on file, Colonial Williamsburg Foundation, Williamsburg, Virginia.

Myerson, A.

1920 *The Nervous Housewife.* Little, Brown, Boston.

Myrdal, G.

1944 *An American Dilemma: The Negro Problem and Modern Democracy.* Harper and Brothers, New York.

Nash, G. B.

1982 *Red, White, and Black: The People of Early America.* Prentice-Hall, Englewood Cliffs, New Jersey.

1988 *Forging Freedom: The Formation of Philadelphia's Black Community, 1720–1840.* Harvard University Press, Cambridge.

Neiman, F. D.

1993 Temporal Patterning in House Plans from the Seventeenth-Century Chesapeake. In *The Archaeology of Seventeenth-Century Virginia,* edited by T. R. Reinhart and D. J. Pogue, pp. 251–283. Dietz Press, Richmond.

Nichols, E.

1989 *The Last Miles of the Way: African-American Homegoing Traditions 1890–Present.* South Carolina State Museum, Columbia.

Noble, M.

1997 *Sweet Grass: Lives of Contemporary Native Women of the Northeast.* C. G. Mills, Mashpee, Massachusetts.

Nobles, G. H.

1989 Breaking into the Backcountry: New Approaches to the Early American Frontier, 1750–1800. *William and Mary Quarterly* 46:641–670.

Noël Hume, A.

1978 *Food.* Colonial Williamsburg Archaeological Series 9. Colonial Williamsburg Foundation, Williamsburg, Virginia.

North, S. N. D.

1908 *Heads of Families at the First Census of the United States taken in the year*

1790, Massachusetts. Government Printing Office, Washington, D.C.

Norton, M. B.
1976 Eighteenth-Century American Women in Peace and War: The Case of the Loyalists. *William and Mary Quarterly* 33:386–409.

Oakley Collection
1817–1945 Papers of the Matthews Family. Audubon State Commemorative Area, West Feliciana, Louisiana.

O'Connell, B., editor
1992 *On Our Own Ground: The Complete Writings of William Apess, a Pequot.* University of Massachusetts Press, Amherst.

Oldfield, J. R.
1995 *Popular Politics and British Anti-Slavery: The Mobilization of Public Opinion Against the Slave Trade.* Manchester University Press, Manchester.

Olmsted, N., and R. W. Olmsted
1994 History of West Oakland. In *West Oakland: "A Place to Start From,"* edited by M. Praetzellis, pp. 9–138. Anthropological Studies Center, Sonoma State University, Rohnert Park, California.

Olwell, R.
1996 Becoming Free: Manumission and the Genesis of a Free Black Community in South Carolina, 1740–90. In *Against the Odds: Free Blacks in the Slave Societies of the Americas,* edited by J. G. Landers, pp. 1–19. Frank Cass, London.

OMB (Office of Management and Budget)
1995 Office of Management and Budget Standards for the Classification of Federal Data on Race and Ethnicity. *Federal Register* 60:44,674–44,693.

Omi, M., and H. Winant
1986 *Racial Formation in the United States: From the 1960s to the 1980s.* Routledge, London.

Orser, C. E., Jr.
1988a The Archaeological Analysis of Plantation Society: Replacing Status and Caste with Economics and Power. *American Antiquity* 53:735–751.
1988b *The Material Basis of the Postbellum Tenant Plantation: Historical Archaeology in the South Carolina Piedmont.* University of Georgia Press, Athens.
1990 Archaeological Approaches to New World Plantation Slavery. In *Archaeological Method and Theory,* vol. 2, edited by M. B. Schiffer, pp. 111–154. University of Arizona Press, Tucson.
1991 The Archaeological Search for Ethnicity in the Historic United States. *Archaeologia Polona* 29: 109–121.
1994 The Archaeology of African-American Slave Religion in the Antebellum South. *Cambridge Archaeology Journal* 4:33–45.
1996 *A Historical Archaeology of the Modern World.* Plenum, New York.
1998a The Archaeology of the African Diaspora. *Annual Reviews in Anthropology* 27:63–82.
1998b The Challenge of Race to American Historical Archaeology. *American Anthropologist* 100:661–668.
1999 Negotiating Our "Familiar" Pasts. In *The Familiar Past? Archaeologies of Later Historical Britain,* edited by S. Tarlow and S. West, pp. 273–285. Routledge, London.

Orser, C. E., Jr., and B. M. Fagan
1995 *Historical Archaeology.* HarperCollins, New York.

Ortner, S.
1991 Reading America: Preliminary Notes on Class and Culture. In *Recapturing Anthropology,* edited by R. G. Fox, pp. 163–189. School of American Research Press, Santa Fe.
1998 Identities: The Hidden Life of Class. *Journal of Anthropological Research* 54:1–17.
1999 Generation X: Anthropology in a Media-Saturated World. In *Critical Anthropology Now,* edited by George E. Marcus, pp. 55–88. School of American Research Press, Santa Fe.

Otto, J. S.
1980 Race and Class on Antebellum Plantations. In *Archaeological Perspectives on Ethnicity in America: Afro-American and Asian American Culture History,* edited by R. L.

Schuyler, pp. 3–13. Baywood, Farmingdale, New York.
1984 *Cannon's Point Plantation 1794–1860: Living Conditions and Status Patterns in the Old South.* Academic Press, Orlando.

Packard, V.
1957 *The Hidden Persuaders.* Pocket Books, New York.

Pacquet, G., and J.-P. Wallot
1987 Nouvelle-France/Quebec/Canada: A World of Limited Identities. In *Colonial Identity in the Atlantic World, 1500–1800,* edited by N. Canny and A. Pagden, pp. 95–114. Princeton University Press, Princeton, New Jersey.

Padgett, T.
1978 *Final Report on the Test Excavations at the William Johnson House, Natchez, Mississippi.* On file, Preservation Society of Ellicott Hill, Natchez, Mississippi.

Park, R. E.
1928 The Bases of Race Prejudice. *The Annals of the American Academy of Political and Social Science* 140: 11–20.

Parker, C. H.
1897 The Use and Abuse of Ornamentation in the House. *The Boston Cooking-School Magazine* 2(4): 7–11.

Patten, M. D.
1997 Cheers of Protest? The Public, the *Post,* and the Parable of Learning. *Historical Archaeology* 31(3):132–139.

Patten, S. N.
1907 *The New Basis of Civilization.* Macmillan, London.

Patterson, T. C.
1995 *Toward a Social History of Archaeology in the United States.* Harcourt Brace, Fort Worth.
1997 *Inventing Western Civilization.* Monthly Review Press, New York.

Patterson, T. C., and F. Spencer
1994 Racial Hierarchies and Buffer Races. *Transforming Anthropology* 5(1–2): 20–27.

Patton, S.
1995 Antebellum Louisiana Artisans: Black Furniture Makers. *International Review of African-American Art* 12(3):15–22, 58–62.

Patton, V. K., and R. J. Stevens
1999 Narrating Competing Truths in the Thomas Jefferson–Sally Hemings Paternity Debate. *Black Scholar* 29(4):8–15.

Paynter, R.
1988 Steps to an Archaeology of Capitalism: Material Change and Class Analysis. In *The Recovery of Meaning: Historical Archaeology in the Eastern United States,* edited by M. P. Leone and P. B. Potter, Jr., pp. 407–433. Smithsonian Institution Press, Washington, D.C.
1990 Afro-Americans in the Massachusetts Historical Landscape. In *The Politics of the Past,* edited by P. Gathercole and D. Lowenthal, pp. 49–62. Unwin Hyman, London.
1992 W. E. B. Du Bois and the Material World of African-Americans in Great Barrington, Massachusetts. *Critique of Anthropology* 12:277–291.
1995 Practicing Critical Archaeology: Problems and Methods. Paper presented at the annual meeting of the Society for American Archaeology, Minneapolis, Minnesota.

Paynter, R., S. Hautaniemi, and N. Muller
1994 The Landscapes of the W. E. B. Du Bois Boyhood Homesite: An Agenda for an Archaeology of the Color Line. In *Race,* edited by S. Gregory and R. Sanjek, pp. 285–318. Rutgers University Press, New Brunswick, New Jersey.

Paynter, R., and R. H. McGuire
1991 The Archaeology of Inequality: Material Culture, Domination, and Resistance. In *The Archaeology of Inequality,* edited by R. H. McGuire and R. Paynter, pp. 1–27. Blackwell, Oxford.

Paynter, R., R. Reinke, J. R. Garrison, E. Hood, A. Miller, and S. McGowan
1987 Vernacular Landscapes in Western Massachusetts. Paper presented at the annual meeting of the Society for Historical Archaeology, Savannah, Georgia.

Perdue, C. L., Jr., T. E. Barden, and R. K. Phillips, editors

1976 *Weevils in the Wheat: Interviews with Virginia Ex-Slaves.* University Press of Virginia, Charlottesville.

Perry, W. R.

1997a Analysis of the African Burial Ground Archaeological Materials. *Update: Newsletter of the African Burial Ground & Five Points Archaeological Projects* 2(2):1, 3–5, 14.

1997b Archaeology as Community Service. *Society for the Anthropology of North America Newsletter,* pp. 1–3.

Peterson, J. L.

1981 The People in Between: Indian-White Marriage and Genesis of a Metis Society and Culture in the Great Lakes Region, 1680–1830. Doctoral dissertation, University of Illinois, Chicago. University Microfilms International, Ann Arbor, Michigan.

Peterson, J. L., and J. S. H. Brown, editors

1985 *The New Peoples: Being and Becoming Métis in North America.* University of Nebraska Press, Lincoln.

Phillippo, J.

1843 *Jamaica: Its Past and Present State.* John Snow, London.

Phyn, J., and A. Ellice

1767–1776 *Letterbooks.* Vols. 1–3, 1767–1776. Buffalo Historical Society Microfilm Publication 1. Microfilm copy in the collections of the Mackinac Island State Park Commission, Lansing, Michigan.

Pickett, D. W.

1996 The John Page House Site: An Example of the Increase in Domestic Brick Architecture in Seventeenth-Century Tidewater Virginia. Master's thesis, College of William and Mary, Williamsburg.

Pierre, J.

1999 African Immigrants in the United States and the "Cultural Narratives" of Ethnicity. Manuscript on file at the University of Texas, Austin.

Piersen, W. D.

1988 *Black Yankees.* University of Massachusetts Press, Amherst.

1993 *Black Legacy: America's Hidden Heritage.* University of Massachusetts Press, Amherst.

Pinderhughes, J.

1990 *Family of the Spirit Cookbook: Recipes and Remembrances from African-American Kitchens.* Simon and Schuster, New York.

Polanyi, K.

1957 The Economy as Instituted Process. In *Trade and Markets in Early Empires,* edited by K. Polanyi, C. M. Arensburg, and H. W. Pearson, pp. 243–269. Free Press, Glencoe, Illinois.

Pond, P., F. Graham, and T. Williams

1773–1775 Accounts of Peter Pond, Felix Graham, and Thomas Williams, 1773–1775. Originals in the Thomas Williams Papers, Burton Historical Collection, Detroit Public Library. Typescript copies in the collections of the Mackinac Island State Park Commission, Lansing, Michigan.

Potter, P. B., Jr.

1991 What Is the Use of Plantation Archaeology? *Historical Archaeology* 25(3):94–107.

1994 *Public Archaeology in Annapolis: A Critical Approach to History in Maryland's Ancient City.* Smithsonian Institution Press, Washington, D.C.

Powers, B. O., Jr.

1994 *Black Charlestonians: A Social History, 1822–1885.* University of Arkansas Press, Fayetteville.

Praetzellis, A.

1998 Introduction: Why Every Archaeologist Should Tell Stories Once in a While. *Historical Archaeology* 32(1):1–3.

1999 The Archaeology of Ethnicity: An Example from Sacramento, California's Early Chinese District. In *Old and New Worlds,* edited by G. Egan and R. L. Michael, pp. 127–135. Oxbow, Oxford.

Praetzellis, M., and A. Praetzellis, editors

1999 *Cypress I-880 Replacement Project, Phase III.* Draft. Sonoma State University Academic Foundation, Rohnert Park, California. Prepared for

CALTRANS, District 4, Oakland, California.

Propper, D. R.

1990 *"The Property of Eben'r Williams": The Family Library of Ebeneezer Hinsdale Williams (1761–1838); A Bibliographic Study and Survey Together with a Catalogue of Its Contents, and an Interpretation.* On file, Historic Deerfield, Deerfield, Massachusetts.

1997 *Lucy Terry Prince: Singer of History.* Pocumtuck Valley Memorial Association and Historic Deerfield, Deerfield, Massachusetts.

Puckett, N. N.

1969 *The Magic and Folk Beliefs of the Southern Negro.* Dover, New York.

Quaife, M., editor

1921 *Alexander Henry's Travels and Adventures.* Lakeside Press, Chicago.

1922 *John Long's Voyages and Travels in the Years 1768–1788.* Lakeside Press, Chicago.

1928 *The John Askin Papers,* vol. 1, 1747–1795. Detroit Historical Society, Detroit.

Raboteau, A.

1980 *Slave Religion: The "Invisible Institution" in the Antebellum South.* Oxford University Press, New York.

Randolph, M.

1993 *The Virginia Housewife, or, Methodical Cook: A Facsimile of an Authentic Early American Cookbook.* Dover, New York.

Randolph, P.

1969 *Sketches of Slave Life.* 2nd ed. Historic Publications, Philadelphia.

Ransford, H. E.

1977 *Race and Class in American Society: Black, Chicano, and Anglo.* Schenkman, Cambridge, Massachusetts.

Rawick, G. P.

1972 *From Sundown to Sunup: The Making of the Black Community.* Greenwood, Westport, Connecticut.

———, editor

1972–1979 *The American Slave: A Composite Autobiography.* 41 vols. Greenwood, Westport, Connecticut.

Raymer, L.

1996 *Macroplant Remains from the Jefferson's Poplar Forest Slave Quarter: A Study in African-American Subsistence Practices.* New South Associates, Stone Mountain, Georgia.

Realey, F. D.

1939 Do You Remember—. *West of Market Boys' Journal* (June):11.

Reed, C. R.

1999 The Black Presence at "White City": African and African American Participation at the World's Columbian Exposition, Chicago, May 1, 1893–October 31, 1893. Paul V. Galvin Digital History Collection, Illinois Institute of Technology http://columbus.gl.iit.edu/reed2.html

Reinke, R.

1985 The Presentment of Rank. Paper presented in the symposium "The Archaeology of Inequality," chaired by R. Paynter and D. R. Gumaer, at the twenty-fifth annual meeting of the Northeastern Anthropological Association, Lake Placid, New York.

Reinke, R., J. R. Garrison, J. E. Hood, R. Paynter, A. Miller, and S. McGowan

1987 Transformations of Landscape: Historical Archaeology at Deerfield. Paper presented at the annual meeting of the Northeastern Anthropological Association, Amherst, Massachusetts.

Reitz, E. J., T. Gibbs, and T. A. Rathbun

1985 Archaeological Evidence for Subsistence on Coastal Plantations. In *The Archaeology of Slavery and Plantation Life,* edited by T. A. Singleton, pp. 163–191. Academic Press, Orlando, Florida.

Reitz, E. J., and M. Scarry

1985 *Reconstructing Historic Subsistence with an Example from Sixteenth-Century Spanish Florida.* Special Publication Series 3. Society for Historical Archaeology, Tucson, Arizona.

Revis, S.

1991 *Hannah Jackson: An African-American Woman and Freedom.* Alexandria Archaeology Publications 33. City of Alexandria, Virginia.

Richardson, B. J.

1910 *The Woman Who Spends: A Study*

of Her Economic Function. Whitcomb and Barrows, Boston.

Riis, J. A.

1890 *How the Other Half Lives.* Scribner's, New York.

Roberts, D.

1997 *Killing the Black Body.* Vintage, New York.

Robertson, C. C.

1997 Black, White, and Red All Over: Beans, Women, and Agricultural Imperialism in Twentieth-Century Kenya. *Agricultural History* 71: 250–299.

Robinson and Leadbeater

c. 1885 *Catalogue of Figures.* Robinson and Leadbeater, Stoke-on-Trent, England.

Roediger, D. R.

1991 *The Wages of Whiteness: Race and the Making of the American Working Class.* Verso, London.

1994 *Towards the Abolition of Whiteness,* Verso, London.

———, editor

1998 *Black on White: Black Writers on What It Means to Be White.* Schocken, New York.

Rogers, J. D.

1990 *Objects of Change: The Archaeology and History of Arikara Contact with Europeans.* Smithsonian Institution Press, Washington, D.C.

Romanucci-Ross, L., and G. De Vos, editors

1995 *Ethnic Identity Creation, Conflict, and Accommodation.* Alta Mira Press, Walnut Creek, California.

Roosens, E. E.

1989 *Creating Ethnicity: The Process of Ethnogenesis.* Sage, Newbury Park, California.

Rose, M.

1996 Race Obliviousness and the Invisibility of Whiteness: The Court's Construction of Race—*Miller v. Johnson,* 115 S. Ct. 2475 (1995). *Temple Law Review* 69:1549–1570.

Rose, W. L., editor

1976 *A Documentary History of Slavery in North America.* Oxford University Press, New York.

Roseberry, W.

1988 Political Economy. *Annual Review of Anthropology* 17:161–185.

1989 *Anthropologies and Histories: Essays in Culture, History, and Political Economy.* Rutgers University Press, New Brunswick, New Jersey.

Rosengarten, D., M. Zierden, K. Grimes, Z. Owusu, E. Alston, and W. Williams

1987 *Between the Tracks: Charleston's East Side During the Nineteenth Century.* Charleston Museum, Charleston, South Carolina.

Rothenberg, D.

1980 The Mothers of the Nation: Seneca Resistance to Quaker Intervention. In *Women and Colonization,* edited by M. Etienne and E. Leacock, pp. 63–87. Bergin and Garvey, New York.

Roundtree, H. C.

1989 *The Powhatan Indians of Virginia: Their Traditional Culture.* University of Oklahoma Press, Norman.

Rowlands, M.

1994 The Politics of Identity in Archaeology. In *Social Construction of the Past: Representation as Power,* edited by G. C. Bond and A. Gilliam, pp. 129–143. Routledge, London.

Rutman, D. B., and A. H. Rutman

1984a *A Place in Time: Middlesex County, Virginia 1650–1750.* W. W. Norton, New York.

1984b *A Place in Time: Explicatus.* W. W. Norton, New York.

Ryan, M. T.

1981 Assimilating New Worlds in the Eighteenth and Seventeenth Centuries. *Comparative Studies in Society and History* 23:519–538.

Sacks, K.

1994 How Did Jews Become White Folks? In *Race,* edited by S. Gregory and R. Sanjek, pp. 78–102. Rutgers University Press, New Brunswick, New Jersey.

Sadoques, E. M.

1929 History and Traditions of Eunice Williams and Her Descendants. *History and Proceedings of the Pocumtuck Valley Memorial Association, 1921–1929* 7:126–130.

Sahlins, M.

1965 On the Sociology of Primitive Exchange. In *The Relevance of Models for Social Anthropology,* edited by M. Banton, pp. 139–227. Tavistock, London.

Said, E.
1978 *Orientalism.* Routledge, New York.

St. George, R. B.
1983 Maintenance Relationships and the Erotics of Property in Historical Thought. Paper presented at the American Historical Association meetings, Philadelphia.

Samford, P.
1991 *Archaeological Investigations of a Probable Slave Quarter at Rich Neck Plantation.* Report on file at DAR, Colonial Williamsburg, Virginia.

Sangster, M. E.
1897 *Home Life Made Beautiful in Story, Song, Sketch, and Picture.* Christian Herald, New York.
1898 *The Art of Home-Making in City and Country, in Mansion and Cottage.* Christian Herald, New York.

Santayana, G.
1936 *The Last Puritan.* Scribner's, New York.

Saunders, Rebecca
1996 Mission-Period Settlement Structure: A Test of the Model at San Martin de Timucua. *Historical Archaeology* 30(4):24–36.

Savage, K.
1997 *Standing Soldiers, Kneeling Slaves: Race, War, and Monument in Nineteenth-Century America.* Princeton University Press, Princeton, New Jersey.

Savitt, T. L.
1978 *Medicine and Slavery: The Diseases and Health Care of Blacks in Antebellum Virginia.* University of Illinois Press, Urbana.
1989 Black Health on the Plantation: Masters, Slaves, and Physicians. In *Science and Medicine in the Old South,* edited by R. L. Numbers and T. L. Savitt, pp. 327–355. Louisiana State University Press, Baton Rouge.

Savulis, E.-R.
1991 Continuity and Change in Historic Native American Settlement and Subsistence Traditions: The Simons Site, Mashpee, Massachusetts. Paper on file, Department of Anthropology, University of Massachusetts, Amherst.
1996 Continuity and Change in Historic Native American Settlement and Subsistence Traditions: The Simons Site, Mashpee, Massachusetts. Paper presented at the annual meeting of the American Anthropological Association, San Francisco.

Savulis, E.-R., and C. Carlson
1989 *An Archaeological Excavation at the Historic Simons House Site, Mashpee, Massachusetts.* University of Massachusetts Archaeological Services Report 89B. University of Massachusetts, Amherst.

Schmidt, P. R., and T. C. Patterson
1995 Introduction: From Constructing to Making Alternative Histories. In *Making Alternative Histories: The Practice of Archaeology and History in Non-Western Settings,* edited by P. R. Schmidt and T. C. Patterson, pp. 1–24. School of American Research Press, Santa Fe.

Schuyler, R. L., editor
1980 *Archaeological Perspectives on Ethnicity in America: Afro-American and Asian American Culture History.* Baywood, Farmingdale, New York.

Schwartz, M. J.
1996 "At Noon, Oh How I Ran": Breastfeeding and Weaning on Plantation and Farm in Antebellum Virginia and Alabama. In *Discovering the Women in Slavery: Emancipating Perspectives on the American Past,* edited by P. Morton, pp. 241–259. University of Georgia Press, Athens.

Schwarz, P. J.
1988 *Twice Condemned: Slaves and the Criminal Laws of Virginia, 1705–1865.* Louisiana State University Press, Baton Rouge.

Schwerin, R.
1981 Former West Oakland resident. Taped interview, October 28, 1981, for the Oakland Neighborhood History Project, Oakland. Verbatim transcription on file at the Anthropological Studies Center, Sonoma

State University, Rohnert Park, California.

Scott, E. M.

1985 *French Subsistence at Fort Michilimackinac, 1715–1781: The Clergy and the Traders.* Archaeological Completion Report Series 9. Mackinac Island State Park Commission, Mackinac Island, Michigan.

1991a Gender in Complex Colonial Society: The Material Goods of Everyday Life in a Late Eighteenth-Century Fur-Trading Community. In *The Archaeology of Gender,* edited by D. Walde and N. D. Willows, pp. 490–494. Archaeological Association, University of Calgary, Alberta.

1991b "Such Diet as Befitted his Station as Clerk": The Archaeology of Subsistence and Cultural Diversity at Fort Michilimackinac, 1761–1781. Doctoral dissertation, University of Minnesota. University Microfilms, Ann Arbor, Michigan.

1996 Who Ate What? Archaeological Food Remains and Cultural Diversity. In *Case Studies in Environmental Archaeology,* edited by E. J. Reitz, L. A. Newsom, and S. J. Scudder, pp. 339–356. Plenum, New York.

1997 Faunal Remains from House D of the Southeast Rowhouse, British Period (1760–1781), Fort Michilimackinac. Report submitted to L. L. M. Evans, Mackinac State Historic Parks, Mackinaw City, Michigan.

1998 Some Thoughts on African American Foodways. *African-American Archaeology Newsletter* 22:5–6.

Scott, S. M.

1933 Chapters in the History of the Law of Quebec, 1764–1775. Doctoral dissertation, University of Michigan. University Microfilms, Ann Arbor, Michigan.

Serjeantson, D.

1989a Animal Remains and the Tanning Trade. In *Diets and Crafts in Towns,* edited by D. Serjeantson and T. Waldron, pp. 129–146. BAR British Series, B.A.R., Oxford.

1989b Introduction to *Diets and Crafts in Towns,* edited by D. Serjeantson and T. Waldron, pp. 1–12. BAR British Series 199. B.A.R., Oxford.

Severens, K.

1988 *Charleston: Antebellum Architecture and Civil War Destiny.* University Press of Tennessee, Knoxville.

Shackel, P. A.

1992 Modern Discipline: Its Historical Context in the Colonial Chesapeake. *Historical Archaeology* 26(3):73–84.

1993 *Personal Discipline and Material Culture: An Archaeology of Annapolis, Maryland, 1695–1870.* University of Tennessee Press, Knoxville.

1994 Town Plans and Material Culture: An Archaeology of Social Relations in Colonial Maryland's Capital Cities. In *Historical Archaeology of the Chesapeake,* edited by P. A. Shackel and B. J. Little, pp. 85–96. Smithsonian Institution Press, Washington, D.C.

1998 Maintenance Relations in Early Colonial Annapolis. In *Annapolis Pasts: Historical Archaeology in Annapolis, Maryland,* edited by P. A. Shackel, P. R. Mullins, and M. S. Warner, pp. 97–118. University of Tennessee Press, Knoxville.

Shackel, P. A., and B. J. Little

1992 Post-Processual Approaches to Meanings and Uses of Material Culture in Historical Archaeology. *Historical Archaeology* 26(3):5–11.

Shapiro, G.

1978 Early British Subsistence Strategy at Michilimackinac: An Analysis of Faunal Remains from the 1977 Season. In *Excavations at Fort Michilimackinac, 1977: House One of the South Southeast Row House,* by D. P. Heldman, pp. 161–177. Archaeological Completion Report Series 2. Mackinac Island State Park Commission, Mackinac Island, Michigan.

Sheehan, B. W.

1980 *Savagism and Civility: Indians and Englishmen in Colonial Virginia.* Cambridge University Press, Cambridge.

Sheldon, G.
1893 Negro Slavery in Old Deerfield. *New England Magazine* 8(1):49–60.
1972 *A History of Deerfield.* 2 vols. New Hampshire Publishing, Sommersworth, New Hampshire.

Shephard, S. J.
1987 Status Variation in Antebellum Alexandria: An Archaeological Case Study of Ceramic Tableware. In *Consumer Choice in Historical Archaelogy,* edited by S. M. Spencer-Wood, pp. 163–198. Plenum, New York.

Shepperson, G.
1993 African Diaspora: Concept and Context. In *Global Dimensions of the African Diaspora,* edited by J. E. Harris, pp. 41–49. Howard University Press, Washington, D.C.

Sheridan, R. B.
1985 *Doctors and Slaves: A Medical and Demographic History of Slavery in the British West Indies, 1680–1834.* Cambridge University Press, Cambridge.

Sherwood, M. E. W.
1881 *Amenities of Home.* D. Appleton, New York.

Sider, G. M.
1986 *Culture and Class in Anthropology and History: A Newfoundland Illustration.* Cambridge University Press, Cambridge.
1987 When Parrots Learn to Talk, and Why They Can't: Domination, Deception, and Self-Deception in Indian-White Relations. *Comparative Studies in Society and History* 29:3–23.

Sider, G. M., and G. Smith, editors
1997 *Between History and Histories: The Making of Silences and Commemorations.* University of Toronto Press, Toronto.

Silverman, R.
1986 *The Moundbuilders.* Ohio University Press, Athens.

Simmons, L.
1942 A Study of the History of Public Relief in West Feliciana Parish, Louisiana 1824–1932. Master's thesis, Louisiana State University, Baton Rouge.

Simmons, W. S.
1986 *Spirit of the New England Tribes: Indian History and Folklore, 1620–1984.* University Press of New England, Hanover, New Hampshire.

Singleton, T. A.
1984 The Slave Tag: An Artifact of Urban Slavery. *South Carolina Antiquities* 16:41–66.
1985a Textiles in South Carolina. In *Social Fabric: South Carolina Traditional Quilts,* edited L. Horton and L. Myers, pp. 5–10. McKissick Museum, Columbia, South Carolina.
1988 An Archaeological Framework for Slavery and Emancipation, 1740–1880. In *The Recovery of Meaning: Historical Archaeology in the Eastern United States,* edited by M. P. Leone and P. B. Potter Jr., pp. 345–370. Smithsonian Institution Press, Washington, D.C.
1990 The Archaeology of the Plantation South: A Review of Approaches and Goals. *Historical Archaeology* 24(4):70–77.
1991 The Archaeology of Slave Life. In *Before Freedom Came: African-American Life in the Antebellum South,* edited by E. D. C. Campbell Jr. with K. S. Rice, pp. 155–175, 188–191. Museum of the Confederacy, Richmond; and University Press of Virginia, Charlottesville.
1995 The Archaeology of Slavery in North America. *Annual Review of Anthropology* 24:119–140.
1997 Commentary: Facing the Challenges of a Public African-American Archaeology. *Historical Archaeology* 31(3):146–152.

———, editor
1985b *The Archeology of Slavery and Plantation Life.* Academic Press, Orlando, Florida.
1999 *"I, Too, Am America": Archaeological Studies of African-American Life.* University Press of Virginia, Charlottesville.

Singleton, T. A., and M. D. Bograd
1995 *The Archaeology of the African Diaspora in the Americas.* Guide Series. Society for Historical Archaeology, Tucson, Arizona.

Singleton, T. A., and B. Crane

1995 Engendering African-American Archaeology. Paper presented at the annual meeting of the Society for Historical Archaeology, Washington, D.C.

Skinner, E. P.

1993 The Dialectic between Diasporas and Homelands. In *Global Dimensions of the African Diaspora,* edited by J. E. Harris, pp. 11–39. Howard University Press, Washington, D. C.

Smart-Grosvenor, V.

1992 *Vibration Cooking: Or the Travel Notes of a Geechee Girl.* Ballantine, New York.

Smedley, A.

1993 *Race in North America: Origin and Evolution of a Worldview.* 1st ed. Westview, Boulder, Colorado.

1998 "Race" and the Construction of Human Identity. *American Anthropologist* 100:690–702.

1999 *Race in North America: Origin and Evolution of a Worldview.* 2nd ed. Westview, Boulder, Colorado.

Smith, B., editor

1983 *Home Girls: A Black Feminist Anthology.* Kitchen Table: Women of Color Press, New York.

Smith, D.

1991 In Search of Our Mothers' Cookbooks: Gathering African-American Culinary Traditions. *Iris: A Journal about Women* 26:22–27.

Smith, T. H.

1994 *Conjuring Culture: Biblical Formations of Black America.* Oxford University Press, New York.

Sobel, M.

1987 *The World They Made Together: Black and White Values in Eighteenth-Century Virginia.* Princeton University Press, Princeton, New Jersey.

Spelman, W. A.

1885 *Spelman's Fancy Goods Graphic.* W. A. Spelman, Chicago.

Spires, W.

1994 West Oakland and the Brotherhood of Sleeping Car Porters. In *West Oakland: "A Place to Start From,"* edited by M. Praetzellis, pp. 205–223. Anthropological Studies Center, Sonoma State University, Rohnert Park, California.

Stanton, L.

1993 *Slavery at Mount Vernon.* Thomas Jefferson Memorial Foundation, Monticello, Virginia.

Stavney, A.

1998 "Mothers of Tomorrow": The New Negro Renaissance and the Politics of Maternal Representation. *African American Review* 32:533–561.

Steevens, G. W.

1897 *The Land of the Dollar.* Reprint, Books for Libraries, Freeport, New York, 1971.

Stewart, J.

1808 *An Account of Jamaica and Its Inhabitants.* Longman, Hurst, Rees, and Orme, London.

Stewart, R. J.

1992 *Religion and Society in Post-Emancipation Jamaica.* University of Tennessee Press, Knoxville.

Stewart, S.

1993 *On Longing: Narratives of the Miniature, the Gigantic, the Souvenir, the Collection.* Duke University Press, Durham, North Carolina.

Stewart-Abernathy, L. C.

1992 Industrial Goods in the Service of Tradition: Consumption and Cognition on an Ozark Farmstead before the Great War. In *The Art and Mystery of Historical Archaeology: Essays in Honor of James Deetz,* edited by A. E. Yentsch and M. C. Beaudry, pp. 101–126. CRC Press, Boca Raton, Florida.

Stiebing, W. H., Jr.

1993 *Uncovering the Past: A History of Archaeology.* Oxford University Press, New York.

Stine, L. F., M. A. Cabak, and M. D. Groover

1996 Blue Beads as African-American Cultural Symbols. *Historical Archaeology* 30(3):49–75.

Stiverson, G. A., and I. P. H. Butler

1977 Virginia in 1732: The Travel Journal of William Hugh Grove. *Virginia Magazine of History and Biography* 85:18–44.

Susman, W. I.

1984 *Culture as History: The Transformation of American Society in the*

Twentieth Century. Pantheon, New York.

Swartz, D.
1997 *Culture and Power: The Sociology of Pierre Bourdieu.* University of Chicago Press, Chicago.

Sweeney, K. M.
1984 Mansion People: Kinship, Class, and Architecture in Western Massachusetts in the Mid-Eighteenth Century. *Winterthur Portfolio* 19:231–256.
1985 From Wilderness to Arcadian Vale: Material Life in the Connecticut River Valley, 1635–1760. In *The Great River, Art and Society of the Connecticut Valley, 1635–1820,* edited by G. W. R. Ward and J. W. N. Hosley, pp. 17–27. Wadsworth Atheneum, Hartford, Connecticut.
1994 High-Style Vernacular: Lifestyles of the Colonial Elite. In *Of Consuming Interests: The Style of Life in the Eighteenth Century,* edited by C. Carson, R. Hoffman, and P. J. Albert, pp. 1–58. University Press of Virginia, Charlottesville.

Sypher and Company
1885 *The Housekeeper's Quest: Where to Find Pretty Things.* Sypher and Company, New York.

Tate, T. W., and D. L. Ammerman, editors
1979 *The Chesapeake in the Seventeenth Century: Essays in Anglo-American Society.* University of North Carolina Press, Chapel Hill.

Taylor, J. G.
1974 *Louisiana Reconstructed, 1863–1877.* Louisiana State University Press, Baton Rouge.
1984 *Louisiana: A History.* W. W. Norton, New York.

Templeton, A. R.
1998 Human Races: A Genetic and Evolutionary Perspective. *American Anthropologist* 100:632–650.

Terrill, T. E., and J. Hirsch
1978 *Such as Us: Southern Voices of the Thirties.* University of North Carolina Press, Chapel Hill.

Thomas, B. W.
1998 Power and Community: The Archaeology of Slavery at the Hermitage Plantation. *American Antiquity* 63:531–552.

Thomas, D. H.
1993 The Archaeology of Mission Santa Catalina de Guale: Our First Fifteen Years. In *The Spanish Missions of La Florida,* edited by B. G. McEwan, pp. 1–34. University Press of Florida, Gainesville.

Thomas, H.
2000 You Are What You Eat. Paper presented at the University of Texas, Department of Anthropology, and the African Diaspora Graduate Program, Austin.

Thomas, J.
1996 *Time, Culture, and Identity: An Interpretative Archaeology.* Routledge, London.

Thompson, E. P.
1963 *The Making of the English Working Class.* Vintage, New York.

Thompson, R. F.
1983 *Flash of the Spirit: African and Afro-American Art and Philosophy.* Random House, New York.
1993 *Face of the Gods: Art and Altars of Africa and the African Americas.* Museum for African Art, New York.

Thoreau, H. D.
1854 *Walden, or, Life in the Woods.* Reprint, Modern Library, New York, 1937.

Tregle, J.
1991 Creole and Americans. In *Creole New Orleans: Race and Americanization,* edited by A. R. Hirsch and J. Logsden, pp. 131–185. Louisiana State University Press, Baton Rouge.

Trigger, B. G.
1989 *A History of Archaeological Thought.* Cambridge University Press, Cambridge.

Tucker, S.
1988 *Telling Memories Among Southern Women.* Louisiana State University Press, Baton Rouge.

Tuma, M.
1999 Ethnoarchaeology of the Subsistence Behaviors among a Rural African American Community in Southwestern Mississippi. Paper presented at the Southeastern Archaeological Conference, Pensacola, Florida.

Turner, M.
1998 *Slaves and Missionaries: The Disin-*

tegration of Jamaican Slave Society, 1787–1834. University Press of the West Indies, Kingston.

Union Publishing

1887 *Secrets of Success in Love, Courtship, and Marriage, Showing Also How to Obtain and Retain Health and Wealth.* Union Publishing, Newark, New Jersey.

Upton, D.

1982 The Origins of Chesapeake Architecture. In *Three Centuries of Maryland Architecture: A Selection of Presentations Made at the Eleventh Conference of the Maryland Historic Trust,* pp. 44–57. Society for the Preservation of Maryland Antiquities and Maryland Historical Trust, Annapolis.

1985 White and Black Landscapes in Eighteenth Century Virginia. *Places: A Quarterly Journal of Environmental Design* 2:59–72.

1986 *Holy Things and Profane: Anglican Parish Churches in Colonial Virginia.* Yale University Press, New Haven.

1988 White and Black Landscapes in Eighteenth-Century Virginia. In *Material Life in America, 1600–1860,* edited by R. B. St. George, pp. 357–370. Northeastern University Press, Boston.

1990 Imagining the Early Virginia Landscape. In *Earth Patterns: Essays in Landscape Archaeology,* edited by W. M. Kelso and R. Most, pp. 71–86. University Press of Virginia, Charlottesville.

Usner, D. H., Jr.

1987 The Frontier Exchange Economy of the Lower Mississippi Valley in the Eighteenth Century. *William and Mary Quarterly* 44:165–192.

1992 *Indians, Settlers, and Slaves in a Frontier Exchange Economy: The Lower Mississippi Valley Before 1783.* University of North Carolina Press, Chapel Hill.

1998 *American Indians in the Lower Mississippi Valley: Social and Economic Histories.* University of Nebraska Press, Lincoln.

Van Kirk, S.

1980 *Many Tender Ties: Women in Fur-Trade Society, 1670–1870.* University of Oklahoma Press, Norman.

Veblen, T.

1973 *The Theory of the Leisure Class: An Economic Study of Institutions.* 1893. Reprint, Houghton Mifflin, Boston.

Vernon, R.

1988 Seventeenth-Century Appalachee Colono-ware as a Reflection of Demography, Economics, and Acculturation. *Historical Archaeology* 22(1):76–82.

Vlach, J. M.

1991 Plantation Landscapes of the Antebellum South. In *Before Freedom Came: African-American Life in the Antebellum South,* edited by E. D. C. Campbell Jr., and K. S. Rice, pp. 21–47. The Museum of the Confederacy and the University Press of Virginia, Richmond.

VMHB (*Virginia Magazine of History and Biography*)

1913 Appraisement of the Estate of Phillip Ludwell Esqr Decd. *Virginia Magazine of History and Biography* 21(1):395–416.

Voget, F. W.

1975 *A History of Ethnology.* Holt, Rinehart, and Winston, New York.

Walker, A.

1973 *The Color Purple.* Washington Square Press, New York.

Walker, F. A.

1872 *Ninth Census.* Vol. 1, *The Statistics of the Population of the United States.* Government Printing Office, Washington, D. C.

Walker, K. J.

1988 *Kingsley and His Slaves: Anthropological Interpretation and Evaluation.* Volumes in Historical Archaeology 5. South Carolina Institute of Archaeology and Anthropology, University of South Carolina, Columbia.

Walker, S.

1988 The Eighteenth-Century Landowner as Entrepreneur: The Business Career of Alexander Lindsay, Sixth Earl of Balcarres, c. 1785–1825. Doctoral dissertation, Lancaster University, England.

Walker, S. S.
2000 Everyday Africa in New Jersey: Wonderings and Wanderings in the African Diaspora. In *African Roots/American Cultures: Africa in the Creation of the Americas,* edited by S. S. Walker, pp. 2–74. Rowman and Littlefield, Lanham, Maryland.

Wallace, W. S., editor
1934 *Documents Relating to the North West Company.* The Champlain Society, Toronto.

Walsh, L. S.
1993 Slave Life, Slave Society, and Tobacco Production in the Tidewater Chesapeake, 1620–1820. In *Cultivation and Culture,* edited by I. Berlin and P. D. Morgan, pp. 170–199. University Press of Virginia, Charlottesville.
1997 *From Calabar to Carter's Grove: The History of a Virginia Slave Community.* University Press of Virginia, Charlottesville.
1998 Slavery at Carter's Grove in the Early Eighteenth Century. *Virginia Cavalcade* 47(3):110–125.

Walsh, L. S., A. S. Martin, and J. Bowen
1997 *Provisioning Early American Towns: The Chesapeake, a Multidisciplinary Case Study.* National Endowment for the Humanities Grant RO-22643-93. Colonial Williamsburg Foundation, Williamsburg, Virginia.

Warner, M. S.
1990 *Archaeological Testing at Gott's Court, 18AP52, Annapolis.* Historic Annapolis Foundation, Annapolis.
1998 Food and the Negotiation of African American Identities in Annapolis, Maryland, and the Chesapeake. Doctoral dissertation. University of Virginia, Charlottesville.

Warner, M. S., and P. R. Mullins.
1993 *Phase I–II Archaeological Investigations of the Courthouse Site (18AP63), an 1850–1970 African American Neighborhood in Annapolis, Maryland.* Historic Annapolis Foundation, Annapolis.

Warner, W. L.
1936 American Caste and Class. *American Journal of Sociology* 42:234–237.
1941 Deep South: A Social Anthropological Study of Caste and Class. In *Deep South: A Social Anthropological Study of Caste and Class,* by A. Davis, B. B. Gardner, and M. R. Gardner, pp. 3–14. University of Chicago Press, Chicago.

Warren, R. P.
1930 The Briar Patch. In *I'll Take My Stand,* pp. 246–264. Louisiana State University Press, Baton Rouge.

Waselkov, G. A.
1993 Historic Creek Indian Responses to European Trade and the Rise of Political Factions. In *Ethnohistory and Archaeology: Approaches to Postcontact Change in the Americas,* edited by J. D. Rogers and S. M. Wilson, pp. 123–131. Plenum, New York.

Washington, B. T.
1993 *Up from Slavery: An Autobiography by Booker T. Washington.* Gramercy, New York.

Watts-Roy, J.
1996 Signaling Identity on the Frontier. Paper presented at the annual meeting of the Society for Historical Archaeology, Cincinnati, Ohio.

Webb, S. S.
1966 The Strange Career of Francis Nicholson. *William and Mary Quarterly* 23:515–548.

Wells, C.
1998 The Multistoried House: Twentieth-Century Encounters with the Domestic Architecture of Colonial Virginia. *Virginia Magazine of History and Biography* 106:353–418.

WHC (Wisconsin Historical Collections)
1855–1931 Collections of the Wisconsin Historical Society, edited by R. G. Thwaites. Vols. 1, 8, 11, 18, 19. State Historical Society of Wisconsin, Madison.

White, C. P.
1989 *Chesapeake Bay: A Field Guide.* Tidewater Publishers, Centreville, Maryland.

White, D. G.
1985 *Ar'n't I a Woman? Female Slaves in the Plantation South.* W. W. Norton, New York.
1991 Female Slaves in the Plantation South. In *Before Freedom Came: African-American Life in the Antebellum South,* edited by E. D. C. Campbell Jr., and K. S. Rice, pp. 101–121. The Museum of the Confederacy and the University Press of Virginia, Charlottesville.

White, R.
1983 *The Roots of Dependency: Subsistence, Environment, and Social Change among the Choctaws, Pawnees, and Navajos.* University of Nebraska Press, Lincoln.

Widder, K. R.
1987 Magdelaine Laframboise, Fur Trader and Educator. In *Historic Women of Michigan,* edited by R. R. Troester, pp. 1–13. Michigan Women's Studies Association, Lansing.
1999 *Battle for the Soul: Métis Children Encounter Evangelical Protestants at the Mackinaw Mission, 1823–1837.* Michigan State University Press, East Lansing.

Wilkie, L. A.
1994 Childhood in the Quarters: Playtime at Oakley and Riverlake Plantations. *Louisiana Folklife* 18:13–20.
1996 Medicinal Teas and Patent Medicines: African-American Women's Consumer Choices and Ethnomedical Traditions at a Louisiana Plantation. *Southeastern Archaeology* 15:119–131.
1997 Secret and Sacred: Contextualizing the Artifacts of African-American Magic and Religion. *Historical Archaeology* 31(4):81–106.
2000a *Creating Freedom: African-American Material Culture and Identity at Oakley Plantation, Louisiana, 1845–1950.* Louisiana State University Press, Baton Rouge.
2000b Not Merely Child's Play: Creating a Historical Archaeology of Children and Childhood. In *Archaeologies of Childhood,* edited by J. Sofaer-Derevenski, pp. 100–113. Routledge, London.
2001 Black Sharecroppers and White Frat Boys: Living Communities and the Construction of Their Archaeological Pasts. In *The Archaeology of the Contemporary Past,* edited by V. Buchli and G. Lucas. Routledge, London.

Wilkie, R. W., and J. Tager, editors
1991 *Historical Atlas of Massachusetts.* University of Massachusetts Press, Amherst.

Willey, G. R.
1968 One Hundred Years of American Archaeology. In *One Hundred Years of Anthropology,* edited by J. O. Brew, pp. 29–53. Harvard University Press, Cambridge.

Willey, G. R., and P. Phillips
1958 *Method and Theory in American Archaeology.* University of Chicago Press, Chicago.

Willey, G. R., and J. A. Sabloff
1993 *A History of American Archaeology.* 3rd ed. W. H. Freeman, New York.

Williams, E.
1944 *Capitalism and Slavery.* Putnam's and Sons, New York.

Williams, J. M., and G. Shapiro
1982 *A Search for the Eighteenth Century Village at Michilimackinac: A Soil Resistivity Survey.* Archaeological Completion Report Series 4. Mackinac Island State Park Commission, Mackinac Island, Michigan.

Williams, R.
1990 *Hierarchical Structures and Social Values: The Creation of Black and Irish Identities in the United States.* Cambridge University Press, Cambridge.

Williams, R.
1982 *Dream Worlds: Mass Consumption in Late Nineteenth-Century France.* University of California Press, Berkeley.

Willis, W. S., Jr.
1974 Skeletons in the Anthropological Closet. In *Reinventing Anthropology,* edited by D. Hymes, pp. 121–132. Vintage, New York.

Wilson, S. M., and J. D. Rogers
1993 Historic Dynamics in the Contact Era. In *Ethnohistory and Archaeology: Approaches to Postcontact*

Change in the Americas, edited by J. D. Rogers and S. M. Wilson, pp. 3–15. Plenum, New York.

Wobst, H. M.

1977 Stylistic Behavior and Information Exchange. In *For the Director,* edited by C. Cleland, pp. 317–342. Museum of Anthropology, Anthropological Papers 61. University of Michigan, Ann Arbor.

1999 Style in Archaeology or Archaeologists in Style. In *Critical Approaches to the Interpretation of Material Culture,* edited by E. S. Chilton, pp. 118–132. University of Utah Press, Salt Lake City.

2000 Agency in (Spite of) Material Culture. In *Agency in Archaeology,* edited by M-A. Dobres and J. Robb, pp. 40–50. Routledge, London.

Wolf, E. R.

1982 *Europe and the People Without History.* University of California Press, Berkeley.

1999 *Envisioning Power: Ideologies of Dominance and Crisis.* University of California Press, Berkeley.

Woolsey, E. H.

1881 *Annual Report of the Health Officer to the City Council of Oakland, California for 1880.* Daily Times Book and Job Printing House, Oakland.

World's Columbian Exposition

1999 Tour the Fair. http://xroads.virginia.edu/~MA96/WCE/tour2. html.

Worsley, P.

1981 Marxism and Culture: The Missing Concept. *Dialectical Anthropology* 6:103–121.

WPA (Work Projects Administration)

1994 *The Negro in Virginia.* 1940. Reprint, John F. Blair, Winston-Salem, North Carolina.

Wray, M., and A. Newitz, editors

1997 *White Trash.* Routledge, London.

Wright, C. D.

1887 *The Census of Massachusetts, 1885.* Vol. 1, *Population and Social Structure.* Wright and Potter, Boston.

Wright, L. B.

1940 *The First Gentlemen of Virginia: Intellectual Qualities of the Early Colonial Ruling Class.* Huntington Library, San Marino, California.

Wurst, L.

1999 Internalizing Class in Historical Archaeology. *Historical Archaeology* 33(1):7–21.

Wylie, A.

1995 Alternative Histories: Epistemic Disunity and Political Integrity. In *Making Alternative Histories: The Practice of Archaeology and History in Non-Western Settings,* edited by P. R. Schmidt and T. C. Patterson, pp. 255–272. School of American Research Press, Santa Fe.

Yakubik, J-K., and H. Franks

1997 *Archaeological Investigations at the Site of the Cabildo, New Orleans, Louisiana.* Prepared by Earth Search, Inc., for the Louisiana State Museum, New Orleans.

Yentsch, A. E.

1992 Gudgeons, Mullet, and Proud Pigs: Historicity, Black Fishing, and Southern Myth. In *The Art and Mystery of Historical Archaeology: Essays in Honor of James Deetz,* edited by A. E. Yentsch and M. C. Beaudry, pp. 283–314. CRC Press, Boca Raton, Florida.

1994 *A Chesapeake Family and Their Slaves: A Study in Historical Archaeology.* Cambridge University Press, Cambridge.

Yetman, N. R.

1970 *Life Under the Peculiar Institution.* Holt, Rinehart, and Winston, New York.

Zafar, R.

1999 The Signifying Dish: Autobiography and History in Two Black Women's Cookbooks. *Feminist Studies* 25: 449–469.

Zimmer-Tamakoshi, L.

1997 We Call Ourselves "Americans." In *Cultural Diversity in the United States,* edited by L. L. Naylor, pp. 35–48. Bergin and Garvey, Westport, Connecticut.

Zuckerman, M.

1987 Identity in British America: Unease in Eden. In *Colonial Identity in the Atlantic World, 1500–1800,* edited by N. Canny and A. Pagden, pp. 115–157. Princeton University Press, Princeton, New Jersey.

Contributors

James A. Delle
Department of Anthropology
Franklin and Marshall College
Lancaster, Pennsylvania 17604-3003

Ywone D. Edwards-Ingram
Department of Archaeological Research
Colonial Williamsburg
P.O. Box 1776
Williamsburg, VA 23187-1776

Terrence W. Epperson
Independent Scholar
25 Bank Street #2
Philadelphia, PA 19106

Maria Franklin
Department of Anthropology and the Center for African and African-American Studies
University of Texas
Austin, TX 78712

Gladys-Marie Fry
Department of English
University of Maryland
College Park, MD 20742

Mark. P. Leone
Department of Anthropology
University of Maryland
College Park, MD 20742

Christopher N. Matthews
Department of Sociology and Anthropology
Hofstra University
Hempstead, NY 11549

Paul R. Mullins
Department of Anthropology
Indiana University—Purdue University at Indianapolis
425 University Boulevard
Indianapolis, IN 46202

Charles E. Orser Jr.
Department of Sociology and Anthropology
Campus Box 4660
Illinois State University
Normal, IL 61790-4660

Robert Paynter
Department of Anthropology
Machmer Hall
University of Massachusetts
Amherst, MA 01003

Elizabeth M. Scott
Zooarch Research
P.O. Box 285
St. Mary, MO 63673

Theresa A. Singleton
Department of Anthropology
209 Maxwell Hall
Syracuse University
Syracuse, NY 13244-1200

Laurie A. Wilkie
Department of Anthropology
University of California, Berkeley
Berkeley, CA 94720-3710

Index